SIGNAL SUCCESS

SIGNAL
SUCCESS

Tommy Thomas

The Book Guild Ltd
Sussex, England

This book is sold subject to the condition that it shall not, by way of trade or otherwise, be lent, re-sold, hired out, photo-copied or held in any retrieval system, or otherwise circulated without the publisher's prior consent in any form of binding or cover other than that in which this is published and without a similar condition including this condition being imposed on the subsequent purchaser.

The Book Guild Limited
25 High Street
Lewes, Sussex

First published 1995

© Tommy Thomas 1995

Set in Baskerville

Typesetting by Dataset
St Leonards-on-Sea
East Sussex

Printed in Great Britain by
Bookcraft (Bath) Ltd.

A catalogue record for this book is
available from the British Library

ISBN 0 86332 995 0

CONTENTS

	Foreword	7
	Acknowledgements	9
1.	Voyage to India	11
2.	Early Childhood	22
3.	School	30
4.	Apprenticeship	35
5.	Recruit Days	40
6.	Technical Training	48
7.	Life in India	54
8.	Baluchistan	77
9.	Home Service	90
10.	Sojourn in France	107
11.	The Battle of Britain	117
12.	Voyage to Egypt	134
13.	The Desert War	142
14.	The Lebanon and Syria	177
15.	The Holy Land	196
16.	Homeward Bound	205
17.	United Kingdom 1945-47	231
18.	East Africa 1948-51	247
19.	East Africa 1951-52	280
20.	Mumbo-Jumbo	297
21.	Postwar Germany	302
22.	Bound for Singapore	320
23.	Germany – Second Time Round	342

24.	Aphrodite's Island	360
25.	Retirement Looms	385
26.	Semi-Retirement	394
27.	Retirement	422

FOREWORD

Although there is only a few years' difference in our ages and most of our respective lives have been spent in the Royal Corps of Signals, we did not meet until 1990 when both of us had been retired for some time. Our Corps is a large one and there was a tendency for half of it to be abroad and the other at home and so we probably passed each other by, almost literally like ships in the night.

It was therefore a great pleasure to get to know Tommy when we formed the East Kent Branch of the Royal Signals Association, on whose committee we both serve, and a singular honour to be asked to provide this foreword.

I mean no disparagement when I liken Tommy's book to a ride on a roller-coaster – there is no way to get off: it makes compulsive reading as one is carried along through the ups and downs with little nuggets of unexpected events and observations.

Throughout, the reader cannot fail to discern the thread of ambition tempered by modesty and loyalty that made this young soldier into a man and subsequently one of the few who gained the higher ranks of the Quarter-Master Commission.

The Corps awards a special Badge for those who have served it for fifty years or more; there are not so many of them, but there are even fewer who have recounted that half-century of service in such a delightful and interesting way as Tommy has done in this book.

Read on, young man, there is much to emulate.

Major-General J. M. W. Badcock, C.B., M.B.E., DL
(Master of Signals 1980-1990)

ACKNOWLEDGEMENTS

This book could not have been produced but for the tireless effort of my wife Edith, who in her seventy-sixth year mastered the art of operating a word processor and devoted most of her time during the past year to typing, correcting and rearranging the format in which my story has been written.

I am much indebted to Juanita Carberry, whose extensive knowledge of Kenya in general and the events of early 1941 in particular, leading to the murder of the Earl of Errol, dispelled some preconceived idea I held about the background of the case. My information had been gained from stories related to me by some of the early settlers, handed down to them by the pioneers, and like all tales some of the facts became distorted in the retelling.

Bid, the widow of John Lawrence-Brown, has been able to refresh my memory on the way of life of ordinary hard-working Kenyans who, unlike the dissolute Happy Valley set described by General Erskine as 'shady people living in a sunny spot', operated the railways, organised the post office and telephone system, managed departmental stores and worked in the notoriously low-paid Government departments. I am very grateful for their kindness shown to us during our five years in the colony.

I have been encouraged and supported throughout by Major-General John Badcock, who not only consented to write the Foreword but whose experience and knowledge I was able to call upon for guidance in the section dealing with the Suez operation. And who better to advise me – after all, he took part in it!

Librarians are often thought of as people issuing books on loan in exchange for tickets, but they also give invaluable advice to researchers and I should like to record my thanks to the librarian and her assistants at the Swalecliffe Library, Kent, for their patience and help in providing dates and data which my ageing brain had long forgotten.

1

VOYAGE TO INDIA

A party of young soldiers wearing full marching order and carrying kitbags could be observed standing outside a barrack room in Gaza Lines Catterick Camp in North Yorkshire. They were awaiting transport to convey them to the railway station, the starting-point for what was to prove a long and arduous voyage to the subcontinent of India.

The party included 21-year-old No. 2322350 Signalman W. J. Thomas, who had volunteered for service in India and whose story is related below.

It was the morning of 14th February 1934 and the draft had been awakened early to prepare for the journey to Southampton. We said our farewells to those of our chums remaining behind and were driven to Catterick railway station – and that was the last I saw of Catterick Camp for upwards of twenty years.

All movements to overseas stations at that time were by sea transport. Several vessels owned by the Bibby Line were chartered to the War Office after being adapted from cargo vessels to troops' accommodation, and these included HMTs *Somersetshire*, *Devonshire*, *Oxfordshire*, *Lancashire* and the *Dilwara*. The *Lancashire* was later converted to a hospital ship and saw service in the 1939-45 war. Because of the high temperatures prevailing in the Red Sea during the summer months and the primitive ventilation system installed in these ships, trooping was confined to the winter season, usually commencing in November and terminating in March. Senior officers and their families travelling overseas were unaware of the discomfort endured by the troops who spent six weeks or longer at sea in these troop-ships, because they travelled first class in comfortable passenger liners.

Having reached Southampton the next step was boarding. The troops were hustled from here to there by the embarkation staff. Their job was not an easy one and the difficulty of shepherding hundreds of soldiers wearing full equipment and carrying kitbags up swaying gangplanks can be imagined. Their task was not made easier because the departure of the ship depended on the state of the tide and, as is well known, 'time and tide wait for no man'. Embarkation completed, the troops were ushered to their accommodation, relieved of their kitbags and equipment, and paraded on the decks to listen to the strains of a regimental band playing patriotic tunes. Eventually there was a blast on the ship's siren, lines were cast and HMT *Lancashire* was nosed from the quayside and commenced her slow progress down to the Solent.

Thinking that they were already in the English Channel, some of the innocents remarked that they were in for an easy passage but were soon disillusioned, because very soon after leaving Southampton, we were instructed into the mysteries of 'ship's routine'. Unlike the relative comfort of Catterick where we had a bed on which to sleep and a locker to contain our kit, we learnt that beds were out and hammocks in. These were drawn from the hammock store in the evening and slung wherever hooks could be found to support them. There were insufficient hooks to accommodate everyone and the unlucky had to make do with sleeping on the hard deck.

Hammocks were numbered and had to be returned to store half an hour after reveille, and anyone handing in one badly rolled up was rebuked and sent away to make a better job of it.

The dining-tables were massive things suspended from the upper decks, which swung with the movement of the ship to prevent the dinner-plates sliding off. Seating was on wooden forms with twelve men to a table. Each of the sitters took it in turn to report to the galley and collect and share out the food. This could be a dodgy exercise in foul weather – carrying a large metal tray down wet and slippery steps was no joke.

Smoking was forbidden below decks for obvious safety reasons, and a large number of men were deployed as sentries in high fire risk areas to give warning of any outbreak and take action where possible to deal with it. It was my bad luck to be nominated as one of these sentries on my first night aboard and my post was in a well of the deck outside the disinfectant store. Already feeling queasy now that we were in mid-Channel, the smell of carbolic and coal-tar soap did nothing to ease my discomfiture. Morning came, and ended the most miserable night of my life.

The sleeping and eating arrangements having been described, the other bodily needs have to be mentioned. 'The heads' is the nautical term for lavatories and ablution rooms. The urinals consisted of open drains flushed by a plentiful supply of sea water. For more pressing needs lavatory bowls and a supply of square sheets of latrine-paper tied at one corner were provided. Wash basins were of the galvanised-iron type inserted into slate slabs about two feet apart. We washed and shaved in cold sea water, using salt-water soap which did not produce much lather. The showers were open cubicles but no one used these until the weather and the water became warmer. It should be mentioned that toilet-paper was supplied on the basis of four sheets per man per day, without regard for the needs of those suffering from constipation or contracting dysentery. In the depot it had been compulsory for everyone to have a hot shower once a week and a record of this was maintained in the 'bath book', which was available to the medical officer in cases of infection.

Each morning at 11 a.m. 'ship's rounds' were conducted by an officer nominated by the captain. The troops were paraded on the deck at the lifeboat station nearest to their sleeping-area, wearing life-jackets of primitive design and made of canvas filled with kapok. These jackets were slung over the head so that half rested on the chest with the other half on the nape of the neck, and they were kept firmly attached to the body by means of straps tied around the waist. Woe betide anyone parading for ship's inspection with a loose life-jacket; it was instantly spotted by the vigilant ship's officer, who often gave it an upward push causing some pain to the victim's jaw. The purpose of these life-jackets was to support a man in the sea until he could be rescued by a lifeboat or raft, but it is now generally accepted that anyone jumping into the sea from any height would end up with a broken neck.

Not content with this daily parade at lifeboat stations, there were irregular drills carried out to assess the response to the emergency alarms sounded on the ship's siren. After a few days at sea we accustomed ourselves to this routine and looked forward to our first port of call, which was said to be Gibraltar, five days' steaming away.

To reach Gibraltar we crossed the English Channel with the Channel Islands on our port side and headed towards the dreaded Bay of Biscay, which turned out to be living up to its reputation. Most of the troops were seasick and the situation did not improve until we passed Cape Finisterre in Spain, well known for its magnificent lighthouse whose beams can be seen fifty miles out to sea.

The weather conditions improved as we sailed down the coast of Portugal and it became warmer so that we were able to relax on deck. Three hundred miles or so after passing Cape Finisterre we were south of Cape Trafalgar, where Nelson vanquished Napoleon's French Fleet in 1805, and soon we were nearing Gibraltar. Long before we entered the straits, the massive fortress loomed into view and we looked forward to stretching our legs on dry land; but this privilege was denied to us. Perhaps because we were behind schedule due to stormy weather in the Bay of Biscay, the *Lancashire* remained in port only long enough for provisions and fresh drinking-water to be loaded, and twelve hours later the ship was set on a course for Malta. By this time we were into March, and although the western Mediterranean can be quite cool in early spring, it was far preferable to North Yorkshire.

Because of this improvement, more and more of the troops were spending their leisure time on deck, and to relieve the monotony equipment for simple deck games was provided – which helped to tone up those who had been idle for too long. One of the most popular was deck quoits with two teams of three men sliding their hoops of rope along the deck towards a target. The trick was to move an opponent's hoop away from the target and deflect one's own towards it. One of the simplest ways of making a profit was the 'stick game'; the man running this racket provided himself with twelve strips of wood of equal length and reduced one of them by an inch or so. He then invited the punters to buy a stick for a penny, and the winner was the person drawing the shortest strip, his prize being tenpence. Income a shilling, outgoings tenpence: a profit of twopence in as many minutes. It was at night that the real gambling took place below decks, and although this was frowned upon by the ship's officers it still flourished. It was run by selected crew members and the most popular game was 'crown and anchor'.

As everyone knows, the captain of a ship is the highest authority aboard, hence the expression 'Master under God'. The discipline of soldiers on board was the responsibility of the ship's Regimental Sergeant-Major, whose appointment lasted the whole of the trooping season, and it was in his gift to engage a number of the non-seamen staff such as cabin stewards and ancillary workers not directly concerned with navigation and engine-room duties. It was these crew members who organised the shipboard gambling, and so profitable was this sideline, particularly on homeward-bound vessels, that they were reputed to pay the RSM up to a hundred pounds for engaging them for the season.

We had taken on a chaplain at Gibraltar and he soon made his presence known. Although a chaplain has the status of an officer he does not hold any military rank and has no powers of command. He belongs to the Royal Army Chaplain's Department, which is headed by the Chaplain-General to the Forces, and according to his seniority is graded Chaplain 1st Class down to 4th Class, and is invariably addressed or referred to as 'Padre'. It did not take him long to organise a church service held on deck and was of a non-denominational character. His service was well attended possibly because the troops were bored and any change to ship's routine was welcome. Further he was accepted as a 'soldier's padre' – one who went down well with the men. For the rest of the voyage he was regularly on deck pointing out to his audience places of biblical and general interest as we went along.

The grandeur of the snow-capped Atlas Mountains stood out as we passed the coast of Morocco and it was here that we passed another ship of the Bibby Line, the *Oxfordshire,* homeward bound from India with its complement of time-expired men. Signals were passed, the soldiers crowded on to the decks and there was much waving of caps as we wished them a safe return. The next place of interest was the Italian island of Pantelleria, situated between Sicily and Tunisia, and at that point we were only a day from Malta.

By this time the troops were becoming restive through lack of exercise and our hope was that on arrival at Valetta, that great British naval base which was home to the Mediterranean Fleet, we should be allowed ashore for a route march. Ten days cooped up in a ship where every square foot counted was no joke. One morning the islands of Malta and Gozo were sighted and our spirits rose, but were soon deflated when it was announced that no shore leave was permitted. Shrugging aside our disappointment we left for Port Said, in Egypt, and the remainder of the trip proved uneventful.

Despite the cramped conditions on the ship, there had been no outbreak of infectious disease so there was no need to fly the yellow flag indicating to the shore health authorities that the ship was in quarantine. We were boarded by the pilot, who guided us to our berth, and a retinue of Egyptian officials then appeared, including the immigration authorities and the Egyptian police, to ensure that only bona fide visitors were allowed aboard. Strict anti-theft precautions were adopted, including the securing of all portholes. We were surrounded by bumboats whose occupants tried to sell their wares to the onlookers above. When a bargain had been made, a line attached to a small basket was thrown up to the deck, the purchase was examined and if it was satisfactory the agreed amount came down to the vendor. Most of the transactions were for 'feelthy pictures', pornography at its worst, depicting women in all sorts of lewd sexual acts. Port Said was a den of iniquity and we had been told by old soldiers that a huge sign hung there bearing the words

'Abandon Hope All Ye Who Enter Here'. We saw no such sign but passed a bust in memory of Ferdinand de Lesseps, the French engineer responsible for the construction of the Suez Canal. One huge sign that we did see was an advertisement for Johnnie Walker whisky showing the picture of John Bull with the caption 'Born 1820. Still going strong'. Whisky then cost 12s 11d (63p) per bottle!

Many years later, following the ending of the 1956 Suez Operation, an observant Sapper officer spotted a small bust of de Lesseps which had been knocked off its plinth and had it crated to return to England as a souvenir. The Signals learnt of the plan and during the night removed the bust from its crate and substituted it with rubble. The figure was then re-crated by a Signals party and it found its way to Maresfield Barracks in Herford. The bust was eventually returned to the Royal Engineers, who showed their appreciation by having a plaster reproduction made for presentation to 7th Signal Regiment and this now reposes in the Corps Museum.

Having restocked with fresh provisions and water obtained from the Sweet Water Canal, the pilot arrived, the mooring ropes were cast off and the ship approached the ninety mile Suez Canal at very slow speed and steamed towards the Gulf of Suez. Our progress was leisurely, to avoid damage to the embankment from the wash caused by the ship. At that time the convoy system had not been introduced and vessels passed each other in the canal, which is only ninety yards wide. The rule in force was that apart from naval vessels, which always had right of way, priority was given to homeward-bound ships, outward-bound vessels having to tie up at the canal bank. Being at sea level, there was not a lot to see apart from the odd camel and its rider plodding their way on the road running alongside.

The ship did not call at Suez and the only historical feature pointed out to us on the 200-mile passage through the Gulf was Mount Sinai, where Moses is supposed to have written the Ten Commandments on tablets of stone. Having reached the southern-most point of Sinai, where the Red Sea enters the Gulf of Aqaba terminating in the Israeli port of Eilat, orders were given for us to pack away our khaki serge uniforms and change into tropical gear. This was welcome with the exception of the topi, a huge pith helmet designed to minimise the danger of sunstroke. Our next stop was to be Aden, then a British protectorate garrisoned by British troops and some 1,300 miles from Suez.

From this stage onwards life became almost intolerable. There was little fresh air circulation in the sleeping-quarters and as the humidity increased men started to perspire and the fetid atmosphere assailed one's nostrils. Primitive methods were taken to overcome this, including huge canvas funnels which caught whatever breeze existed and diverted air down below. Permission was granted to sleep on the open deck and I was one of the lucky ones able to find six feet of deck space on which to stretch out. In my youth my father had told me of the dangers of sleeping beneath the night sky in the tropics, particularly in full moonlight, saying that it could cause 'moon madness'; but I took that risk. Awakening with the dawn, it was a pleasure to be able to buy a mug of tea or coffee at the canteen and watch the sun rising like a red ball of fire in the east, by which time it was necessary to go down below for breakfast. The stench that greeted one going down the companion-way to the mess deck was overpowering and enough to put one off one's food, but sea air promotes a healthy appetite and man must eat to survive.

The Red Sea averages a hundred miles in width and as a ship traverses a middle course there was nothing much to see except passing ships and Arab dhows carrying their cargoes to and from Africa. Although we could not see the coastline, the padre kept us informed of our progress. We passed Jidda, the Saudi-Arabian port which thousands of the Muslim faithful go through to make their pilgrimage to the holy city of Mecca. Port Sudan in the Sudan, Massawa in Eritrea and Djibouti, the French naval base in French Somaliland, were ports that we passed on the starboard side. Another place of interest was a group of huge rocks, known to seamen as 'The Twelve Apostles'. By now we were nearing Aden, where we were to refuel. In its day Aden was the largest bunkering station in the world (bunkering being a nautical expression for taking on coal or oil fuel). It was also one of the most humid places in the Red Sea. This humidity brings on a distressing condition, prickly heat, which results in skin rashes developing particularly beneath the armpits and other hairy regions of the body. There was no remedy for it and the only relief was copious applications of calamine lotion to the affected parts.

Having arrived there and taken up our berthing-station we found it extremely uncomfortable. In the open sea even if there are no breezes the movement of the ship creates its own air circulation but being stationary in a metal ship beneath a hot sun is most unpleasant. Aden was an eye-opener in another respect. Coal was conveyed to the ships in large lighters which sat low in the water, and it had to be carried up to the deck for tipping into the coal hold. The method used was archaic. It was carried in wicker baskets borne on their heads by women, in an endless procession resembling a trail of ants, and it seemed an age before the ship was loaded up and ready to leave.

The oil-burners were more fortunate. For refuelling, they were moored near to stand-pipes on the sea bed, which contained oil pumped from the shore.

We were not displeased to leave Aden and were now looking forward to our final destination: Karachi, 1,500 miles away. After emerging from the Gulf of Aden we entered the Arabian Sea. From then life on board became more tolerable, so we felt that the worst part of the voyage was behind us.

The route to Karachi was an easterly one and the ship made good progress along the coasts of the protectorates of the South Arabia Federation and Muscat and Oman. At this point we met many oil-tankers emerging from the Persian Gulf carrying their cargoes, some of them to replenish the oil-tanks at Aden.

At last the morning of 7th March dawned and a watchful sailor called out 'Land ahoy'. After three weeks on HMT *Lancashire* we were not sorry to leave our temporary home as we trudged along the gangplank with full kit and equipment, to reach *terra firma*. At the docks the disembarking troops were met by the movements staff responsible for transportation to our new units, which were widely dispersed throughout the subcontinent. We had made many friends on the ship, a few of whom we would meet up with again in five years' time.

Karachi was not the only port in India used for troop movements. The British Army in India was dispersed widely throughout the country, and if large units were changing station, Bombay and Calcutta were used. Bombay was the best-known, possibly because of that popular war time song:

> *A troop ship was leaving Bombay*
> *Bound for Blighty shores,*
> *Heavily laden with time-expired men*
> *Bound for the land they adored.*
> *And we'll say goodbye to them all,*
> *The long and the short and the tall*

One thing that struck us forcibly after reaching the quayside was that we had without noticing it acquired 'sea-legs' and walked with a sailor's gait. The movements staff had long experience of somewhat bemused soldiers arriving in a strange country and it did not take long for them to sort us out into groups travelling to different destinations. Our draft was handed over to the movement control NCO by Sergeant Pedlar Palmer, the draft-conducting NCO, and we were told our destination.

One of the first essentials for a traveller arriving in a foreign land is to possess local currency, and what remained of our English money was exchanged into rupees and annas. Each of us was then handed a *dhuree* and three blankets. Rather mystified by the *dhuree*, which was a green rug-like length of material, the more inquisitive asked its purpose and were told that they would find out later.

Our destination was Meerut in the north of the country and as we were a large group a special troop-train had been provided. We were briefed about the length of the journey, with dire warnings about buying iced water and sweetmeats at railway stations en route and the need to wear our pith helmets at all times when the sun was up.

As HMT *Lancashire* steamed steadily eastwards the thought struck me that I had been impetuous in volunteering to serve a stretch of five years so far away from home. There was also time to reflect on my upbringing and how my life had followed its course up to the time I joined the Army.

2

EARLY CHILDHOOD

I was born in a village called Porth-y-Felin near the town of Holyhead in the County of Anglesey on 7th September 1912 – the year in which the *Titanic*, the ship that was claimed to be unsinkable, collided with an iceberg and sank with the loss of so many lives on its maiden voyage to New York. Porth-y-Felin is a Welsh name and loosely translated it means the path to the mill. It was in fact a water-mill but I cannot recall it functioning, because the stream leading to it had silted up so that any heavy rainfall overflowed on to the pasture land on each side of it. What little water flowed past the mill meandered down to a creek four hundred yards away and ended in the sea. Often boats from sailing-vessels calling at the harbour were rowed in to the creek so that their crews could collect its unpolluted water to replenish their supplies.

The village was situated about a mile from Holyhead, a port serving the sea traffic between North Wales and Ireland. It nestled near the shore line, protected from the ravages of northerly gales sweeping the Irish Sea by a magnificent breakwater built in the last century. Holyhead itself was deemed to be the main Gateway to Ireland.

My parents were of working-class stock who had ventured away from home to seek employment. My father had spent his early adult life at sea, sailing around the world in 'wind-jammers' – sailing-vessels built of wood and entirely dependent on winds and breezes to propel them. Without steam to provide mechanical and electrical power, there were no winches, and any loading, unloading or moving of cargo had to be done manually with the aid of derricks or blocks and tackle. The only means of illumination for cabins, working-areas and navigational lights were kerosene lamps. Not for them the luxury of air-conditioning or electric fans when sailing through the tropics. Sail produced a tough and hardy seaman sometimes contemptuous of his brethren who sailed in steamers, and gave rise to the saying 'Iron men in wooden ships, wooden men in iron ships'.

My father was introduced to his first ship, the *Celtic Queen*, by my uncle, a ship's officer named Ebenezer Evans who later on in life became a well-known character in Far Eastern waters and spent years voyaging in the China seas. Because my father had learnt about carpentry and joinery, the job to which he was best suited was that of a ship's carpenter, the sea-going equivalent of a shipwright, whose task it was to make any necessary structural alterations to the ship's accommodation, subdivide cargo holds and carry out any joinery repairs needed to keep the vessel 'ship-shape'. At sea these functions were delegated to the ship's carpenter, who had one very important extra responsibility. He was answerable to the ship's master for the replenishment of fresh water supplies before sailing, taking on fresh supplies where possible and the daily logging and monitoring of water consumption to ensure sufficient stocks were kept in hand until the ship reached the next port of call where it was possible to top up the water-tanks. Vessels travelling to varied destinations encountered changeable weather conditions and, unlike the tea-clippers which travelled the trade routes and enjoyed trade winds, were liable to meet abnormal conditions, from the Roaring Forties around Cape Horn to the doldrums, where they could be becalmed for weeks. The captains of these ships never knew how long it would take them to reach their next port of call, so every effort was made to conserve water supplies, even to the extent of collecting rain-water in tarpaulins and transferring it to the tanks. A man can survive for weeks on short rations of food, but without water he soon dies of thirst.

After years afloat some men tire of the sea and seek a job ashore. This happened to my father, who married and settled down. He found employment with the firm of William Wild, a Sheffield-based business making fire-bricks for the furnaces of that once great steel-producing city. Wild's also quarried a special type of stone from Holyhead mountain which was rich in minerals. The bricks and stone were carried in wooden wagons on a light railway and loaded on to coasting vessels berthed alongside a jetty in the harbour, and my father's job was to keep this rolling stock in good repair.

During the 1914-18 war the production of steel was vital, and all the employees of William Wild were kept on because of their contribution to the economy.

My mother Margaret was one of six children, one of whom died in infancy, another married and with her husband emigrated to the United States before World War I. Yet another became a governess, the fourth was trained as a teacher and her brother was Ebenezer Evans of South China Sea fame. Feeding and clothing a large family is never easy. My mother, being the eldest, went into service. At that time job opportunities for women were limited and the great majority of them had no option but to take up domestic work, usually far away from home in large cities such as London or Liverpool. It was my mother's good fortune to gain employment with a kind family residing in Mayfair and she eventually became their cook.

In due course she met my father and they married in 1910. They rented an end-of-terrace house in Porth-y-Felin owned by a Mr Pearson, a retired industrialist who lived in a large house called Soldier's Point built on a promontory with a landing-stage to the sea, and it was in this terraced house that I was born. The rent of our house was derisory and was collected by his head gardener, Holden, one of whose perquisites was to retain the rents he collected from the tenants. Many years later Mr Pearson decided to sell his houses to sitting tenants on very favourable terms and my parents became property owners at a cost of £110.

Having acquired a property, the next thing was to improve it. My mother had long complained about the cramped conditions in the scullery, so we had an extension built which housed the paraphernalia connected with laundering and also served as a sun lounge which gave us extra space for sitting out.

My earliest recollections are those of our home and surroundings. The house had three bedrooms, a parlour and a kitchen/dining room. A coal-burning range provided heat for cooking and warmth, and illumination was by paraffin lamp or candles. There was no bathroom and the obligatory weekly bath was taken in the scullery, using a galvanised bath with water heated in large kettles on the kitchen range. Fuel was then relatively cheap, South Wales household coal costing £2 10s per ton.

The outside lavatory was primitive by modern-day standards and had to be flushed with buckets of water, but, unlike some of the villagers, we didn't have to put up with cesspits. A large attic fitted with a skylight provided extra sleeping-space when needed and the view from this part of the house was superb. Vessels could be seen entering and leaving or at anchor in the harbour, while further out at sea ocean-liners and freight vessels headed to and from Liverpool and the Firth of Clyde. The Skerries lighthouse, built on a small islet five miles away and a navigational hazard, beamed its warning lights to alert ships of its presence, and on a very clear day the Isle of Man could be seen with the naked eye, as could the Wicklow Mountains in Ireland. During the 1920s we were a great maritime nation and Liverpool was a busy port serving the ships travelling the North Atlantic routes to the United States and elsewhere. Pacific and Orient, White Star and Blue Funnel ships were a common sight.

We were still a great sea power, but the nation was impoverished after emerging from a world war costly in lives and resources. Food rationing was still in force and, although there was no black market, luxury foods were only available to those with money to spare. DORA, the Defence of the Realm Act, still restricted public-house and shop opening hours.

No present-day child can visualise life without television, radio, calculators, computers and the sophisticated toys available to them today, but children of that generation had to be content with simple playthings, and the more inventive made their own. The most popular of these, which provided a lot of entertainment, was the go-cart, easily constructed out of the discarded chassis of a child's pram and a wooden box. Two inverted cans with strings attached to them provided ideal mini-stilts. Marbles was a popular game, and marbles were often used in lieu of cash to exchange for other things, but the real gamblers played pitch-and-toss for halfpennies. Cigarette-card collecting was in vogue and it was the ambition of many to acquire a complete collection of famous footballers, cricketers, motor cars and whatever else the cigarette manufacturers produced. Groups of small boys would gather outside tobacconists' and with a winning smile say, 'Cigarette card, sir?'

An annual event very much looked forward to was the Sunday school trip to Rhyl, the holiday resort on the North Wales coast. The chapel hired a special train to carry those who had qualified by regular attendance to this charming seaside town with its long sandy beaches and busy promenade where tricycles and canoes could be hired at a modest price. My first sea trip was from Holyhead to Douglas on the Isle of Man, organised by a department of the London Midland and Scottish Railway and coinciding with the TT races, an annual event covering a tortuous ninety-mile course, with the spectators enjoying the thrill of motor cyclists hurtling along at 60 m.p.h.

To prevent me from becoming bored, my parents encouraged me to read and take part in local activities, one of which was the fancy-dress procession held on St David's Day, when the village children would walk in colourful costumes singing 'God bless the Prince of Wales'. I joined the Wolf Cubs, and one of my cherished memories was forming up with my fellow cubs to line the route taken by the Prince of Wales, later King Edward VIII but better known as the Duke of Windsor. The Prince was unveiling the North Wales Heroes Memorial at Bangor in North Wales to commemorate those fallen in the Great War.

George Borrow in his book *Wild Wales* described Holyhead as a town of lime-washed houses built on the seaside, skirted by a mountain, and beneath a blue sky reminding him of a Moorish piratical town. It developed in the early nineteenth century because of its close proximity to Dun Laoghaire, the port of Dublin, and it was the shortest sea route between Ireland and the mainland. Holy Island, on which the town is built, is connected to the Isle of Anglesey by means of a causeway carrying the railway line and road traffic, and Anglesey in turn is separated from North Wales by the Menai Straits, which are navigable by shipping at high tides. The Menai Straits were traversed by two bridges: Telford's suspension bridge carrying road traffic, and the Britannia tubular bridge used for the railway line, but as a result of a disastrous fire in 1970 a new bridge has been constructed to carry road and rail traffic.

The dominant feature of Holy Island is Mynydd Twr, the mountain referred to by Borrow. The cliffs beneath it are steep and treacherous on its seaward side, and the tides vicious with swirling races. Because of the danger to shipping presented by this rocky coast a lighthouse had been built at each end, and these were known as the North Stack and the South Stack. Access to these lighthouses could only be gained by means of narrow and tortuous paths cut into the mountain side with sheer drops in places to the sea below. All provisions to sustain the crews had to be carried by donkeys as, unlike some other lighthouses, the Trinity House relief ships could not reach them.

Another imposing feature was the breakwater, constructed to give safe anchorage and shelter to passing sailing-vessels and coasters in stormy weather. The original packet-boats carrying the mail to Ireland were berthed in the inner harbour, which was too small to accommodate any other vessels.

Because the port lacked a natural harbour, in 1800 the Government of the day funded the construction of a massive breakwater. The stone used to build it was quarried from the local mountain and conveyed to the site by a light railway. It was a colossal feat of engineering and took nearly thirty years to complete and a suitably imposing lighthouse was built at the end of it.

During the time the breakwater was being built the port was visited by the *Great Eastern,* one of the earliest iron ships designed by Isambard Kingdom Brunel, the most talented designer and engineer of his time. He also built the GWR (nicknamed God's Wonderful Railway), which ran from the West Country to London.

The *Great Eastern* was a paddle-ship powered by steam and assisted by sail. It boasted five funnels and six masts, dwarfing any other vessel near to it, and it was this ship that was used to lay the first transatlantic cable to the United States.

In the wars that followed, the harbour was of great strategic value in keeping the sea lanes open for commerce and troop movements, so a naval base was set up there to protect the Irish Sea from German submarines. The townspeople had always been dependent for their livelihood upon the service between Ireland and Holyhead; the contract for the conveyance of the Royal Mail was vested in the London and North Western Railway (later to become the LMS) and the mails were carried between Euston and Holyhead stations by the Irish mail train whose punctuality was legendary. The mail-boats covered the sixty mile crossing in three and a half hours and were seldom late. The transfer of mail and passengers from ship to train took little time and there were no passport inspections to hold things up.

Three of the vessels in service were *Cambria*, *Hibernia* and *Scotia*, and the latter was to figure in a tragic incident during World War II. The original *Hibernia* had seen service in the Mediterranean in the Great War; after being converted into an armed cruiser she was renamed HMS *Tara* and proceeded to the eastern Mediterranean with a complement of ninety local officers and men, where she was sunk by a German submarine off the coast of Libya. The survivors reached the shore in lifeboats and were interned by the unfriendly Libyans. The Duke of Westminster, hearing of their plight, led an armoured column to rescue them and they returned home to continue their war effort.

The LMS Railway Company boasted proudly and justifiably that the mail was never late in reaching its destination at Euston Station. A mobile postal sorting-office formed part of the mail train, and as it sped towards London letters were sorted out for distribution to large centres such as Chester, Crewe and Rugby. In the 1920s we had no first- and second-class post, and a letter stamp cost only 1½d. Anyone missing the last collection at the main post office could walk the short distance to the railway station, affix an extra ½d stamp, and rest assured that the letter would reach its destination in time for the early morning delivery.

3

SCHOOL

Formal education began at the age of five and I joined St Cybi's, a primary school located about a mile from home. School meals were not provided, and the four miles a day walking there and back was good physical exercise. Life here was uneventful and the only exciting thing I can remember was an accident to a boy in my class-room who was playing with a detonator found at a disused quarry. It exploded, blowing off part of his hand and lifting the wooden lid of his desk. Pandemonium set in but the teacher restored calm and the injured lad was given first-aid treatment before being moved to the cottage hospital. Fortunately for him, tinkering with the detonator had removed some of the explosive, otherwise he might have ended up with one hand.

Two memorable events took place whilst I was at St Cybi's. King George V followed the example of Queen Victoria, who had passed through the port on her return from a visit to Ireland in the Royal Yacht *Prince Albert*. The King, the Queen and the Princess Royal boarded the Royal Train at the pier head and the route to the railway station was lined with school children waving Union Flags and cheering the royal party on its way.

One day a rumour circulated that Gene Tunney was due to arrive on the Irish mail train from Euston to visit the birthplace of his ancestors. Tunney was an American ex-marine who defeated Jack Dempsey for the title Heavyweight Boxing Champion of the World and his arrival caused a mass evacuation of school pupils to the railway station, which was crowded with expectant admirers. As soon as he boarded the mail-boat the reigning champion made his way to the bridge and kept on waving to his delighted fans.

The town of Holyhead was home to a seaman known as 'Will V.C.' who had been decorated at Buckingham Palace by King George V for the part he played as a crew member on a 'Q' ship hunting German submarines in the Irish Sea. To combat the U-boats, relatively small marine craft were converted to act as decoys. They carried at least one naval gun and the crews were armed but did not wear uniform, which would have identified them as combatants. Their ships were fast and manoeuvrable, making them less vulnerable to torpedo attack, and the biggest danger to the crew was from a boarding-party intent on taking prisoners.

One day the decoy was spotted and hailed by an enemy submarine. Finding it within range of their gun, the crew opened fire and sank it. This exploit evoked high praise from the Admiralty, and the King agreed to award the highest decoration for valour, the Victoria Cross, to a crew member. No one in particular had played an outstanding part in this episode, so lots were drawn to decide who was to receive the highly prized decoration.

I was a plodder getting by with average school reports, the remark 'Must work harder' summing up my progress, and everyone was surprised when at the age of ten and a half I gained a scholarship to the county school, administered by the Central Welsh Board and considered to be one of the jewels in its crown. The examination had taken place in April, and at the end of the summer term I was met by the headmaster and told that I had done well, passing top of the school and seventh in the county.

One of the more eminent pupils educated at the county school was Cledwyn Hughes, who became MP for Anglesey and attained high office in a Labour government, one of his posts being Colonial Secretary. He is currently the Leader of the Opposition in the House of Lords.

At about this time Miss Megan Lloyd George was adopted as Parliamentary candidate for Anglesey by the Liberal Party and was supported by her father David, who addressed a meeting at Garreg Lwyd, the home of the shipowner Sir Robert Thomas. My father took me along to it. The election address over, Lloyd George passed us by, exchanged a few words, patted me on the back and said that he liked to see the young taking an interest.

Politics aroused a lot of passion then and there was no lack of fervent orators to espouse a cause. Some of these speakers were lay preachers experienced in rousing the passions of their listeners and capable of pouring scorn on their opponents. In her first election campaign Megan was opposed by a Labour candidate named Robert Lewis Jones, and at one election meeting a supporter of hers was in good voice.

'The name of David Lloyd George,' he thundered, 'will live when Robert Lewis Jones is rotting in his grave.'

Helped by emotional words like these, she went on to become the first woman MP for Anglesey.

In 1927 Holyhead was chosen as the venue for the Welsh National Eisteddfod, that well-known cultural festival in which archdruids, druids and bards voice their knowledge of religion, history, prose and verse. It attracted visitors from all over Wales and overseas, notably from Patagonia, which had earlier been colonised by Welsh people seeking a better life. There were few hotels in the town and the organisers spent months arranging rooms in private homes for the visitors, but unfortunately the festival attracted some unsavoury characters whose morals were not in keeping with the religious upbringing of the locals.

It was fashionable for women at that time to wear fancy garters to hold up their stockings, and these multi-coloured supporters were very much in evidence as couples lusted on the beaches and in the fields, although the less brazen of them found privacy beneath upturned rowing-boats, where their activities were hidden from the public gaze.

When the decision was made to hold the Eisteddfod in the town, the local council arranged to erect shelters along the promenade. It was here that old gentlemen met in the daytime to chat and girls lost their virginity at night, one of them, known as 'Fornicating Cissy', being particularly notorious.

Very few trees grew in Anglesey and so there were no

lovers' lanes where couples could do their courting. The nearest place to relax was known as the 'rocky coast', a small headland covered with heather and springy turf, ideal for lying on, and here they could do as they wished provided they did not mind the odd Peeping Tom concealed in disused slit trenches.

Those were the years of the great depression following the Great War. Unemployment was rife and wage rises were unheard of. Pay cuts were made frequently, and this prompted the coal-miners of South Wales to withdraw their labour and led to the General Strike of 1926, dealt with firmly by the Prime Minister, Stanley Baldwin.

Although the price of basic foodstuffs remained static, there were other expenses to be covered, such as the repayment of the mortgage, new clothing and shoes, boot repairs and other incidentals. I realised that my parents were finding it difficult to cope so I found a Saturday-morning job. This involved carrying a large tray of cakes and pastries from a nearby bakery to a stall in the market-place and replenishing the stock as it was sold. My reward for this was 6d plus a paper bag full of unsold cakes, which the family enjoyed at tea-time.

From this beginning I went on to better things and found morning employment on Saturdays and Sundays on a milk round. The local dairy farmer delivered milk to his customers from a large churn mounted on a pony-drawn trap, measuring it directly into the housewife's jug. My main responsibility was to take charge of the pony while the farmer collected his debts or called at the local pub for his Saturday-morning drinks. This was a well-paid job which earned me 2s 6d for a weekend.

In the summer months when milk was liable to curdle, domestic refrigerators being non-existent, the guest-house owners expected evening deliveries to be made and I carried these on foot in small containers. The extra money I received for this job was sufficient to pay the weekly instalments on a Hercules bicycle which I bought for £5 17s 6d, thus saving on shoe leather.

My earnings from this part-time job enabled me to make a small contribution to the running of the home, but I felt that my parents were making sacrifices in order to maintain me at school. I was now in my fourth year and realised that I was not keeping up the promise shown in my entrance examination. Although I remained in the A stream, I considered that I was not keeping pace with my fellow students.

This state of affairs was resolved when an electrical engineer named R. J. Williams offered to take me on as an apprentice. The headmaster was loth to release me, although after some persuasion he agreed, but by leaving at the end of the fourth year I had to be content with passing the Junior School Certificate. The decision to leave school early was a difficult one to make, but my reasoning was that unless I achieved brilliant results in the School Certificate examination, that was the end of the road. To gain entry to university one had to be academically outstanding and fortunate enough to gain one of the few bursaries offered by philanthropists to cover living expenses. The days of universities in every town, and government grants, were then a long way off.

4

APPRENTICESHIP

In 1927 the age of electricity was dawning, but less than fifty per cent of homes had it installed, so there was plenty of scope for development. My new boss operated from small premises in a good position and undertook house-wiring, battery-charging, electrical-plant maintenance and retailing domestic appliances. Some of these were rented out, and an Electrolux carpet sweeper could be hired for 2s 6d a day. My starting pay was 5s a week for the first year, increasing by 5s each year until the end of my five-year apprenticeship.

Labour and material costs were low and the charge for installing electricity in a building was £1 per 'point', a point being a light fitting or plug. Wireless receivers were powered by secondary batteries and it was one of my jobs to run the battery-charging room.

Trearthur Bay, with its sandy beach and ready access to the sea for dinghy-sailing, had been discovered. The people who could afford to have homes built there were not content with kerosene lamps, so they were dependent on their electric power plants, as the bay was too remote from the generating station for cables to be laid to it.

My first outside job was rewiring the electric bell installation at the workhouse in Valley, then a small hamlet four miles from Holyhead and later well known to thousands of RAF personnel who served at the base nearby. The bell system was an archaic method of summoning servants for help but simple in concept. It was activated by pressing a bell-push connected to a glass-lidded box containing small 'flags' which moved to indicate the location of the caller. The system was energised by Leclanche cells, which were virtually self-charging. In this case the bell and flags were located in the office of the work master, the wiring connecting the system being laid in the ceiling.

No one had taught me to tread on the wooden beams, and in my naivety I gaily walked on the lath and plaster ceiling until suddenly I ended up with one leg protruding into the room below, to the amusement of the inmates, and had to be yanked up by my workmate.

Social conditions at that time were at their worst. Lloyd George had introduced the old-age pension in 1908 when Chancellor of the Exchequer, and this amounted to 7s 6d a week on attaining the age of sixty five. The destitute had to rely on the sympathy of the Poor Law Committee, who considered their cases and doled out pittances in very needy cases. Local charities organised collections and flag days for the 'Sick and Needy'. There was no free health service.

Now Lloyd George was trying to rally the nation with his election slogan 'We can conquer unemployment'. Because of the plight of homeless men seeking employment, workhouses had been set up in rural areas every twenty-five miles or so. In return for a bed, supper, breakfast and a bath, they were given a task such as chopping firewood, filling the coal-scuttles or washing up. Apart from caring for the travellers, the work master, an understanding and kindly man, had another heavy responsibility.

The insane were kept in lunatic asylums, but those women who were feeble-minded were segregated, often for their own good, in institutions like the workhouse. Imagine my anxiety when told to enter their common room to repair some wiring: a virile youngster of sixteen surrounded by females, some of whom had not set eyes on a man for years.

The responsibility of keeping the women within the confines of the building was a cross that the work master had to bear. Sometimes one or two of them managed to slip out, spent an hour or two in the hay with farm labourers and returned satiated with sex – with dire results and an official enquiry to follow. The job at the workhouse took a week and I was glad to leave the place.

The cinema provided evening entertainment, and old favourites included Charlie Chaplin, Buster Keaton, Fatty Arbuckle, Laurel and Hardy, Tom Mix and a host of other black and white silent films. Before the film was shown and during the interval, a pianist played the popular tunes of the day. It was in the Empire Cinema that I saw my first talking picture, which featured Al Jolson in the 'Singing Fool'.

Unlike present-day Anglesey, where the crime rate is high and vandalism rife, breaches of the law were rare, the most common offences being riding a bicycle at night without lights and drunkenness, suitably dealt with by the magistrates. Any serious cases were heard by a judge at the quarter sessions. More often than not his visit was unnecessary, and as consolation he was presented with a pair of white gloves.

The local police superintendent, John Fair, sensed the despair of young men unable to find a job and did something about it. He acquired an empty building and had it converted into a gymnasium with the help of local traders and charitable townspeople. His constables, most of them ex-servicemen, volunteered as physical-training instructors, and this enterprise raised the morale of the town's youths. Superintendent Fair insisted on a simple oath being taken by all who joined the club. It was: 'Live clean, help others, fear God and honour the King'.

In 1928 the local electricity company extended its cables to our village, and our house was one of the first to have electric light installed. This was a boon especially to my mother, who no longer had to spend time on chores like removing candle grease, cleaning oil-lamp shades and trimming wicks.

'The wireless' was gaining popularity, and I came upon a blueprint which showed enthusiasts how to build a simple set from a kit or spare parts. The set recommended was the Mullard Straight Four, and having purchased a quantity of thermionic valves, transformers, fixed and variable condensers, headphones and other bits and pieces, I assembled the set and was delighted to hear a voice announce 'This is 2 L O London calling'.

Such was the public interest in the wireless that within a

few years sets were being marketed by firms like Cossor, Ferguson and Mullard, fitted with a built-in speaker and encased in a moulded bakelite container. However, the days of mains-operated sets were a long way off as far as the domestic user was concerned.

At the age of eighteen I became friendly with a boy named David Green who had spent a few years at sea, starting as a cabin-boy until qualifying as seaman. His tales of adventure and visits to far-off places aroused a desire in me to travel.

Many seafarers of the time spent years at sea accumulating money, and the more enterprising saved sufficient to start off a business of their own. This happened to David, who by 1950 was running a thriving grocery shop and became a well-respected town councillor. His father had served with the British Army in India and in the Great War and was in receipt of a pension, payable every three months, and for days after its receipt there was much imbibing at the 'Harp', our local pub. He was proud of his Army service and could yarn for hours about places he had visited in India. A scroll hung in his parlour bearing the words:

> *His King and Country called him,*
> *The call was not in vain.*
> *On Britain's Roll of Honour*
> *You'll find this Hero's name.*

Reverting to my apprentice training, Bill Roberts was a competent tradesman well versed in the theory of electricity and he advised me to enrol on a correspondence course to further my knowledge of the subject. Heeding his advice, I took a course with the Technical Institute of Great Britain and completed their syllabus in general electrical engineering. In November 1930 I was sent a diploma of associate membership of this august-sounding body, designated by the letters A.M.Tech.I. (Gt.Brit.) signed, sealed and delivered from Temple Bar House, London EC4.

My mother was ailing, suffering from a complaint that modern medical knowledge could have cured. She died at the early age of forty-seven and was interred in Maeshyfryd cemetery. This left a void in my life, so I devoted my leisure time to keeping fit in the youth club and running middle distances.

Meanwhile, my apprenticeship ran its course until it ended on my twentieth birthday. I asked my employer if he would keep me on as an improver for a further year but he declined on the grounds that business was slack, so I became unemployed. My ambition was to obtain a job as ship's electrician, but because of the continuing depression shipping was still in the doldrums.

Five weeks of unemployment was long enough for me, and when I told my father of my intention to join the Army his response was: 'You haven't got the guts'. That decided me.

There were other openings available to young men, including the police service, but UK Forces could afford to be selective, preferring recruits who were six feet tall. Colonial police forces, such as Northern and Southern Rhodesia, Hong Kong and Kenya, and protectorates like Palestine, welcomed UK citizens who were adventurous and of good physique, but having acquired some technical knowledge my preference was to enlist as a tradesman in the British Army.

5

RECRUIT DAYS

Having decided to enlist in the Army, I called at the local police station, stated my intention and was given a railway warrant to travel to Caernarfon, the nearest recruiting centre.

Being a tradesman with a reasonable educational background, my preference was for the Royal Engineers, so I was disappointed to learn that they had no vacancies. The recruiter, a Regimental Sergeant-Major from The Royal Welch Fusiliers (the county regiment) tried to steer me into the RWF, whose battle honours were legendary and motto: 'Death before Dishonour', but life in an Infantry battalion did not appeal to me. His next tactic was to try and lure me into the Welsh Guards, which he said would be a better bet for a lad of my physique, and the pay was higher, half a crown (2s 6d) a day, recently reduced from 2s 11d.

I was about to leave when he asked me to stay, saying that a new corps had been formed at Catterick Camp and that he would telephone their depot to find out if they had any vacancies. The answer was reassuring, and after passing a simple literacy test I was sent home on ten days' paid leave plus ration allowance and told to await further instructions. In due course I was ordered to report on 7th November 1932, and enclosed was an encouraging letter from the RSM, the gist of which was that to succeed in my new career I should acquire an Army certificate of education 1st class and become a Class 1 tradesman. The inference was that having achieved these standards (and kept my nose clean) with God's help I might even reach the elevated rank of RSM. The enormity of my commitment to serve eight years with the colours and four in the reserve weighed heavily upon me.

Having bidden farewell to my family and friends and after a long train journey to North Yorkshire, I reported to the guardroom of the depot battalion late at night and was met by a kindly sergeant, who showed me how to make my bed. It did not help matters that I was the first arrival of number 16 squad and my first night was a lonely one.

The first thing that struck me was the intense cold, which contrasted so sharply with the mild and equable climate of Anglesey, so near to the Gulf Stream. I was preoccupied in the morning handing in my civilian clothing, drawing my Army kit and having a further medical examination.

More recruits arrived gradually and soon we were sufficient in number to form a drill squad. Our accommodation was primitive, the huts having been erected during World War I to house German prisoners. Heating was by means of two large coal-burning stoves, the fuel for which was kept in a huge metal container the size of a modern-day skip.

In the absence of the squad NCO, his duties were delegated to the senior soldier, and being the first arrival I was the 'fall guy'. The policy was to keep everyone on the move, and we were 'marched' from place to place even before we learnt to march. To keep us occupied before starting life on 'the square', as the parade-ground was called, we were given menial tasks such as scrubbing, polishing, coal-carrying and any other activity that the NCO could dream up.

We were well fed in a communal mess room which had a detached area for washing up our eating utensils, and it was here that I met Johnny Magee, a Holyhead boy whose father managed a bottling-store where Guinness brought over from Dublin in huge casks was transferred into bottles and distributed throughout the realm. Johnny hoped to become a wireless operator but sadly failed the aptitude test and was earmarked to be trained as a driver HT (Horse Transport) until his father secured his discharge by purchase for the sum of twenty five pounds.

Ironically, Johnny Magee finished his career as the ship's master of a supertanker!

One of the first things instilled into us when we enlisted into the Royal Corps of Signals was respect for our cap badge and *esprit de corps*. In 1932 the Corps cap badge consisted of the winged figure of Mercury standing on a globe and carrying a caduceus surmounted by the Imperial Crown, the globe being embellished by a scroll bearing the Corps motto *Certa Cito* (Swift and Sure), the whole being enclosed in an oval band bearing the words 'Royal Corps of Signals'.

In 1932 we were still in the depths of a very severe world slump with international trade virtually stagnant, and because of this our merchant fleet and its crews were idle. The Corps was very selective in its choice of recruits. Wireless operators holding Class I Post Master General certificates in wireless telegraphy were eager to enlist and were a bonus because they were capable of transmitting and receiving upwards of thirty words per minute on a keyboard and needed only to learn Army operating procedures. On the technical side there was no shortage of electricians and mechanics available to maintain the uncomplicated equipment in use at the time.

After weeks of fatigues, space was found for us on the parade-ground and we were taught foot drill leading to the execution of complicated and intricate movements. From these foot movements we graduated to 'whip drill'. The Royal Corps of Signals had been formed in 1920 out of the Royal Engineers, a horsed regiment, and we maintained most of their traditions, with trained soldiers wearing spurs and carrying a whip. From whip drill we graduated to rifle drill, and the rifles in use at the time were Lee Enfields, relics of World War I. Using these weapons, we were taught how to carry out orders such as slope arms, present arms, ground arms, port arms, and order arms. Constant practice at these movements achieved near perfection, and after sixteen weeks the squad was ready for 'passing out' or 'passing off' the Square. The parade-ground was used solely for organised drill, and woe betide the innocent who strayed on to this hallowed ground: not only was he bawled out by watchful

NCOs but quite often given extra drill to teach him a lesson.

It was during my recruit days that I met Jack Dineen, an Irishman who hailed from County Clare on the west coast of Ireland, and being fellow Celts we chummed up. The Easter break was approaching, but it was of short duration and did not allow him time to visit home, which entailed the train journey to Holyhead, the sea crossing to Dublin and the long train journey across Ireland to his home. Feeling sympathetic towards him, I invited him to spend Easter at our house, and it made a pleasant break from hours spent on the drill square. Jack was over-sexed and missed his Irish colleen, and he prevailed upon me to find him a girl – so I organised a foursome and headed for the rocky coast. Jack's partner was very obliging, but mine played the innocent and kept her legs crossed, which is the surest method of birth control.

We were nearing the end of our initial training and looking forward to our trade training when one morning we found that Jack Dineen was absent. Because of my friendship with him, I was questioned about his sudden departure but satisfied the authorities that I had not connived at his desertion, so no further action was taken. Jack was posted as absent without leave and later as a deserter and was not seen again. It then transpired that his brother was an officer in the Irish Republican Army and that Jack was earmarked to follow in his footsteps. Lacking the training facilities enjoyed by the British Army, they would persuade their more promising members to enlist in the UK, where they could complete their basic training, including the use of firearms. Having attained proficiency as soldiers, they would return to Ireland, the British taxpayer having to foot the bill for their pay, uniform, keep and training.

Life at the depot was not all drill. We were lectured on military law, as enacted in the Army Act, and warned of the dire consequences of offending against some of its sections. Two of the more awe-inspiring sections reflected the punishment for any soldier showing cowardice by deserting in the face of the enemy, or being a soldier acting as a sentinel falling asleep at his post. Anyone found guilty by court martial of these crimes was 'to suffer death'.

Before passing out, one was taught Corps history and subjects leading to the certificate of education 2nd class, which had to be passed before a soldier qualified for trade pay. Lectures were also given by the medical officer and a course in the gymnasium had to be completed. Athletic standards had to be achieved and recruits participated in cross-country running.

Although the rations were lavish by civilian standards, the constant exercise and the cold climate induced pangs of hunger, and most of a soldier's pay was spent on food in the canteen. The problem was alleviated by the messing officer providing a mug of cocoa and biscuits, or some left-over dishes such as rissoles, which were available from the kitchen from Tuesday to Thursday. The more astute of us had learnt another trick or two, and after tea on Sundays, the only time that a pat of butter was served, we hurried to the house of the Methodist padre, who was at home to anyone wishing to call, and were regaled with cups of tea and home-made cakes baked by his wife. After a decent interval, we made our apologies and left for Sandes Soldiers' Home in time to listen to a talk by a visiting missionary, and were rewarded with more cups of tea and a plate of rice pudding or some other dish. So the Sabbath day passed and we were well rested and nourished, ready to face the rigours of another working week.

Rather than have an interminable queue lining up with plates at the servery hatch, meals were served in flat dishes holding rations for six men and issued in exchange for a metal tally left on each trestle table by the NCO. A man was designated to collect the food and divide it up into six portions, watched closely by his five fellow diners, who made sure that each of them received an equal share.

On one occasion the NCO left two tallies for the dessert course by mistake and one of them was hurriedly pocketed. The 'waiter' rushed to the hatch to collect the sweet – and to our delight it was roly-poly pudding and was soon devoured. To avoid the risk of recognition, another man took the second tally to the servery and returned with a further tray of pudding. While this was going on, the empty tray was concealed beneath the table and propelled by soldiers' feet from one place to another to avoid the culprits being detected.

Television viewers often see so-called 'dramas' portraying life in the Army as sadistic and brutal, but many of these scripts are written and produced by dramatists with sick minds and fertile imaginations. Soldiers do sometimes let off steam as a result of being mocked by a comrade, and this could lead to blows. At the depot, they had the answer to grudges in the form of the 'blood tub', a part of the gymnasium set aside for boxing training and tournaments. Fist fighting was never resorted to, and anyone with a score to settle was advised to sort it out in the ring. Although the difference was not resolved under the Queensberry Rules, one of the physical-training instructors was always present to ensure fair play.

Soon after the departure of Jack Dineen I became friendly with Ernie Mitchell, a well-proportioned ex-miner from Chesterfield in Derbyshire, who related his Sunday afternoon exploits to me. He had lived in a village near to a large house bequeathed to his two unmarried daughters by a wealthy coal-owner. The ladies had no wish to marry but, being human, needed to have their sexual appetites fulfilled in a discreet way.

Attracted by his physique, they arranged for him to visit them on Sunday afternoons to demonstrate his prowess in bed, and so virile was he that he could satisfy them both, at the same time earning himself a substantial retainer for his services.

It is a maxim in the Army that every soldier, serving in a technical unit, whatever his skills, is a soldier first and tradesman second, and with this in mind he had to complete a course of weapon training in which he learnt to use the arms issued to him and take care of them. The old saying, 'A rifle is a soldier's best friend' still applies; so, in common with other arms of the service, we in the Royal Corps of Signals had to become proficient shots. To achieve this we practised on a miniature range, using small-bore .22 ammunition, and then graduated to an open-air range where .303 rounds were used. Recruits were required to be at least class two shots before being classified as trained soldiers.

Rifle practice and classification over, the long-awaited day arrived when we could say goodbye to recruit training on the square, and the one hurdle left was the 'Pass off'. Several hours were spent on polishing our leatherware until it shone like glass. Great care had to be taken in polishing the brasswork lest traces of metal polish showed on the leatherwork or uniform. We were carefully inspected by the squad instructor, who put right minor faults, and awaited the arrival of the assistant adjutant, Lieutenant E. R. Nanney-Wynn Nanney-Wynn, our inspecting officer. He subjected the squad to the most exacting inspection – front and rear – before inviting the instructor to put us through our paces at drill. On being satisfied with this the squad was re-formed, but Nanney-Wynn Nanney-Wynn had another duty to perform before marching off: to award the Commandant's Whip to the best recruit. Unlike the normal issued fibre whip, this one was special, made of whalebone, and I was the fortunate recipient! During my later service we chanced to meet again, once at Bulford, again in Damascus and lastly in London, where he was running an Army postal unit. Nanney-Wynn had been commissioned in 1927 and retired in 1950 in the rank of major to his home county of Merionethshire in West Wales.

In the days before leaving the depot we were tested on our knowledge of Corps history. The Corps had been formed in 1920 out of the Royal Engineers by General Fowler, whose portrait hangs in the ante-room of the HQ mess at Blandford, and the King had graciously conferred the honour of the word Royal being added to its title in the same year. Its cap badge has been described earlier, but the central figure of Mercury had been affectionately known as 'Jimmy' from the start.

During the early days of the Corps, blazer badges bearing the figure of 'Jimmy' were awarded to outstanding athletes like Jimmy Emblem (Corps, Army and ABA heavyweight boxing champion), Joe Cottrell, the outstanding amateur runner of his day, Spud Murphy (Army hurdles champion) and many more. Somewhere along the line the name of the Corps was abbreviated to Royal

Signals, possibly because ours was the only 'Royal Corps' in the British Army until the formation of the Royal Corps of Transport much later on.

Now that we were trained soldiers, we were allowed to have our breeches 'winged' and to wear spurs. Instead of being confined to the Catterick Camp area, we could travel to places as far away as Richmond and Darlington, or further afield with a pass. One such excursion took us to York, at that time the headquarters of Northern Command, to attend the Northern Command Tattoo held on York racecourse. Most of the young women living in York at the time were employed at the Rowntrees chocolate factory, and because we had become accustomed to living the life of single men in barracks, many of us were unnerved at being ogled by pretty girls and were too shy to respond to their advances.

6

TECHNICAL TRAINING

After sixteen weeks of what amounted to basic Infantry training, we were ready for the next phase and our squad was dispersed. Those earmarked for the workshop trades of electrician fitter and instrument mechanic were posted to D Company, and the potential wireless operators to E. The weeding-out process had brought to light that a number of men did not have the acumen to be trained for the more highly skilled jobs, so according to their aptitude they were categorised as motor-cycle despatch riders, linemen, and horse drivers, who were the lowest in the scale and were ranked as drivers as opposed to the superior grade of signalman.

The job of a lineman entailed laying and repairing field cables spewed out from a horse-drawn waggon travelling at great speed over difficult terrain, and in wartime under fire, so it was essential for him to be a proficient rider. Equitation training for both linemen and drivers was undertaken in the riding-school of the mounted wing of the Depot Battalion under the supervision of Lieutenant Wilfred Ponsonby and his team of experienced instructors, some of whom had qualified at the Army Equitation Centre as rough riders. Drivers were mainly employed as carters who carried the tentage, stores and heavy baggage of marching men in their waggons. Despatch riders were trained in F Company under the able direction of Captain Henry Firth, who was also involved in the formation of the White Helmets and later achieved international fame at displays demonstrating their expertise in handling their motor cycles.

In view of my electrical experience, it was my hope to be

trained as an electrician fitter. To this end I had been given a theoretical test on electricity and magnetism and a practical test in machine fitting as a prelude to joining the Training Battalion, but I was devastated to learn that I had been selected for training as a wireless operator.

After spending two weeks at E Company trying to master the intricacies of the Morse code, I was nearing despair when my discomfiture was noticed by the instructor. On hearing of my disappointment, he advised me to apply for an interview with the Workshop Officer, Lieutenant Ian Meiklejohn. He was sympathetic and said that he would look into the matter, and within a few days I was told that my test papers had been mixed up with those of another recruit. He confirmed that I was suitable material for workshop training and I lost no time in moving to D Company.

Technical instruction involved the production of simple tools made to exacting standards with the aid of micrometers and Vernier gauges, stripping engines down to their constituent parts before reassembling them and lectures on mechanical and electrical engineering.

We were taught the fundamentals of the internal combustion engine evolved by Dr Ottomann, the German engineer who discovered that a measured amount of petrol inserted into a cylinder under pressure and ignited by a spark caused an explosion which drove a piston down and thus created power, and the Ottomann sequence of compression, ignition, firing and exhaust was instilled into our memories.

Alternative means of producing the energy to propel motor engines was now being developed by scientists who discovered that if a foreign body was pumped into pressurised air it caused an explosion, and this led to the evolvement of the diesel engine.

Cannibalised sections of motor vehicles were available with cut-away sections of engines and gearboxes on display to enable students to understand more readily how these components worked, and trainees were encouraged to make copious notes for inclusion in their own self-written manuals.

Life at D Company was not confined to technical

training, and other activities such as sport and guard duty took up a lot of time. When I enquired about facilities for education, it was made clear to me that no provision was made in working hours. There were classes for coaching men with ambitions to pass their Army 1st examination, but attendance was purely voluntary and of a spare-time nature.

This attitude did not deter me, and I applied to attend educational classes run under the supervision of a sergeant in the Royal Army Education Corps – and this did not pass unnoticed by the corporal in charge of our barrack room. Unlike the officers and technical instructors, the NCOs forming the permanent cadre were unambitious and in a rut with no hope of achieving further promotion, so they were content with performing supervisory duties of a routine and domestic nature. A typical example was the post corporal, whose main job was to collect incoming letters from the orderly room and hand them over to those for whom they were intended by calling out the name of the recipient, who stepped out of line to collect his mail.

The post NCO had an additional responsibility in that he was required to assemble the occupants of each barrack room on a rota basis at the cookhouse for the evening ritual of potato-peeling, and if this chore clashed with educational classes he ensured that sufficient potatoes were left unpeeled for any absentee students to complete their quota before breakfast on the following day.

Despite the discouragement, I persevered with my studies and when the result of the 1933 examination was announced I was presented with a parchment certificate, the gist of it was to the effect that at an examination held in October 1933 under the authority of the Army Council, I had passed in English, Mathematics, Geography and Mapreading, with a distinction in English, having obtained more than eighty per cent marks.

It was rubber-stamped by Major-General A. E. McNamara, Director of Military Training, and a footnote read: 'The examination in these subjects is approximately of the standard required for the School Certificate.'

So, despite discouragement from some of the 'twostripers', I was some way to reaching the goal set by my recruiter back at Caernarfon – and all within a year of enlisting.

From time to time we were detailed to form the 'quarter guard', which normally consisted of a corporal and five men. After a thorough inspection by the orderly officer, the smartest man on parade was nominated as 'stick man' and the scruffiest 'waiting man' before the old guard was ceremoniously relieved and the new guard dismissed to the guardroom.

One of the duties of the orderly officer was to visit the quarter guard during the hours of darkness to ensure that it was alert and obeying orders, and this could be any time between 'lights out' and the dawn, depending on the whim of the adjutant, who stipulated the time of 'visiting rounds'.

The flaw in this arrangement was that the orderly officer was known, his room could be seen from the sentry's post and he always used a bicycle on his rounds; so when the light in his room was extinguished and a bicycle lamp lit up, there was ample time to warn the guard commander of his approach.

The last eight weeks of our training were spent learning to drive, starting off on waste ground within the camp area, and as we gained experience moving on to the roads within its perimeter. Finally we were permitted to drive on the public highway, and the ultimate thrill was to travel on almost deserted roads to Darlington and back, a round distance of some twenty miles.

The vehicles used were sturdy thirty hundred weight lorries, not very manageable, and it was essential to learn the art of 'double declutching' to avoid clashing the gears. This involved depressing the clutch, moving the gear lever to neutral, pausing to allow the engine revolutions to die down, again depressing the clutch, before engaging a higher gear and repeating the process until top gear was reached. Changing down was even more hazardous as the engine speed had to be raised before a lower gear was engaged. The introduction of synchromesh gears has made motoring somewhat simpler!

Finally the red-letter day arrived for our road test,

which the Army insisted upon before entrusting its vehicles to inexperienced drivers although the compulsory testing of civilians was years away. When the driving licence arrived, we felt very proud of our achievement and pleased that its cost of five shillings was borne out of Army funds.

We now found more time in which to explore our surroundings. The old Catterick Camp is shown on current road maps as Catterick Garrison and is four miles from Richmond, that charming little town with its cobbled square built soon after the Norman Conquest. The town lies on high ground with a commanding view of the countryside, and its most dominant feature is Richmond Castle, which was used as a fortress throughout the Middle Ages to keep the peace in that part of North Yorkshire. The River Swale flows beneath it, and there is a wide pathway along its bank which climbs steeply to Easby Abbey, now taken over by English Heritage. The garrison is also near to some charming villages with ancient taverns where we spent an hour or so drinking a glass of beer and eating cheese sandwiches, sometimes being invited by the local customers to join them in a game of darts or shove-halfpenny, the losers paying for a round of drinks.

Recreational facilities within the camp included a billiard table on which some of the novices practised their strokes. There was a saying that proficiency at the game was the sign of a misspent youth but from what we saw the players had led blameless lives. The supervision of the billiard hall was entrusted to Leslie Bainbridge, a Yorkshire lad who had enlisted at the age of sixteen after giving a false date of birth. Bainbridge had completed his training and was awaiting a passage to China, and we were to see much of each other during the course of the next fifty years.

We were now nearing the end of our training. As progress reports were submitted regularly it was reasonably certain that the students in our class would pass their class 3 trade test, and those who wished to apply for overseas postings were invited to do so. My choice was India and I was accepted on condition that I qualified at the forthcoming trade testing board, which proved to be no problem. The posting to 3rd Indian Divisional Signals, stationed at Meerut in the United Provinces, was confirmed and extended leave was granted covering the Christmas period and ending on 31st January 1934. With my accrued 'credits' – money kept back from the 14s per week basic pay, an extra 1s a day trade pay for which I had recently qualified and the ration money advanced to pay for my keep – I felt as rich as Croesus.

A soldier appearing in a small town with money in his pockets and wearing a smart uniform attracts the attention of females, and I was ogled by a girl of Irish descent named Kelly, who told me that she was engaged. Anyone told this on a casual encounter can be sure that he is on to a good thing, and from the outset it was evident that she was not being faithful to her fiancé. She was more than willing to help me forget the months of enforced chastity at Catterick Camp. As the liaison continued she became more demanding and was not averse to performing in daylight in the breakwater storm shelters in full view of those obververs on the beach using field-glasses. After five weeks I was drained and eager to return to Catterick to face the great adventure ahead.

Our party, now referred to as 'the draft', spent two weeks in Hut 16 being kitted out with tropical uniforms and equipment, in addition to being vaccinated and inoculated against diseases such as smallpox, then prevalent, typhoid fever and tetanus. Our departure date from Catterick was scheduled for 14th February so we all adjourned to the canteen for a few last drinks in the UK. One of the concessions made to us was that the strict rule about lights being turned off at 10.15 p.m. would be relaxed, and on our return to the barrack room some of the party, keyed up with excitement and unaccustomed to alcohol, started a singsong. The noise and the lights attracted the attention of the provost sergeant, a martinet whose sole purpose in life was the maintenance of discipline, and he burst into the room full of indignation and bombast and ordered us to bed.

7

LIFE IN INDIA

As far back as 1930 India had an extensive railway network, run by the Indian State Railways, serving the large centres of population. Because of the distance between them, stops were infrequent and the trains were not equipped for catering, Europeans preferred to eat at the excellent restaurants provided at major railway stations, while the Indians carried their food with them or bought it from hawkers lining the platform to sell iced water, sweetmeats and fly-clustered slices of melon.

As we were travelling in a special train, field kitchens were set up at suitable points to coincide with meal-times. The distance between Karachi and Meerut was 800 miles and the journey lasted two days, with frequent stops for refuelling, meals and change of train crews. Whenever we stopped, professional beggars clamoured for money and fought amongst themselves for any coins thrown to them. It was a sad sight to see some of the younger ones whose limbs had been deformed by their parents in order to attract sympathy.

Our route lay through the Sind desert, past Hyderabad on the River Indus, Jodhpur (famous for its riding boots) and Jaipur in Rajasthan. Sleeping accommodation was not de luxe but preferable to that on the troopship, consisting of foldaway slatted wooden bunks over which blankets were spread out. At least the air was fresh and the compartments airy, and it was also a pleasant change to be able to wash and shave in fresh water.

The train rumbled on and there was great excitement as it neared Delhi, the capital city of India. The stay here was brief and two hours later we arrived at Meerut. Twelve of us were posted to 3rd Indian Divisional Signals and were met at the station by a representative of that unit. Our kit was loaded on to a horse-drawn waggon and we travelled the four miles to the unit lines in the cantonment. On the way there we passed a number of small villages and became aware of cooking smells – the food was being heated over fires burning dried cow-pats.

Tongas passed us by, drawn by undernourished and tired ponies. The tonga wallah sitting on the driving-seat would flick his whip occasionally to encourage the animal to maintain its leisurely trot. Good-humoured badinage greeted us as we neared the unit headquarters, and the older hands advised us to get our knees brown.

The first essential now was for a change of clothing and a bath, so without further delay we proceeded to the shower rooms and spent a delightful twenty minutes under the taps, using soap that produced a lather which brought a tingle to the skin, before changing into clean clothes and handing the soiled garments to the dhobi wallah. The dhobi was the laundryman whose job it was to wash, starch and press our khaki drill uniforms. Each newcomer was alloted a 'dhobi mark' that was unique, and wherever one travelled in India the garments and their owners could be linked by this clever identification system.

Tiffin was now ready and was served in an airy dining-room with bearers in attendance. There was a choice of soup or curry, followed by the main meal and dessert. After the indifferent food served on the ship this was indeed *haute cuisine*.

On returning to the barrack-room we found boot boys looking for employment. The boys usually worked for five sahibs, and apart from cooking attended to all their domestic needs from bedmaking to button-polishing. They were paid about 4d a week by each employer.

The standard currency in use in India was the rupee, which was divisible into four four anna pieces; the anna in turn could be divided into four pice. The official rate of exchange was twelve rupees to the pound sterling, but British forces serving in India received the concessionary rate of sixteen rupees. The value of a rupee to an Indian was so great that wholesale counterfeiting took place. A spurious coin was so difficult to detect that the only sure way of proving it genuine was to drop it on a hard surface, when it gave a ringing sound.

After a good night's sleep it was nice to be awakened by an orderly with a cup of tea and a biscuit. The morning parade was held at 8.30 a.m. but the draft was excused this. We proceeded to the clothing stores instead, where we were kitted out with a full set of tropical clothing, including three sets of headgear, a Wolseley helmet for ceremonial parades, a pith helmet to replace the one used on the troop-ship and a dark blue cap with a polished peak and chin-strap. This initial issue of clothing was free but its upkeep costs had to be met by the owner out of a generous clothing allowance.

The accommodation for British other ranks in Meerut consisted of three large buildings: the elephant hut and two blocks of modern bungalows. The Indian soldiers lived in a separate area some distance away. I had been posted to No. 1 Company, which was housed in the elephant hut. This was a very old high building capable of sleeping fifty men. The old soldiers explained that before the British reached this part of India the maharaja governing the province had actually used the building to stable his elephants. The modern blocks were referred to as the new bungalows, and personnel of unit headquarters, the DR Section and No. 2 Company lived in these.

Having a very high roof, the elephant hut was quite cool even in very hot weather, whereas the bungalows – although fitted with electric fans – were uncomfortably warm. At the height of the hot weather season 'tatty' boys were employed to splash water on to reed fixtures fitted to the outside of the open windows, and this had a cooling effect on the air inside.

After a settling-in period, the adjutant gave us a talk on the role of the British Army in India and how our unit functioned. The primary role of the Indian Army was to prevent invasion by a foreign power; it had also to deter tribesmen from making incursions into that part of the country administered by the Government of India. To guard against the main threat, the largest concentration of troops was positioned in the north-western part of the country facing Afghanistan – with the USSR beyond. Signal communications for these garrisons were provided by Royal Signals units stationed at Rawalpindi, Quetta, Peshawar, Waziristan and Kohat, with a reserve force at Karachi.

There was no threat of invasion in the north-east of the country, protected as it was by the Himalayas, and our function was internal security, which covered everything from civil unrest to the containment of ambitious maharajahs who sometimes posed a threat to their neighbours. Normally a regiment of cavalry was capable of dealing with any such misdemeanours and restoring peace and tranquillity.

Meerut is situated sixty miles from New Delhi, the capital of the United Provinces, now known as Uttar Pradesh, and the seat of government during the cool weather season. The Indian Mutiny of 1857 occurred at Meerut on a Sunday morning when most of the garrison were at church. Disaffected Indian sepoys gained access to firearms and ammunition, massacring every British soldier. The mutiny spread like wildfire to Lucknow and Calcutta, and reinforcements took a year to suppress it.

As a result of being caught unprepared, stringent measures were taken to prevent a repetition. Rifles were locked in racks and magazines kept in stout padlocked boxes, the keys to which were kept on the person of the room orderly.

Church parades continued as soon as normality was restored, but the Army had learnt its lesson and no large body of men was allowed to leave barracks unless armed. Those detailed to attend Church paraded in full ceremonial dress carrying arms and rounds of ammunition. After a meticulous inspection by the orderly officer, he led them to and from church. Newcomers to a unit are always interviewed by the commanding officer but in our case this duty was delegated to the adjutant, Captain R. M. Lunt, because the CO, Lieutenant-Colonel O. P. Edgcumbe, was away on duty. 'Joe' Lunt had served in India for longer than he cared to remember and was an understanding officer who at the outset made it clear that we had joined a happy and well-behaved unit.

In his homily he explained that the Indian Army was made up of 180,000 all ranks, 60,000 of them being British. A brigade consisted of one British battalion and two battalions of Indian troops. As far as we were concerned, the Indian element was comprised of fifty per cent Punjabi Mussulmans and fifty per cent Sikhs. The British and Indian other ranks were integrated into sections according to their trade qualifications, but workshop and operating trades, together with despatch riders, were British. The Indian ranks, although under the command of British officers, had their own. These had been promoted from the ranks and were known as Viceroy's commissioned officers, being graded subedar major, subedar and jemadar in that order of seniority. Their duties were mainly to look after the welfare of their Indian subordinates and maintain discipline. The Indian ranks of havildar and naik corresponded to sergeant and corporal in the British service. British other ranks (BORs) did not salute VCOs but always addressed them by their rank, followed by the word sahib; similarly a BOR was called sahib unless his name was known to the VCO.

Entry to the Indian Army was only open to men with an excellent background, usually associated with a line of military heritage, and in the caste system a soldier ranked one below a priest. Jiwan Singh, our subedar major, was a magnificent figure of a man who had served with distinction in France in the Great War and was destined to receive the King's Commission before retiring as a lieutenant-colonel. Before the adjutant dismissed us he paid tribute to one of our British officers, Captain (QM) E. W. Anderson, who had served in the Boer and Great Wars and had been commissioned from the ranks. Andy had been decorated with the Distinguished Conduct Medal, a distinction only surpassed by the Victoria Cross.

The basic rate of pay for a lieutenant in 1934 was 11s 10d, and this included an emolument for those qualifying for Corps pay at the RMA Chatham or the School of Signals. Those passing a colloquial language test and in command of Indian troops were granted Indian Army rates of pay which were far higher than the British rates. Supplementary allowances such as 'hard lying pay' could be claimed by anyone sleeping in a tent whilst on exercises to compensate for having to sleep on a camp-bed.

Promotion was abysmally slow and it was not uncommon for a subaltern qualified and recommended for promotion to serve as long as thirteen years as a lieutenant. There were compensations for this and most officers could live quite comfortably on their pay, even to the extent of running a polo pony or two. Life for the rank and file was comfortable too, all the polishing of boots and equipment, bedmaking, laundering of uniform and linen being left to the bearer.

The first works parade was at 0830 hours and routine work was found to while away the time until 1230 hours when it ceased for the day except for those who had horses to care for. In their case, duty commenced at 0700 hours with rough exercise, each horseman taking out one or two horses for a trot or canter lasting an hour to keep the animals in good shape, and on return to the stables watering and feeding them. Once the animals had been fed it was their turn to eat. After a shower and breakfast they would return to the stables to groom their mounts for an hour before calling it a day. The evening water and feeds could be managed by a minimum of horsemen, and this duty was arranged on a rota basis.

The hard work in the stables was performed by the syces, whose job it was to clean the saddlery, remove horse-droppings and lay fresh hay for the animals' beds. Water to quench their thirst was carried in canvas buckets by the bhisties (water-carriers) who inspired Rudyard Kipling to write the poem 'Gunga Din'.

As an electrician fitter I was part of a team operating a mobile wireless station mounted in a thirty hundred weight vehicle, and it was my job to see that the lorry was properly serviced and to ensure that the set batteries were kept charged. The charging plant to do this was manufactured by Stuart Turner and was relatively trouble-free. Nineteen thirty four was a quiet year with few training commitments and in these circumstances all batteries were removed to a central battery-charging room for periodic maintenance. The battery room was run by an elderly lance-corporal who had difficulty in pronouncing his aitches, omitting them from where they should be and inserting them where they should not be. He was due to accompany his wife to Mussoorie hill-station for the summer months and I was to relieve him.

Sport was encouraged at all levels and we were well provided with playing-fields for hockey, soccer and tennis, as well as facilities for swimming and indoor sports. Hockey and tennis were played on hard surfaces kept in first-class condition by a gang of youngsters who repaired damaged surfaces with mud. Tennis was my favourite and a small group of us played in the afternoons, despite the handicap of having to wear topis while playing.

One afternoon diversion was to cycle to the bazaar, where merchants displayed intricate carvings of ivory, ebony and other hardwoods, mingled with exotic silks from China and items of jewellery. One of the show-pieces was a carved ivory bridge of elephants, trunk to tail, with the tusker in front and the calves in the rear. Few of these precious items were ever sold; tourism was non-existent and the soldiers feared the amount of customs duty they would be charged on returning home.

Thursday was always a special day, being set aside for anti-malarial precautions. In order to contain the breeding of mosquitoes, every Thursday anti-malarial squads drained stagnant water and sprayed wet areas with bamber oil. The shower rooms were closed until after lunch and clay ewers used for keeping drinking-water cool were emptied. Mosquitoes cannot live without water and it takes ten days for them to breed, so denying them a pool of stagnant water would eliminate them.

The Times of India, an English-language newspaper, announced that a hockey match was being held in New Delhi between Delhi Selected and All India, the 1932 Olympics gold medallists. Four of us applied for tickets and were lucky in the draw. One snag was that wearing military uniform was not permitted in New Delhi, so the regimental dherzi (tailor) was called upon to produce a civilian suit for each of us. He completed the job within three days. My memories of New Delhi have dimmed over the years and most of the photographs in my album have been filched, but I remember All India winning by four goals to two.

Most serving soldiers and their families are familiar with the NAAFI, which provided the services with foodstuffs, tobacco and drinks through the medium of their shops and mobile canteens. The NAAFI could not get a foothold in India because they could not compete with the local contractors. During the summer of 1934 the service that our contractor, Moti Ram, provided deteriorated to such an extent that we decided to boycott his canteen facilities. Not a meal was taken there, not a pint of beer or packet of cigarettes was sold, and this boycott extended to the man selling tea on the verandah because he was subcontracted to Moti Ram.

We transferred our custom to Brij Lall, who kept a well-stocked shop and delicatessen half a mile away. After three weeks a distraught Moti Ram appealed to the second-in-command. A meeting was called and our demands stated. Everything we asked for was granted, including small snacks in the bars, imported English beers and an improved waiter service. Consumer power had won the day!

News leaked out that our commanding officer, Lieutenant-Colonel Edgcumbe, whom some of us had never seen, had been promoted and would not be returning. He was being relieved by Lieutenant-Colonel A. C. Sykes, who had been serving with Armoured Fighting Vehicles at Tidworth.

The monsoon season was now approaching and the atmosphere became humid. Anti-malarial precautions were enforced and it was an offence for anyone not to sleep beneath his mosquito-net. These nets were slung over metal rods fitted above the bed and tucked in below the mattress. Apart from mosquito bites there was another hazard, the 'piss beetles'. These insects, no larger than a ladybird, would settle on top of the net and deposit their waste on the sleeper, causing a nasty blister if the fluid dropped on an uncovered part of the body. Although not dangerous unless burst, the blisters were most uncomfortable for a day or two, particularly those in the hair or on an eyelid. Mosquitoes were attracted by the moisture in boots, which had to be shaken out before being worn, sometimes dislodging a scorpion.

The south-east monsoons arrived with a flourish accompanied by ear-splitting claps of thunder and vivid flashes of sheet and forked lightning. A camera with its shutter left open and placed under cover produced dazzling pictures. The *maidan,* a large grassy area around the buildings, resembled a lake until the rain-water subsided, and was impassable except to riders. The duration of the monsoon was usually five weeks but the rain did not fall continuously and it was possible to venture out at times.

During one of these dry spells some of the old hands introduced us to a new game – cobra-hunting. Armed with staves and with a trained dog in attendance, we would walk along a tree-lined road to the Abu Nullah, a drainage canal three miles from barracks and a notorious nesting-place for snakes. Cobras, their underground lairs flooded with rain-water, could often be found there. The peasants were terrified of them and alerted us to their presence with the words '*Sap*, sahib'. Using the dog to divert the attention of a solitary cobra, we would kill it with our sticks, taking care not to damage its skin. The skin was a prized trophy which the *moochie* could make into a belt or a pair of sandals after it was cured. This snake-hunt was not a pastime for the faint-hearted because, unlike the cobras we had seen in the bazaars fighting a mongoose, their poison sacs had not been removed.

Precautions had to be taken against snakebite and a first-aid kit was always carried, comprising a box of sulphur matches, razor-blades and permanganate of potash. The razor-blade was to cut the flesh around the wound so that the poison could be sucked out, the potash to neutralise any remaining venom and the lighted matches to cauterise the cut. The bitten one then prayed to his God that he lived long enough to reach hospital for an injection of anti-snakebite serum.

Bijnor was a village forty miles to the north of Meerut and its farmers used camel and bullock-carts to carry their agricultural products to markets at Delhi and other large towns. The animals plodded along the solitary road from Bijnor and as darkness fell and their drivers slept continued to their goal unguided. The carts were unlit and a danger to any motor traffic using the road. An approaching vehicle driver could spot bullock carts in time because the bullock's eyes reflected his headlamps, but a camel's eyes were above the beams because of its height. It was not unusual for an Indian vehicle-driver to dismount and turn the carts round in the roadway, their drivers still asleep and the animals quite happy to head for home.

The monsoons finally cleared and training for the winter manoeuvres began. I took the opportunity to sit an examination for my class II trade, and qualification brought its reward in the form of an increment of 9d, so I was passing rich on 3s 9d a day. It also brought nearer the target of 1st Class Education and Trade set by the recruiting RSM at Caernarfon. There was only one snag to this: Captain Joe Lunt, the adjutant, did not consider a soldier experienced enough for promotion until he had served five years!

The next momentous event in the life of the unit was the arrival of our new CO. Some of the troops had read Dicken's *Oliver Twist*, and from the moment of his arrival he was known to the troops as 'Bill' Sykes. The colonel drove to his office in a large American yellow-painted Chrysler car, which was immediately dubbed 'the Yellow Peril'. The uncharitable asserted that the gift of a new car was made by the contractor to every new CO as a sweetener, but that was unkind and untrue.

It was not long before the colonel got to hear about the 'blue lights' racket. Those who ate heartily or drank heavily in the canteen found themselves short of money by mid-week. In order to help them out, an obliging pay sergeant distributed vouchers, referred to as 'blue lights'. The vouchers were to purchase food or drink from the canteen, redeemed at the pay table on Friday. No doubt the pay sergeant received a commission from the contractor for his spare-time activity, but it was a vicious system which left the borrower with a reduced pay-packet to start the week. The new CO soon put a stop to the custom.

He summoned me to his office in late October to tell me that he was sending me on an advanced MT course at Chaklala, near Rawalpindi, the home of the Indian Army Service Corps. He commanded me to do well and not let the unit down.

After a luxurious two-day train journey travelling in a second class coach through Ambala, Ludhiana, Lahore, Jhelum and the Sikh holy city of Amritsar, I reached Rawalpindi and was transported to Chaklala, where I reported to the adjutant, Lieutenant Addison. He explained that the lowest rank serving there was sergeant and he proposed to appoint me to that rank. I protested that on my pay I could not afford the extra messing supplement charged in the sergeants' mess nor could I keep up with their drinking habits. A compromise was reached: sleeping-accommodation was found for me in the medical centre and food supplied from the sergeants' mess kitchen at no extra charge. I did, however, accept the local rank of corporal so that I could visit my Signals friends in nearby Rawalpindi.

The course assembled and I had never seen so many officers in one room. The chief instructor explained in his opening address that instead of relying on horses and mules, the Indian Government had decided on partial mechanisation of the Indian Army and as a consequence the IASC would expand. Several of the senior officers attending the course came from illustrious cavalry regiments but were getting on in years, and the intention was to transfer them to the IASC to carry out sedentary duties provided they qualified.

Two exceptions were Major (QM) Jimmy Hawke, O.B.E., and Captain (QM) J. T. Cussens, both of them Signals officers, who it was thought would acquire experience which would be useful to them in running their unit transport. Jimmy Hawke and I were teamed up and I was able to help him with the more difficult jobs we were given in the workshop.

In appreciation he asked me if I would like to spend a weekend at Peshawar District Signals, and I was delighted at the prospect. We left early on a Saturday to cover the eighty miles to the garrison fort of Peshawar, travelling through the Royal Artillery base at Nowshera, and at Attock traversing a massive bridge spanning the River Indus. Major Hawke told me that this river was navigable from its mouth at Karachi nearly seven hundred miles away. A few miles further on, the Indus was joined by the River Kabul, which had its source in the Hindu Kush range.

On arriving at Peshawar he handed me over to one of his staff with instructions to attend to all my needs. I slept well and on awakening at dawn was horrified to see a cut-throat razor held by a grinning native an inch from my throat. The custom there was for soldiers to be shaved in bed, sometimes while still asleep.

Because of its strategic importance so close to Afghanistan, Peshawar had developed into a well-fortified garrison guarding the Khyber Pass. The first line of defence was Jamrud fort, ten miles away, formerly the scene of spirited fighting by its Sikh defenders. Feeling adventurous, I hired a bicycle on that bright Sunday morning and headed for the fort.

Before reaching it I passed a huge and impressive building called the Islamia College, which was attended by the followers of Islam for miles around.

I boldly decided to cycle a little nearer the Khyber until being pulled up short by a notice which read:

> FRONTIER OF INDIA. Travellers are not permitted to pass this notice board unless they have compiled with The Passport Regulations.

I could go no further and cycled back to Peshawar. Major Hawke collected me early on the Monday and we returned to Chaklala in time for the first session.

As the course progressed a few amusing diversions were introduced. The Albion was fitted with a hand throttle and had irreversible steering. The instructor would find a level area, set the hand throttle to a slow speed, lock the steering-wheel and step out, leaving the unmanned vehicle to run around in circles.

Another monstrosity was a motor cycle fitted with three wheels in line, the two rear wheels being tracked. It was designed for cross-country work but was too heavy to handle and proved to be a white elephant.

The president of the sergeants' mess invited me as a mess guest for Christmas and Boxing Days, and it was at one of the parties that I met a lady whom shall be called Mrs Dee, the wife of a senior warrant-officer. She was very hospitable and invited me to play tennis at the Rawalpindi Club. I met her at the club several times and she often asked me where I intended to spend my next leave.

The hill-station for that area was Murree, and wives were sent there to live in comfortable accommodation while their husbands remained behind on the plains. Mrs Dee kept extolling the virtues of Murree, and when we finally said goodbye remarked, 'Come to Murree for your holiday. You'll have a good time there.' And on that enigmatic note we parted.

The course dispersed on 9th February and I was invited to apply for transfer to the IASC in the rank of staff sergeant. As gracefully as I could I declined, a decision I was to regret. The train journey back was uneventful and two days later I rejoined my unit.

The Silver Jubilee of King George V was approaching and it was decided that the Royal Signals' contribution would be a display of trick riding by a team of experienced motor cyclists. The venue for the celebrations was the hill-station of Simla. The responsibility of organising the team was delegated to the Meerut unit, and selected riders were trained by Sergeant 'Puncher' Fee, a veteran who had seen active service in Russia at the end of the war.

The machines were crated and sent by rail to Dehra Dun, a station in the foothills which was then the railhead. From there they were carried on the backs of porters – one machine to two porters – thirty miles to Simla. The riders travelled by native buses whose drivers were well used to the hairpin bends and tortuous road.

Soon after their arrival, news trickled back that all was not well, and Foreman of Signals Bill Paget and I were sent up to sort things out. We thought that the problem was likely to be carburation trouble brought about by the rarified atmosphere at six thousand feet.

There was nothing mechanically wrong with the machines: it was man management. Like many small men,

Puncher was bombastic and domineering, and the team, tiring of his bullying, had resorted to doctoring their machines.

The rehearsals took place on the arena at Annandale, a vast level area capable of accommodating several soccer, hockey and polo pitches. The noise of the motor cycles exasperated some of the elderly senior officers out exercising their horses and they would bawl, 'Get those infernal machines away from here.'

The horses were unused to noise; the only motor cars allowed in Simla belonged to the Viceroy and the Commander-in-Chief and they were driven sedately.

By today's standard the Signals display was primitive and far below the standards of the 'White Helmets' who entertain television viewers and military tattoo spectators with their expert performances. The bands of the Highland Light Infantry and the Cameron Highlanders provided the accompaniment for the many tableux and march-pasts which took place. On a hillside overlooking the arena a huge sign had been erected bearing the letters GVR surmounted by the Imperial Crown, the whole being illuminated by multicoloured electric bulbs.

When the festivities were over, Their Excellencies The Viceroy and Countess of Willingdon invited all the participants to a garden party at their home, Viceregal Lodge, where they were lavishly entertained. The Commander-in-Chief India, Field-Marshall Sir Phillip Chetwode, was also present and together with the Viceroy strolled through the grounds posing for those of us who owned cameras.

On returning from Simla I thought it time to explore the area beyond the environs of the cantonment and one day, having a vehicle to road-test, I instructed the driver to visit the native city. Driving a thirty-hundredweight truck through the narrow streets with stalls of produce on each side proved a hazardous business. Apart from the cyclists, pedestrians and bullock carts travelling along, cows sauntered from side to side helping themselves to cabbages or any other tasty morsel that they fancied. We gave them a wide berth because cows were considered to be sacred animals by the Hindus and any injury to one would cause a storm of protest. Animals were often the cause of civil disturbances between Muslims and Hindus. Occasionally the Muslims would slay a cow and in response the Hindus would set a pig loose in a Muslim mosque, the result being turmoil.

A group of us was out walking one day when we sighted an unusual number of vultures circling overhead and so we investigated. It was then that we found the casting-ground for horses.

The Indian Army was heavily dependent on the horse for its cavalry regiments and for drawing field guns and supply wagons. These animals were bred in New South Wales, shipped to India and trained in the remount depot at Saugor. The horses were well fed and cared for by a dedicated veterinary service. When they reached the end of their useful working life they were destroyed to prevent them falling into the hands of civilians who were likely to undernourish them and work them to death.

'Casting' was the term used to denote humane slaughter and we watched in fascination as four of the carcases were disposed of. They were skinned and their hides removed for curing in order to provide valuable leather. When they were disembowelled the vultures alighted. After five minutes we disturbed them to find little flesh on their bones, and on returning to the scene thirty minutes later nothing remained except the skeletons and hooves, which the natives carried away for conversion to glue.

The hay for their fodder and bedding was grown in nearby military grass farms well watered by irrigation channels, and was stored in huge silos for future use.

Sometimes a party of us would take a sack of beer to the local cholera graveyard to imbibe after the official closure of the canteen. It was here that we came across a headstone bearing the epitath: THE BUFFS, MEN WHO DIED FROM CHOLERA BURIED HERE 1867. It listed the names of two colour-sergeants, one sergeant, two corporals, two drummers and twenty-five privates. If the curator of the Buffs Museum contacts me I will send him a photograph.

Apparently in the year 1867 Meerut was afflicted with an epidemic of cholera, and to avoid the spread of the disease the victims were interred in mass graves.

The officers of the unit took an active interest in sport. Many of them were talented horsemen and played polo. Others had a passion for aquatic sports, although the swimming-pool available to us was very small indeed. Hockey was the most popular of the sports, and the Indians took to it as a duck takes to water; it was a rule that every Indian eleven fielded a British officer.

Some of them spent their furloughs in the jungle. They would hire a bullock cart and set off with a bearer and beaters in search of tigers. These predators terrified the villagers and preyed on their livestock, and a tiger-hunting sahib was more than welcome in their midst. The hunter would arrange for his bearer to buy a goat from the peasants, tether it to a tree, and find a suitable hide within view of the bait. The tiger, hearing the bleats of the goat, would stalk its prey and attack it. With luck, the hunter would shoot the tiger, and earn the gratitude of the local people in addition to bagging a valuable trophy.

One of the outstanding subalterns was Lieutenant P. M. P. Hobson. Blessed with a fine physique, he commanded admiration as he stood on the diving-board of the pool and then plunged the whole length of it. Pat Hobson was to gain fame later in Burma when he and his men routed a superior force of Japanese attacking his HQ, 7th Divisional Signals. For this spirited action he was awarded the Distinguished Service Order.

Another personality was Lieutenant Nick Pocock, who met with an unfortunate accident. Because of his knowledge of wild animals he was asked to act as an observer for a team of visiting zoologists studying the habits of the big cats. Unfortunately, he was attacked by one of the tigers and badly mauled – but happily he survived and is still alive.

The R.S.M. was 'Sammy' Hughes, a veteran of 1914-18. Soon after joining the unit, Sammy won the first prize in the prestigious Calcutta Sweepstake. He was about to retire on a sizeable pension and was happy to complete his service quietly.

In late May 1935, news was received on the wireless link that Quetta, the capital of Baluchistan, had been devastated by an earthquake which caused horrific damage and great loss of life. It had lasted only thirty seconds but caused great havoc in the native city and the RAF quarters. Much later, we found that our pattern of life was to be changed because of this event.

In 1935 King George V honoured the Corps by appointing his daughter Princess Mary, the Princess Royal, as our first Colonel-in-Chief, an appointment she was to hold for thirty years.

The monsoon season was approaching and the temperature soared. *The Times of India* recorded the daily readings under the heading 'The Hot Weather Stakes'. Hyderabad in the Sind desert and Multan in the Punjab often headed the list with shade temperatures exceeding 120°F, with Meerut not far behind. The families had moved up to the hill-stations of Mussoorie and Chakrata for the summer months to escape the enervating heat, as had many of the soldiers to undergo trade training and upgrading. Those of us remaining on the plains carried out essential duties only.

Later in the year we were due to take part in the Eastern Command manoeuvres in an area near the Ganges Canal at Roorkee. It proved to be a large-scale exercise commencing in late November and continuing well into December, with the RAF also participating. The canal was built by the Bombay Sappers and Miners and provided water and irrigation for a vast area of the United Provinces.

An unusual incident took place at this camp featuring Lance Corporal Dick Turpin, our former mess room NCO at Catterick, who had joined us for this exercise. He was disturbed one night by an animal entering the tent and in the dim light of a hurricane lamp recognised it as a fox. Wrapping a sheet around his fist, he struck out at the intruder and chased it out. It was seen by an alert sentry, who killed it with a blow from his rifle butt. It was concluded that the fox was rabid, and as Dick's hand had been grazed in the encounter I was ordered by the adjutant to drive him, together with the dead fox, to the British Military Hospital at Meerut for anti-rabies treatment.

When the admissions officer saw the fox he was

nonplussed and evidently did not know that the carcase had to be beheaded and the brain sent to the Pasteur Institute at Dehra Dun for forensic examination. I left Dick Turpin in the hospital and the dead fox in the grounds. Dick was treated and showed no ill effects but the medical authorities should have been aware of the procedure for dealing with suspected rabid animals.

Christmas was approaching and our thoughts were with our families at home. The flying-boat air mail service had not then been introduced and surface mail took two weeks to reach India. To reduce transit time, newspapers and mail were carried overland to Marseilles and then loaded on to fast passenger ships bound for the Orient.

Christmas Day started off with the arrival of the warrant-officers and sergeants, who served us tea, laced liberally with rum, in bed. A generous grant was always made from regimental funds to pay for the dinner which was prepared by the contractor's cooking staff, and the meal was served in the canteen by the senior NCOs of the unit. The room was well decorated, and glasses and cutlery were provided by the contractor, so obviating the chore of carrying and washing one's own 'eating-irons'.

Some more good news reached me that Christmas in the form of confirmation of my entitlement to an extra 1s a day on completing three years' service, which meant that I was earning 4s 9d a day, £1 13s 3d per week. Not so welcome was the news that King George V was ailing and prayers were being offered in churches throughout the land for his speedy recovery.

Nineteen thirty six dawned and the unit prepared for an exercise in the Lucknow area due to commence in mid-January. As Lucknow was four hundred miles away, everyone looked forward to a change of surroundings, especially the MT drivers, who were bored by carrying out routine cleaning of their vehicle. Some preliminary training was carried out on our arrival, but on emerging from my tent on the morning of 21st January I met a dejected-looking Subedar Major Jiwan Singh, who said to me, 'Thomas Sahib, the Burra Sahib (the King) is dead.' Out of respect for His late Majesty, the exercise was curtailed – but not before we were given an opportunity to visit places of historic interest.

The Siege of Lucknow has been well documented in early history books and I was interested in seeing the old fort which the Resident, Sir Henry Lawrence, and his garrison had defended for so long until the seige was lifted. No attempt had been made to repair the damage caused to the buildings by cannon shells and it had become a museum. Various notices were displayed; one of them read: 'IN THIS ROOM SIR H. LAWRENCE WAS WOUNDED BY A PIECE OF SHELL ON THE 2ND JULY 1857'. The wall of the church had been demolished and the reason for this given in another notice: 'THE WALL WAS BREACHED HERE SO THAT THE GRAIN STORED IN THE CHURCH COULD BE REMOVED TO THE RESIDENCY'. The epitaph on his white marble tomb read:

HERE LIES HENRY LAWRENCE, WHO TRIED TO DO HIS DUTY
MAY THE LORD TAKE MERCY ON HIS SOUL.
BORN 28TH JUNE 1806. DIED 4TH JULY 1857

A magnificent zoological garden with leafy trees had been laid down a short distance from the fort, where tigers roamed in their natural habitat and humans were protected by a substantial railed fence. A tigress strolled up to a group of spectators and gazed at them disdainfully. An Indian boy teased her with a bamboo stick, whereupon she turned her back to him and drenched him with her urine.

There were other edifices: the Harcourt Butler Memorial, the tombs of the Raja Nawab Ali and his Begum, the Council Chambers and the Bara Emimbara, which it was claimed had the world's largest unsupported roof. Having seen these wondrous sights we returned to our base station.

A soldier is useless if he is not conversant with the weapon issued to him and skilled in its use, and for this reason he is required to pass an annual qualification test on the range. A Lee Enfield rifle posed few problems but a revolver was more difficult to handle. The personal weapon issued to officers, fitters and despatch riders was the Webley .45, which was heavy to hold. The technique taught was to raise the weapon at arm's length until it pointed at the target, and fire. Taking aim was not encouraged, because it caused the firer to waver and miss. Another maxim was never to point a loaded weapon at anyone unless the intention was to shoot. A firearm is a lethal weapon only to be used against an enemy.

The Signals Research and Development Establishment at Woolwich was responsible for the design and production of new wireless models but because of financial stringency only prototypes were ever constructed. However, a new set, the No. 2 set, was produced, two of which were shipped to Meerut for extensive field tests. The War Office directed that the efficiency of these sets was to be assessed after trials conducted under extreme atmospheric conditions and to the limit of their range, and this meant just before the monsoons broke. A team of experienced operators was assembled under the supervision of Sergeant Bill Pack to carry out the War Office edict.

The mobile set was installed in a thirty-hundredweight vehicle with separate transport for the NCOs and crew. The final destination was Kanpur, in the south of the province, 450 miles from our base. The mobile crew were to communicate with the set at base at intervals of fifty miles on the outward and return legs of the route.

To my surprise, I was sent out with the detachment in charge of a lorry carrying the rations, spare batteries, fuel and a charging-engine. My crew consisted of a driver and two cooks. The plan was for me to travel ahead of the group in order to replenish our water and provisions from military units on our route and have meals prepared for the detachment in advance of its arrival. This suited me quite well as it allowed time to deviate in order to visit places of interest on the way.

As we neared Ghaziabad, on the Meerut-Delhi road, we came across an unusual spectacle. A bullock detached from its cart was lying on the road with its legs bound, and when we asked the reason were told that it was being shod. Up to that time I had thought that horses were the only animals fitted with iron shoes.

The party reached Kanpur without incident and after a suitable break prepared for the return trip. Instructions had been received from control that we were to return by another route, which passed through Agra on the Jumna River.

Before reaching Agra I was giving the driver a rest when suddenly a large porcupine crossed the road ahead. I tried to avoid it but failed, and the driver suggested that we stopped. The animal was not mutilated so the cook covered the carcase with moistened mud and cooked it at the roadside. The quills came out easily and we shared a succulent meal.

Arriving at Agra well before the rest were due, we made for the most famous mausoleum in the world, the Taj Mahal, a breathtaking spectacle even in the moonlight. The entrance to the tomb was guarded by a massive gate which housed the sentries, and on emerging through the portal we saw a wide and very long waterway teeming with goldfish. This canal was flanked by broad pathways leading to the Taj itself, and behind the paths were two avenues of luxuriant trees. I took a photograph a hundred yards from the Taj, and the only visitors in sight were two Indian gentlemen. How different from these days of mass tourism, with millions of viewers treading the pathways and staircases.

The curator explained that the Emperor Shah Jahan was so saddened by the death of his wife that he resolved to have a fitting edifice built in her memory. The imposing entrance hall was still encrusted with jewels and other precious stones, but the curator said that these were only those that remained after the marauding hordes from the north had desecrated the temple and pillaged the country. I saw the tomb of the Shah, who had been laid to rest here after the death of the Begum. An elaborate hanging lamp presented by Lord Curzon, a former Viceroy, graced the hall. The four minarets were as high as the dome, and could be climbed in easy stages, pausing at the viewing-platforms on the way up.

The party rendezvoused to the south of Delhi, and after a midday meal Sergeant Pack told me to return to Meerut independently.

This gave me an opportunity to visit the Quit'b Minar near Delhi, which the curator at Agra had told me was erected by the Shah to enable him to see the Taj Mahal. It proved to be a colossal column near his home, having a winding granite staircase leading to the top. From this great height it was possible to see the Taj Mahal all those miles away.

This was an opportunity, too, to visit the Old Fort at Delhi, where a detachment of Royal Signals was based, and I was greeted and taken to their canteen. After many days of total abstinence the cold beer offered me tasted like nectar. The single obstruction between Delhi and base was the bridge over the River Jumna, which was only wide enough for one lane of traffic in each direction. As the bullock carts trundled along to the city at two miles an hour, we were pleased not to be held up by anything moving ahead of us.

The news that greeted us on our return was that we were to exchange places with the Quetta unit later in the year. Meanwhile, it was back to routine. By this time I had spent over two years on the plains and had despaired of seeing the hill-stations of Mussoorie, Chakrata or Raniket. I now learnt that it was medical policy for no one to spend more than two hot-weather seasons without a break in the hills, so the medical officer arranged for me to be sent to Chakrata at once.

The change of air and the new environment acted as a tonic. As soon as I was accustomed to the rarified atmosphere at 6,000 feet, I went for some pleasant walks. The nearest mountain was Nanda Devi, 25,645 feet in height, and with the sun shining on its snow-covered surface it was a superb sight.

There was no work for me to do, so Captain E. V. McCormack, the OC, asked me to do a private job – and it was then that I saw a V8 engine for the first time. Its owner, the CO of the Bedfordshire and Hertfordshire Regiment, could not start the engine. I diagnosed fuel starvation and stripped the pump, only to find that the diaphragm had perished. The nearest spares depot was at Calcutta, more than 1,200 miles away, but I was able to make an improvised job using shoe leather. He was so pleased that he gave me a half a sovereign.

We were to lose that respected officer Captain E. W. Anderson, D.C.M., before we moved to Quetta. He exchanged jobs with Captain (QM) T. Jones, who arrived from Trimulgherry with his wife and grown-up daughter. Soon after his arrival he asked me to call at his bungalow to fix a fault on his car, and it was there that I learnt the correct way to eat a mango.

Details soon emerged of the planned move to Quetta, which was to take place in October for climatic reasons, both units leaving behind their vehicles, animals, stores and equipment, and travelling by train. Like ships that go by in the night, we should pass each other in the Great Indian Desert. One of their number was Eric Swainson, who after spending years in the ranks was commissioned and became a Signal Officer in Chief.

We were hoping to leave behind the kite hawks, those scavengers who swooped down and snatched anything eatable out of the hand of anyone foolish enough to carry it in the open.

8

BALUCHISTAN

Quetta, now in Pakistan, was the capital city of Baluchistan until the partition of India in 1947 and was strategically placed to defend any incursion from Afghanistan through the Khojak Pass. It stands at 6,000 feet and access to it is gained through the Bolan Pass by railway and road. The nearest Afghanistan town of any size is Kandahar, about 120 miles away.

Because of its defence importance it had become the headquarters of Western Command and consisted of a garrison of twelve thousand men, supported by a large contingent of RAF used mainly for reconnaissance. In the event of trouble in the North-West Frontier region, the Quetta Garrison could be called upon to reinforce formations quelling the dissident tribesmen.

The great earthquake of 1935 had destroyed three-quarters of the city and caused the death of thousands of people, but the barracks housing the Royal Signals element had escaped serious damage. Fearing a repetition of the earthquake, orders were given that sleeping-quarters still standing were not to be used, so the troops were accommodated in tents as a temporary measure. The tents were adequate during the summer months, but because of the extreme cold other arrangements would have to be made in the winter. The solution was to erect Wana huts, which had been found effective in the bitterly cold outpost of Wana in Dera Ismail Khan.

The walls of the huts were constructed of sandbags, reaching to a height of seven feet and were covered by a canvas roof incorporating an EP/IP (Egyptian Pattern/Indian Pattern) tent. Each hut was large enough for five single metal beds. Fitted with a draught-proof entrance door and containing a coal-burning stove, it was comfortable and snug. Very much later on, the former Lord Mayor of Canterbury, Councillor Pat Burke, revealed to me that he had been born in a Wana hut at Quetta in 1939.

After two days and three nights on a train which had to climb up the Bolan Pass we arrived at our destination and were driven to the camp. After a hearty breakfast we were shown to our accommodation. There was no lack of seasoned NCOs to show us the ropes and we quickly settled down in our new surroundings.

The first impression of Quetta was the arid nature of the area. There was hardly any vegetation, in marked contrast to the lush pastures and leafy trees we had left behind. The reason for this was that the south east monsoon rains petered out before reaching this outpost. Although Herculean efforts had been made to clear up the city and its surrounding cantonment, the scars still remained; but a massive reconstruction project was in hand and earthquake-proof single-storey sleeping-accommodation was being erected. The cinema had been demolished and an open-air one set up as a morale-booster, and the massive Matheson swimming-pool was undamaged. Meals were taken in a well laid out dining-room, and the canteen facilities provided a corporals' room and wet and dry bars.

The old hands told tales of the aftermath of the earthquake: the rescue of orphans, removal of the injured to improvised hospitals, disposal of the dead in huge funeral pyres, the restoration of the railway line, demolition of unsafe buildings, repairs to the drainage system, restoration of the telegraph lines, and hygiene measures taken to combat disease. They recalled the ever-constant guard against the marauders who came from far afield to loot and pillage – and were despatched by a rifle bullet if discovered. And they added with pride that they had been commended by the Commander-in-Chief India for their valiant efforts.

Back at Meerut, the contractor providing a poor service had been boycotted until he saw the error of his ways. From the muttering heard at Quetta it was time for our current one to improve his image. Every soldier looks forward to his Christmas dinner, the cost of which is usually heavily subsidised from regimental funds.

After a hearty breakfast some activity such as a comic football match is usually arranged and favoured ones are invited to the sergeants' mess for a drink. Instead of eating the meal in the dining room it was usual to sit down in the contractors' canteen with senior NCOs in attendance serving the meal. It was also the practice at Quetta for the men to be 'stood down' from Christmas Eve to 2nd January.

From the moment that we entered the canteen, things were seen to be wrong. Table utensils were of inferior quality, paper serviettes were provided instead of linen, some of the glassware was chipped, and when the serving began it was obvious that the food had been cooked indifferently. The contractor's face appeared in the servery and had oranges thrown at it. He was replaced by the sergeant-major smoking a large cigar, who was taunted with cries of 'Is that a contractor's bribe?' The stems of spoons and forks were bent and serviettes torn up, the place was left in a shambles.

Naturally this incident reached the ears of the colonel, and it was said privately later that he was prepared to fine the contractor but could not condone the action of his men.

His first reaction was to have the orderly officer inspect the barrack rooms and take disciplinary action against any NCO whose room was untidy. Needless to say, this intention had been leaked on the grape-vine, and by the time the orderly officer carried out his duty everything was spick and span. As a follow-up after the Christmas holidays, every officer and every man paraded to hear these words by the colonel:

'I have been in the Army for twenty-seven years and I have commanded units for twenty-five years. I've commanded good units and I've commanded bad units but I've never commanded a unit that I've been ashamed of. And I'm ashamed of you! I order company commanders to pay to me by 1200 hours today the sum of X rupees to make good the damage.'

The sum he specified was the total cost recoverable from those attending the dinner and it was deducted from individuals on the next pay day. It was noticeable that Captain Joe Lunt, considered as some to be the father of the unit, paled visibly while these words were being spoken and seemed to have aged considerably.

Changes were now taking place in the personnel of the unit. Captain Joe Lunt was due for promotion and left us to be replaced as adjutant by Captain C. H. Barker. RSM Price was posted home, and his relief was RSM 'Jimmy' Noonan.

The policy at Meerut had been that a Signalman was not ready for appointment to lance-corporal until he had served five years. The policy adopted at Quetta was that if a Signalman had not been appointed to lance-corporal within five years there was something lacking in him. At this time I had served for upwards of four and was slowly becoming what was termed an 'old sweat'.

Because of the nature of the terrain, massive manoeuvres on the scale held in the United Provinces were not possible, but all units were kept in a state of immediate readiness for any contingency. This involved parading in full marching order ready to leave barracks within thirty minutes of the alarm being sounded.

These practices, held monthly, became routine until one day the colonel decided to inspect us closely, paying particular attention to water-bottles which should have been full. On reaching Lance-Corporal Fabian he shook his water-bottle and found it to be empty. 'Werp' Fabian was a veteran of the Great War and not likely to rise any further. The normal punishment for an offence of this nature would have been 'deprived of lance appointment', but the CO decided not to take any formal action, no doubt because of Werp's long service and good conduct. He was given an unofficial punishment of marching twelve miles away from camp and twelve miles back, carrying an empty water-bottle. He was accompanied by the orderly sergeant to see that the order was complied with. So as not to punish the sergeant too, he was allowed to ride a bicycle.

Other exercises in which we became involved quite

frequently were the TWETs (Tactical Exercises Without Troops) that were held in the proximity of the Quetta Staff College. These were designed to train the senior officers attending a course in the use of wireless communications.

Annual summer camp was held in May at a place called Bostan, thirty miles from the border with Afghanistan and not much further from the Khojak Pass with its British-manned fort at Chaman. The soldiers had to march or ride horses there, but this was no great problem as it was only twenty-four miles away.

By now we had taken delivery of several Austin 7 cars designed to carry portable wireless sets. They could also be used for reconnaissance purposes, and one day the colonel asked me to deliver one to his office tent as he wished to study the terrain. On his return, as he drove past the transport office tent he passed a message in Morse code on the horn button: 'Come and get it.'

An amusing incident happened at this camp – although it was not so amusing to the victim. The area contained many abandoned artesian wells, and Signalman H. K. Witt had the misfortune to fall down one of them. Hearing his cries for help, a rescue party was formed and by linking vehicle tow-ropes together managed to reach him. All the time the rescue operation was proceeding, small pebbles around the hole were being displaced and falling on him. Eventually he was hauled to the surface and miraculously had suffered no serious injuries apart from the lumps caused by the pebbles. From that time onwards he was known as H. K. Twitt.

Following this, a serious accident occurred when a havildar was out exercising his horse along the escarpment. They came to a sudden dip, the rider was unable to stop the animal which had the bit in its teeth and they both plunged down the cliffs to their deaths below. The death of the havildar was unfortunate but the loss of a weapon or a horse was a very serious matter for the authorities at GHQ in Delhi.

Quetta is well known for its extremes of temperature. In late May the rays of the sun are intense and aggravated by the rarified atmosphere, and I have seen Sikhs, who normally have a pallid complexion and whose faces are protected by their beards, suffering from sunburn. Anyone having a fair complexion is particularly vulnerable, and after two years or more their faces are burnt brick-red. Newcomers arriving during the summer season were told to roll down their shirt sleeves and wear slacks instead of shorts on alternate days. In contrast, the cold in the winter is intense. Sentries were issued with *poshteens* – evil-smelling sheepskins which reached down to their boots – and instead of the usual two hours the sentry beat was reduced to thirty minutes. There was no rationing of fuel for the stoves and the coal-sheds were left unlocked, so that the occupants of the Wana huts had only themselves to blame if their sleeping-quarters were cold. That hoary myth about a dripping water-tap never freezing was exploded here, and I have seen a pinnacle of solid ice rise from the base to the mouth of a tap which had not been properly turned off.

In due course summer camp ended and the unit returned to normal duties. Considerable progress had been made in the construction of the new earthquake-proof bungalow but until they were completed we had to revert to the Wana huts. One of the five sharing my hut was Signalman Langmaid, a scruffy fellow who used his enamel drinking-mug to heat his shaving-water on the stove. Very often he did not bother to clean the whiskers from it before drinking his tea.

By this time I had joined the 'wet bar clique', five or six chaps who preferred drinking beer to sipping tea. A frequent visitor to our bar was 'Guts' Murray, a huge Glaswegian who had remained in India since the end of the war and had never left to go on UK leave. He had a black tailless dog which he called Monkey, his constant companion. Guts was a very experienced wireless operator on a chain called the VV group, which communicated to all stations in India. Another of our party was Reg Everson, who was in charge of sanitary arrangements. He had an office adjacent to the boilers which provided hot water for the showers, and very often we would buy sacks of beer and carry them to his room after the bar was closed at 9.30 p.m. For some reason, beer-bottles were enclosed in hessian sacks instead of the convential crates – possibly because jute was readily available and cheaper.

Quetta city had now returned to normal and the dealers and traders had replenished their stocks.

Captain Jones, the Quarter-Master, called me to his office one morning, handed me 600 rupees and asked me to buy him a used car. I selected an ancient Armstrong Siddeley which was in reasonably good mechanical condition, with comfortable upholstery and well-polished bodywork. It had been adapted for cold-weather conditions, and by pulling a lever the radiator could be blanked off until the engine attained a good running temperature. On returning with it to his office he said, 'Good. Now you can teach my daughter to drive.'

Pellier's cinema, devastated in the earthquake, had been rebuilt and reopened, and a unit bus was purchased to carry the cinema-goers. It was driven in his spare time by Signalman 'Smudger' Smith, who received extra-duty pay for his pains.

Six of us, reading daily orders one day, found that we had been appointed unpaid lance-corporals. Fortunately, because I was senior in length of service, I headed the list. This position was important because it meant that I would be paid for the rank before those whose names appeared below mine and an unpaid appointment was lost on being posted back to England. The six of us were then interviewed by the RSM, who explained that promotion had hitherto been blocked by the large number of NCOs who had elected to carry on serving at the end of the war, and these now held the senior positions. He further explained that most of them would be leaving the service, after completing twenty-one years, in 1938 or 1939.

In August 1937 my unit was instructed to send a representative to an army school at Minora Island, near Karachi, to attend a ten-day course on 'The Art of Education'. In fact, this simply meant instructing the student on how to instruct. Nine mornings were spent in the class-room, learning the art of instruction; but the afternoons were free and we made friends on the beach with some Gunners who were stationed on the island. They willingly lent us one of their boats to go fishing and even grilled the fish we had caught for us. The sea in these parts was unpolluted and dozens of turtles could be seen swimming in the clear water.

One more exercise took place that year before the arrival of the cold weather. It was to test the efficiency of wireless transmission in the hills, and the area chosen was near to the Afghanistan border in the Toba Kakar Hills, which had an unusual configuration, consisting of a number of high hillocks with bases all on the same level. A British signalman was despatched to a map reference, with a wireless set carried by a mule and accompanied by a havildar, and instructed to transmit signals at hourly intervals. Nothing was heard from his set and nightfall was approaching. A worried commanding officer then converged all vehicles in a small area and ordered the headlights to be elevated to form a continuous beam in the hope that this beacon would guide the party back to base.

This ploy proved to be ineffective and a further day passed without contact being made with the detachment. The matter was now becoming serious and on the third day the help of the RAF and The Guides – a famous cavalry regiment – was enlisted to search for them. At the end of the third day a patrol of The Guides located them and led them back, thoroughly exhausted, to base. After this incident it was conceded that the exercise was a failure!

Christmas was now approaching and I was given the job of organising the draw. The draughtsman produced a board large enough to contain two thousand spaces for the insertion of all the names, and each Friday following pay parade two of us carried this board from room to room, raising money for the draw. Ten days before Christmas the spaces were filled; the next job was to invite some local merchants to the camp to compete for the contract to supply the draw prizes.

When the goods arrived and were displayed they covered a line of six-foot trestle-tables extending the length of the dining-room. Two thousand rupees could buy a lot of goods in those days when a bottle of Drambui cost only five rupees.

Soon after this the colonel left, as he was approaching

the end of his service. His replacement was Lieutenant-Colonel Guy Tayleur, who had joined us from the depot at Catterick Camp.

We moved from the Wana huts to the new quarters early in 1938, and as each room housed sixteen men stricter discipline was enforced, largely because the new CO had become so used to depot routine. At Catterick there had been a large parade-ground well surfaced with tar macadam, whereas Quetta was built on a mountain top and had no topsoil. Any foot movement disturbed the stony surface, making drill impossible. It was good marching-country but not suitable for a barrack square. A check parade was instituted and everyone turned out at 6.30 a.m. under the command of the RSM. Wheelbarrows were provided and for half an hour each day we picked up stones to fill the barrows and wheel the contents to the edge. For every pebble removed three more appeared, and had the folly continued the parade-ground would have become a pit.

The unit pay documentation was the responsibility of a sergeant who kept a ledger sheet for everyone on the payroll. It was the custom for each of us to report to the pay office on the first Sunday of the month to agree his balance in hand at the end of the previous month. The pay clerk, Lance-Corporal Cooke, with his dog Sandy in attendance, usually met us when we arrived. Sandy was a friendly dog and was always made a fuss of. On one of these occasions I made to pat him but he growled and snapped, just grazing my skin. Later in the day I heard that several others had received the same treatment so suspected that he was developing rabies, whereupon I reported the matter to the RSM, who arranged for all who had contact with the dog, including his owner, to report for sick-parade in the morning.

As the senior present, I handed the sick-report to the MO, who questioned me about the incident and asked me if I had seen anyone die of rabies. When I said 'No', his remark was, 'Well, it's a horrible death!'

The treatment consisted of inserting a hypodermic needle into the walls of the stomach and injecting anti-rabies serum, taking care not to pierce the stomach lining.

On completion of the parade, I saw that we had all been 'excused duty with bed down' and thought this was a joke. After three days I was unable to kick-start my motor cycle and travelled with the rest to the hospital in a truck. None of us could stand up straight – so then we understood the reason for being excused duty. Some were luckier than others; in my case, having only been grazed, I got away with seven days' treatment, whereas those who had been bitten suffered for two weeks. What alarmed me was having to sign a form at the end of the treatment headed 'If this man is still alive six months from now GHQ Delhi must be informed.'

Leslie Hore-Belisha had now taken over the job of Secretary for War and he soon introduced sweeping changes. No longer were officers expected to serve half their service as subalterns, and all those who had held the rank for eight years were promoted to captain, which meant that most officers in the British service were upgraded and from then on were referred to as '1938 captains'. Another innovation which he introduced was the rank of warrant-officer III, which was intended to replace officers in charge of sections or platoons. His idea was good, because the senior NCOs promoted to this new rank were experienced in man-management and administration.

This new arrangement was not favourably received by the Government of India, and those promoted were soon on their way home to join British units. It was a retrograde step on their part because war was looming and they lost a considerable number of seasoned soldiers at a critical time for the Indian Army.

In my last year at Quetta I contracted malaria. Prior to the earthquake the few mosquitoes in Quetta were non-malarial. Many of the construction coolies brought up from southern India had been victims of the malaise, and this was transmitted to the mosquitoes who sucked their blood. I was feeling unwell one evening and on the following morning found myself in bed at the BMH. The treatment was to keep warm and take liberal doses of quinine. The normal length of time spent in hospital with malaria was ten days but after five days my fellow patients and I were discharged. We found out the reason later. An exercise was being held involving battalions of Infantry, and malaria victims were being brought to the hospital by the truck-load. A further five days in my own bed, attended by the medical orderly, completed my cure. Fortunately, it was only a bacterial type and not the malignant type of malaria which can recur for years.

One of the most detested duties which still existed was the Quarter-Master stores piquet. This had been set up in 1935 to protect the contents of the store from looters and no one had thought fit to discontinue it. One NCO and three men, dressed in the awful *poshteens*, were detailed for this duty; each sentry spent thirty minutes on his beat. Most of us realised the futility of the chore, and as soon as the orderly officer had visited, what remained of the night was spent by all in the warmth of the Wana hut.

Trouble was now flaring up on the North-West Frontier; the tribesmen had harvested their crops and had little to do except annoy the Army. As the covering force for the frontier, we were responsible for reinforcement, and many of our operators were sent there. In order to discourage the tribes, the RAF would destroy some of their villages in the hope that the dissidents would withdraw to rebuild their homes before the winter. Whenever a village was to be bombed, the RAF dropped leaflets warning the inhabitants of its intentions.

The biggest thorn in the side of the Indian Army was the Fakir of Ipi, a religious fanatic who warned the villagers that the big birds in the sky would drop bombs on them. 'But do not fear,' he said, 'their bombs will turn to paper.' This was a dilemma for the RAF, who did not want to cause loss of life.

The trouble on the frontier subsided, and our pals, having earned themselves a General Service Medal, returned with lurid tales of action further north. Their biggest fear was the loss of a rifle – a court-martial offence – and when they slept at night in the open their weapons were kept in a shallow trench beneath them. The wily Pathans and Afridis were adept at crawling up to a sleeping soldier and tickling his face with a bird feather, causing him to turn over in his sleep, so they could make off with his rifle. To guard against waking a soldier and being grabbed, they smeared their arms with animal fat so that the alerted soldier lost his grip and they could escape.

In the autumn of 1938 my appointment as a paid lance-corporal was promulgated, which brought my daily rate of pay to 6s, so the ignominy of returning to the UK holding the same rank as five years earlier was removed.

Our last Christmas in Baluchistan was drawing near, and after the festivities were over, a large draft was warned of its impending return to the UK. Soldiers leaving India were allowed to carry a suitcase in addition to a kitbag, and most of us, wanting to return in style, bought solid hide cases in the bazaar.

Those of us who were careful with our money were well in credit and on leaving India this money had to be withdrawn. The canny ones discovered that the banks gave a better rate of exchange if English coins were accepted rather than paper currency.

In late January the home-going draft was ordered to prepare for entrainment to Karachi on 5th February, and on the preceding Friday I withdrew all the surplus cash in my account, took it to the bank and exchanged it for English coins, which I carried in a small canvas bag packed into my kitbag.

The draft left early on 5th February 1939 to cheers and farewells from the friends we left behind, some of whom were to remain in India or Burma until the end of the war. Meals were served on this train and as we neared Rohri Junction it was breakfast-time. Since we had left Meerut in 1936 I had seen no hawks and very few birds on which they preyed. As I stood at the carriage window holding my tin plate and eating my breakfast, a hawk swooped down, knocked the plate from my hand and stood on the track eating my food. One never learns!

There was a hold-up at Rohri Junction to await another troop-train joining us from the northerly stations of Rawalpindi, Peshawar and Nowshera, and when it arrived it was connected to our own and we proceeded to Karachi.

The first sight that greeted us at the docks was HMT *Lancashire,* on which we had made the outward voyage. Formalities at the docks were kept to a minimum; we handed in our blankets, exchanged our remaining money and boarded the troop-ship.

9

HOME SERVICE

From the moment we boarded the *Lancashire* and left Karachi we were deemed to be on the home establishment, having severed all links with India. Conditions on board were far more tolerable than they had been in 1934 and to some extent the improvement was due to the efforts of the War Minister, Leslie Hore-Belisha. Faced with the growing influence of Hitler, the Government had been forced to introduce rearmament; but the young men of 1938 were not hurrying to join the forces.

A study was carried out to find the reason for their reluctance. From the result it was obvious: no one wanted to join the Army in order to carry out menial tasks such as potato-peeling, scrubbing floors, polishing buttons and the like. To eliminate these irritants civilians were employed to perform non-military duties, and this improved recruitment and reduced the dole queues. No longer did soldiers have to line up at the galleys to carry food to the mess tables, waiter service was available.

Realising that we were not still callow youths, the ship's staff treated us with respect. But the excitement of seeing places of interest on the voyage out had given way to wondering about the changes we would find on reaching home. In order to relieve the boredom, groups of men were inveigled into card schools, others could not resist playing housey housey – the original name for bingo – and sometimes the stakes were high.

Daily news bulletins received over the ship's radio were displayed on the notice-boards, and they made gloomy reading. On our route through the Red Sea we passed a number of Italian naval vessels and freighters travelling to

Mussolini's new conquests, Eritrea and Ethiopia.

At night the vultures organised the crown and anchor tables in secluded but well-lit areas between decks. I watched one of them laying the ground bait with the dice, and queens came up time and time again. In a moment of folly I hurried below to retrieve my money bag and decided to gamble, starting with a shilling stake and doubling it every time the dice were thrown. After the tenth throw my savings had halved and, remembering the old maxim 'In for a penny, in for a pound', I divided what remained of my kitty into three lots, still hoping that queens would turn up trumps. On the thirteenth throw queens had not appeared and my kitty was expended. Two throws later three of them were exposed! In 1939 the £100 that I had lost in ten minutes would have bought a Ford 10 motor car, so I consoled myself with a few lines of Kipling's 'If':

> *If you can make one heap of all your winnings*
> *And risk it on one turn of pitch-and-toss,*
> *And lose, and start again at your beginnings*
> *And never breathe a word about your loss . . .*

A daily event that most people looked forward to was the ship's mileage sweepstake. On leaving port a line was cast overboard and towed in the wake of the vessel, and in some mysterious way the distance travelled each day was logged. Those lucky enough to guess the mileage covered shared the prize-money less ten per cent retained for seamen's charities.

At the end of February we reached the Western Approaches, and it was not long afterwards that The Needles hove into sight. Much time was taken up in concealing contraband in kitbags or suitcases. There was no smuggling as such but many of us had bought the unexpurgated version of *Lady Chatterley's Lover* – still banned in the UK – and did not wish to have the book confiscated by HM Customs. As we waited to disembark an English bobby made an appearance and was greeted by loud cheering. The order came for us to leave the ship and, heavily laden with our gear, we walked past the

Customs men. Every tenth soldier was asked if he had anything to declare but few were searched, possibly because the Customs officers were invariably called 'sir' by those they challenged.

The disembarkation staff were at the dockside to meet us and sort us out into groups for onward movement to our new units. I was put in charge of twelve men, handed their documents and instructed to conduct them to Bulford Camp near Salisbury, where I was to report to the adjutant of Mobile Divisional Signals.

On arrival there, the draft was shown into accommodation, given a meal and told to relax until the following morning, when we were to proceed on twenty-eight days' leave. The accommodation allocated to me was a bunk within a large wooden building housing twenty-four men for whom I had responsibility.

I reported to the office at 8.30 a.m. and was told that I was improperly dressed. Apparently my promotion to corporal had been promulgated whilst still at sea and this left me nine pence a day better off. The next formality was to collect a leave pass, twenty-eight days' pay and ration allowance, and a return railway warrant to Holyhead.

Pausing only to change into civilian clothes, I was soon on my way to London. There, feeling conspicuous in my light-weight Indian-made suit, my first visit was to Austin Reed, where I bought a top-of-the-range off-the-peg suit for six guineas. The salesman became suspicious when I asked him to discard my old suit, and took pains to write my name on the lining of the inner pocket of my new one. Perhaps he thought I was a fugitive from justice. As I proceeded to Lyons Corner House in the Strand for tea and cakes, I was terrified of London's traffic and took great care in crossing the road.

It was relaxing to sit in the cafeteria eating pastries and listening to the orchestra, but I had a train to catch. The ladies lurking about outside the entrance door looking for clients gave me meaningful glances, no doubt noticing my bronzed complexion and thinking I was an easy touch, but I had other thoughts on my mind.

I sent a telegram home announcing my arrival and reached Euston station in time to catch the evening *Irish*

Mail. As always, the carriages were spotlessly clean and even in the third class compartments waiter service was at hand to supply beer or sandwiches. A bottle of Bass cost less than 6d and the waiter was delighted when told to keep the change. The express train sped on, stopping only at Rugby, Crewe and Chester, and shortly before midnight I arrived home.

Holyhead had not changed. The 10 m.p.h. speed restriction sign, erected in the horse-and-cart days, still stood at the entrance to the High Street. Many of my old friends had left the town in search of more lucrative employment. Some had heeded the call of the sea, others had enlisted in the services, and the more talented had left to take up jobs in industry.

One day I read a notice announcing that a dance was being held at my old school and former pupils were welcome. Some of the masters recognised me and appeared eager to hear of my experiences in India. Young pupils, noting the attention paid to me by the staff, crowded around asking questions until I felt like a celebrity.

My father was a total abstainer and a pillar of the chapel, but one day I persuaded him to celebrate my home-coming by having a few drinks at the George Hotel, the oldest tavern in the town. He elected to drink port wine and seemed to enjoy it. The hotel served a very palatable bitter beer which was brewed in Burton-upon-Trent. Every time the barman drew me another beer he refilled the old man's glass and I thought my father was becoming a convert to alcohol until I glanced in his direction and saw him tipping his drink into the aspidistra pot.

One thing that struck me forcibly on my return was that the price of most commodities had remained stable since I left the country in 1934. They were the days of nil inflation.

I was not sorry when my leave drew to a close as I looked forward to getting down to work. Mobile Divisional Signals was destined to be part of the 1st Armoured Division in the British Army, and Lieutenant-Colonel F. S. Straight, M.C., and his adjutant, Captain Smythe, had spent two years planning the establishment of manpower and equipment.

The unit was woefully undermanned, although strenuous efforts had been made to stiffen it with an influx of seasoned NCOs and men over the past six months. I was told that my job was to give driving-instructions to those earmarked as drivers.

On the Friday after my return from leave we were parading for pay when a distinguished-looking officer wearing red tabs and a red-banded cap walked past with his escort, looked at the parade and said to the sergeant-major, 'I want to talk to the NCO in the supernumerary ranks wearing an IUL cap.' He was referring to me, so I stepped up to him, gave a smart salute and recognised him as our old CO from Quetta. On returning to the UK he had been given a staff appointment in the rank of colonel and was now our Chief Signal Officer. He asked about present-day life at Quetta, chatted for a minute or two and ended by wishing me luck in my new unit. It is always pleasant to be recognised and remembered by a senior officer.

We were allowed to wear our IUL – India Unattached List – caps for six weeks after disembarking to distinguish us from the *hoi polloi*.

Driver-training was interesting and enabled me to get to know the surrounding country. We passed through charming villages and hamlets such as Middle Wallop, Nether Wallop, Over Wallop, Ludgershall, Amesbury and Andover, always stopping for a mid-morning cup of tea at a café. Amesbury was then a quiet rural village, unlike the sprawling town of today, and Stonehenge was just a cluster of giant rocks that no one paid any attention to.

Soldiers prided themselves on their appearance in those days, and Aldershot was known as the town of England's well-dressed men. When off duty we could wear either civilian dress or on more dressy occasions blue patrols, purchased at our own expense and invariably tailor-made. They consisted of a smart tunic fitted with brass buttons and collar badges. The headgear was a side cap in Corps colours of light blue, dark blue and green.

For ceremonial occasions the dress was a khaki serge

tunic with brass buttons and collar badges, riding-breeches and spurs, and puttees – long lengths of woollen material wound round the legs starting below the knee and finishing at the ankles. The rural dwellers in these parts described our linesmen as 'they those telegraph soldiers with the twisted trousers'.

When out walking in the camp one day I met our old RSM Jimmy Noonan, who was now a commissioned officer holding the appointment of Quarter-Master. He chatted for a while and asked what my job was. On being told, he said that Fred Kitchen, his CQMS running the MT Section, was joining the Territorial Army at Cardiff and asked if I would take on the job. My first reaction was that asking a corporal to take over the duties of a company quartermaster sergeant was cheap labour, and I told him so. In reply he said that he would look after me, so I accepted.

My new responsibility was to take over all MT vehicles and stores, maintain the ledgers and liaise with the Ordnance workshops at Tidworth. I was provided with an eight-hundred weight pick-up with a driver named Gunn and a storeman, 'Chippy' Woods. Both Gunn and Woods were very old soldiers and wore World War I medal ribbons.

It was an onerous job and on most days I worked well into the evenings in order to reorganise the stores and records. Within a month of taking over the job I was promoted to the rank of temporary sergeant, bringing my daily pay up to 8s 3d.

One of my sisters had married a seaman working for Trinity House, based at East Cowes on the Isle of Wight, and very often at weekends I would visit them. Beer brewed in the Isle of Wight could be bought in the saloon bar of his local public house for 4½d a pint. Whenever I visited them on a Saturday Pat and I would spend the evening at the pub and the ten-shilling note that I placed on the counter was sufficient to pay for all our drinks with enough change left over to buy fish and chips for three on our way home.

Hitler by this time had taken over Austria and was threatening Poland. It was obvious that war with Germany was imminent, and my curiosity was aroused when a new officer joined us with the reputation of being a wireless expert. His name was Lieutenant Henn-Collins.

Speculation grew when several NCOs and men, all experienced wireless operators, were re-accommodated in a block of their own, where a number of black-painted crates were delivered. This seemed odd as the Army does not waste paint on wooden crates. A few days later an unusual sight was seen in Kiwi Barracks, Bulford: a group of soldiers dressed in regimental mufti – blue blazers, dark grey trousers and black shoes – appeared outside this block, from which a quantity of heavy wooden crates had been removed and loaded on to trucks. By the following morning Lieutenant Henn-Collins and his party had left us.

It was many months before some individuals of the party were seen again, and under the fifty-year secrecy rules the general public was not to hear the story of their adventure – which can now be revealed.

General Carton-de-Wiart, V.C., known as the one-eyed, one-armed V.C., had settled in Poland on his retirement after an illustrious career in the British Army. He was recalled from retirement to head the British Military Mission to Poland and had requested Royal Signals support to augment his communications. It was in response to his appeal that the party from Bulford had been set up.

The problem confronting the War Office was how to get it to Warsaw. Travel through Germany was out of the question, so arrangements were made for them to travel by rail to the South of France and by sea to Alexandria, where they were issued with false papers. A group of soldiers, whether in uniform or civilian clothing, always stands out; to avoid suspicion it was split into small groups, which eventually reached Warsaw using different forms of transport. These small groups reached the capital of Poland safely and Henn-Collins organised them into a small communication unit which enabled the head of mission to pass vital intelligence to the Cabinet.

Hitler invaded Poland on 1st September 1939. Although the Poles offered fierce resistance, they were powerless to hold back the German armour and within three weeks Poland, stabbed in the back by Russia, was overwhelmed. General Carton-de-Wiart, realising that the position was hopeless, gave orders for the Signals equipment to be destroyed, before disbanding the group and instructing the operating crews to make for Egypt in small numbers. Fortunately, they all reached Cairo safely many months later, and the general too survived the war.

Two of my best friends at the time were Martin Cullen, who had served for five years in India, and Tim Cole, who had served in Palestine. The three of us would often stroll to a very old tavern in Amesbury and sit in the saloon bar drinking beer and chatting. The barmaid was a tall blonde who was unusually reserved for a lady in her occupation, and although we were regular customers, and sometimes the only customers, we were never given a friendly greeting on our arrival. It was not until 1942, while serving in the desert campaign, that I heard she had been arrested as an enemy agent.

Kiwi Barracks was the home of 3rd Divisional Signals, who were under strength and had spare accommodation, which is why Mobile Divisional Signals, having no base of its own, was housed there. Towards the middle of 1939 reinforcements started arriving, which caused the barracks to be overcrowded. It was decided that my unit would move into tented accommodation in Bulford Fields, two miles away, but I was to remain behind to safeguard the MT stores. I was therefore attached to 3rd Division for messing purposes and became a member of their sergeants' mess.

It was in this mess that I met 'Tich' Henshaw, a cheerful West Countryman whose job was pay sergeant. Like many of us he had spent most of his service abroad, where he was excused wearing shorts for obvious reasons. He also had a wry sense of humour. He later rose to the rank of RSM and was supervising his unit on a jungle warfare course which involved crossing a river by means of a rope bridge. When half-way across, a company sergeant-major lost his grip and fell into the water, whereupon a sergeant dived in to rescue him. Tich called out, 'Sergeant, you won't get promotion that way.'

I had noticed that their Captain Quarter-Master, an exceptionally tall man, wore the ribbon of the Distinguished Conduct Medal amongst many others. The orderly-room sergeant told me that as an Infantry soldier before transferring to Signals he had been awarded this coveted decoration during the Great War and his citation read: 'For conspicuous bravery in charging and routing an enemy machine-gun post armed only with a shovel GS.' (GS meaning General Service).

The vehicles I had taken over were a varied collection of anything Ordnance could supply to meeting the training needs of the crews who had to operate the wireless sets installed in them. An establishment of vehicles had been agreed but industry could not meet the requirement. A case in point was the armoured command vehicle. An ACV is a large vehicle capable of housing all the wireless and telephone equipment needed for a commander to conduct a battle. It is the nerve-centre of any operation and it should be well protected by armour to ensure the safety of the staff and operators from small-arms fire. The ACVs issued to us in 1939 were mock-ups and consisted of a fifteen-hundredweight chassis covered by panels of plywood. They were just large enough to contain a small wireless set and operator.

Because many of the vehicles issued to us were obsolescent, it became increasingly difficult to obtain spares for them through Ordnance channels and much of my time was taken up in trying to buy suitable replacement parts from local garages. My storeman, Chippy Wood, was good at keeping the place tidy but not a great help technically, so I was given an assistant named Nick Carter.

The reservists were called up early in August and they were greeted with relief. Most of them had served in the Corps for eight years and all of them were experienced soldiers and competent tradesmen. Despite the circumstances of their call-up there were many happy reunions in the messes and canteens.

When the 1914-18 War ended there was a serious shortage of shipping to carry the overseas contingents home and thousands had to be found accommodation until transport was available to repatriate them. Hundreds of the New Zealand veterans had occupied Bulford Camp, hence the name Kiwi Barracks. In order to commemorate their stay in Wiltshire, they shaped a giant kiwi on the hillside overlooking the camp. It could be seen for miles, and by 1939 this memorial was recognised as part of the heritage and wardens were employed at public expense to keep it tidy.

After a heavy session in the wet bar one moonlit Friday night, a group of reservists, armed with spades and hoes, climbed the hillside towards the kiwi to do their infamous work, and in the light of day anyone glancing in the direction of the kiwi noticed that it had laid an egg!

The propaganda war was hotting up and we were aware that Poland had been invaded and that the Prime Minister had given Hitler an ultimatum.

Just before midday on Sunday, 3rd September 1939, I switched on my wireless set to hear Mr Chamberlain announcing that a state of war now existed between the UK and Germany. A few minutes later the Quarter-Master called and asked if I had heard the news. When I said to him that at least the tension was over, he remarked, 'War is a terrible thing.'

The new battledress had now arrived at the QM stores and was in course of issue to all ranks. It was not welcomed by the old soldiers, who took a pride in polishing their buttons and leather belts, but it was comfortable to wear.

The outbreak of war did not change our lives, apart from working extended hours. Although we were supposed to be a mobile unit we lacked mobility because of the shortage of transport. This state of affairs was soon remedied and I was advised to expect a fleet of vehicles within a week as the Army was commandeering commercial vans and trucks. These impressed vehicles arrived and caused eyebrows to be raised. They consisted of transport formerly used by Thomas Tilling, Sangers Circus, Pickfords and several other firms who wished to dispose of unwanted vehicles; I shuddered to think of the maintenance problems they would cause.

Word was passed that we were soon to leave the Bulford area and billeting officers were detailed to find a suitable venue. The area selected for us was near to Blandford

Forum and the unit was deployed in the villages of Spettisbury, Charlton Marshall and Blandford St Mary. A warrant-officer III named Lancaster met me and said he had found accommodation for both of us in the guest room of a pub at Spettisbury. It proved to be very comfortable, but there was one snag: the bedroom contained a pump which drew water from a well below to supply the whole pub and we were expected to operate it! A disused building was found for storing the MT spares and it took three of us a week to sort them out into bins.

I had by now chummed up with Ronnie Drake, who owned a car, and invited him to the bar of the billet for a drink. We were the sole customers until a florid elderly gentleman entered, accompanied by a young lady whom I took to be his daughter. He introduced himself as Victor before buying us a drink. After a couple of drinks he told us that he farmed at Sturminster Marshall and had served in the Dorsetshire Yeomanry during the Great War. Victor often called in for a drink, and it became clear that Eileen was not his daughter. She was, in fact, the wife of one of his farm-workers. Victor had made an arrangement with him that she should become his social companion. She went to markets with him, to pubs with him but never to bed with him.

One evening they arrived earlier than usual. It appeared that Victor had had a profitable day at Salisbury market and wanted to celebrate, so Ronnie and I were invited to a country club at Lytchett Matravers. Before the outbreak of war it had been a popular rendezvous for the people of Poole and Bournemouth wishing for some night-life. It did not take us long to discover that it functioned as a club on week nights and became a bawdy house at the weekends.

The motoring organisations had been campaigning for years to have road-marking to indicate the middle of the road. Driving a vehicle at night was particularly hazardous because wartime regulations forbade the use of car headlights unless they were masked. In no time at all road-workers appeared with pots of white paint, and the sarcastic ones said that it took a war to bring about the change.

Moving to Spettisbury was a temporary expedient. After a month it became obvious that the venue was unsuitable and we were ordered to move to Hertfordshire. The RHQ took over a Territorial Army barracks and the squadrons serving their armoured brigades were located at Baldock, Bishops Stortford and Great Dunmow.

Our establishment of manpower and vehicles had been approved by the War Office in mid-September. New vehicles were arriving but not in sufficient quantity, and we were extremely short of spare parts.

Captain Smythe asked me what items we needed most, so I gave him a list of urgent requirements. He must have telephoned the Command Ordnance Depot at Nottingham, for within an hour he called me to his office and told me to bring my driver. He paid us both our subsistence allowance and told me to report to the COD for everything we needed and to leave after lunch.

We reached Leicester, then a small straggling town, and we realised that we would not get to the depot that day, so we paused for a smoke in the main street. A soldier wearing the chevrons of a sergeant was nearing us, and I recognised him as Douglas McManus, a townie of mine. He was serving in the RAPC and was billeted in Leicester, so he said he would ask his landlady if she had any spare accommodation. Regrettably all she could offer was a double bed. It was a court-martial offence for two soldiers to share a bed, but as the sailor said, any port in a storm.

In 1939 Hertford was a delightful market town and its people went out of their way to make our stay there a happy one. Many of the girls worked in the Halex toothbrush factory and no soldier was short of one of their products. Good use was made of the Territorial Army drill hall, and other rank dances and similar entertainment were held there to repay the hospitality shown by the townspeople. The town had been denuded of most of its young men, who had volunteered to join the forces.

Hertford was popular with many of our members because of its proximity to London, which could be reached by train in thirty minutes. Weekend passes were not difficult to get. Our working hours were from 8 a.m. to 7 p.m., except at weekends, when work stopped at noon.

Hertford pubs were kept open until 4.30 p.m., so it was possible to drink from 11.30 a.m. until lunch-time and then repair to the market area and continue to quaff ale until tea-time.

The Corn Exchange was opened as a social centre on Saturday evenings, with music for dancing and a bar for the thirsty. The entertainment fraternity was mobilised with touring parties in order to keep up the morale of the troops, before leaving for the sergeants' mess after the show to be entertained themselves.

I met a pleasant girl in her middle twenties rumoured by some of her friends to have had an affair with a married man. I took her out a few times but never made any advances. On one of these occasions she said, 'I'm not innocent, you know,' but I preferred her friendship. She must have thought that I was a queer! Jimmy Noonan had no such qualms. After he had spent his lunch-time in a pub, he rushed into the stores one afternoon, grabbed two blankets and drove off, leaving his staff exchanging knowing glances.

RSM 'Darkie' Penfold left us on being commissioned as a Quarter-Master. He was posted to a unit in North Yorkshire, where he spent the war years. His replacement was 'Lottie' Collins, who arrived with a reputation. Some remembered him from their days at Colchester when he was their section sergeant in a horsed unit. When he left them on promotion, they presented him with a horsewhip to remind him of how he had treated them.

Christmas arrived, and soon we were into the New Year of 1940. The British Expeditionary Force was building up under the command of Field-Marshal Lord Gort, V.C. The RAF showered pamphlets on Berlin and it was being called 'the phoney war'. Soldiers sang patriotic songs in the canteens and pubs, including 'The Long and the Short and the Tall' and 'We'll Hang Out Our Washing on the Siegfried Line'. The French were smug in their Maginot Line, believing it to be impregnable.

We had our Webley revolvers withdrawn and were reissued with Smith and Wessons, which used .38 calibre rounds. The bullets fired from the Webley were capable of knocking a man over and if they struck a bone would shatter it. The reason given for the change of weapons was that the Germans claimed the ammunition, made in the Ordnance factory at Dum Dum near Calcutta, was in breach of the Geneva Convention.

Vera Lynn made an occasional private appearance at the Royal Oak in Faircross, near Barking, and sang in public, entertainment aimed at keeping up the morale of the troops and the nation. She was soon to be known as 'the Forces' Sweetheart'. For her services to the war effort she was later elevated to Dame Commander of the Order of the British Empire. Another frequent visitor was Tessie O'Shea, a large and jolly person mentioned later, whom my wife knew well.

Rationing was imposed and queues formed outside confectioners' and tobacconists'. Many people joined a queue not knowing what was on sale at the counter.

All good things come to an end, and once again it was learnt that another change of location was planned. It was with real regret that we left Hertford and its hospitable people.

Our venue this time was Downton, five miles south of Salisbury on the A338. A billeting officer had been sent in advance to secure accommodation for messes and individual soldiers, as well as parking-spaces for our vehicles. Sergeants and above were entitled to a bed, and the inconvenienced house-owner was rewarded with 6d a day for providing it. Lower ranks slept in barns, for which the farmer was paid 3d per man.

I was sent on ahead of the main party, driving the MT stores lorry, a clapped-out vehicle which had been 'commandeered' from a willing seller anxious to dispose of it. We passed through Alton, then a straggling town, and stopped at a Strong's pub for a midday refreshment break. Whatever happened to those freshly made succulent pork pies filled with fresh meat and juices? Wherever anyone travelled in Hampshire, whether by rail or road, one saw imposing signs which read 'You are now entering the Strong country'. After sampling a pint or two of this fine ale and eating a pork pie we sped on to Downton.

The main party was not so lucky. The CO had decided to treat the move from Hertford as a communication exercise, and as bad luck would have it they encountered foul weather with freezing temperatures on the way.

The reception was rather frosty too, which was understandable. The villagers' placid way of life was upset by the arrival of a large body of troops, but the atmosphere thawed gradually and the local parish council arranged local dances to entertain their girls and the troops. There was ill feeling between the residents of Downton and a hamlet on higher ground they referred to as Upton, and this came to a head when we were invited to attend a dance at Upton. The reason for the friction emerged later and sounded rather silly. The inhabitants of Downton earned their living from agriculture and cattle-raising but those living on higher and less fertile soil were dependent on raising sheep for their livelihood and were looked down upon by their neighbours.

The sergeants' mess was a disused church in the local cemetery, so Leslie Bainbridge and I found more congenial surroundings for our leisure time. There was a reasonable bus service to Salisbury so we decided to investigate. There were five taverns in one street bordering on the market square and we found one to our taste. We always preferred to drink in the saloon rather than the 'spit and sawdust', where pints were a halfpenny cheaper. The main bus station was visible from the pub, and as 10 p.m. approached we kept an eye out for our bus. If we delayed our departure from the pub too long we missed the last bus and faced a five-mile walk back – not too funny if snow had fallen.

Most of the villagers attended church service on a Sunday morning, and the local farmer drove there with his wife and two daughters, sometimes waving as they passed by. I got to know one of them and invited her to the cinema at Salisbury. After one or two meetings I was invited to the farmer's house, an imposing building surrounded by many acres of arable land. I sensed then that she was becoming too serious, so Bainbridge and I spent our evenings playing darts against the locals in the village pub.

Most of us guessed the reason for our move to Downton, which was within twenty miles of the port of Southampton. It was obvious that we were to reinforce the BEF as soon as we were fully equipped. Ominously enough, we were encouraged to go home on leave on a rota basis and I took advantage of this. Life at Holyhead was dreary so I curtailed my furlough and returned two days early.

The sight that greeted my eyes as I walked along the village staggered me. The village green was chock-a-block with a hundred or so brand-new Army vehicles which had arrived there that day. The second-in-command and the Quarter-Master were in a tizzy because they all had to be handed over to the various squadrons. Another difficulty was that we were still on peacetime accounting and any missing tools had to be paid for.

I was handed a distribution list of vehicles by the adjutant, transport representatives were called in from the detached squadrons, and the hand-over was completed within the hour.

Two weeks later block leave was granted, which I declined for reasons stated earlier. So did Major 'Dizzy' Duncan, whom I had left behind at Meerut, where he commanded the 3rd Cavalry Brigade Signal Troop. While cycling through the village he spoke to me and asked why I hadn't taken leave.

Shortly after the unit was assembled after embarkation leave the orderly-room sergeant told me that my name had been submitted to Divisional headquarters for promotion to warrant-officer Class III, but as bad luck would have it the War Office had followed the example of the Indian Army and discontinued the rank in the very week I was recommended for it.

Ten days later, and long before the days of Dr Beeching, we formed up at Downton Station and entrained for Southampton. The station platform was crowded with well-wishers, including the farmer's daughter, the guard blew his whistle and we were on our way.

The train party consisted of Regimental Headquarters and No. 1 Squadron, our vehicles had been driven to the port to be loaded on to freighters. The Support Group and Brigade Signal Squadrons travelled with their Formation Headquarters, to which they were now permanently attached.

Ordnance had failed to produce our new armoured command vehicles but had promised to deliver them to the ports for onward shipment. All but one arrived, which meant that one of the armoured brigades went into action with a mock-up ACV flanked by a protective tank on each side of it.

10

SOJOURN IN FRANCE

The train arrived at Southampton Docks two hours later and stopped opposite a camouflaged ship whose name and port of registration had been obliterated. The lines of the ship looked familiar and I asked a Mercantile Marine Officer her name. It was an indiscreet question from a security point of view and he asked where I came from. On being told, he asked my father's name and this satisfied him. He introduced himself as Devnald and said that he was the chief engineer of the *Scotia*, a Holyhead mail-boat now in use as a troop transport.

After chatting for a few minutes he asked me if I had met the chief officer and when I said 'No' he took me along to meet him. The chief asked me if I had eaten, and on being told that we had only had a packed meal on the train invited me to the first class saloon for dinner, adding, 'and bring a mate'. My friend Bainbridge thought I was joking when I asked him to join me. The chief officer greeted me and I had to apologise for Bainbridge, saying that he was shy. Ships' chief officers are not fools, and he simply said, 'Go and get him.' A chastened Leslie Bainbridge then came along and joined us.

I was disconcerted to find that the second table was occupied by the CO and his officers. I noticed that our late second-in-command now wore the badges of rank of a lieutenant-colonel. The unusual news that two sergeants were dining in the first class saloon passed through the ship like wildfire. RSM Lottie Collins could not believe it, and half-way through the meal I caught a glimpse of him peeping through the saloon door with a look of envy on his face.

The table steward had leaked the news to other crew members, and after dinner we were pressed to join them for a drink in their quarters. The chief had told me that we would be sailing at midnight for Le Havre, and as he would be on bridge duty all night his cabin was at my disposal. When bidding me goodnight he asked me to report to the bridge to pay my respects to the captain before disembarking.

The ship's master, Captain W. M. Hughes, spoke a few kindly words before offering me a tumbler of whisky, which he insisted that I drank before leaving the bridge.

A week before we left Downton, RHQ and No. 1 Squadron had been reinforced by an Ordnance Light Aid Detachment consisting of a captain RAOC, a class II warrant-officer and several technicians, and responsibility for the maintenance and repairs to the unit vehicles was now theirs.

Disembarkation took place without a hitch and transport was ready at the dockside to take us to a staging-area at Honfleur, a few miles away, while our own vehicles were unloaded.

We landed on French soil on 16th May in what was described later as 'that amazing summer'. Alarming news reached us that the Germans had opened up an offensive to the north of the country but were being stubbornly resisted by the Allies. Eventually our transport arrived and we moved in an easterly direction towards Rouen. We stopped for a few days at the small village of Yevetot, where the wireless equipment was checked and found to be in good working order.

A 'stand to parade' was now in operation. The unit assembled at dusk, when the roll was called to ensure that there were no absentees. Whilst this was in progress the RSM and I visited one or two cafés to sip cognac. The rate of exchange at the time was 240 francs to the pound sterling, and a cognac cost four francs!

Orders were given for us to move and we ended the day to the north of Rouen. The RHQ and No. 1 Squadron remained near Rouen for a week and everything appeared quiet, apart from the odd dogfight in the air – which usually resulted in a French plane being shot down.

The German armour broke through at Arras, and Abbeville was taken. The BEF was fighting a rearguard action which culminated on the beaches of Dunkirk, Calais and St Valery. We were joined at Rouen by a Corporal Hicks, a huge man who had got away from the Germans at Neufchâtel, not far from where we were.

Busty Hicks had found a frightened and half-starved jackdaw. He fed and watered the bird and it attached itself to him. Everywhere that Hicks went, the jackdaw could be found perched on his shoulder.

The plan had been for the 1st Armoured Division to reinforce the BEF and protect its right flank, but because of French intransigence it was unable to get anywhere near its objective. Tanks are not designed to travel long distances on metalled roads, and tank-transporters were a thing of the future. The French had been asked to provide railway flats to carry the armour nearer to its destination, but these were not forthcoming. Consequently they had to be driven on their tracks, which resulted in wear to the sprockets. The French commander, Weygand, held frequent conferences and bemoaned the lack of British support. When Major-General Evans, our divisional commander, pointed out that his tanks had been held up due to track failure, he railed and said, 'If you can't fight them with your tanks fight them with your fists.'

Although I was nominally still the MT sergeant, my responsibility for vehicle maintenance had been taken over by the LAD, and as I had no longer to account for spare parts there was little for me to do. My main purpose was to liaise with Ordnance for replacement trucks, motor cycles and major items of equipment. To this end I made contact with an RAOC stores depot at Louviers and told our new adjutant my intentions. As travelling to Louviers meant a road journey of forty miles, he issued me with an *ordre du mission* which was an authorisation for despatch riders or individual truck drivers to travel on French roads. All convoy movements were notified to the French by their liaison officer, who was attached to us. The RAOC stores officer at Louviers was helpful and I persuaded him to issue me with a new Matchless motor cycle, and this enabled me to move about the countryside unencumbered by Signalman Gunn and his eight-hundredweight pick-up.

Things were now going badly for the BEF, who were in the middle of a two-pronged attack by the Germans, and the decision was made to fall back to Dunkirk and Calais. Seeing that the situation was desperate, the War Cabinet ordered evacuation and organised a massive rescue operation involving all craft capable of carrying passengers, with orders to proceed to Dunkirk post-haste. All types of craft took part in the operation including Thames barges, ships' lifeboats, fishing-boats and sailing-dinghies.

The troop-transport *Scotia* was one of the larger vessels sent there, and because of its draught had to remain well out from the beach and accept survivors ferried to it by the smaller craft. Her size attracted the attention of the German bomber crews and she was singled out for a determined aerial attack. She was hit by one of their bombs, which exploded in the engine-room – killing Chief Engineer Devnald and all his staff. The vessel was doomed and the captain and crew made valiant efforts to rescue as many survivors as they could. Ships' lifeboats and rafts were lowered into the sea, and the majority of the survivors boarded these or were rescued by other small vessels. Captain W. M. Hughes took a leading role in the rescue operation, and for his heroism, leadership and disregard for his own safety he was awarded the Distinguished Service Cross – a decoration very rarely given to a Merchant Navy officer.

Reinforcement of the BEF did not now arise, and the next aim was the defence of Paris. The German Air Force had now taken possession of many French airfields, and as our unit was in an exposed position north of Rouen it was decided to move further south. As we re-entered Rouen I noticed several metal signs attached to buildings advertising anything from cough mixture to brandy, but the most prominent advertisement was for 'Pernod Fils'. The field security service later discovered that beneath the Pernod signs enemy agents had hidden directions for the Germans, detailing the best route to take southwards in order to avoid Allied strongpoints.

We arrived at Elbeuf, a village near the River Seine, and

camped in a large forest on its outskirts where we were free from aerial observation. The uncertainty was now having an adverse effect on morale, and when one of the younger operator sergeants came into the mess tent he blurted out that there were forty-eight German divisions on the other side of the Seine. I told him to shut up in no uncertain terms.

The position was depressing. We saw hundreds of French vehicles moving south, some with solid tyres, field kitchens and horse-drawn waggons, their crews dispirited and scruffy in appearance. In contrast to this, a visit to the towns, particularly Evreux, revealed hundreds of French officers sitting at outside cafés sipping cognac or promenading in the streets, all of them obviously on leave from the front.

Tiring of living in a forest, I motor-cycled to Evreux one evening in early June and sat down to watch the scene. The French people did not seem to have a care in the world and the street cafés were thronged with people relaxing after work. I sat at a pavement table drinking some French beer and noticed an attractive young woman observing me. We exchanged glances and she gave me a meaningful look, whereupon I toyed with the idea of staying the night in Evreux but had second thoughts – which was just as well. On returning to the forest at dusk I sensed an air of expectancy. Orders to prepare to move had gone out earlier in the evening and the code word 'Scram' was passed around. This led to some confusion later when a driver named Nobby Clark who had a limited vocabulary and used the word frequently uttered it. Engines were started up and the drivers prepared to move off before hurried orders to switch off came from the command vehicle. At about 11 p.m. the code word 'Scram' was passed around and this was the real thing.

Emerging from the forest was not easy; vehicle lights were vetoed and trees had to be avoided. Another problem was the order of march, each vehicle having to take its correct place in the column. For illumination we were dependent on a small tail-light fitted beneath the chassis to make it invisible from the air. We formed up on the road eventually and moved off. Vehicles were driven nose to tail, and to anyone riding a motor cycle the exhaust fumes from the larger vehicles were troublesome and a strain on the eyes. The column drove through the night and by daybreak had covered only fifty miles.

We stopped for breakfast, after which a briefing session was given to the officers and senior NCOs by the second-in-command. He explained that the CO was at Divisional HQ advising the GOC on communication matters and told us the reason for the hurried departure the previous night. It seems that Marshall Pétain, the hero of Verdun, was suing for an armistice; the French had given up their intention to defend Paris and decided to declare it an open city, to avert damage by aerial attack or gun-fire. All British Forces remaining in France were given five days to leave the country or risk internment. We were told by the second-in-command to treat this information as confidential.

The organised withdrawal of what was left of the BEF posed a considerable problem to the movement-control staff. Thousands of men and vehicles were converging on the channel ports of Le Havre, Brest and St Nazaire, and care had to be taken to avoid bottle-necks at some of the smaller towns on the route. Fortunately, we were not hampered by the presence of refugees, who had cluttered the roads in the north.

We travelled in a south-westerly direction, passing through Chartres, and reached Le Mans by early evening. I was sent forward to direct the convoy off the main road at some minor town, and when I reached it was puzzled because there were two roads leading to the left and I chose the further one as the more likely.

As I sat astride my motor cycle in the middle of the road, a group of ill-disciplined soldiers emerged from a café and one of them approached me with a revolver in his hand and said, 'I don't like sergeants.' He was obviously drunk and, not knowing if his hand-gun was loaded or whether the safety-catch was on, I had a problem. There is only one way to deal with a drunk and that is to humour him. Leaving the motor cycle on its stand, I sauntered with him to the pavement and asked if he had a problem. He appeared to relax, but I was taking no chances. When he seemed to be off guard I thumped him on the chin and held his revolver with my left hand. The drunken soldier bumped his head against the wall of a building and slid to the pavement. I 'broke' his revolver to find that the chamber contained six rounds of ammunition, which I strewed on to the road. By this time it was dark. The convoy had not turned up so I rode back five or six miles but saw no sign of it. I then assumed that the leader had taken the first road to the left but decided I would follow my original instructions and, passing the spot where the gunman had had his fun, I turned left.

Riding a motor cycle with dimmed headlamps on an unlit road is no fun. After four or five miles I came upon some hooded figures walking towards me wearing what appeared to be gowns.

Some publicity had been given to the story that the Germans were dropping paratroopers disguised as nuns behind our lines, but I was not shot at and passed them. A mile or so further on, a vast building looked up which I took to be a university – so the 'nuns' were probably students out for a stroll.

I rode on for hours without seeing any sign of the convoy. I had not slept for two days and nights, but my bedding had been packed on one of the trucks and it was too cold to sleep in a dry ditch. Just before dawn, I noticed a large heap at the roadside. It was a manure mound, and quite warm, so I slept on that for a few hours until the warmth of the rising sun awoke me. I remounted, and with the sun behind me rode on. Two hours later I rejoined the convoy. There was not much respite; after an hour-long break we moved off.

We approached Rennes and saw sad-looking Breton women outside their front doors, some of them weeping openly. As I passed a well-spoken lady she asked why we were leaving them to the Boche. When I tried to explain that the war was over, she retorted that the French were still fighting in the Maginot Line. We were nearing Brest, and the convoy commander decided to halt at a village ten miles short of the port to await instructions. It was an opportunity to relax and catch up on some sleep.

The headquarters had been set up in a vacant private

house, and as I walked past it on the following morning, the second-in-command, who had just completed his conference, called me in to say that he was leaving me behind in charge of a rear party of twenty men. I demurred on the grounds that a party of twenty men merited an officer to command it and said that his staff included two technical officers. He could not be moved, so I insisted that I should be given an NCO as back-up. He agreed to this and Corporal Busty Hicks was included in my party. The adjutant later stipulated my duties, which were to destroy all vehicles and equipment, burn all spare uniforms and clothing and get rid of all the secret papers in the safe. I was also handed over two Boyes anti-tank rifles, which the War Office in its wisdom considered to be an effective deterrent to German armour. He emphasised that these were to be brought back to the UK by my party. Shortly afterwards the convoy moved off in the direction of Brest.

I think it was Napoleon who said that an army marches on its stomach. For the past two days we had survived on indifferent meals and were hungry. The most likely place for sustenance was the officers' mess truck, so I told Busty to organise a small party to denude it of its most appetising foodstuffs and drinks. I found a suitable place on high ground for dumping the vehicles and then returned to enjoy the feast. The truck had, amongst other delicacies, crates of beer brewed in commemoration of King George Fifth's Coronation!

The vehicles were driven to the destruction site in the morning, with the exception of one three-ton lorry to return the drivers to our temporary camp. I opened the safe expecting to find the secret documents, which I intended burning in a stove at the camp, and was surprised to find it empty. Having packed the vehicles nose to tail in readiness for a huge conflagration, we returned to the estaminet for lunch. The meal was interrupted by the arrival of a Royal Signals despatch rider with a message which read:

From: Brest Garrison HQ
To: All detachment commanders

> It is the intention to embark all troops today. Detachments will proceed soonest to dockside on foot. *Nothing to be destroyed by fire or gun-fire.*

Our orders were clear but I decided to have a final look around the area where our vehicles had been dumped with a view to draining them of water and oil and running their engines so that they seized up. On arrival there we were confronted by a sizeable party of hostile-looking gendarmes armed with rifles. Telling my party to cover me, I walked up to their officer and bade him goodday in my inadequate French. He was not communicative and it occurred to me that the party had been sent there to ensure that 'no burning' orders were complied with. Not wishing to start a private war with the French, we left them there.

On returning to the temporary camp area we found two visitors, a Sapper warrant-officer and his sergeant, who were proceeding east to carry out demolition work to hold up the Germans. They had authorisation to take over any arms which might be of help to them in their task and showed an interest in the Boyes rifles, so I was happy to hand them over.

We then proceeded towards Brest in our remaining truck and noticed many British soldiers lying on the pavements either drunk or suffering from fatigue. Not wishing to flaunt the fact that we had misinterpreted the orders about marching on foot, we dismounted from the truck and walked the remaining half-mile.

There was a large ship at the dockside. As we neared it a ship's officer called out, 'Hurry up, sergeant, we are the last ship to leave.' I gave the orders 'Party attention. Quick march. Double march'. When Hicks started to run, the jackdaw was jolted from his shoulder and flew away. There was a lone figure standing at the quayside beside a line of valises. As I drew level I recognised him as the Ordnance LAD officer and he called out, 'What about the officer's kit?' I told him what to do with the officer's kit, mounted the gangway and found sleeping-space between decks.

When we woke up in the morning it was to find that the

ship on which we had embarked, the SS *Bellerophon*, berthed at Plymouth. It was 18th June and our stay in France had lasted only thirty-four days.

11

THE BATTLE OF BRITAIN

Disembarkation took a long time because the vessel was crammed with troops. There were no HM Customs formalities to go through, which was just as well for some as many of the less-disciplined soldiers had passed abandoned NAAFI depots and disposed of their kit in order to stuff their kitbags with cigarettes and tobacco.

We were all touched by the kindness shown to us by the ladies of the WVS and other bodies who greeted us with cups of tea and biscuits. When my party was ready to move off, transport was arranged to take us from the docks to a large municipal building on Plymouth Hoe, where Drake had completed his game of bowls before putting the Spanish Armada to flight. We had no beds but were quite happy to lay our bedding down on a wooden floor, and after a substantial midday meal Corporal Hicks and I strolled down to the shopping centre. It was pleasant to see smiling English faces and to hear Devonian accents, and we spent a pleasant afternoon gazing at shop windows.

When we returned to the billet, our kit and equipment had been removed to an adjoining park. We asked the reason and were both shocked to hear it. The SS *Lancastria* had left the port of St Nazaire crammed with troops evacuated from the Nantes area, and whilst on passage she had been spotted by German bombers and sunk. Some of the survivors were picked up by naval vessels and merchant ships and brought into Plymouth. The wounded were being cared for at local hospitals and some of the remainder, shocked by their experience, had been moved into our billet. The sinking of the *Lancastria* with appalling loss of life was described by Churchill as the biggest single disaster of the war. Coming so soon after Dunkirk, the news was suppressed from the nation because of the demoralising effect it would have had if released.

I was not looking forward to spending another night beneath the stars so we both walked to the nearest pub. Strong English beer tasted so much better than the weak watery French variety and we remained there until the bar closed. When the landlord heard that we were sleeping in a field he insisted that we put up in his saloon bar, and we woke up in a room filled with other soldiers in a similar plight.

My party was moved later that morning to a barracks in Plymouth where we were expected to stay for a few days before rejoining our unit. In the thirty-four days spent in France I had not been able to have a hot bath, and I had not changed my underwear for a week. I found a bathroom block well supplied with hot water and spent the next hour soaking myself.

On emerging I found that my party had been rounded up and was on its way to the railway station. One of the movements NCOs said that he had searched for me before despatching it but had not thought of checking the bathroom.

Two days later I was summoned to the orderly room and given a railway warrant to take me to Aldershot. From there the movement-control unit provided transport to take me to Mons Barracks, which housed an officer cadet training unit. I reported to the adjutant, who asked how the destruction had gone. He was shaken when I told him that there had been no destruction, and produced the signal from Brest Garrison. When I told him that there were no secret documents in the safe, he paled. Had he pursued the matter I was prepared to say that it was the responsibility of an officer to destroy classified documents, a duty that should not be delegated to a sergeant.

There were many faces in the sergeants' mess that I recognised from my days in India. The instructors and staff were mostly elderly and too old for active service life. One of them whom I had known at Meerut looked at me twice when he saw that I was wearing a sergeant's chevrons.

We heard of the tragedy that befell the 1st Support Group Signal Squadron, who with the remainder of their group were cut off at Calais and St Valery. All except two of the squadron were killed in action or taken prisoner. The town of Tidworth, the home of the Infantry battalions of the group, was now called 'the town of widows'. It was a time for reflection and assessing the present situation. We were all that remained of a mobile force, living as lodgers in Aldershot, having abandoned our vehicles and equipment in France and without a role to play in the war effort.

Winston Churchill, having replaced Chamberlain, was now in full spate. he had delivered his famous speech about the miracle of Dunkirk and declared that we would fight them on the beaches and in the streets but would never surrender.

Impatient as most of us were to play an active part, there was an awareness that plans were in hand for our future deployment and until these were finalised we had little to do. There was a sprinkling of ATS serving in Mons Barracks, most of them clerical staff and upper class. Many of them were pleased to have a drink with what they termed 'real soldiers'. One of them was a corporal who owned her own sports car and another a buxom girl from Oxfordshire, and two of us caused a stir when we invited them to the sergeants' mess for a drink.

The members of the Royal Engineers mess extended an invitation to visit them and it was there that we were introduced to the ritual of the 'CRE'. A volunteer was called upon to sit on a bar stool above screwed-up newspaper, and the conductor led the onlookers in the singing. The words of the song have had to be changed out of deference to the Race Relations Act but went roughly like this:

> *I saw a little boy sitting by the fire*
>   *I saw a little boy playing with his lyre*
> *Ooh-la-la let me get near him*
>   *Ooh-la-la here's a penny for his hoop.*

(Refrain) *And we're marching down to Laffins Plain*
To Laffins Plain, to Laffins Plain
Where they can't tell clay from barley water.

As the first words were uttered the newspaper beneath the victim's stool was set alight, and unless he remained seated while the song was sung he had to pay a forfeit.

Two weeks after arriving at Aldershot our future role was disclosed. The 1st Armoured Division was to proceed to Surrey and deploy around the Dorking area. The HQ and No. 1 Squadron were based at Betchworth, and it had been decided to form a new support group with its HQ at North Holmwood and the Signal Squadron a mile or so away at South Holmwood. I was to report to the new squadron on promotion to SQMS (squadron quartermaster sergeant). Oddly enough, the group was still to be known as the 1st Support Group, despite having lost the original first group in France.

On reaching South Holmwood I found that we were billeted in spare accommodation in the vicarage – and I was met by Sergeant-Major 'Spriggo' Feltham, whom I had last seen at Simla in 1935 during the King George V Jubilee celebrations.

I was not impressed by our two officers. One of them I had known as a warrant-officer Class III before he was granted a short service commission, and the other had been recalled from the Reserve. Nor was I impressed when I saw the store-room, which was a large loft above the unused stables. It meant that every item received or reissued had to be manhandled up or down the wooden stairs.

Over the course of the next two weeks we were reinforced by personnel and equipment and reached our establishment of four senior NCOs. This left the problem of setting up a sergeants' mess for the six of us. With the arrival of petrol rationing, The Holly and Laurel public house on the old Worthing road had lost its thriving lunch-time trade catering for the needs of motorists passing by. So the landlady, Mrs Turner, agreed to let us use her dining-room as a mess and also said that she would do our cooking. This was Utopia! Six daily rations were delivered to her kitchen, and with the extra 3s 6d a week we each gave her we lived on very fine fare. Mrs Turner also gave us a valuable concession by allowing us to buy drinks in the saloon bar at 'spit and sawdust' prices.

A load of stores arrived one morning and my storeman and I were sorting them out when we were visited by the commander, Brigadier 'Freddy' Morgan (later Sir Frederick Morgan, K.C.B.). When he saw the jumble he remarked with a twinkle in his eye, 'This looks like the aftermath of the Battle of Waterloo,' but I think he took in the point about the inadequacy of the stores accommodation. Brigadier Morgan achieved fame later in his career and became the chief planner for Operation Overlord, the code-name given to the Allied Second Front. He was to retire as an Honorary Lieutenant-General and was appointed Colonel Commandant Royal Artillery.

Negotiations had been going on with the United States for the procurement of equipment to make up for that lost in France and in the evacuation of Dunkirk, and finally the Lend-Lease arrangement was agreed. In return for the use of some British military bases, the Americans offered to supply us with *matériel* for the duration of the war, including fifty destroyers that had seen service in World War I.

This was now being delivered and our squadron was issued with an 'Indian' motor cycle for the use of the sergeant-major. It was a high-powered machine used by the American speed cops and seen by cinema-goers worldwide. Spriggo was thrilled with the machine and invited me along for a test run as a pillion passenger. We rode in the direction of Horsham. After a few miles we spotted something bright lying at the roadside and stopped to investigate. It looked like a large aircraft cannon shell, so we decided to recover it for expert examination. I picked it up gingerly and held it in my handkerchief until we reached the HQ. Brigadier Morgan passed by and asked what I was carrying, and on being told it was suspected German ammunition said, 'Get it out of my headquarters.' He had evidently come across booby traps in World War I!

Overhead aerial combat was now a daily occurrence and one afternoon I heard a screaming noise. I thought it was a bomb, and rushed out of the store – to see a German fighter plane crash to the ground two hundred yards away. Grabbing a loaded rifle, I ran to the scene hoping to take a prisoner, but the pilot had baled out before the plane crashed.

Intelligence reports were coming in of a massive build-up of barges in the Dutch and French ports. As Hitler had threatened an invasion of the UK, the massing of these craft was ominous. Tank-traps were erected around the coasts and pillboxes appeared everywhere. The Home Guard, as yet unarmed because of the lack of rifles, went through its defence drills with pitchforks. ARP wardens wearing steel helmets and carrying anti-gas respirators patrolled the streets at night, bawling out the careless ones who allowed a glimmer of light to emerge from behind their black-out curtains.

The German Air Force was in possession of all the continental airfields from France to Norway. German long-range heavy artillery was brought up to threaten any vessels trying to run the gauntlet of the English Channel and to train its guns on Dover Castle, which was often shelled. These preparations by the Germans were the *raison d'être* for the presence of the 1st Armoured Division in the area, so that it could help in protecting the sandy south coast beaches from invasion.

As our build-up of vehicles continued, frequent exercises were held to teach the drivers convoy discipline and to familiarise us with the countryside. Knowledge of map-reading was essential as all road signs and names of railway stations had been removed. We began to know the area around Steyning and Shoreham-by-Sea like the backs of our hands.

Spriggo Feltham received sad news one day concerning his wife. While serving at Cologne with the British Occupation Army between the wars he had met and married a German lady, and when the British were withdrawn from their role she had left Germany to live with him in Army quarters at his new station. The authorities had now decided to treat all former German nationals as potential enemy aliens, and Mrs Feltham was interned on the Isle of Man for the duration of the war.

Food rationing was now beginning to bite. The civilian ration per person per week was:

Sugar	12 ozs	Butter	4 ozs	Meat	1 lb
Tea	2 ozs	Margarine	2 ozs	Cooking fat	2 ozs
		Cheese	2 ozs		

There was also a paper shortage; newspapers were reduced drastically in size and the wrapping of goods bought in shops was forbidden. People started to queue for cigarettes but this did not affect the services, who received a free ration of fifty cigarettes a week, or two ounces of tobacco. The tobacco was packed in four-ounce tins, and as I was one of the few pipe-smokers I was often issued with a tin.

The farmers were making valiant efforts to increase the supply of foodstuffs to reduce dependency on overseas supplies. They could be found ploughing and cultivating their land until late at night, using a small searchlight on their tractors.

Our CO, Lieutenant-Colonel Duncan, did not rejoin us on our return from France, and a new CO now took over, Lieutenant-Colonel M. S. Wheatley, who had recently served in Egypt.

It was not long before he made his presence felt, and after he inspected the squadron at South Holmwood there were changes at the top. A new OC arrived within days, and immediately morale improved. He was Captain D. C. Harris, a young officer who was cool, calm and collected.

RSM Lottie Collins, whom we now rarely saw as he was with RHQ at Betchworth, was commissioned as a Quarter-Master and was replaced by RSM Fraser, who had started life in the Army as a boy soldier. He was a good organiser and raised the social life of his mess at Betchworth by promoting dances to which young ladies working for firms in the area were invited. Spriggo and I took time off one evening to visit our old friend Tim Cole at the Betchworth mess and found to our consternation that a dance was in progress. As we were fully dressed for walking out and wearing 'ammunition boots' we made a hurried departure – but not before I had received a smile from a young lady on the dance-floor.

The officer cadet training units were by now fully established and young officers were coming off the production line in a steady stream, so we were up to strength in troop commanders. Field training involving the movement of vehicles had to be restricted to conserve petrol supplies as it was no longer possible for oil-tankers to negotiate the English Channel to deliver their cargoes. Construction had begun on an underground oil pipe-line running from the Bristol Channel to carry crude oil to the refineries on the River Thames. Brand names of petrol were no longer available at the pumps, and the new term 'pool petrol' was introduced. Fuel supplies to the forces was dyed to prevent it falling into the wrong hands.

The invasion threat receded and as many men as possible were granted weekend leave to visit their families or friends.

My twenty-eighth birthday fell on Saturday 7th September and I decided to spend the evening in Dorking, but changed my mind when the bus reached North Holmwood. There had been heavy aerial activity that afternoon, and as I alighted from the bus I saw the result of it. German bombers had made a savage attack on London's dockland in an attempt to destroy shipping and warehouses. The capital was ablaze and the glow from the fires was clearly visible from as far as Holmwood, thirty miles away. The Battle of Britain had started in earnest.

So had the Battle of the Atlantic. German submarines were sinking our ships bringing over supplies from the United States, despite the presence of naval escorts. German aircraft dropped mines in our estuaries, and they had invented the magnetic mines which were strewn in the sea lanes. The steel hulls of the ships attracted these mines in the same way as a magnet attracts iron filings, and the resulting explosions at sea-level caused havoc. The answer to this threat was degaussing – demagnetising ships – by an ingenious method of encircling the hull of a ship with a special wire hawser attached below the water-line, rendering the mines harmless by neutralising their magnetic field. The minesweepers, some of them from the Royal Netherlands Navy, did a magnificent job of mine disposal around the ports and their approaches.

A skilful German submarine-commander, plotting a course between the Dogger Bank and the Kent coast, reached the Orkney Islands and was able to penetrate the booms guarding the entrances to Scapa Flow and sink the battleship HMS *Hood,* a great victory for the German propaganda machine. Depressing news, but the postmen and the paper-boys still whistled cheerfully as they carried on with their jobs.

Despite the gloomy tidings on the home front, encouraging reports were coming in from Africa. Two seasoned divisions of Indian regular troops had been sent to Africa to reinforce the British; the 4th landed in Egypt and the 5th was sent to the Sudan. The 4th Indian Division was the one in which I served in India but it had been redesignated. The British 7th Armoured Division and the 4th Indian were the only British forces available in the Western Desert to face the Italians, who had sided with the Germans. The Italian force of seven divisions which had occupied Cyrenaica advanced towards the Egyptian border but were easily repulsed by the Allied force under their commander General 'Jumbo' Wilson (later Field-Marshal Lord Wilson of Libya). The Italians had no stomach for the fight and surrendered in their thousands. Cinema-goers at home were delighted to see on their *Pathe Gazette News* columns of Italian POWs marching to captivity escorted by only a few armed Tommies.

Autumn was now approaching and there was not much entertainment for the troops at South Holmwood. Many of the soldiers were married and were sending money home to support their families so could not afford to patronise public houses and other places of public entertainment. Captain Harris realised this and arranged with some helpful local organisations to hold weekly dances in the village hall. The WVS ladies laid on tea and cakes and music was provided by gramophone records. It was a good move on his part. Some of the larger firms evacuated from London and now located nearby provided transport for their female employees to attend the dances.

I decided to go along one evening, and to my surprise

the lady who had smiled at us in Betchworth was there. Later on in the evening we chatted and I was pleased that she accepted my invitation to escort her home. She was living in a bed-sitting-room in Dorking, three miles from my billet, and the six-mile walk there and back was good exercise.

She told me that her name was Edith Clarkson and that she had left her parents' home when the firm she worked for, W. T. Henley's Telegraph Co. Ltd, had moved from London to Milton Court, a mansion on the outskirts of Dorking, at the outbreak of war. We saw a lot of each other in the coming months and I spent less time at the Holly and Laurel and more in Dorking. Eventually I plucked up the courage to propose to her and was accepted.

The next formality was to meet her parents, who lived in Essex on a new residential development at Upney on the District Line. I obtained formal permission from her father to marry his daughter and, unknown to the parents, we planned the wedding for 1st February 1941, four months after we first met. When she told her parents of our plans they tried to dissuade her from marrying a soldier whom she had not known for any length of time.

Nevertheless, with only three weeks to make the preparations friends rallied round and brought chiffon velvet in white and blue down from London, which Edith fashioned into a wedding dress in her spare time. She also found the energy to produce the bridesmaids' dresses for her life-long friend Gladys Williams and her landlady's little girl. Another very good friend, a florist from London, arrived on the day and took charge of all the floral arrangements – Edith's was a sheath made of orchids, and the bridesmaids had velvet muffs with floral decorations.

The banns were called at the parish church in North Holmwood on the requisite three Sundays and I asked Sergeant George Comfort to be my best man. He was a journalist by profession and had been astute enough to buy two properties in Cheam. He asked Mrs Turner at the Holly and Laurel if she would undertake the catering arrangements, and it proved to be an excellent choice. Mrs

Turner, as an experienced caterer, held large reserves of cooking ingredients in her store-room before rationing began and she made a three-tier wedding-cake. As icing sugar was unavailable it was encased in white cardboard but beautifully decorated and had ribbons flowing from the top tier in the Royal Corps of Signals colours: light blue, dark blue and green.

The church was packed with my Army friends and Edith's work colleagues. After a moving service, the vicar gave us the usual homily before we posed outside the old stone building for photographs. A friend of Edith's named Arthur Lowe took some excellent photographs of professional standard and many photos were taken by friends some with the old-fashioned Brownie box camera. Captain Harris kindly lent us his staff car to take us to the wedding reception, held in the Turners' restaurant, and some witty speeches were made – including the ditty:

And when I was single my pockets did jingle.
Oh I wish I was single again.

I paid for a 56-gallon cask of beer to be drunk by members of the squadron and our local wellwishers after we left for Dorking station en route to Guildford, where we had booked a hotel room for the night. For the whole of the day I had worn my blue patrol suit, and this attracted curious glances from some of the officers billeted there who had never seen the peacetime walking-out uniform. From their close scrutiny I imagined some of them took me to belong to the Allied forces, so numerous were the varieties of uniforms to be seen around. There was even a joke going the rounds that if a German officer walked the streets of London in full dress uniform he would pass by unnoticed.

We left the charming town of Guildford after lunch on the following morning for Combe Martin on the North Devon coast. It was wartime travel at its worst, the carriages were unheated and the train stops interminable. Eventually we reached our destination by breakfast-time and settled in at the guest house. My new wife had once stayed there and was greeted warmly by the landlady. It had a long south-facing sun lounge and by mid-morning it was filled with elderly ladies basking in the late winter sun. We learnt that they were expatriates who had settled on the Mediterranean coast of France and decided to return home rather than be interned as enemy aliens.

We went for long walks along the coast and this unaccustomed exercise induced hunger. I now knew what it was like to live on civilian rations, although we did reasonably well on the meals provided. Landladies in rural areas had many friends and could usually acquire a few rabbits, game-birds and sometimes a pig that had not been declared to the registration agency.

The honeymoon was over and we returned to Dorking to resume our respective jobs. My wife was one of two secretaries working for Henley's chief engineer. The work was classified and she could not be released to join any of the women's services. Dr Dunsheath, the chief engineer and one of the directors, was heavily involved in War Office plans and was constantly rushing in and out of his office in between chauffeured drives to London. She was able to keep a secret, and it was not until the Normandy landings were over that she disclosed that Dr Dunsheath headed the team of scientists responsible for the design and development of PLUTO (pipe-line under the ocean) that carried fuel from southern England to supply the armies on the beach-heads of Normandy.

It was at about this time that our squadron was moved from South Holmwood to be nearer group HQ. Our former billeting area had become too small to accommodate the increasing number of men and vehicles reinforcing us. Our new base was a very large country house near North Holmwood and it was big enough to cater for office and store accommodation plus sleeping-rooms for the men, all beneath one roof. As my wife was living in rooms at Dorking I was granted a 'sleeping-out' pass on the condition that I could report for duty within fifteen minutes if needed. My means of transport was a ladies' bicycle!

Edith and I were invited to visit her parents at Upney and I obtained a weekend pass. We arrived there for lunch and passed the day in desultory talk. They lived quite close to the Thames, which was festooned with barrage balloons to deter the German bombers. Her parents had adopted the habit of sleeping in the Anderson air-raid shelter which covered a large hole dug into the ground at the end of the garden.

In the early hours of Sunday morning we were awakened by the wailing of sirens followed by anti-aircraft fire and spent a very uncomfortable night hearing bombs exploding not too far away. The raid ceased at about 3 a.m. and when we gathered for breakfast we heard the BBC proclaim that it was the heaviest air raid of the war and that the Germans had lost well over a hundred aircraft shot down or destroyed by fighter aircraft as they returned across the English Channel.

Forseeing difficulties in returning to Dorking, we left early and travelled by bus to Victoria Station. The scene along the route was one of utter devastation. Air-raid wardens were in evidence everywhere, ambulance crews were exhausted through rescuing people trapped in houses or buried in the rubble, smoke was pouring from bombed buildings, firemen were still putting out fires and station staff were trying to cope with passengers wishing to get out of London. Once we reached Victoria Station the position improved. The damage to the railway track had been repaired and we were able to reach Dorking without further delay. The BBC claimed that the German losses were so great as to discourage them from mass air raids over London in future.

It was at this stage that Sergeant-Major Feltham left us on promotion and he was replaced by SSM Peacock, who was posted in from another squadron. Peacock was an excellent operator but poor at man-management and lasted only two months. I was sounded out if I wished to replace him and accepted without hesitation. Sadly Peacock never rose higher than warrant-officer second class throughout his service and ended up in the Chelsea Royal Hospital as an in-pensioner, better known as a Chelsea pensioner.

As the summer approached, the area to the east of us became crowded with troops. Lieutenant-General Bernard Law Montgomery (later Field-Marshal Viscount Montgomery) arrived at Reigate with his corps, and the pubs of Dorking were inundated with Canadian soldiers. They were a difficult lot and were not used to drinking spirits. To prevent drunkenness their commander issued an edict to publicans that liquor was not to be served in bars to Canadian soldiers. Unfortunately, some of the landlords interpreted it as a ban on sales to everyone in battledress and harsh words were spoken by those of us who could hold our drink.

The time came when I had to say goodbye to my wife because the division was moving to the Salisbury Plain area. My group was based around the small town of Hungerford and we were housed on an estate surrounded by racing stables. However, the valuable racing stock had been removed to safer quarters in more rural areas. The reason for the move was the abundance of training-ground, owned by the War Department, that became available to the tank crews to practise mobility of movement.

Brigadier Morgan was destined for higher rank and soon after our arrival he left us and was replaced by a middle-aged ex-Royal Artillery officer wearing Great War medal ribbons. The first thing he noticed was the size of his HQ. The strength of our signal squadron was 120 all ranks, and the group HQ consisted of another 60 clerks, cooks, batmen, orderlies and drivers. The new brigadier said that he did not need 180 officers and men to pass on his orders to four regiments and I was asked my views on combining the signal squadron and group HQ into one body with the resultant saving of manpower. I said that it was feasible providing that his three warrant-officers first class confined themselves to their specialist duties and left me to run the sergeants' mess and discipline. He agreed, and the new arrangement worked very well. Much later on, in 1960 or 1961, a Royal Signals major serving in BAOR hit upon the same idea, sold it to the staff, who thought it was the best thing since sliced bread, and within a short space of time every Signals unit from division down to brigade was amalgamated with its formation HQ.

Shortly after this we were reinforced by a platoon of Sherwood Foresters who were to act as an Infantry protection group to the HQ. They came from a mining district in Nottinghamshire and most of them had served in the TA before being embodied into the Army. Their sergeant amused me by explaining the method of selection into their local TA unit. Apparently the officers were all colliery managers or under-managers, the NCOs consisted of deputies or foremen and the other ranks were composed of ordinary miners. Like all those of the mining fraternity they made very good soldiers.

Captain Harris had been with the squadron for nearly a year when he broke the sad news that he was departing on being promoted to the rank of major and joining one of our armoured brigade signal squadrons. It was not too long before the reason for this move became generally known.

Lieutenant-Colonel Wheatley had brought the unit up to a high state of efficiency and decided to make an informal inspection of his unit HQ one morning. On entering one of the troop stores he discovered the troop commander, Captain Alistaire Beattie (not to be confused with Lieutenant-Colonel Bruce Beattie, who has rendered sterling service to the Corps) asleep on a camp-bed, evidently sleeping off the excesses of the previous evening. The colonel was not one to tolerate such an example to the men and gave Beattie two hours to pack his kit. It was a maxim in those days that a good commander did not off-load poor material on to another unit, so he was obliged to retain him under his command. Unfortunately, he joined us at Hungerford, a poor replacement for Captain Harris.

There were soon to be more changes and Lieutenant-Colonel Wheatley left us for duty at the War Office. From 1954 to 1957 he held the highest appointments in the Corps, those of Director of Signals and Signal Officer in Chief. Lieutenant-Colonel Doyle joined us as our new CO. He came from the Middlesex Yeomanry, which had been converted from a Cavalry unit to Signals before the war, and was joined later by Major The Viscount Malden as his second-in-command. It was said at the time that the viscount joined the Middlesex Yeomanry not knowing that it had been converted to Signals.

The new CO spent some of his time visiting his

detached squadrons and encouraging the discussion of current affairs on a question-and-answer basis, and as the oldest soldier amongst them I was more often than not the one questioned.

In the meantime we were training for war.

Edith was able to visit Hungerford some weekends, staying with a water-bailiff on the nearby River Kennet who rented out a room to Army wives.

It was not many months later that the division was warned for overseas service, and embarkation leave was granted to all ranks. The destination was not given in those days of high security; but when we were issued with tropical kit, including topis and khaki drill it was fairly obvious that we would be proceeding to join the Eighth Army.

Reinforcements arrived so that we would be fully up to strength by departure day. Our vehicles were to be left behind for another armoured division and we were told that new vehicles would be ready for us on our arrival. All stores were packed and crated with the exception of the 'comfort' wireless-receiving sets which had been issued by HQ Southern Command to keep the troops from being bored. These comfort sets were to be returned, but by an oversight the one issued to the sergeants' mess was not.

One morning my new OC told me that we were expecting a visit from some VIPs, and I was instructed to line up the troops on the roadway. I took up my position on the right of the formation and saw a solitary police car approach. Twenty yards behind it a limousine came into view bearing the royal standard. Its passengers were King George VI and Queen Elizabeth, and as I saluted the royal couple the King returned my salute and the Queen smiled. They had come all the way from Windsor Castle to wish the division 'God-Speed' – and this was the royal couple whom William Joyce – 'Lord Haw Haw', the British renegade serving Dr Goebbels' propaganda machine and hanged after the war as a traitor – referred to in his broadcasts from Germany as 'your stuttering King and your grinning Queen'.

At a secret briefing warrant-officers and above were told that the 1st Support Group would be embarking shortly in a separate convoy from the remainder of the division. As enemy bombardment of the south coast ports made the passage of convoys dangerous, we guessed that our embarkation port would be Liverpool or Greenock near Glasgow.

In the event, and after a long train journey lasting all night, we arrived at Liverpool. As we neared the docks the devastation caused by German bombs was all too evident. Most of our group were embarked on the passenger liner *Empress of Canada,* and we pulled out of the docks to form up the convoy in Liverpool Bay.

12

VOYAGE TO EGYPT

Warrant-officers travelling abroad by sea were entitled to cabin accommodation, and four of us shared a large cabin containing four beds. It was lavishly appointed and kept tidy by a cabin steward, who even brought us early morning tea. A bathroom steward asked at what time we wished hot water to be drawn for our evening bath. Two of the warrant-officers belonged to 1st Support Group HQ, whilst our fourth cabin mate was a company sergeant-major of the King's Royal Rifle Corps, whom I was to see in action in the Western Desert some months later.

The second-class saloon was roomy, the dining-tables were covered with linen and the silver gleamed. The food was excellent and well up to peacetime standards. There was a large smoke-room open only in the evenings but soft drinks were available at any time.

Lifeboat drill was introduced on the day of embarkation, even though we were still at anchor in Liverpool Bay, and it continued daily throughout the voyage. Apart from attending boat drill and troop inspections, we did not spend much time on deck as autumn was with us and unless the sun shone it was chilly in the open air. While waiting for the convoy to assemble we attended lectures on hygiene and how we should respond if taken prisoner of war. The Geneva Convention was explained and the legend about 'Number, rank, name' emphasised. The need for the stringent enforcement of black-out orders was reiterated and there was a massive master-at-arms ever present after dusk to enforce them.

On the voyage to India warnings had been given about

dropping lighted cigarette ends over the rail. The reason given then was the fire risk from a butt-end entering an open porthole and igniting bedding. Consequently discarded cigarettes had to be dropped in the scuppers.

In wartime there was a more serious risk, and a ship's officer explained that a trail of debris left behind by a convoy was certain to attract the attention of enemy submarines. For this reason, as we were to discover later, all garbage from every ship in the convoy was dumped into the sea at twelve noon precisely, and as the convoy altered course frequently an enemy had no idea of its position.

The convoy formed up eventually and left Liverpool Bay on 27th September 1941. Its course was to take us into the North Atlantic, passing through the North Channel between Scotland and Northern Ireland. The convoy commodore was given sealed orders, only to be opened at sea and at specific times, which enabled the Admiralty to pin-point our position at any time, despite strict wireless silence.

Ours was a large convoy escorted by two destroyers and it covered many square miles of ocean. It was comforting to see the way in which the destroyers mothered the merchant ships, using loud hailers to coax the laggards on and to maintain formation. A merchant vessel on our port side carried a most unusual deck cargo: a medium-sized steam locomotive bound for some distant possession to augment its transport system. The port shipwrights must have had a challenging job in reinforcing the decks to carry such a heavy load.

Constant vigilance was the order of the day, and although a diligent watch was maintained by the ship's officers the passengers were encouraged to rush up to that holy ground, the bridge, if they noticed anything suspicious. There was a scare when the officer of the watch observed a floating mine not too far away. The incident was reported to the Royal Navy escort by lamp signal and no doubt they were able to dispose of it. We had very early in the war been told that it was forbidden to keep a diary because it could provide useful information to the enemy if captured, but there was little of interest to record on the voyage. It was evident that we were steaming in a south-westerly direction although the convoy changed course frequently.

After two or three weeks at sea it became warmer and I calculated that we were proceeding in the direction of Florida. The warmer weather induced the troops to spend longer on deck, and exercises were arranged to prevent them from becoming bored. There was insufficient space for mass exercises, so small groups were formed in different areas to carry out PT, maintenance of weapons and even rifle-shooting at targets towed behind the ship. Some joker thought up the idea of the Signals personnel learning to communicate with flags using semaphore.

Flag signalling had been introduced to the British Army in India at the time of the Indian Mutiny and could be of considerable value when passing messages from hill top to hill top in difficult terrain. Useful speeds could be attained by experienced signallers, the best of whom sent at twelve words per minute; but we were now living in 1941, were not in the Boy Scouts and not equipped with flags. Not to be outdone, and to further his dreams, the resourceful Signals captain borrowed flags from the ship's store, and little groups of signallers could be seen on deck practising their new skills.

The convoy commodore, having studied his sealed orders, then made a complete change of course and headed south-east. We were aware of the passage of time but had no idea of our position and our next stop had to be on the west coast of Africa. The reason for this was obvious. To run the gauntlet of a passage through the Mediterranean would have been too risky, packed as it was with Italian submarines and surface craft, and German intelligence was aware that the reinforcement of our Desert Force had to be around the coast of Africa. To forestall their efforts, the convoy had sailed nearly to the coast of America before sailing south-east again to avoid the predators lurking in the sea lanes off the coasts of Morocco and Mauritania.

After a few more weeks in soaring temperatures, we found ourselves in Freetown, Sierra Leone, where we were to refuel, replenish food supplies and take on water.

Although we did not stay long at Freetown and were not allowed ashore, it was nice to see land after such a long time at sea. Great quantities of semi-tropical fruit were loaded and the luscious melons, bananas and pineapples made a welcome change to our diet. Freetown is approximately ten degrees north of the equator and the atmosphere there is extremely humid, so we were not sorry when the convoy left.

When it was announced two days later that a crossing-the-line ceremony was to be held on the following day there was great excitement. Marine traditions die hard and it would take more than a war to deprive sailors of the pleasure of meeting King Neptune. At midday the troops and those of the crew who had not crossed the equator before were assembled on the main deck. Then victims were chosen and lathered with soft soap, and no less a person than the captain himself appeared with a huge wooden razor to 'shave' them. The lather removed, they were bundled into a large canvas bath filled with sea water, after which they were free to carry on.

The sun at noon was now almost directly overhead and dire warnings were issued about the dangers of sunburn and heat exhaustion. Salt tablets were issued to replace the minerals lost from the body by excessive perspiration, and huge canvas awnings were erected above the decks to provide shelter from the sun.

There were still almost 2,500 miles of the South Atlantic Ocean to cross before we were impressed by the grandeur of Table Mountain, and from some miles out at sea it really seemed as flat as a table. Our spirits flagged as we left Capetown behind; we had all hoped to spend some days ashore – if only to get some badly needed exercise. The reason why we did not enter port was that it was crammed with vessels from another convoy and there were no wharfs or anchorages available. Some weeks later we learnt that the HQ of 1st Armoured Division with some of its brigades had arrived there in a separate convoy before us.

We were relieved to hear after rounding the Cape that we were to call at Durban in Natal Province, where shore leave was to be granted. The holiday resort of Durban with its long shimmering beaches was beautiful and we could not wait to put our feet on dry land. On the morning after our arrival the troops formed up on the quayside and were told that a five-mile route march had been organised. Unfortunately, the staff officer on the ship had not done his homework regarding the order of march. As the senior formation on board, the Signal Squadron and HQ led the march, followed at five-minute intervals by other groups. What he did not take into account was that we marched at 120 paces to the minute whereas the Light Infantry, who followed us, were trained to do 140 paces. It was not very long before the leading party was brushed off the road by the advancing KRRC and RB! Another difficulty was that for all the time spent on board we had worn plimsolls and the unaccustomed return to marching-boots raised a few blisters. On returning to the ship we learnt that shore leave had been granted from after lunch to midnight.

My platoon sergeant and I decided to stroll into Durban. Being wary of the traffic, we paused at the kerbside before crossing the road, whereupon a civilian stopped his car and asked us if we would like a trip around. Thinking that he was a pimp we ignored him, but he was insistent. We were both much bigger than he was so we decided to take a chance. To our surprise he drove into the grounds of a palatial bungalow and invited us inside to meet his wife, who prepared a sumptuous tea, including freshly baked scones and pastries.

I knew that the Prime Minister of South Africa, then in the British Commonwealth of Nations, was Field-Marshal Jan Smuts of Boer extraction, he was an erstwhile enemy who had served the Empire well in the 1914-18 War. Our hosts briefed us on the political position in South Africa. We gathered that the immigrants of British stock had settled in Natal or Cape Province, where there was also a large proportion of Jewish settlers. These two provinces were making a substantial contribution to the Allied war effort and had already provided two South African divisions, now serving in the Western Desert. While Jan Smuts was alive they had no worries, but he was ageing and they were looking ahead. What they feared was that with an Anglo-Saxon electorate, depleted by war casualties, they would be in a minority compared with South Africans of Boer extraction. They took every opportunity of extolling the virtues of Natal, hoping to encourage further immigrants of British stock when the war ended.

As the sun settled we spent the evening in their well-stocked garden, and then it was time for 'sun-downers' served in crystal glasses. An excellent dinner was prepared by their cook; then, not wishing to outstay our welcome, we made preparations to leave. This did not suit our hosts at all. They said that after so long at sea in a blacked-out ship we should enjoy the illuminations. They took us on a twenty-mile drive around the hills surrounding Durban and it was like fairyland. On reaching home we had a final drink before being driven to the dockside. Early on the following morning a huge hand of bananas was delivered to the *Empress of Canada*, bearing a card made out in our names. I have never met anyone who passed through these South African ports during the war years profess anything but gratitude for the kindness and hospitality shown.

Many of the soldiers were sending presents home and I was amused by the way in which coconuts were shipped back OHMS. A coconut cut down from a palm tree has a smooth outer skin over the kernel and the coir surrounding it. All the sender did was write the name and address of the receiver in indelible ink on the outer skin, and off it went. No wrapping-paper or cardboard box necessary! Letters, of course, had to be censored on the ship and were returned home in sealed mail-bags.

Johnny and I decided to have a swim on the following afternoon, and as we had no swimming-gear had to make do with PT shorts. The only bronzed parts of our bodies were our faces, forearms and knees, and our appearance was in marked contrast with the deeply tanned Durban swimmers. After a lengthy swim in the warm Indian Ocean, we noticed a large tent on the beach. As we strolled towards it we saw several white ladies dressed in uniform and sun-hats with the motif DVL on the crown. They were members of the Durban Victoria League, a similar body to our own WVS, who dispensed tea and cakes to the men on shore leave for a token three pence.

The less responsible spent their evening leisure-time in the bars, and after abstinence on the ship were quite unused to the potency of South African beer. To make things worse for them, the local patrons of the clubs and pubs, trying to outdo each other in hospitality, plied them with drinks – with the result that the shore patrols were kept busy ferrying drunken sailors and soldiers back to the ship. Some of the local farmers whose workers had enlisted in the South African forces found themselves short of labour and were not averse to enticing the soldiery to desert and work for them on their farms. The South African police usually managed to round them up and return them to the military police at the ports. Before leaving Durban I was handed over six deserters who had been arrested in the Pietermaritzburg area, and my first action was to hand them over to the master-at-arms for confinement in the ship's cells for the remainder of the voyage.

On our last night in port Sergeant Johnson and I decided to see the night-life of Durban but did not relish spending the time in the night-clubs and bars along the seafront, where fights were becoming all too common. We noticed a night-club in one of the quieter areas which was not too garish and the music was more subdued. On entering we found ourselves to be the only two customers and thought this odd. However, we bought a drink and considered our next move. At this stage a fat South African lady approached me and asked if I wanted a girl. Being curious, I asked her who the girl was and she said 'Me.' We were rescued from our predicament by the appearance of a posse of South African police, one of whom said that they did not expect to see Britishers in such a place and advised us to depart, so we returned to the ship.

We left the port of Durban on the following morning to the sound of car hooters blaring and flags waving and nosed out into the Indian Ocean. It took some hours for the convoy to assemble, and when the ships were in correct formation we proceeded east. We did not steam through the Mozambique Channel but skirted the southern coast of Madagascar; then in Allied hands, and the course was set for the island of Mauritius. The convoy changed course again, towards the Gulf of Suez.

From the time we left Durban the convoy had been escorted by the newly constructed battleship *Prince of Wales* and the battle-cruiser *Repulse,* and after three days at sea the troops were ordered to line the decks. The reason for this soon became evident. Both Royal Navy warships were leaving the convoy to reinforce the Far Eastern Fleet in its defence of Singapore. As the men-of-war steamed proudly past us with their decks lined with white-clad naval ratings we little thought that these impressive ships would be sunk in Malayan waters by Japanese bomb and torpedo attacks. They went down on 10th December 1941 with the loss of eight hundred lives.

A few days after our naval escort left us, the convoy called at Aden to replenish food, water and fuel stocks before steaming up the Red Sea and reaching our final destination: Port Taufiq at the mouth of the Suez Canal. More bad news was broken to us after disembarking when we learnt of the treacherous attack made by the Japanese upon the US Fleet at Pearl Harbor on 6th December.

13

THE DESERT WAR

Facilities for disembarking were limited at Port Taufiq and not all of the ships were able to tie up at the wharfs. Floating pontoon bridges were used to bring the troops ashore from vessels floating in the harbour. This was a hazardous exercise for the fully equipped soldiers, so progress was slow. By mid-afternoon all were safely ashore and we spent our first night on Egyptian soil in a nearby transit camp. As we listened to the BBC news broadcast we learnt that following the raid on Pearl Harbor, the United States had declared war on Japan, and that Hitler, in a moment of madness, had made a declaration of war against America.

The war in the Far East was going badly and Singapore was in peril. Successive chiefs of staff had always considered the island to be of prime importance to the Far East, and massive sums of money had been spent on its defences. It had been thought impregnable, as had Hong Kong, already lost.

We spent a comfortable night at the transit camp and in the afternoon railway carriages were found to take us the two hundred miles to El Amiriya, near the naval base at Alexandria. As the train trundled along we passed a large camp housing German POWs taken in General Wavell's 1941 push across Cyrenaica towards Benghazi. They were an arrogant lot and one of them, a giant of a man, stood at the camp perimeter holding up his arm in the Nazi salute until we lost sight of him.

Our progress was slow and it was not until dawn that we reached the area allocated to us. It was just a vast area of desert containing a few structures to serve as cookhouses, latrines, shower-rooms and offices. The troops were cold and dispirited and there was nothing to do until our tentage arrived. I knew that one of the group owned a mouth-organ, so I persuaded him to play a few lively tunes. The music and the rising sun raised their spirits and when our tents arrived they set to erecting them with gusto.

El Amiriya was to be our tented home for a further two weeks and every effort was made to make it comfortable. We provided ourselves with a marquee for use as a sergeants' mess and set up a bar with supplies bought from the NAAFI at Alexandria. The mess lacked comfort but we were able to make do with folding canvas chairs and stools. Hurricane-lamps were not the best means of illumination but George Bray, our Ordnance representative, used his influence in acquiring a Tilley incandescent lamp, an issue normally reserved for general officers. After a few days our stores started to arrive from the docks and I was more than pleased when the 'comforts' wireless receiver appeared. Apart from the gloomy BBC news, it provided musical programmes from the Levant and elsewhere.

The purpose of our stay at El Amiriya was to prepare our vehicles for the long trek ahead of us across Egypt and Cyrenaica and there was much work to be done. General-service vehicles were arriving from America under Lend-Lease and they had to be camouflaged with khaki paint. Wireless sets had to be installed in our specialised vehicles and a lot of work was carried out in a huge Ordnance workshop employing Egyptian labour.

The brigadier found plenty to do by visiting the other elements of his group, which were widely dispersed and included the Artillery, Infantry and specialised units under his command, in order to assess their readiness for action. We were joined one day by a newly commissioned ex-ranker who had some experience of the desert and was there to tell us all about it. I decided to check on the camp guard one night and as I approached the sentry heard a rather heated conversation. The newcomer was trying the old trick of surprising the sentry, who was embarrassed because he recognised him as a British officer. I told the sentry in no uncertain terms that if it happened again he was to shoot, and drawing the officer aside, told him that we were not all raw recruits and that I did not expect my soldiers to be humiliated.

The War Office had equipped us with a mobile bath unit, a huge vehicle fitted with pumps and water roses and petrol-burners to heat the water. In civilised areas its hose could be fitted to a fire hydrant, but as these were not too frequently found in the desert three very large tankers had to be provided to carry the bath water.

By now preparations were well in hand for our move. As we were expected to be leaving before Christmas, the customary dinner was cooked and served to the men several days before.

One day I was supervising the loading of the vehicles when smoke was seen emerging from the body of a fifteen hundredweight wireless truck, followed by the odd minor explosion. Being within fifty yards of the vehicle, I rushed towards it and called two drivers to join me. My intention was to off-load the cargo and wireless set, which could have been completed in a minute or two, and then deal with the smouldering. Before I reached the vehicle the brigadier, who was passing, ordered us to stay away. I was inwardly furious because wireless sets and trucks were vital to the communications network; however, I had no option but to obey the commander's orders. The vehicle was salvaged but the wireless set was so badly damaged as to require a replacement. No doubt the brigadier had human safety in mind, but a few small-arms cartridges exploding posed no great threat and I have often wondered about the caution of some senior officers.

The cause of the fire was diagnosed as a slow-acting chemical element placed in the secondary batteries of the set by a disaffected workman in the Ordnance workshop. Egypt was teeming with Nazi sympathisers and agents who knew how to cause most damage.

HQ 1st Support Group left El Amiriya and travelled along the metalled coast road, passing through El Daba, Fuka and Baggush, reaching the area of Mersa Matruh by late afternoon. It was decided to make camp there for the night. The field kitchens were set up and a substantial meal was prepared and enjoyed, apart from the yams – sweet potatoes grown locally. Our first night stop gave the soldiers an opportunity of using their newly issued bivouacs, low tents issued one for two men, but sergeants and higher ranks were more fortunate in having one to themselves.

The border between Egypt and the Libyan province of Cyrenaica was only 120 miles distant, and the convoy left the coast road to travel along sandy tracks to Halfaya Pass (nicknamed 'Hell-Fire Pass' by the 8th Army) near to what was invariably called 'the wire'. This was the frontier fence erected along the border on the orders of Mussolini to keep the Libyans from escaping to Egypt with their camels and donkeys. It was heavily mined but it proved no obstacle to the British Army engineers clearing the way for General Jumbo Wilson's advance. Not wishing to negotiate the pass in the fading light, the brigadier ordered a halt and we spent another night in bivouacs beneath the escarpment.

The convoy climbed up the notorious pass on the following morning and from the top we noted its strategic position. Observers on its heights had a clear view for forty miles into Egyptian territory, and Mussolini had constructed Fort Capuzzo a few miles from the wire as a defence bastion. Its garrison had, of course, been killed or taken prisoner in earlier British advances. General Wavell had relieved the beleaguered Tobruk Garrison in his advance to Benghazi the previous year, so our progress across Cyrenaica was unimpeded. At the time that we crossed the border the 7th Support Group of the 7th Armoured Division (the Desert Rats) were holding a line at El Agheila, 350 miles to the west.

Major-General Lumsden had by now taken over as GOC 1st Armoured Division. He was experienced in desert warfare and considered to be the finest tank-warfare tactician in North Africa. He scorned using the coastal road to reach his objective and aimed straight across the desert. From the time that the division came under his command, convoy discipline was enforced rigidly; but we did not move as a solid group, for the presence of a large force moving west would have been apparent to German and Italian reconnaissance planes and given timely warning to Rommel.

The procedure therefore was for the divisional HQ with its Signals unit to lead the way, flanked by its six protection tanks and with armoured scout cars spying out the ground ahead. The remainder followed in self-contained groups, sometimes days later. The role of a support group required us to be the last formation of the force.

Although aerial attack was unlikely because of our distance from enemy airfields, dispersal of vehicles was imperative because it discouraged air attack. Each vehicle in the convoy was driven at a minimum distance of two hundred yards between vehicles and this would not have been possible on the coast road. Another factor was the dust raised by a large number of tanks and vehicles which could not be missed by aerial observers.

At night we moved into close laager for administrative and defensive purposes. (Laager is an Afrikaans word for an encampment; the Boers formed a defensive block made up of trail waggons on the outside and people and oxen within the protective defences.) It was essential that all vehicles were once again properly dispersed before first light in the morning, but when we reached a place called Agedabia we stayed there for some days. Our Signals OC was now becoming restive, and on the excuse that the men were idle ordered me to hold a morning parade of the personnel. This went entirely against the principle of dispersal, so I made a spirited protest – but he was adamant. I considered complaining to the brigadier, but as he was busy thought better of it. The parade was duly formed up at 9 a.m. on the following day and rifles were inspected. There was no point in inspecting anything else as the strictest orders had been given that nothing should be polished because it attracted attention from the air. Polished brasses and shining toe caps were a sure way of nullifying the effort of camouflaging the vehicles. That very afternoon a staff officer of the HQ whose regiment wore a red sidecap was spotted in the open by an enemy fighter pilot who mistook him for a general and made a determined effort to shoot him up by cannon fire. That stopped the nonsense of morning parades.

That, too, was the end of close laager, and instead of everyone forming up in a queue for meals at the cookhouse 'vehicle messing' was introduced. The quartermaster sergeant issued rations including water to the crews of a vehicle, who were then responsible for preparing it. This was no great problem because we were so far from base that fresh provisions could not be provided and we were entirely dependent on tinned food supplies and hard biscuits. Bully beef is all very well for a change but when eaten for breakfast, dinner and supper it begins to pall. Once a week or so we were lucky enough to receive American tinned bacon, wrapped in paper, but this was difficult to cook without proper utensils and was usually eaten raw. There were ample supplies of tinned jam and I discovered a way of making hard biscuits more palatable by immersing them in a mixture of jam and water to soak overnight.

There was a problem, too, with water supplies. Although there were several water wells on our route, this source of supply was suspect as it was rumoured that the Italians and Germans were in the habit of poisoning the wells when retreating. Water was carried in two-gallon petrol-cans loaded on to the floor-boards of lorries travelling for hundreds of miles. The desert is not all flat, bumping and vibration damaged the cans, so there was much loss of water on the way. At best the ration of water amounted to one gallon per man per day, but for long periods this was reduced to half a gallon, with the sole exception of the general so that he could have a daily bath. This daily ration was for all purposes: drinking, tea-making, shaving and topping up of radiators. None of it could be spared for laundering clothes, which had to be dipped into a receptacle containing petrol. The mobile bath unit was still with us, but since leaving El Amiriya, now 750 miles behind us, it had not provided anyone with a bath. Each unit was equipped with a 250-gallon tanker, but its water was for emergency use only and the key to it was in the safe custody of the quartermaster.

Because our stay at Agedabia was longer than expected, stricter hygiene rules were enforced. When the Desert Force captured Fort Capuzzo they found the sand ridden with lice and attributed this to the unhygienic habits of the Italians. The biggest risk in this area was dysentery and so steps were taken to counter the danger. A mobile force does not have time to dig deep latrine trenches and the method adopted for disposing of human waste was by means of a shovel. Anyone wishing to relieve himself could be seen walking away from the perimeter with a shovel, in order to dig a hole a full spit deep, which was filled up with sand after use.

The reason for our lengthy stay at Agedabia was to enable our division to take over in an orderly fashion from the 7th Armoured and the 4th Indian Divisions, who had launched an offensive in November and driven the Axis forces almost into Tripolitania, Libya's western province. Once the GOC 1st Armoured Division had decided on a suitable location for his HQ and armour, we were free to take up our position between him and the enemy. The military tactics at the time were that the tanks captured territory and the supporting group moved up and relieved them by defending, where possible, a natural defensive position, while the armour withdrew to regroup and prepare for a further attack.

Plans were now sufficiently well advanced for us to relieve 7th Support Group, but some internal reorganisation had to take place and the group was split into two formations. The commander, his staff officers and the operational side of the Signal Squadron, together with the Sherwood Foresters protection platoon, were to form a small advanced tactical group facing the enemy. The echelons – that is, the supply vehicles supporting the tactical group – were to remain ten miles or so to its rear, from which position they could ferry rations, charged batteries and ammunition forward. In this instance the echelon was 'brigaded' and consisted of all supply vehicles for the forward elements such as gunners, engineers, ordnance and infantry. A recalled elderly major was put in charge of the brigaded echelon and provided with a mobile wireless set to communicate with the tactical HQ.

The HQ moved off after giving the echelon orders to proceed two hours later. As we moved westward we passed over an extensive area of flat ground which resembled the dry bed of a lake, unlike the corrugated tracks that had been encountered before. After travelling for two hours or so we met a fiendish duststorm which made driving very difficult, and the drivers, instead of maintaining the distance of two hundred yards between vehicles, had to reduce it to keep within sight of each other. Dusk was falling when the convoy major called a halt, and the duststorm had not abated. A desert storm has to be experienced to be believed. It gets into the nostrils, the mouth, the hair and, worst of all, into the barrels and working parts of rifles and pistols. The first priority was to clean the small arms so that they were ready for instant use and the second to prepare a light meal.

I awoke at dawn and was appalled at what I saw. No vehicle was more than seventy-five yards apart, and as we were within range of enemy airfields the echelon presented a tempting bombing target. I asked the commander to order the front vehicles a mile or so forward so that we could redeploy. He was unwilling to do so, so I told him that if the brigadier visited he would be court-martialled. This startled him and he told me to ask the commanders on our flanks to move sideways and increase the distance between their vehicles from front to rear.

I was in the process of doing this when I noticed nine planes approaching. We had not been strafed by enemy planes from the time we left Egypt and had grown careless; most of the time our respirators and steel helmets being hooked up in the vehicles. As I eyed these planes I saw bombs being dropped from them. All hell then broke loose, with bombs exploding over a wide area. The noise was increased by the gunfire from our Bofors light anti-aircraft battery.

The normal drill was to dig shallow trenches adjacent to the vehicles, which would provide some protection from blast; but it was still early morning and this precaution had not been taken. I heard a screaming noise above me and threw myself flat on the ground. Something went *plop* and I glanced out of the corner of my eye to see a red-hot smoking piece of shrapnel the size of a man's fist within two feet of me. It was either a bomb fragment or a piece of gun shrapnel from our own Bofors.

The German planes departed, leaving some severely wounded soldiers on the ground and a few vehicles ablaze. It was not very long before a fleet of ambulances arrived and conveyed the more badly wounded and shocked soldiers to the medical reception station. But for a freak of weather on the previous afternoon we would have been well dispersed and not offered such a tempting target to the Luftwaffe; but even so our casualties were light, taking into account the number of aircraft attacking us. I made a tour of our own HQ and Signal Squadron area and, surprisingly, saw no evidence of damage to vehicles or their crews.

On my way back to the truck I was startled to find hundreds of vehicles retreating through our lines and discovered that they belonged to two Infantry regiments which had been ordered to withdraw from further west. Scout cars, armoured personnel carriers and other vehicles sped past for ten minutes or so. The echelon commander told me that orders had come through for us to withdraw, and he was not slow in following the Infantry eastwards.

Before leaving the spot, I scoured the area for any injured men, but finding none decided to follow up in the rear. I had not gone very far when the brigade RASC officer approached me in his Bedford truck and asked what was happening. He suggested that we return to the vacated area to make doubly sure that no one had been left behind. After satisfying ourselves that this was so, we followed on. After a mile or so we caught up with the King's Royal Rifle Corps, now regrouped and facing the enemy, and I recognised the CSM, freshly shaved and looking spruce, who had been our cabin-mate on the *Empress of Canada*. We waved, and a little later on came upon our 250-gallon water truck, which had become stuck in soft sand. Apart from being our only reserve of water these vehicles were especially prized by the Germans, who could use them for the same purpose. My Bedford truck was not powerful enough to recover it and reluctantly it was left behind, but we learnt that it was dug out later and returned.

Because of these distractions my driver and I had fallen behind the echelon, but we followed an easterly course as set by the sun compass. Having travelled about twenty miles and not seen our party, we espied a spread-out group of vehicles ahead. They belonged to rear division, the supply element of 1st Armoured. I found Tim Cole, an old Bulford friend, and explained our predicament, just as a divisional staff officer passed by. He asked me my business, and I told him I was looking for 1st Support Group. He said they were in the position they had been before we withdrew. When I corrected him he became awkward and muttered darkly about deserters, saying that they had arrested two on the previous evening. I heard afterwards that there had been a delay in the code lists reaching him and he was out of touch with the situation. On the same evening, trying to establish contact with his divisional HQ, he blundered into a German patrol, was taken prisoner, and spent the remainder of the war as a captive.

Having said goodbye to Tim Cole, we searched the desert and eventually came upon the group five or six miles away. Rommel was held at El Agheila, which was perhaps the furthest he wanted to go in view of his supply position.

At a subsequent court of inquiry the truth emerged. The divisional HQ staff were required to send a signal message to their corps HQ each day, giving the numbers of tanks fit for combat. These messages were enciphered, but through a serious breach of security one was sent out in clear language on a South African wireless set attached to our division. The report was intercepted by German Signals Intelligence and also by our own monitoring teams. The German commander was passed this information, which could have been a hoax by the British to lure him forward.

Following the duststorm, heavy rain had fallen at Antelat, the nearest RAF base, causing aircraft to be grounded. Rommel knew this too and decided to make a reconnaissance in force towards the British position. At the same time two British columns were probing the area in front of Support group headquarters, and Rommel's column drove a wedge between them and almost captured the HQ. Fearing deception on the part of the British, he remained at El Agheila with his staff but allowed some of his armour to roam the desert and do what damage it could.

We stayed in our present situation for several days and became aware that our supplies were dwindling. Everything that we needed had to be transported from the port of Tobruk or from the railway terminus at Fuka. The strain on the transport system was enormous, because of the distance all supplies had to be carried.

Things were becoming critical, and I was sent out with a wireless vehicle and as many load-carriers as could be spared to search for any forward supply dumps which could be found and load up with essential supplies, with the emphasis on petrol. When about ten miles out, I saw a sign indicating the position of a forward supply depot and sent an NCO to verify it was still there. We stopped near to a track and heard the rumble of tanks approaching and heading west. It was our own 4th Armoured Brigade, and as it passed I saw Major Harris standing up in the hatch of a leading tank. He gave a wave of recognition and I saluted my officer commanding of South Holmwood days.

A few minutes after the column had passed we heard a roar overhead and three German Stukas were seen and heard screaming over a low escarpment. Everyone ran as fast as possible away from the vehicles and threw himself flat on the ground. We need not have worried for they were after bigger game than our six vehicles, their target being the armoured brigade. I did not hear if they caused any damage, but found out later that the brigade was proceeding to Antelat to protect our aircraft from a possible German thrust.

Our scout returned and reported the presence of a supply dump four miles away, so we proceeded there and loaded up. This took some time and when we returned to the vicinity of the Group it was dark. The desert is no place to wander about with vehicles at night, so I asked the group by wireless to fire a flare to indicate its position, but this request was refused. I was told instead to rendezvous at a given point in the morning. The engine of one of the three-ton vehicles was being temperamental so I decided to load its contents on to the other trucks and travel on it in case the driver should need help.

After a fitful night's rest we set off in the morning to meet the group at the appointed place, with my three-ton truck in the lead and the remainder spaced out behind me. I did not like the appearance of the meeting-place at all; there were too many smokescreens and flares about for my liking.

A captain of the Rifle Brigade, whom I shall never forget because he had a dewdrop at the end of his nose, then appeared and asked why I was there. When told he said, 'I am Roberts Column and I am withdrawing and I advise you to do the same.'

Simultaneously the RASC captain appeared in his Bedford, travelling as fast as the engine would drive it, and instead of stopping to talk to me, waved us back. The drivers behind me took heed of his signal and started to follow him, so instead of mine being the lead vehicle I brought up the rear.

Calamity then struck; after a few hundred yards our engine coughed and the truck stopped. At the same time the corporal operator of the wireless truck appeared and said that the brigadier wanted to speak to me on the set. I told the commander that I had been ordered to withdraw by Roberts Column, and he was most anxious to know its position and gave me a map reference at which we should meet. I had a difficult decision to make, being the only one to know the rendezvous, and with my supply vehicles in front I was not prepared to leave the driver behind in a broken-down vehicle, so we both piled into the wireless truck and abandoned the lorry. My uncle Ebenezer told me once that the captain of a ship has only a split second to reach a decision but the board of inquiry has months to reach its verdict.

We overtook the other vehicles gradually, only to be confronted by another problem. The course I had set brought us to a huge expanse of water and for a moment I thought we had reached the sea. That, of course, was impossible, the sea being behind us, and I realised that we had reached the edge of the plateau that we had crossed a few days earlier, now turned into a lake by the recent heavy rain. It was necessary to skirt this in order to reach our meeting-point, and by this time we had recovered all the stray vehicles.

Being sure of my position I called a halt near the water's edge. Very soon afterwards a formation could be seen approaching from the south. There was no way of telling whether it was friendly or enemy, and when it was a mile away a reconnaissance vehicle detached itself from the main body and sped in our direction. We were elated to find that it belonged to 1st Support Group and that we had succeeded in delivering much-needed supplies.

Later that evening the brigadier called his staff officers to give orders for the following day and to receive reports. When he called out Alistaire (my OC), I said, 'Not here, sir.' We heard later that the Signals and RASC captains had ended up in Tobruk – 250 miles away!

We slept fitfully that night and were awake at dawn, just in time to see flares and rockets exploding, and once again we were withdrawing. It must have been fifty miles on before a halt was called and we were able to re-form into some sort of defensive force. During this latest withdrawal, having lost the truck earlier on, I had to travel on any vehicle available, but fortunately we came upon an abandoned Italian horse-box, left behind in an earlier Allied advance, which we were able to hook to one of our towing vehicles. This proved very useful later as it contained a wide shelf along one side and was long enough to serve as my bed for many months.

In the course of this latest skirmish General Lumsden suffered a shrapnel wound and was evacuated to a field hospital for treatment. His place was taken by General Messervey, the commander of 4th Indian Division, who summed up the position very quickly. Rommel was dependent for his supplies on shipping discharging at the port of Tripoli. The vessels carrying his reserves across the Mediterranean from Italy were being continuously harassed by British submarines based at Alexandria and Malta, and many of his reinforcement ships were being sunk. As a consequence he was short of supplies and a very long way from his Tripoli base.

General Messervey realised this and decided that Rommel was so far stretched as to make a counter-offensive feasible, particularly as most of the British armour was intact. He stood in the communications centre, the armoured command vehicle, and pleaded with Corps HQ to allow him to attack. Permission was not granted and the general was thwarted in his plan to encircle the German force by means of a pincer movement.

In the course of this latest withdrawal, the mobile bath unit still followed us, but because of its weight and bulk was finding it difficult to keep up. The crew then decided to abandon it, and by removing the bolts securing the structure to the floor they managed to heave it off the vehicle. The German forces pursuing us saw this massive structure in their path and were so suspicious of it that their advance was delayed sufficiently long for the bath unit to catch up. We were then approaching the Msus area, and it was obvious that the Afrika Corps had been reinforced from its Tripoli base. Rommel's objective must have been apparent to our force HQ: to capture the ports of Benghazi and Derna, enabling supply vessels to be discharged there – thus cutting his lines by seven hundred miles, with a consequent saving in fuel and other supplies consumed in transporting them over the land route.

The nature of the terrain was different here; instead of the relatively flat nature of the ground further south, we came upon a number of wadis and hillocks. We were travelling by the compass in a north-easterly direction when the leading vehicle made an abrupt change of course and headed almost due east. The reason for this was revealed later that evening; we had become isolated from the remainder of the division and were heading straight for a German column advancing on our left flank. Unknown to us, and at the very time we changed direction, a tank battle was taking place and both our own and enemy shells were passing over our heads. But for the prompt action of a staff officer at divisional HQ in diverting us, we would have driven straight into the hands of the Afrika Corps.

Our troubles were not yet over. After travelling another

few miles we received orders to halt on a low escarpment. The news that the major passed to me was gloomy. We were cut off from the remainder of the division and boxed in by the German forces. There was a ray of hope, however, in the form of a staff officer who was also a talented amateur astronomer. Our position was known, and he was to join up with us after nightfall and guide us back to safety with the help of the stars. Strict instructions were given to prevent giving our position away by vehicle lights or smoking, and in due course we commenced our tortuous journey driving nose to tail. There was one scare when a column of tanks could be heard approaching from ahead of us and it was with relief that we learnt it was the 4th Armoured Brigade advancing under cover of darkness to engage the enemy at dawn.

It had been a mistake to send a mobile bath unit into desert country where water was desperately short, and a high-level conference was held to assess the suitability of a support group in country where there was very little natural defence. Unlike the 1914-18 War, when vast armies dug into positions for months on end to defend territory, desert warfare was fluid and ground given up was not important, provided vital seaports and men and *matériel* were not captured. The conference decided that desert terrain was not suitable for the deployment of support troops and a decision was reached to disband 1st Support Group and replace it with a motorised brigade.

When the news was announced I was called upon to form up the HQ and Signal Squadron to hear a final address by the brigadier. After it was all over he came along and shook my hand. Sadly, he was to lose his command and report to Cairo, where there was no job for him. My work was not yet completed; the next task was to break up the remainder of the unit. We had lost a few men, including the OC Sherwood Foresters platoon, missing in action, and his platoon was the first to go. Our remnants were posted as reinforcements to other Signals units short of manpower, together with the remaining vehicles. I was now without a job and found myself attached to rear division of the 1st Armoured, where I caught up with former friends. Ted Cornish, now a captain, was the administrative officer, and the second-in-command, Major The Viscount Malden, was also based here.

It was not long before I was found a job. RSM Edwards was on his way back to Egypt and for want of anything more to do he had been running a mobile unit canteen to serve the needs of the troops. Supplies were bought from the nearest NAAFI depot and sold to the men, thus making a ten per cent profit for unit funds. It should not have been necessary for unit personnel and transport to be misused in this way, because the NAAFI charter stipulated that on mobilisation their staff, most of them reservists, donned uniform and were referred to as the Expeditionary Force Institute. The crews were expected to drive their canteens to forward units to sell them the small luxuries that did not come up with the rations, but experience showed that a minority of them preferred to keep away from the sound of gunfire and dispose of their stocks to units nearer their depots. Their supervisors were not aware of this because the stocks were readily saleable and they always returned to their base with full cash boxes and empty shelves.

Running the unit canteen was a simple job. All that was necessary for me to do was draw a hundred Egyptian pounds from the unit accountant, assess the requirements of the troops, stock up and return to base to sell it off. The main preference was for tinned fruit, packets of biscuits, chocolate and cigarettes. Canned beer was available on the scale of one per man per week, and in order to buy beer I had to take a certificate, signed personally by the commanding officer, showing the ration strength of officers and men under his command. The cans were not provided with the modern easy openers but had to be punctured by means of a marline-spike, which was part of a soldier's jack-knife. Just imagine cans of beer having travelled in the back of a lorry and shaken up for fifty miles or so being pierced by a marline-spike in two places. Most of it went up in froth, but the wiser ones buried the can in sand and opened it in the cool of the evening.

Some of the officers expressed a liking for gin and this was no problem. The ration of spirits for officers and senior NCOs was one bottle per head each month, but there were few buyers because neither Angostura nor tonic water was available and the ration of water was too precious to waste on diluting gin. On the odd occasion, however, I was able to trade a bottle of gin for a two-gallon can of water, and this kept my friends happy.

There was less tension at rear division than there had been at Support Group HQ, mainly because of our distance from the front line. We had sufficient members to form a small warrrant-officers' and sergeants' mess, and were fortunate in having a qualified chef to cook for us. He was Paul Gaultier, whose father had run a number of restaurants in Paris until the capitulation of France. Paul had assisted him in this family business until things became desperate, when he escaped to England and joined the Royal Armoured Corps. His culinary ability soon became known and he was offered employment as cook to the general, but declined because he was of an extrovert nature and preferred the company of his fellow sergeants.

Rear Division was very much part of a mobile force and ready to move at short notice should the need arise. An impending move was signalled by hoisting a flag on the command vehicle in daylight or firing a single flare from it at night. This signal was a warning to move off in fifteen minutes; should it not be heeded there was no one to chase up the laggards, who were simply left behind. There was a recognised order of march and each vehicle had a set place, so there was no confusion in the event of a hurried evacuation. The last people to leave the site were the Ordnance Light Aid Detachment, who were responsible for recovering any vehicles breaking down on the route.

Now that we were reasonably stabilised, mail from the UK started to arrive and this raised morale. It had been possible to write home from the time we arrived in Egypt but this amounted to only one air-letter card a week, and these cards were censored by an officer and subject to further censorship at base. The incoming mail was not censored and the senior ranks were warned to look out for discarded letters written by wives, mothers or sweethearts complaining about conditions at home. If they fell into the wrong hands they would serve as useful ammunition for the Nazi propaganda machine. One day I found such a letter caught in a clump of bush and picked it up to have it incinerated. My attention was attracted by a red pattern and I wondered at its significance. What I read shocked me. The female writer had painted the mouth of her vagina with lipstick, impressed it on the letter card and written a crude message below the impression. I wasted no time in applying a match to it.

The lower formation that I had served with was dependent for its instructions on the Signals Despatch Service, which made regular runs to carry the longer messages and administrative orders. Shorter operational instructions were sent by radio-telephony, with map references and sensitive data disguised by simple codes, changed daily for security reasons.

Whenever we had participated in major exercises while serving in India, the provision of these codes had been the responsibility of the Army Education Corps. In 1939, when war seemed imminent, the need for educational instruction ceased and the Army schoolmasters, together with some members of the Intelligence Corps, were trained in the use of sophisticated methods of secure communication and attached to the higher formations of Signals, where they were referred to as cipher operators. With the expansion of the Army, other sources of manpower had to be found. Ideally, wireless operators from within Signals, given a short course of instruction, would have filled the gap – but the Corps was desperately short of operators and it took months of training before signallers became proficient. The solution was to call for volunteers from other arms of the service to undergo a crash course in elementary codes and ciphers. No great intelligence was required, and provided a man had a clean conduct sheet, was literate and numerate, he was accepted. The irony of it was that having qualified he was promoted to the rank of corporal, and worse still was allowed to wear the Royal Signals cap badge. This was at a time when experienced operators with years of service in the Corps, some of them operating hundreds of miles behind enemy lines with the Long Range Desert Group, and most of them capable of sending upwards of thirty words per minute on the morse key, were serving in their basic rank of signalman.

Shortly before the disbandment of 1st Support Group a new commanding officer had been posted to the unit whose name sounded like Smith. The former Signals captain also appeared and was attached to Rear Division, albeit without a job, and the reason for his appearance soon became known.

When the group was located at Agedabia he had withdrawn the sum of a hundred Egyptian pounds from public funds and with George Bray, the RAOC Sub-Conductor, had spent it on canteen goods of dubious origin and dumped them on to me. I was instructed to distribute these items amongst the troops and obtain temporary receipts, which were to be converted into acquittance rolls later by the pay clerk. These acquittance rolls would in due course find their way to the chief paymaster in Egypt, the amount due would be debited against each man's account and the public funds reimbursed. I did not like this arrangement because public funds had been spent on goods that could have been lost or unsaleable. The distribution was made, however, and temporary receipts given on sheets of paper attached to a millboard. Very soon afterwards and before the authentic acquittance rolls could be signed, the Germans attacked at El Agheila and the temporary receipts were lost when my truck had to be abandoned.

The chief paymaster in Cairo, having been advised of the disbandment of the Signal Squadron, requested the imprest account be closed and returned to him. With a hundred pounds missing, there was no way in which this could be done, and an inquiry was held into the affair. The new CO, having read the evidence, decided to make me a scapegoat. I was told that as he had no power to try a warrant-officer, I would have to face trial by court martial.

I was charged with losing acquittance rolls to the value of one hundred Egyptian pounds and the loss of my truck. The truck had, of course, been recovered on the same day! My sole defence witness was the brigadier, who by this time was somewhere in Egypt. His evidence would have been sufficient to clear me, but a field general court martial was convened. It took only two hours for the cases for the prosecution and the defence to be stated, another twenty minutes for the court to reach a verdict and for me to be recalled to hear the President say, 'You have been charged with losing acquittance rolls to the value of one hundred Egyptian pounds and the loss of your truck. You have been found "Not Guilty" and you are dismissed.'

It was not the end of the affair, because the general, promulgating the verdict of the court, ordered further inquiries into the whole affair. The chief clerk of the HQ told me later that the general, had the circumstances been explained to him, had the authority to write off such a small amount!

By this time it was early May and becoming warmer. Despite the lack of water no one smelt. There are two theories for this, one being that in the arid atmosphere of the desert perspiration did not stay on the skin, and the second that we all smelt to such an extent that it passed unnoticed. The second theory is borne out by a friend of mine who was in a party evacuated to a base hospital. On their arrival a young nurse was heard remarking to one of her colleagues, 'My! Don't they pong.'

With the advent of the warmer weather, the question of a summer offensive by either side was much discussed. Up to now any attacks had been made in the cooler seasons. One school of thought was that in the summer months tank warfare could be ruled out because of the extreme risk of heat exhaustion to the crews. Our intelligence, however, suggested that Rommel would attack on the night of the full moon. In preparing our defence position the Sappers had laid thousands of mines between the opposing forces, but little did we know that the Afrika Corps had rounded up hundreds of camels and herded them into an enclosure.

The night of the full moon came and nothing happened, so we all thought that our intelligence was at fault. It was not. On the following night, having driven the camels through the minefield to create a safe path for his sortie, the enemy surprised everyone by reaching our advanced divisional HQ at breakfast-time. General Lumsden, who was at his HQ, would have made a prize captive, but with remarkable presence of mind he tore off his badges of rank, threw away his hat, seized a tin plate from a trooper and joined the breakfast queue. He was captured but the Germans, believing him to be an ordinary soldier, relaxed their guard and later that day he regained his freedom, together with many other members of his HQ. This thrust of Rommel's was soon repulsed and, surprisingly, the HQ communication centre and other office trucks were left unharmed.

The Eighth Army at the time came under the command of General Ritchie, who was supported by two Army corps, the 13th and 30th, but he was short of divisions. From time to time hardened troops experienced in desert warfare had been withdrawn to participate in actions in Eritrea, the Sudan, Greece, Crete and other operational theatres without being completely replaced. Faced with the lack of manpower and firepower, the commander decided to hold the Gazala-Bir Hakeim Line. Gazala was on the Mediterranean coast, and his right flank was given a measure of protection by the Royal Navy, who could pound Rommel's positions from the sea. The Free French force was brought up to defend the left flank and, provided this position was held, a frontal attack by the Afrika Corps was unlikely to succeed. Bir Hakeim had been chosen because it was at the extreme south of traversable ground, and beyond it were escarpments and large areas of soft sand which even camels could not cross.

The nearest NAAFI depot from which we could obtain supplies was now Tobruk, and as my driver Harvey and I wound our way down to the docks we saw the damage caused to the town by aerial bombardment. Following General Wilson's rout of the Italians in 1940, General Rommel, heavily supported by air force squadrons, had launched a counter-offensive which succeeded in driving the British forces to the Egyptian border by March 1941; but in doing this he had to bypass Tobruk. The garrison was besieged for several months but supplied by surface craft and submarines of the Royal Navy. An attempt was made by General Wavell in June to raise the siege with the

4th Indian Division, but it was not until November 1941 that the garrison was finally freed. This episode became known as the 'long siege'.

The damage to the port was not serious, mainly because it was well defended by anti-aircraft guns and the firepower of vessels sheltering there, but havoc had been caused to the villas and bungalows on higher ground, and only the cellars were habitable. There was a lot of shipping in the harbour, including a hospital ship clearly marked with the Red Cross and a Palestinian vessel discharging a load of oranges. The Jewish settlers were unable to sell their citrus crop and had chartered a ship to deliver a free load of luscious fruit for the use of the Allied forces. As we skirted the perimeter defences on the way back, we came to an airfield and were just in time to see it attacked by a Luftwaffe fighter plane. This followed the usual pattern of the RAF engaging the enemy planes and running out of ammunition. When this happened the Germans followed them down and shot them up on the ground. We were safe enough; shooting down a Kittyhawk plane and finishing it off on the ground was more rewarding to an enemy pilot than destroying a single truck, and at least he could claim a kill.

An unfortunate incident occurred on our return to the laager. Our truck had barely stopped in its position when the shriek of bombs was heard almost overhead and as we jumped out we saw Tim Cole and his staff do the same. His vehicle was two hundred yards away and next to ours. Three of them managed to take shelter beneath their vehicle but the fourth, an RAOC cobbler attached to us, was too slow. A bomb dropped near the tail-board and killed him. As my driver and I rushed to the scene, we found the remainder shaken and smoke-blackened but uninjured. 'Shoey' had joined the unit as a reservist in Bulford in 1939 and was a quiet and respected man. His job was to keep us well shod, but as far as I am aware had not repaired a pair of boots since he joined us.

In letters from home we heard that Winston Churchill, in order to save fuel at the pumping stations, was exhorting the nation to use only five inches of water for a bath! My wife wrote to say that she had applied to join the

Women's Land Army but her application had been rejected because she was in a reserved occupation. One of my sisters said that she wished to visit the other one living in the Isle of Wight but was refused entry because the island had been created a defence zone. My reply was heavily censored!

Not all the Germans played the game by the rules of the Geneva Convention. A staff sergeant I know was taken prisoner for a short while with the general, and on his escape he was without a watch. A German, he said, had demanded it. Anticipating this, he had concealed it, but the Hun pointed to the white skin on his othewise tanned wrist and, drawing his pistol, insisted on the watch being handed over.

The tales of the Gurkhas' prowess are legion. These little men, recruited from the hills of Nepal and whose fathers and grandfathers had served the British Raj since before the days of the Indian Mutiny, formed part of the 4th Indian Division. They were adept at patrolling and stalking, particularly at night. A patrol of them was sent out one night to deal with a troublesome German observation post perched on a hilltop not too far from Bir Hakeim and directing artillery fire on the Free French positions. Two of the Gurkhas moved silently up the hillside and found a single German awake on sentry duty while the remainder slept. One of the Gurkhas, with a sweep of his kukri, decapitated him. On their return to base they were asked why they had not dealt with the remainder. Johnny Gurkha replied, 'When they wake up and see the sentry's head they will die of fright.'

With the German front not too far away, contingency plans were in hand to strengthen the defences of Tobruk and a pioneer battalion of East African troops was brought up. Their sole European officer was a British major and, not knowing their customs, he was not very popular. He woke up one morning to find that the battalion to a man had deserted him during the night. That was one way of losing a command!

There was a tale in circulation of an officer who had raised a fictitious unit of colonial troops. By some means he had obtained authority to open an imprest account which entitled him to draw money to pay the wages of his men. As most of them had not learnt to write, a thumb-mark was considered a sufficient receipt and as one thumb-print was similar to another he was able to amass a considerable sum of money through his trickery. Suspicions were aroused when it was discovered that his unit did not draw rations. The chief prosecution witness at his court martial was a Metropolitan Police fingerprint expert who had been called up and was serving in the Special Investigation Branch of the Military Police!

Rommel launched an attack on the Gazala line, but it was resisted and he could find no way of piercing the front. He then concentrated on the Free French position at Bir Hakeim. This onslaught continued for days, with the French putting up determined resistance – at one stage they sent a signal to the Corps commander which read: 'Keep sending us ammunition, we can manage without rations.' Finally, after determined aerial and artillery bombardment, their resistance was broken; the British and Indian divisions were outflanked and more ground had to be given up to the Afrika Corps.

The Eighth Army regrouped for one of the last battles to be fought on Libyan soil in Rommel's present offensive. This took place at what was known as the 'Knightsbridge Box'. The whole of the fighting force was formed up into a square formation so that all of its fire-power was directed outwards. The 'soft' vehicles (supply vehicles) were ordered to withdraw well away from this action so that tanks from the fighting units did not have to be disengaged to protect them.

The NAAFI source of supplies was now changed to Bardia near to the Egyptian border, so to be first in the queue in the morning Harvey and I left on the previous day to reconnoitre its position. We found it located on a large area of ground in use as a petrol and ammunition dump, well dispersed. As darkness fell we prepared to settle down for the night when we heard the noise of anti-aircraft batteries and soon afterwards the drone of approaching aircraft. It was not long before they dropped their flares and the whole area was lit up. We heard a piercing noise and crept as close to the vehicle as possible for protection. A few seconds later, the piercing noise ended in a thud. A bomb fragment or a lump of shrapnel from an exploding gun-shell had dropped on the track beside us.

Not wishing to be incinerated by exploding petrol, I urged Harvey into the truck and he drove away. The surface of the track was badly corrugated, what the Americans called a washboard surface, and ignoring the risk of damage to the springs he drove as fast as he could until we reached the coast road leading to Tobruk. There was no parking-space along the road, which was bordered with dannert wire bearing notices *Achtung Minen*. As we had no means of knowing if the mines had been cleared we carried on. A few miles further along we came to a road barricade manned by soldiers carrying hurricane-lamps, and we halted.

They were Free French on their way from Syria to reinforce their comrades fighting alongside us, and they were the soul of hospitality. We were given a meal with wine, and the French adjutant insisted that I had the use of his bed that night, saying that he was on all-night duty. It was the first time I had slept in a bed since leaving the transit camp at Port Taufiq.

It was only a few days after returning from Bardia that the news was broken that the Eighth Army had been disengaged from the Knightsbridge Box and had given ground to the Afrika Corps. The situation was now critical and General Auchinleck, known affectionately to the soldiers as 'the Auk', and later to become Field-Marshall Sir Claude Auchinleck, had himself come up from Cairo to take over command of the Eighth Army.

The protection of the supply echelons had been a worry to the senior officers conducting the fighting, who were constantly preoccupied with the danger of being cut off from their supplies by enemy raiders. It was decided that all soft vehicles would be withdrawn to the safety of Tobruk, from where they could supply the fighting troops when safe to do so. As a consequence we were given orders to proceed to Tobruk, one hour's driving-time away. As we drove along I noticed in the rear mirror a passenger in a vehicle driving behind me make frantic signs. Thinking it indicated an aerial attack, I stood up in the cab and looked out of the hatch – only to see the wireless set bumping along the ground in our wake.

As we approached Tobruk, I saw General Auchinleck driving a Jeep and waving to us. We entered the outer defences in the late afternoon and were directed by the Military Police to a spot near one of the beaches. The sea looked inviting and I organised the swimmers to have a dip. Shortly afterwards, one of the crew members came along with the wireless set which had fallen from my truck. Outwardly, apart from a damaged lid, it appeared all right – and when I switched it on, miraculously it worked.

The RASC was aware of our presence and made a late ration delivery. Although it did not include fresh meat, there was a plentiful supply of McConochies stew. The cooks prepared an appetising meal, including fresh bread rolls baked in Tobruk that day. It was the first time that we had eaten bread in six months.

The meal over, I was about to switch on the set to listen to the BBC 9 p.m. news when the instruction 'Get ready to move' was passed around. There was consternation, but as we were well drilled in unexpected departures things went smoothly and the unit formed up ready to move off.

The reason for this change of plan was not given at the time but it transpired later that General Auchinleck, who had now relieved General Ritchie, had planned to concentrate the whole of his remaining armour on destroying Rommel's supply lines and thus deprive him of fuel and foodstuffs. However, things went wrong. The Afrika Corps had prepared a tank-trap of its deadly 88-millimetre guns and the Eighth Army drove straight into it, losing in one single action almost the whole of its tank strength. There was now no effective defence force left in Cyrenaica, and orders were given to evacuate Tobruk of all except its planned defence force.

Rear Division drove in stops and starts throughout the night and by dawn had only reached the coast road skirting the garrison. The situation was alarming. As far as the eye could see, the road was jammed with stationary vehicles with their engines cut off to conserve petrol. To make things worse, the sound of approaching aircraft could be heard. Prominent notices warning of uncleared mines were displayed on each side of the road, but these went unheeded as the vehicle crews rushed to get as far as possible from their stationary trucks. The tension was eased when an officer shouted, 'They are ours,' after which calm was restored. Had the planes belonged to the Luftwaffe, devastation would have resulted and the coast road would have been blocked for months. The reason for the hold-up was made known later in the morning. Some of the more irresponsible elements at the head of the long procession had felt sleepy and decided to pull off the coast road to rest. When they tried to manoeuvre their vehicles back on to the road, only frantic efforts by the Military Police enabled order to be restored.

It now became clear that the column occupying the whole of the coast road between Tobruk and Salum were on the retreat to Egypt. The remnants of the Eighth Army had been regrouped and were fighting a rearguard action to enable their supply echelons to reach safer ground.

Ours was an orderly withdrawal and not a rout as has been described by some over-imaginative journalists. We travelled in measured stages, skirting Bardia, Salum and Sidi Barrani, passing by a large formation of dummy tanks intended to deceive the Axis forces into believing that there was a build-up- of armour for an impending attack. The 'tanks' were constructed of plywood and mounted on three-ton chassis. It was thought that these dummies would attract aerial bombardment and so deplete enemy stocks of bombs, but the aircraft observers noted that no tracks showed up on their aerial photographs and so ignored the bait. In due course we reached the massive store dumps built up in the area near Mersa Matruh, and it was evident that stores were being back-loaded as fast as trains could carry them.

Baggush and El Daba were bypassed and we were nearly halfway to the naval base of Alexandria. The HQ did not have very far to go and when level with the small railway station of El Alamein turned south towards the desert. After a few miles a halt was called. Orders were given to dig slit trenches and await further developments.

Within a day or so the advance element of the division joined us and the divisional commander had us organised into a defensive force. At that stage of the war six tanks were allotted to the HQ of an armoured division to protect it from being overrun by a marauding task force, but General Lumsden had surrendered his protective tanks for use in more critical areas.

It was not long before we heard of the capture of Tobruk. It had been thought that the port could be defended and prove a thorn in the flesh of the Axis forces, but it was not to be. The saga of Tobruk has been written by many eminent historians, but the basic facts are worth repeating. The defence of the garrison was entrusted to the 2nd South African Division, and when it fell there were mutterings about treachery. On the other hand its defence was not made any easier by intelligence gained by the Germans in the earlier siege, when their patrols were constantly probing its outer defences to look for weak points to attack. Some of the defenders had fallen into the deplorable habit of smoking when on sentry duty, and German Intelligence had been able to build up a complete picture of its outer defences from glowing cigarettes or the smell of tobacco.

The disruption of the previous week had disorganised the ration system and my canteen supplies were now exhausted, so I obtained permission to stock up at the NAAFI stores at Alexandria. As my driver and I approached the coast road we were stopped at a Military Police post. When I gave a friendly nod to the sentry and said that I was going to 'Alex', he became suspicious and asked for our identity papers, which he took to the guard tent for examination. Obviously they were taking no chances with infiltrators.

The fifty miles separating us from Alexandria was devoid of traffic, but when we reached it the place was agog with rumours. The Jews had left by the train-load, making for the Lebanon because Palestine could not accommodate them. Alexandria, shimmering in the sunlight, with the blue Mediterranean in the background, was very impressive. Harvey and I bought our supplies and when we left the compound drove along the Corniche (promenade), where there were still some shapely females disporting themselves on the sandy beaches.

Within days reinforcements started to arrive to help us hold the line. The 10th Corps travelled from Syria, and with it the 9th Australian Division – most of them hard nuts from Sydney – the 2nd New Zealand Division and a British division whose sign was a battleaxe. The choice of El Alamein as a defensive position could not have been bettered. On the right flank there was the sea and on our left the Qattara Depression, a vast area of desert consisting of soft sand which neither man nor beast could cross.

The Australians, known as the Diggers, very quickly set to making their position impregnable. They were not content with slit trenches to shelter them from bomb blast and erected deep affairs from which they could stand up to fight. Our New Zealand friends protected the Ruweissat Ridge, and there was no way in which their flank could be turned without the Germans bogging themselves down in soft sand. Our whole front was reduced to thirty miles, which made its defence easy.

Day by day, reinforcements arrived, mines were laid between us and Rommel and heavy artillery was brought up to deter the Germans from a further attack.

From time to time we were subjected to sneak raids by enemy planes which would overfly the Qattara Depression and escape over the sea, but they did little damage. On the other hand we were heartened by the aid given to us by the RAF in harassing the German positions and supply lines. From the time that we stabilised the line, twelve four-engined Wellington bombers flew over us in perfect formation and they all returned an hour or so later. This was a daily occurrence and their sorties became almost routine. There was disappointment and sadness one day when only eleven flew back over our heads. Our concern reached the corps commander, who got in touch with the RAF Command in Cairo. Everyone was delighted to hear that one of them had developed engine trouble on its outward run and the pilot had thought it prudent to return to base over the sea.

Now that we were in a static position, the importance of hygiene was more fully stressed. Deep latrines were dug, with a pole straddling the length of the trench. Urinating on the sand attracted flies so 'desert roses' were invented. These were metal tubes driven deep into the sand with metal funnels fitted to the top of the tube.

Reading material was at a premium, so the welfare branch produced the *Eighth Army News,* a broadsheet which was read with interest. One of its most popular features was a cartoon by an artist calling himself Jon. It depicted two rather eccentric officers, one fair and one dark, both with long moustaches and wearing felt desert boots and neckerchiefs, who made pithy comments to each other about the state of the war.

Letters from home revealed that the cheese ration had been cut to one ounce per week and the German blockade of the British Isles was tightening. The Prime Minister was complaining of having useless mouths to feed, meaning presumably the prison population, inmates of lunatic asylums, the black marketeers and those unable to contribute to the war effort.

Rumours now began to circulate that the Prime Minister had visited Cairo and that a conference had been held at Giza to determine future strategy. It was evident that Hitler's long-term aim was to eliminate our naval base at Alexandria, gain access to the Suez Canal and link up with Turkey, with whom he had a treaty of friendship. Oil is vital to the conduct of a war and up to now he had been dependent on his supplies from the Rumanian oilfields; if he succeeded in gaining Egypt, there was nothing to prevent him from exploiting the rich mineral resources of Iraq and also gain access to the Soviet refineries at Baku, either through the Dardanelles or overland through Turkey.

Churchill had viewed the withdrawal to El Alamein with alarm because the capture of the Suez Canal and Cairo would have severed our lifeline to India and the Far East. His solution was to appoint another general to command the Eighth Army in the person of Bernard Law Montgomery. It was not long before the accredited press got to know the story, and reports were published in the UK newspapers announcing that an 'unknown' general had been appointed to take over a 'dispirited and demoralised

Eighth Army'. These reports were resented by the Desert Force. Churchill had once said 'Give us the tools and we will finish the job.' The tools were simply not there, and the American Honey tanks with their two-inch peashooter guns and inadequate armour wilted before the superior armament of the Afrika Corps tanks.

Neither was General Montgomery unknown, at least to military men. He had been commissioned into the Royal Warwickshire Regiment in 1908 and served throughout the 1914-18 War, reaching the rank of Lieutenant-Colonel. His appointments included Brigade Commander Southern Command, Divisional Commander Palestine and Trans-Jordan, Corps Commander Home Forces, GOC-in-C Southern Command. Hardly a nonentity!

His first message of the day to the defenders of El Alamein was to the effect that there would be no further retreat and the line had to be defended at all costs – which was what the Eighth Army men were doing.

On one of our visits to the NAAFI stores at Alexandria, my driver and I were attracted by an unusual sight. We passed a tented encampment whose guard tent was visible half a mile away because its tent ropes had been lime-washed. Being curious, we drew up close to it, to come across a guard of honour awaiting the arrival of a VIP. Its turn-out could not have been bettered at the Guards depot. Their boots were highly polished and their brasswork gleamed. We asked what it was in aid of and were told they were being visited by our new general. Needless to say we made a hurried departure. What a target for an inquisitive Luftwaffe pilot who chanced to fly over the area! The scene invited close scrutiny by a passing enemy plane, and had one done so Churchill might well have had to make another appointment.

Life was now becoming boring because we were unused to such inactivity, but the message was passed around that the new commander was waiting for an overwhelming superiority in men and *matériel* before taking on Rommel. Meanwhile, on the home front the Americans were arriving in force. With each delivery of mail some of the soldiers were receiving 'Dear John letters' announcing that their fiancées and girl-friends were no longer faithful to them because their favours had been bought with sticks of chewing-gum, chocolate or nylon stockings.

In September 1942 our division was told that it was being withdrawn and returning to base for re-equipping. We did not have very far to travel as we were being provided with transit-camp accommodation near Cairo at a place called Mena. Things first went wrong as we passed a point named Kilo 10, when a group of Arabs reached up and stole four rifles.

The transit camp offered excellent facilities, ample bars, comfortable messes and camp-beds to sleep on. There was no shortage of beer, and many of the men who had been rationed to a can per week made fools of themselves by shampooing their hair with it. Notices were displayed in the public rooms warning about careless talk costing lives, and others with a propaganda bias urged that 'if she was worth waiting for she was worth fighting for'.

What the troops enjoyed most was music, and they were able to listen to broadcasts of Vera Lynn, now acknowledged as the Forces' Sweetheart, singing her soulful songs. Another keen favourite was 'Lili Marlene'. This haunting song originated in Germany and was adopted by the Afrika Corps as their own. The words were translated into English, and who better to sing them than Marlene Dietrich with her husky voice, herself of German origin and vilified by her former countrymen.

The pace of the war was now hotting up. Liberty ships were being mass-produced in the shipyards on the eastern seaboard of the United States and they ferried war *matériel* to every theatre of conflict. The luxury steamship *Queen Mary* was in use as a transport. She was so fast that she was more than a match for the U-boats and travelled independently of escorted convoys. The speed of a convoy is the speed of its slowest ship, and the *QM* had once held the Blue Riband of the Atlantic. The vessel was capable of carrying a full division of twelve thousand men, but the catering facilities were not sufficient for feeding them all at the same time, nor was there enough sleeping accommodation so the passengers ate, slept and performed their leisure activities in relays. This inconvenience was compensated for by having to spend far less time at sea for a given distance than on a slower ship.

During the time spent at Mena, a friend and I hired a cab to take us into Cairo. We had heard of the Berker and were curious to find out more about it, but the driver was reluctant to take us there as the area was out of bounds to British troops. He changed his mind when the magic word backsheesh was mentioned and drove us to the middle of the notorious red-light area. It was a sordid run-down brothel area and we did not stay long.

In a television series shown by the BBC in the late 1980s – about an odd professor who was incapable of normal relations with his wife – this den of iniquity was portrayed as a glamorous place with merchants' stalls piled high with eastern carpets, rich silks and other exotic goods. Nothing could have been further from the truth.

While in Cairo we stopped at a service club, and it was here that I renewed my acquaintanceship with Charles Severn, a Class I warrant-officer from the Intelligence Corps whom I had met in Dorking the previous year. He had been evacuated from HQ Eighth Army to recuperate from jaundice. Charles had been appointed as personal cipher operator to General Montgomery, and I was one of the first to learn about the layout of Monty's caravan and the photograph of Rommel which faced him over his desk.

I was not impressed by the residents of Cairo I came across. Many of them were pimps and almost all spoke the same sales talk. 'Want to buy my sister, real virgin, only thirteen. Have good time with her and very cheap.' Others were desperate to sell their 'feelthy pictures', some depicting Shanghai Lil having sexual intercourse with a donkey suitably restrained by chains. The biggest nuisance were the boot-boys who insisted on polishing our already highly polished boots. A refusal attracted a mouthful of spit aimed straight at the toe-cap, and one was obliged to pay the next in line to clean it off – who no doubt shared his fee with the spitter.

All good things come to an end, and as we were now fully equipped and ready to return to the line preparatory orders were given for us to vacate the transit camp. Captain Ted Cornish and ten men were left behind as a rear party to strike the tents and return them to Ordnance. Because of the scare resulting from the stolen rifles, he decided that the whole party should sleep in one large tent. Difficult as it is to believe, when they awoke in the morning all of the tents including the one they slept in had been dismantled during the night and removed by thieves.

Our first staging post on the road to El Alamein was fifty miles north of Cairo. We were expected to remain there for a few days, and it was here that a chagrined rear party caught up with us. It was here, too, that I left the 1st Armoured Division with instructions to report to the Royal Signals depot at Maadi. I asked for transport to convey me there and was told none was available, but I was taken to the main road to Cairo with my kit and I thumbed a lift to the depot. As it happened, the division stayed at this staging post for two days then drove straight up into action in the Battle of El Alamein.

On my arrival I was shown to the sergeants' mess, where I found the residents to be in a nervous state because the Chief Signal Officer was paying a visit on the following morning. The company sergeant-major was so disturbed by this news that he reported sick with some obscure complaint. The senior warrant-officer living in the mess had no real job. His last appointment had been to manage a Nile houseboat, bought by the Corps as a floating hotel for the use of units serving in Egypt. Because of the exigencies of war it was now out of commission. Another of the trio was a farrier warrant-officer from the Cheshire Yeomanry. This horsed regiment had arrived in Palestine earlier, complete with its animals, and had promptly been converted into a lines of communication unit. I never did find out what happened to the horses, but the farrier certainly had no shoeing to do. More of Churchill's useless mouths!

On the following morning, and in accordance with the depot standing orders, I was required to report for medical and dental inspection. As I passed the company office a major looked out of the window and asked me where I was going. When told, he asked if I was sick, and when I said that it was a routine check-up in accordance with instructions, he asked me to report back to him.

When I did this I recognised the officer as Major Pronger, whom I had last seen at Catterick Camp as a sergeant in 1933. He explained that his CSM was excused duty and asked me to accompany him to make a preliminary inspection of the barrack rooms housing his staff. What I saw shocked me. Normally any trained soldier avoids the depot as he would the plague. It reminds him of martinet drill instructors, inspections and spit and polish. But this was a shambles, with unmade beds, clothing strewn around and in a general state of untidiness. Between us we straightened out the place as best we could before returning to the office. In the event the Chief Signal Officer was delayed and unable to complete his programme of inspection, which was just as well.

Major Pronger asked me to deputise for Hoppy, the absent CSM, until I received reporting instructions for my next unit. In the few days there I was asked to do a unique job, involving a UK citizen whose parents lived in Egypt, who was liable for call-up for military service. I was asked to prepare a six-week basic training programme for a one-man squad covering all aspects of recruit training.

I was aware that Major Pronger wished to retain me, but the posting branch's answer was firm and clear, 'Thomas is wanted at Ninth Army Signals.' In any case, the depot was the last place in which I wished to serve.

14

THE LEBANON AND SYRIA

The train left Cairo at noon to commence its 450-mile journey to Beirut. It followed the route to Ismailia and crossed the Suez Canal at Qantara, by which time it was dark. The nearest enemy planes at that time were based on the island of Crete, and as this part of Egypt was beyond their reach there were no black-out restrictions. It arrived at the sizeable town of El Arish at daybreak, and there was some commotion as the Egyptian passengers alighted and goods were unloaded. Native hawkers were ever-present on the platform, selling their wares. After a short interval our journey was resumed, and later in the morning the train arrived at Gaza, a short distance from the Palestine border. Then the scenery began to change and instead of flat arid desert we encountered cultivated areas of orange groves. The train reached Haifa early on the Saturday afternoon and to the surprise of the military passengers they were told that the train was proceeding no further that day; instead of travelling to our destination Beirut we were to stay in a transit camp until Monday.

Haifa, overlooked by Mount Carmel, was a modern town and I decided to explore it. As I walked along I heard a voice from behind me calling 'Taffy Thomas' (the name by which I was known at Quetta), and looking round saw two battledressed soldiers approach. As they got nearer I recognised them as Smudger Smith and Langmaid, whom I had not seen for nearly four years. Smith wore the stripes of a sergeant and Langmaid a corporal's. They both wore a ribbon denoting that they had been awarded the Military Medal. We adjourned to a bar for a drink and their story, discreetly told, was an interesting one.

Tiring of the inactivity of military life at Quetta, they had both volunteered for special services and been accepted. Their task was to be dropped from a light aircraft miles behind the Axis lines and to glean useful information from the nomadic tribes of the region, such as the whereabouts of enemy units and the location of water-holes. In return for information the nomads had to be bribed, and as paper currency was of no value to them they were given gold coins and gem stones.

They carried a water-bottle and emergency rations, but no wireless, and after roaming the desert for several days they would be picked up and returned to base to make their report. Their foray over, they would return for a spell of leave after handing back any unused bribes.

Unknown to them, they were being shadowed while on leave and were seen displaying some of the gems. They were arrested, and sentenced to be reduced to the ranks, stripped of their decorations and to undergo six months' imprisonment. While still serving their sentence they were asked if they would volunteer for a special mission in Europe. Both agreed, and it has to be presumed that they were parachuted into Italy or France in preparation for the Allied landings. Nothing more was heard of them.

The train pulled into Beirut station on Monday. I was met and driven up to the headquarters of Ninth Army at Aley. Some of the places mentioned from now on may differ in their spelling from that in modern atlases but their names are spelt as they were known at that time.

My new commanding officer, Lieutenant-Colonel J. C. (Jack) Hardy, impressed me at my interview. He rose from his chair and met me half-way along his office to welcome me to his unit. His was an impressive record: he had served on the North-West Frontier of India in 1930-31 and again in the Mohmand Operations of 1933, having been mentioned in despatches in both operations. He had recently arrived from the desert, where he had served as a general staff officer grade I. He looked young for his thirty-seven years, and had a reputation on the field of sport. He had played rugby football for Ireland and the London Irish. Above all, he was a man prepared to listen.

I had met the members of the sergeants' mess on the previous evening and most of them were seasoned soldiers who had seen active service between 1914 and 1918. The more dominating personalities were the RSM Jack Baxter, M.M., CSM 'Abdul' Pearce and RQMS Bill Ratcliffe. Colonel Hardy said that he was sending me to join one of his detached companies at Ablah.

I reported to Major Hill, the OC, a highly qualified GPO engineer who had been a supplementary reservist before the outbreak of war. Unlike the Territorial Army, which participated in annual training camps, military exercises in conjunction with the Regular Army, tactical training and drills in their own drill halls, the supplementaries were specialists available in wartime who had not undergone any military training, and the most some of them had been taught was how to salute.

The Ablah company was housed in a large complex containing the command ordnance depot, to which it was attached, and provided signal communications for the COD. This included a large manually operated telephone switchboard at the depot itself, in addition to smaller ones at its detachments in Damascus, Homs and Chtaura.

As we were attached to the COD for all purposes, including accommodation, feeding, defence and leisure facilities, I was under-employed, so although it was not my responsibility I took an interest in the operation of the signal centre. On visiting the telephone exchange I noticed that there was a direct line to the local brothel, and as this was out of bounds to all British troops I assumed that it was there for the madam to enlist the help of the Military Police should the need arise.

The barracks housing the COD was originally built for the French Army when France was the protecting power for Syria and the Lebanon. One very noticeable thing was the plumbing, and instead of sitting in comfort on a lavatory bowl one had to squat over a hole to perform one's natural functions. The barracks was guarded by West African troops, who had not qualified to be good fighting soldiers but performed reasonably well as sentries. Being illiterate, they were unable to read the pass that all wishing to gain access had to show, so all passes were typed and signed in red ink. Rommel himself could have gained entry provided he produced a card typed and signed in red.

Ninth Army Signals had a large detachment at a place called Deir ez Zor near the banks of the River Euphrates and deep into Syria. It was here that in earlier times the Syrians had massacred thousands of Armenians by packing them into caves along the river bank and burning them alive. As the crow flies, it was two hundred and fifty miles from Ablah and too remote for snap visits, so I was sent there for four weeks to make an appreciation.

At its nearest point Deir ez Zor was only fifty miles from the border with Iraq. The route lay past the ruins of Baalbek and its ancient Temple of Bacchus and through to Homs, where the road ended. Allowing for deviations, there were two hundred miles of desert to cross, and the route was used so infrequently that vehicle tracks were soon obliterated by the wind. My driver had done the trip once, on his way to collect me, and I determined to make good use of my prismatic and sun compasses. The only place of consequence near the route was the biblical settlement of Palmyra, which was close to the oil pipeline running from Kirkuk in Iraq to Tripoli.

Once past Palmyra, there were no land features to assist in navigation apart from a few clumps of gnarled trees visible ten miles away and a village built on a high hill nearer to our destination. This village had been occupied by French forces resisting the advance of the Allies; the Free French had predicted no resistance by their countrymen, but in fact it had been fierce. From this point there were only fifty miles to cover, and we reached our destination without difficulty.

I had been told that on arrival I was to report to Captain Pearson, the OC of the Signals detachment which provided communications for the sub-area responsible for local administration. I recognised Pearson as a Channel Islander from 16 Squad in the Catterick depot in 1932, when I had been his senior soldier. The place was run down and the discipline slack, so I spent two weeks giving the men a hard time at drill and smartening up their appearance.

Like the Eighth Army they were heavily dependent on tinned food for rations, and in order to procure fresh meat I was persuaded to join a party going out gazelle-shooting. We travelled in two open trucks into a remote part of the desert, armed with .303-calibre rifles, the idea being that two hunters would stand up in the rear of the vehicle and fire over the cab. The noise of the vehicles would alert the small herds, and they would expose their position by the dust trail they left behind. The driver would then follow them, and as the speed of the animals was no match for a vehicle they would soon come into firing range. Everything depended upon the eyesight and skill of the driver, and had he hit an anthill or large tuft of scrub at 40 m.p.h. his passengers would probably have been thrown overboard. Firing a rifle from a fast-moving vehicle can also be fraught with danger, and it was with relief that the exercise ended. We shot six gazelle and despatched the badly wounded ones.

The carcases were certified edible by the camp doctor and shared out between the various messes. It was a brutal way of hunting but the meat made a welcome change from corned beef or McConochies stew.

Before leaving Deir ez Zor I was asked to visit one of our remote detachments on the Turkish border, in a settlement adjoining the Turkish town of Al Qamishli and linked by a bridge spanning a tributary of the Euphrates. The purpose of my visit was to give them their monthly pay and to invigilate at an examination qualifying them for an increase of pay.

As our destination was 150 miles away, Sergeant Harrison and I left early in a fifteen hundredweight open Bedford truck. On the outskirts of the camp we encountered a Syrian who begged a lift. Sergeant Harrison was minded to refuse, but I overruled him on the grounds that if the vehicle had to be manhandled an extra hand would be useful. Steady progress was made for the first hundred miles and then we encountered the most appalling track conditions. Most of the soil had been washed away and in some places we were driving over boulders. Both of us prayed that the springs would survive the stress. Culverts had been built over some of the streams, enabling flocks of sheep and donkeys to cross over, but they were hardly suitable for carrying the weight of a vehicle.

To add to our troubles there was a terrific downpour and the engine cut out. At this point, when we were about ten miles from our destination, our passenger jumped out and made for a rough stone shelter in the distance. The rain stopped and we examined the engine, to find that the battery had been short-circuited by rain-water. We mopped up the water and waited for the battery to revive itself, but it failed to start the engine. Sergeant Harrison then tried the starting-handle. After a couple of turns the engine backfired and broke his arm. We could not have been in a worse position, stuck out in the wilds with no food or blankets and darkness beginning to fall. As the lights of the town began to glimmer in the distance, I heard the sound of a vehicle and fired two shots in the air with my revolver. The flashes were seen and within five minutes a vehicle pulled up. The driver was heading for the town, so I asked him to take Harrison along for medical treatment and to send a recovery vehicle out for me early the following morning.

I then spent one of the most miserable nights of my life. I had no blankets and no spare rations. The side-screens of the cab were constructed of canvas and celluloid and the cold air swept in. To make things worse, I could hear wolves howling in the distance and realised I would be ill-protected from their attentions should they attack.

The dawn came and shortly afterwards a LAD recovery vehicle appeared. I was towed into Al Qamishli in time for breakfast. On enquiring about Sergeant Harrison, I was told that he had been evacuated to base hospital by train on the previous evening. The men were paid out and the examination papers completed and sealed, after which I raised the question of their welfare. It was a surprise to me that their rations were delivered from the train carrying wheat and other essentials from Syria to Baghdad, which travelled for much of its way through Turkey.

Most of the detachment were technicians constructing a telephone exchange in a large house near to the border, for use if the Turks agreed to the Ninth Army entering

Turkey to attack the German positions in Greece and Bulgaria.

After checking that my vehicle was roadworthy, I spent an hour or two in the settlement and saw apples, grown in Turkey, on sale. It was the first time I had seen an apple since leaving the *Empress of Canada*.

I did not relish driving and navigating a vehicle all that way back to Deir ez Zor, but it was unavoidable. Before leaving I asked for some spare rations to tide me over in the event of a further breakdown and I prayed that the sun would shine on the following day to give me a sense of direction. Fortunately, the weather held and I reached the camp in time to hear that I had been recalled and was to leave for Aley two days later.

On my arrival at Aley I was told that the CO was away, and that I had to await his return. This gave me the opportunity of getting to know the place better and learn more about my fellow mess members.

Abdul Pearce had been granted leave to visit his wife in Cairo, where she was serving as a switchboard operator at GHQ. But on reaching Haifa, Abdul learnt that his brother, who was serving with the Australian Army, was also there, and decided to forgo his visit to Cairo. He spent a few days in the company of his brother in the bars of Haifa until their money ran out and he was forced to return.

The submarine HMS *Thresher* had gained an envious reputation for the amount of enemy shipping it had sunk in the eastern Mediterranean, and whenever it returned to base at Beirut its ship's company was always sure of a hearty welcome. The petty officers had been made honorary members of the Signals mess and when a party of them visited they invariably let their hair down. The highlight of these parties was always the 'boat race' in which six visitors faced six of our members, each with a pint glass of beer in front of him. At a given signal the first man of each side lifted his glass and drained it. As soon as the glass was replaced on the table the ritual was taken up by the remaining members of the teams, the winners being the first to lay down six empty glasses. To qualify for membership of a boat race team one had to down a pint of beer in five seconds!

On his return I briefed the CO on the situation at Deir ez Zor, he thanked me and said he would do something about it.

By this time the Eighth Army had cleared the Germans from Libya and were fighting to link up with the British First Army and their American and French Allies who had landed in North Africa. The role of Ninth Army became clear.

The Turks had fought alongside the Germans in the 1914-18 War and had proved to be a formidable fighting force. Their defence of Gallipoli had cost the Allied attacking force of Australians, British and New Zealanders thousands of lives, and the Battle of Gallipoli is still commemorated in Australia and New Zealand on ANZAC Day.

So far the Turks had remained neutral but felt threatened by the German forces occupying Greece and Bulgaria. Now the British renewed their efforts to persuade Turkey to allow access to their territory in order to prevent any incursion by the Germans and, when timely, to attack the German positions in the Balkans.

Ninth Army Signals controlled the static communication systems in both Lebanon and Syria, but if the Turks allowed us entry their rather primitive network would have to be augmented. For this reason the line company was busy practising the technique of cable-laying.

Following General Montgomery's success in Libya, the Turks became more receptive. Ninth Army was reinforced with logistical troops and the Ablah squadron was moved to Damascus.

Here we could see that places described in the Bible actually existed. 'The street that was straight' was really a narrow lane crowded with merchants displaying intricate pieces of jewellery made of gold and silver, delicate carvings of ivory and rich silks and carpets made locally by Syrian women. The lane ended at the entrance to the walls of the city called 'the Eye of the Needle', recalling the proverb about a rich man entering the Kingdom of Heaven.

I was not to stay long at Damascus. Major Hill was

recalled to Aley to command the Operating company and was replaced by Major E. R. Nanney-Wynn Nanney-Wynn of Catterick Camp fame. I was to take over as CSM of the line company, and my replacement was CSM Abdul Pearce, who was out of favour with the CO.

Company HQ was at Aley and its sections were spread around the Lebanon and Syria, carrying out construction work and line maintenance of the permanent communication system. One of my priorities was to visit these detachments in order to meet their officers and men and assess their soldierly qualities, and I was not impressed as many of them had no military training. I had met one of them before and was surprised to see that he wore the badges of rank of a captain. When I had last seen him at Meerut in 1935 he was a corporal in charge of the dining-hall – and now was the OC of a line-maintenance section based at Zahle and responsible for the telegraph route through the Bekaa Valley to Damascus. I learnt that he had held the post of Adjutant 10th Corps Signals and had been left behind when 10th Corps moved to the desert to take part in the 1942 El Alamein offensive. To find him reduced to the role of section OC struck me as odd.

Many of the villas in Aley were owned by wealthy traders from Beirut who wished to escape from the humid atmosphere of the town during the summer months, and these had been requisitioned to house the Army. The Grand Hotel was no longer open to the public, but there were some small hotels and a large restaurant providing music and vocalists.

The warrant-officers often visited this restaurant because it gave us an opportunity of talking to the upper class of Lebanese who could brief us on the history of their small country. One of them was a wealthy wool merchant who was cultivating RQMS Bill Ratcliffe, whose home was at Bradford, noted for its woollen industry. The merchant was unable to dispose of his ever-growing stocks of wool because of shipping restrictions and was hoping that Bill would be a useful contact when the war ended.

Drinks at this place were costly and beer was not on sale, so we usually ordered gin and tonic, and as this was consumed it was replaced with just tonic. As we became better known there we introduced our own supply of gin, carried in hip flasks and, although the management was aware of this, no objections were raised, perhaps because the presence of the warrant-officers discouraged the *hoi polloi* from entering.

The principal entertainer was a girl named Sonia. She had learnt some of the catchy wartime songs but her favourite tune was 'And My Heart Belongs to Danny'. Sonia spent long hours at night entertaining the guests with her repertoire and attending to their needs in another way at her nearby flat in the afternoons.

The Army commander was innovative and made changes to working hours, so that his soldiers could benefit from the good climate. The day was split into two working shifts – 8 a.m. to 1 p.m. and 5 p.m. to 8 p.m. This enabled anyone wishing to visit Beirut for a swim or shopping to do so. This arrangement suited one of our sergeants admirably. Jack Lee was a swarthy and muscular Gypsy who had volunteered for service in 1939 and reached his present rank through application to his job. He had become friendly with a WREN petty officer based at Beirut and their friendship blossomed. They were somewhat thwarted because female quarters were strictly out of bounds to males and vice versa. They got round this my making love in the sea, but had they known it the French madam of one of the smaller hotels was always willing to let one of her rooms to approved customers for a modest sum of money.

Another innovation brought in by the general was to insist that everyone, irrespective of rank, was given a compulsory day off work each week to be spent on some form of physical activity. Mine took the form of traversing a deep ravine to the village of Broumanna, the home of our Christian Lebanese canteen contractor. I became quite friendly with John and his parents and it was he who introduced me to arrack. This spirituous liquor takes many forms; in the East Indies it is distilled from rice, in France it is known as Pernod and in Egypt is called Zibib. Its chief property is that when mixed with water it turns milky. John warned me not to drink arrack which was not produced out of grapes, saying that the Egyptians made it out of figs and too much of that was liable to cause blindness.

My trips to Broumanna reached the ears of the colonel, who thought it good adventure training and arranged for the whole unit to make the journey there and back, after a halt at Broumanna for rest and refreshment.

Frequent liaison visits were made to the headquarters by Glubb Pasha, the commander of the Trans Jordan Frontier Force. Following the untimely death of his father the young Hussein, known as 'the little King', was later appointed to the throne of Jordan, and General Glubb was put in charge of his army. He was respected by the Arabs under his command and with his flowing headdress made an impressive sight. As the young King grew up into manhood he was schooled by Glubb in military matters before receiving training at Sandhurst and eventually taking over command of his own army.

Colonel Hardy was becoming irritated at the way his soldiers walked the streets of Aley and decided that they needed smartening up. An area of ground was found and arrangements were made for each section to be given a ten-day battle-training course. The venue for this was a place called Hammana, eight miles up the hillside on the road to Damascus. I was nominated to take charge of the course, assisted by Sergeant Tom Moon, an infantryman who had transferred to our Corps, and between us we devised a programme with the aim of producing smart and fit soldiers at the end of it. Each subsection was accompanied by its own officer, who was encouraged to take an interest – but it was made clear that I was to be in charge of the training.

On arrival at the site we were met by the landowner, a Djebel Druze who spoke good English and went out of his way to be helpful. He lived in a large house nearby, to which was attached a silk factory employing many young local girls. His name was Georgious, or so he said, and not only was he helpful but he was knowledgeable as well and politically well informed. Georgious detested the French who had occupied his country for so long, and described how they would buy up the wedding rings of widows in order that France with its empire could boast of its high gold reserves, second in the world to the United States bullion stored in Fort Knox. His hope was that when the war ended a friendly great power would act as a protector, because the Lebanese feared their neighbour Syria.

The first section arrived for their training. After they erected their tents it was explained that the training would bring them into peak fitness gradually, culminating in a fifteen-mile route march.

Things went well and Tom Moon and I found time to visit the village. We were surprised to find that many of them spoke good American-English and learnt that some had spent years working in the United States so that on their return they could buy a property of their own and raise a family. We met Hoppy, who ran the local tavern and pressed drinks upon us. The fruit grown at this altitude was luscious; grapes, apricots and pears, ripened by the sun and mountain mists, were handed to us. As we sauntered back to camp from Hoppy's place a small elderly man wearing baggy trousers overtook us and we were startled to hear him say: 'Say, boys, how do you like my house, riding the hill like a ship on the ocean.' It really was an impressive place and blended with the contours of the low ridge on which it had been built.

It was not long before Georgious invited me to his house for a meal, but I was wary of going alone and asked if Tom Moon could come along too. This was readily agreed, so we accepted. To describe it as a meal would be an understatement. A massive oak table was piled high with delicacies, including fresh fish and prawns brought up by taxi from Beirut that day. His father sat with us but knew no English, so we showed our appreciation in sign language. The women of the household who had prepared the feast were not in evidence, it being the custom for them to eat alone. Turkish coffee was served and pipes lit up, while Tom and I waited for the proposition to be made.

It was not long in coming. The father owned land in Syria on which he grew wheat. General Spiers, who headed the mission to Syria and the Lebanon, had introduced a levy on wheat grown in Syria and exported to Lebanon, in order to raise revenue, and this amounted to two Lebanese pounds on each sack. All civilian trucks were searched at the border Octroi (Customs) post and the levy collected. The proposal was for me to drive an Army lorry to Syria, collect a load of wheat, wave to the Customs men as we passed by, and deposit the cargo at a prearranged spot near Hammana. My reward for this was to be £100 Lebanese (£12 10s 0 sterling and not much more than a week's pay). Not wishing to offend our hosts after such lavish entertainment, I prevaricated. The son said, 'English man sits there, smokes his pipe, saying Yes, saying No, thinking all the time.'

I think both father and son realised that they had gone too far and we remained good friends. Before we left they bemoaned the creeping effect of inflation and explained that the workers distrusted paper money and at the first opportunity converted it into something tangible, such as building material. They described how at the onset of war a pedlar travelling on a bicycle had visited every village in the Lebanon and bought up all the sewing-needles he could. Items of this nature could no longer be imported, and as clothes had to be darned he was now able to name his price for a packet.

We returned one morning from a four-mile march to find an elderly man wearing European clothes sitting astride a white horse waiting for us at the camp. He introduced himself as Mr Oliver and said that he lived with his wife and sister in a large house within walled grounds at Broumanna. He invited us all to visit him for tea, explaining that all he could offer was good food, fresh air and tea. I thanked him and said I would bring a party that afternoon. The officer declined to come so we piled into a three-ton truck and drove along the track to his home, which resembled a castle.

Mrs Oliver and her sister-in-law entertained the troops while Mr Oliver showed Tom and me around the house. He said that he was a Quaker belonging to the Society of Friends and had been resident in the Lebanon for several years, helping the local Arabs in their education.

I noticed a photograph of Duff Cooper, a former British Foreign Secretary, hanging on the wall. It had been endorsed in his own hand with the message, 'To Mr

Oliver, who helps the Arabs as well as us', and it did not need an intelligence expert to guess that Mr Oliver had by some means alerted the British that only token resistance would be offered if the Allies entered the Lebanon. He also mentioned that a French department in Beirut intended to arrest him, so he visited another French department, which issued him with a visa to visit Palestine. When the security police arrived at his home he was in Jerusalem. He asked us if we had ever visited Palestine, and when we said no, he remarked, 'You must visit the Holy Land.' I knew a smattering of Arabic and whenever I asked the local children if they knew Mr Oliver they all spoke highly of him.

It took two months to complete the training programme, after which my company was involved in more technical matters. Radio communication is fine for the day-to-day conduct of a battle, but the sheer weight of signal traffic demands the provision of permanent telegraph lines to connect forward formation to their base headquarters. Permanent lines involve the provision of heavy telegraph poles spaced every forty yards or so apart, and this calls for manpower in the construction and maintenance of the route. For that reason it is a slow process.

To provide the cables quickly the multi air line poles system was adopted. This involved erecting shorter and slimmer poles capable of carrying up to twelve telegraph lines easily reached from the ground. The company was split up into subsections, with a sergeant in charge to see how many miles of cable they could each erect in one day. This competitive element caused them to vie with each other, and with practice they all succeeded in laying upwards of six miles a day. The importance of good line communication was proved by a test made by Captain Paterson, a peacetime GPO engineer in charge of land communication, when he made a test call to the Eighth Army in Tripolitania. From his desk in Beirut he called the switchboard in Tripoli, Lebanon, and asked to be put through to Tripoli, Tripolitania – 1,400 sea miles away and considerably further by land line – and then instructed the distant operator to switch his call to another extension in his office. To his delight he was able to talk into the mouthpiece of one telephone and listen to his words in the earpiece of the other.

Whenever an army spends a long time in a static area, some of its members become prone to bribery or racketeering. A case that aroused a lot of interest at the time concerned Major Thompson, an RASC officer. His duties involved the control of a large network of transport operation from the Palestine border to Turkey. His first exploit was to smuggle his Egyptian mistress, who was unable to get an entry permit into the Lebanon, in a coffin across two border check-points.

Emboldened by his success, he embarked upon a more lucrative racket. Opium poppies were still being grown in Turkey, but because of wartime travel restrictions the Turks were unable to get the narcotic drug through to a ready market in Egypt – and Major Thompson became the courier. The Egyptian drugs authorities were aware that opium was reaching the country and knew the likely source, so the Egyptian police alerted the Special Investigation Branch of the British Military Police. Thompson was suspected and a trap laid for him. His staff car was stopped at the border with Egypt and a thorough search was carried out, but nothing incriminating found. By this time he thought himself immune, but a second trap was set and this time he was found to be in possession of the drug. He was tried by court martial and sentenced to be reduced to the ranks and to undergo six months' imprisonment. He served his sentence, and then he was conscripted into the Army and posted to the REME workshops in Beirut as a craftsman. He showed no contrition and boasted that he had salted a large sum of money in South Africa by dubious means as a nest-egg.

Another fiddle was taking place nearer home. A small interception unit had been set up under a Guards warrant-officer, a capable wireless operator named Edwards. Its purpose was to detect clandestine radio transmissions made by enemy agents and to report breaches of communication security by our own operators. The reason for an outside operator being used was that dog does not eat dog. Lofty Edwards carried a document, signed personally by the chief of staff, authorising him unrestricted access to anywhere in the Lebanon so that he was not hindered by Military Police checkpoints. His immediate superior was a grade 2 officer on the staff of the Chief Signal Officer who also carried authorisation papers signed by the chief of staff.

It was known to the police that there was considerable traffic in stolen Army blankets, and Edwards with his freedom to travel was suspect. Following the discovery of some of these blankets in a remote villae on the previous evening, the Special Branch descended on RSM Baxter and demanded to speak to Edwards. When the RSM said that he was at Cairo collecting special equipment they disbelieved him. Jack Baxter offered to contact Edwards by telephone; but they were not convinced until a senior officer at GHQ confirmed that he had positively identified Edwards. It was clearly not Edwards who had sold the blankets on the previous evening, so they arrested his controller, who suffered the same fate as Major Thompson.

There were other instances of misuse of Army property in various parts of the country. During their advance across Syria the Allied forces had suffered a set-back at Raqqah when the French still loyal to Laval had defended and then sabotaged the bridge spanning the River Euphrates. A large detachment of Sappers, aided by the Pioneer Corps employing civilian labour, was busy restoring the damage. At this time of the year the river was fordable. An astute staff sergeant noticed the number of Arabs proceeding towards Aleppo either on foot or in donkey carts, so he decided to put one of his idle three-ton vehicles to good use. He offered the itinerant Arabs passage to Aleppo, a hundred miles away, for ten Syrian pounds each way. His venture proved so successful that he had Army benches fitted into the truck, and for this extra comfort he was paid double the standing rate. His scheme only came to light when his OC, on an official visit to Aleppo, noticed one of his trucks and checked up on its unauthorised presence there.

Some of the more affluent Lebanese who owned motor cars were finding that the treads of their tyres were beginning to wear down. Car tyres were unobtainable locally but plentiful in Palestine, and they hit upon a novel way of having their cars reshod. They offered their car to a serviceman travelling to Haifa, paid his expenses while he was on holiday there and gave him sufficient cash to buy five new tyres.

By now the First and Eighth Armies, together with their American friends, had occupied Sicily and gained a foothold in Italy; but they were encountering strong opposition from the Germans, who were in a position to fortify natural obstacles on ground of their own choosing. In order to keep the Germans guessing, the Ninth Army was being reinforced. Many of us thought that this was a bluff to pin down German divisions near the Turkish border and so prevent them being withdrawn to reinforce their army in Italy or elsewhere.

People living in the towns and villages on the coastal road between Beirut and Homs saw huge convoys, including guns and tanks, carried on transporters being driven in the direction of Antioch in Turkey. What the informers living in the coast area did not see were the same vehicles being driven along the valley route to their starting-point under cover of darkness, and after a day's rest repeating the process.

After a week of this manoeuvring it was our turn to move to a tented camp north of Aleppo to undergo military training. This was much needed as the operators had become soft through leading a sedentary life. Three weeks later we were ordered back to base, and it became obvious that the incursion into Turkey had been called off. Our route back was an interesting one and involved passing through or skirting many biblical towns including Latakia, the nearest point to Cyprus, Tarsus, the birthplace of St Paul, Hamah with its great water-wheel still working, and then to Tripoli with its huge oil refineries.

The line company was disbanded and its sections posted to other theatres for constructing and maintaining line routes which had been sabotaged by enemy forces. I was once again without a job, so I found myself posted to the operating company to rejoin Major Hill. The Deir ez Zor detachment had been left very much to its own devices and it was time for it to be revisited. It was now early 1944, and the air as we drove over the desert was chilly. When we reached the detachment we found that it had changed into winter battledress. News of my visit had preceded me, and the sergeants had done some smartening up on their own account, so I did not stay long.

Because daylight hours were now shorter the driver had instructions to drop me off at Ablah and return that day. From Ablah I was to travel back to Aley on the Signals Despatch Service run. As we neared Palmyra I saw a large complex of temporary buildings ahead of us and went on to investigate. It proved to be one of the pumping stations driving oil along the pipeline carrying fuel from the wells of Kirkuk in Iraq to the coast at Tripoli. These European engineers were quite content to live a quiet life in the desert as they were accompanied by their families.

With Damascus behind us we did not have far to go before reaching Ablah, but the scene that met us as we reached the Bekaa Valley was one of devastation. Heavy snow had fallen there and this had turned to ice. The weight of ice on the overhead cable route and the force of the blizzard had caused many of the telegraph poles to collapse, bringing down others with them.

I learnt the seriousness of the situation when I entered the mess. Virtually all communication with Damascus and within the Lebanon had been cut and an embargo had been placed on telephone calls, except those initiated by very senior officers. Calls from the local switchboard had been banned, and I was unable to report my presence at Ablah to my Aley HQ. To add to the chaos, the mountain pass between the two places was blocked by several feet of snow. Fortunately, I was able to contact the Signals detachment at Zahle and heard that their officer was proceeding to Ninth Army HQ to report on the emergency, and I prevailed on the depot commandant to lend me transport to Zahle.

Reports had come in that the valley road to Homs was blocked in many places by snowdrifts so it was decided to drive into Palestine. We travelled south and reached the border post at Metula, manned by the Palestine police, passing Mount Hermon, a majestic snow-covered mountain over nine thousand feet in height, and travelled into Galilee. Rather than go as far south as Haifa we found a minor road which led to Acre on the coast and went on to Beirut. It was a long detour, caused by miles of mountain road being blocked by snow.

During my short stay away from Aley, further developments had taken place. Colonel Hardy had left the unit on promotion to Chief Signal Officer Air Formation Signals, and the operating squadron was being disbanded. Some of the sections were sent to the Greek islands of Chios and Leros, which had been cleared of German troops. But, realising the threat to their forces on the mainland of Greece, the Germans counter-attacked and regained them, and many of the NCOs and men I knew so well were taken prisoner.

Notification came through that I was to be posted to Paiforce (Persia and Iraq Force) with a hint of promotion, but spending another two years in the heat of Basra did not appeal to me and I was able to talk myself out of it. I was instructed to report to the depot at Maadi, where I learnt that I was to retrace my steps a few days later as my posting was to Palestine.

Maadi was unchanged, and after the ritual of medical and dental check-ups I found time to visit the nearby Pyramids of Giza and the Sphinx. Strangely enough, I chose the day when King Farouk of Egypt was on a pilgrimage to the shrines of his ancestors. As his escort and limousine drove past I gave him the courteous salute to which he was entitled as Head of State, and the King returned it with a friendly wave.

Two days later I was instructed to take charge of a party of sixty NCOs and men and proceed by rail to Jerusalem, the HQ of the Cheshire Yeomanry.

15

THE HOLY LAND

My party reached Jerusalem without incident, and when I reported to the adjutant it was to learn that the commanding officer would see me on the following day. As we were only eight miles away from Bethlehem, I asked for transport to take those of the party who were interested on a visit. The shrine, located in the middle of a square, evoked no interest from the few Arabs who lounged outside their shops and stalls. The days of mass tourism were yet to come and it was a tranquil scene without souvenir shops selling their gaudy wares and touts pleading to be employed as guides.

After my interview the CO said that he was sending me to Haifa, where one of his companies was stationed on Mount Carmel. I was disappointed to find that the subunit was accommodated in a large building with very little ground surrounding it, and I could not see the justification for employing a warrant-officer who had been responsible for the discipline of a company of three hundred tough linemen in such a unit. To make matters worse, it was a mixed company with half its strength consisting of ATS – a new experience for me. Fortunately, the CO, having had time to read my record of service and no doubt referring back to my previous unit, changed his mind and I was sent to Sarafand, near Lydda.

At that time Sarafand was a large garrison of support troops and contained, amongst other units, a military hospital. It was completely enclosed and its main perimeter gate was manned by British Military Police.

For some reason unknown, the Cheshire Yeomanry had been sent to Palestine complete with its horses, although it had been proved in Poland that horses, however well ridden, were no match against armoured cars or tanks. The horses had since been shipped to somewhere more useful and the Yeomanry Regiment, although retaining its cap badge, had been retrained to carry out the functions of a Signals unit in a non-operational theatre, thus releasing fully trained signalmen for use in the active areas.

The OC did not impress me. He told me that his squadron was leaving for home shortly, that his was a 'family' unit which he did not want disciplined by a regular CSM. On the other hand, of the sixty NCOs and men I had brought with me from the depot, thirty had been sent to Sarafand to form the nucleus of a new company and I did not want them to fall into the slack ways of the Yeomanry. I learnt that his peacetime profession was a Barrister-at-Law and that he was a Jew-hater. One of his preoccupations was how to get his black Labrador back to the UK as pets were not allowed to travel on troop-ships, but he circumvented this embargo by declaring the animal to be the regimental mascot.

The build-up of the company continued and the new personnel assumed their duties smoothly. With only a few days to go, the OC called a meeting of all those who wore the Yeomanry cap badge, including some specialist members of Royal Signals seconded to the unit because of their skill at their trade. Having assembled the troops in a large barrack room, I was rather curtly dismissed but remained outside the door to listen to his speech. It was then that his hatred of Jews was confirmed as I heard him gloating about how the fishermen of Acre had carried the bodies of Jews impaled on boat-hooks through the streets of the town.

Three days before he was due to leave, his replacement arrived – and when we met I was not encouraged. He was a wartime Royal Signals major straight from a staff appointment and was suffering from severe stress. I wondered how he was going to run the company, but the situation improved a day later with the arrival of Captain Mack Webster, an experienced soldier who had served in No. 2 Wireless Company as a warrant-officer and was subsequently granted an emergency commission. Mack effectively ran the company, and whenever I entered the office and found them on the telephone line it was he who did all the talking and provided all the answers.

Soon after the Yeomanry left, the garrison commander decided that we should move into vacant accommodation nearer his HQ. We were given a barrack room suitable for use as a sergeants' mess and already fitted with a hatch and bar. The floor of the building was made of wood and not in very good condition, so I asked the Royal Engineers clerk of works if he could supply linoleum as a floor-covering. He was unable to do this, saying that linoleum could only be provided to protect polished floors.

Not to be outdone, I assembled all the sergeants and we spent two nights scrubbing the floors until the floorboards were white. The Quarter-Master then supplied some tubs of Ronuk floor-polish, and with the help of some heavy bumpers and a lot of energy we produced a fine polished floor suitable for dancing. This, of course, was the object. There were many service ladies serving in the garrison, not forgetting the nurses at the hospital, who would be delighted to be given an invitation to dance.

When the clerk of works arrived on his next visit and said that as we now had a polished floor he could provide linoleum to cover it, I was less than pleased.

The mess members voted to buy a radio set as a morale-booster because the fortunes of war were beginning to turn in our favour. The Russians, with the siege of Stalingrad lifted, were advancing on all fronts, and so were the Allied forces in Italy. The Jews living in Palestine had formed a Jewish brigade and were fighting on our side in the advance towards the Austrian border. Marshal Tito's partisans were harassing the Germans in Yugoslavia and pinning down divisions needed elsewhere. Allied aircraft continued their attack on Japanese bases in New Guinea, Guadalcanal and the rest of the Solomon Islands.

Lord Haw Haw, Dr Goebbels' stooge, claimed that the aircraft-carrier *Ark Royal* had been sunk (for the fifth time!) by German bombers. The Italians had long bowed out of the war and Mussolini was a prisoner in Allied hands. The cost of conducting the war had escalated to

£14 million pounds a day in 1943 – a huge increase on the figure of £5 million announced by Churchill in 1941, when a fighter aircraft could be produced for £5,000 and a tank for £25,000.

It is generally accepted that leadership starts at the top; but no matter how good the leadership, the efficiency of a military unit can be made or broken by the quality of its senior NCOs. Was it not Napoleon who said, 'Give me French officers and British soldiers and I can conquer the world.' It was my aim to preside over a contented sergeants' mess, in addition to the somewhat mundane responsibility of taking parades, arranging duty rosters, enforcing discipline, inspecting the cookhouse and barrack rooms, keeping an eye on the sick-reports, organising sports events, ensuring that the men's turn-out was good and any other matter needing attention.

On first moving to our new location I noticed that we were close to a large complex of buildings engaged in the production of mineral water for the NAAFI, so I paid a courtesy call on the manager. He gave his name as Ernie Grunsell and said that the depot had existed for years under his management. I told him that we held a coffee-break in the mess at 11 a.m. and gave him a standing invitation to join us. Ernie said that he preferred beer, so the bar was opened for him to indulge in his favourite beverage. It was a good move on my part because Ernie held officer status in the NAAFI, and it was not long before I was invited to his home for Sunday lunch and to the NAAFI officers' club. The members were really civilians in uniform, but to denote their status they wore an embellishment on their shoulders resembling military stars.

My introduction to their club brought further benefits to our mess. Although beer was nominally rationed, it was usually available as not all messes took up their allocation. One brand, Globus, was not popular, whereas Crown beer, imported from Egypt, was always in short supply because of the demand for it. As a result of my contacts with the NAAFI managers, my caterer always managed to return from the store with more than our fair share of Crown. This caused some embarrassment at a garrison welfare meeting when a unit representative asked why it was that visitors to the Signals mess were served with Crown beer, to which I unblushingly replied that we always saved the best beer for our guests.

It is a truism that an Army marches on its stomach, and for that reason the messing arrangements were not neglected. We were fortunate in having two cooks and three waiters, all of them Italian prisoners of war who preferred life at Sarafand to repatriation to their homeland. Here they had freedom of movement within the confines of the camp, and their work was congenial.

The Italians were housed in hutments quite close to us, and from the sound of music emanating from their area it was evident that they could boast of a talented orchestra. Their OC was a Jewish captain, and with future mess entertainment in mind I asked him if we could engage his band. He agreed to this, providing a small donation was made to the band fund and that we promised to return them to their barracks before curfew.

The seaside resort of Tel Aviv was a mere twelve miles' distance from the camp, and transport was provided at weekends for those off duty to bask on its splendid beach or swim in the warm water of the Mediterranean. The young Jewish girls disporting themselves on the sand were attractive and often ogled by the younger soldiers, to the evident annoyance of the male Jews.

The town of Rishon was a favourite night-spot as its clubs and well-stocked bars were within easy walking-distance of Sarafand camp. The supply of liqueurs was limitless and advocaat seemed to be the favourite drink. Most of us were convinced that this plethora of liqueurs was produced from synthetic materials and the wiser ones gave them a wide berth.

From the operational angle, the company was dispersed widely from Gaza to Haifa on the coast and as far as Jerusalem to the east. Its main function was to operate and maintain telephone switchboards, provide a telegraph network for relaying messages by teleprinter to the Lebanon and those parts of Jordan where British or Colonial forces were stationed, and run the Signals Despatch Service, which carried all official despatches to units within Palestine Command. In addition to this, it was required to operate a train courier service to GHQ Cairo. Because of the incidence of smuggling, a very careful watch was kept on the despatch riders employed on these duties. It was not unknown for a courier to drop a package of drugs from his reserved compartment at a prearranged spot in Egypt and collect his reward later.

Our mess was now well organised and we were ready to entertain visitors. The most popular of these came from the RAF base at Lydda (now LOD airport). They were young pilots who knew how to work hard and play hard and nearly all of them had been decorated for the missions they had flown or the number of enemy planes they had shot down. The RAF boys had a real zest for life; they knew all the party games and the songs, and after they left the mess life seemed dull. One of the snags entertaining the RAF was their transport difficulties – it was easier for them to get authority to fly a bomber aircraft to Cyprus to bring back wine and fresh produce for a party than it was to travel eight miles by road.

The Eighth Army had established a convalescent camp at Nathanya on the coast north of Jaffa, before it moved out of Egypt and Libya. It had served as a rest-centre for soldiers recovering from illness or wounds suffered in battle, but when its usefulness in restoring patients to good health no longer existed it was converted into a leave centre. It was used mainly by soldiers of PAIFORCE who were in need of a break from the debilitating heat of Persia and Iraq.

I received a telephone call one day from Nathanya to the effect that two Royal Signals sergeants staying there wished to spend the weekend with us, and as there was no shortage of dormitory space I agreed they could join us as guests of the mess. They were both linemen by trade and had served with me in the Lebanon. One of them was Sergeant McCann, an athletic type whose speciality was to climb wooden telegraph poles without the aid of a ladder to check the insulation and look for faulty joints in the overhead cables. To do this he wore leg climbers fitted with a metal spike which he would dig into the woodwork as he shinned up to the top supported by his safety belt. It was good to welcome old friends, and the mess members went out of their way to make their stay enjoyable.

The chief clerk, Sergeant Eric Burrows, returning from a duty trip to another unit, caused a surprise one afternoon by bringing along two WREN petty officers. They had been visiting friends at Beirut and had hoped to stay at Tel Aviv and visit Jerusalem before returning to their base at Alexandria. Unfortunately, they were running short of money and, finding holiday accommodation in the resort expensive, asked for a room in our mess. The mess committee bent the rules and offered them a room for two nights, provided they did not expect luxury. At least they were not turned away from our inn!

Eric and I were due for a spot of leave, so we took them up to Jerusalem on the following morning. The girls were interested in the history of the Old City, and we entered by the Damascus Gate. The twelve Stations of the Cross were pointed out to them, and so was Calvary, where a plaque was displayed in English and Arabic which read:

THE GARDEN TOMB

JESUS BEARING A CROSS WENT FORTH INTO A PLACE
CALLED THE PLACE OF A SKULL, WHICH IS CALLED
IN HEBREW GOLGOTHA, WHERE THEY CRUCIFIED HIM.
TWO OTHERS WITH HIM, ONE ON EITHER SIDE WITH
JESUS IN THE MIDST.

We took them to the Wailing Wall and the Golden Gate, and pointed out to them the Mount of Olives, the Garden of Gethsemane and the Dome of the Rock. At one stage two young Arab urchins, unaccustomed to the sight of Naval uniforms and thinking that we were tourists, persisted in pressing their services as guides, and when I told them to go away became abusive and said what they would like to do to 'our English sisters'. It was with difficulty that I restrained myself from banging their heads together. Walking around ancient monuments and climbing granite steps is tiring, and by midday we were ready to return for lunch.

Eric and I took them to Tel Aviv on the following afternoon, and after a stroll along the promenade we sat in a seafront bar and ordered drinks. A young American soldier, wearing the usual two rows of medal ribbons, sat close to us. Wishing to draw attention to himself, he slid nearer to our table. He was ignored until he tried to toy with one of my badges of rank, an imperial crown surrounded by a wreath of laurel leaves. This was going too far, and with my hand on the grip of my pistol I said, 'Out, Yank!' It took him only a split second to reach the door, and by the time I got there it was to see him racing along the promenade as if he was being chased by the Devil. The petty officers were highly amused by this incident when we left them at the railway station to join their train to Egypt.

The RSM who was based at Jerusalem invited a party of us to visit his mess for a weekend and we were pleased to accept. The HQ NCOs lived in a large building within the city and they shared their mess with the Palestine Police CID, whose duty it was to monitor the Jewish elements who were becoming politically active. In a clever move, most of the aggressive members of the community had been persuaded to join the Jewish brigade now serving in Italy, thus leaving fewer potential trouble-makers to be kept under observation.

There were a number of female members present and I got into conversation with an ATS warrant-officer who was the personal assistant to the Chief Signal Officer, Brigadier 'Mutt' Mathews. She had volunteered to join the Women's Service in the summer of 1939 and was surprised that with twelve years behind me I had not advanced further. The explanation was that I had served for a long time in units where vacancies seldom occurred, although quite junior people had gained rapid promotion in Indian units due to their mushroom expansion. She suggested that I wrote a formal letter to the CSO outlining my service and asking GHQ Cairo to review my case. I thought nothing more of it until a letter reached my company saying that my case had been looked into and that I would be promoted as soon as a vacancy occurred in the Middle East.

With the approach of Christmas we were invited to a party being given by members of No. 2 Wireless Company, a specialist unit located at Sarafand but living and operating in their own security compound a mile away from the garrison. The role of this small unit was to eavesdrop on all radio transmissions made from sources in the Middle East, analyse them and re-transmit anything of intelligence interest to the boffins in the UK for further evaluation. Their operators were all experts and many of them were linguists. Because of the secrecy of their job they did not often fraternise with signallers from other units, but Christmas was an exception. One of their number on the administrative side was their Quarter-Master, who was reputed to have spent some time at Aldershot acting as a sanitary orderly. This involved walking round the barracks carrying a spiked stick with which he impaled cigarette packets or any trash dropped by careless soldiers and depositing them in a rubbish bin.

A message was received on 1st January 1945 that I was to report to 5 Air Formation Signals as RSM as soon as I could hand over my present job. We had a terrific party on the night before I left, and the Italian band excelled itself. The Italians are by nature excitable and emotional, and when I said goodbye to Tony, our head waiter, and his staff, they almost burst into tears.

I did not have far to travel because the unit I was to join was stationed in Jerusalem. My new CO explained that his companies were widely dispersed and that we were to concentrate in Egypt before returning to the UK by sea for redeployment.

The HQ travelled by train to the Delta, where offices were found for the staff and tented sleeping accommodation for the soldiers.

16

HOMEWARD BOUND

It took a week for the four companies to hand over their local responsibilities and join the RHQ, but at last we were ready to embark. Although I was now in a position to censor my own letters, subject to base censorship, I had not written to my wife about this move, not even a coded message, which proved to be just as well. With Italy out of the war it was safe for our shipping to travel unescorted through the Mediterranean, and instructions were given that we were to travel on a ship leaving from Port Said. The movement-control staff provided a special train made up of open coaches for the journey. As the engine puffed up a slight gradient we were to meet further embarrassment. Suddenly two Egyptians jumped into the coach from the level embankment, grabbed a rifle each and were back over the top before anyone could stop them. The loss of firearms is a serious matter and the irony was that they were stolen from the carriage in which I was seated.

On arrival at Port Said we embarked on a vessel bound for the UK, its first scheduled stop being Taranto in the heel of Italy. The Mediterranean, considered by some to be a placid sea, was at its worst and our progress was slow. It was not until we reached the Ionian Sea, separating Greece from Italy, that conditions returned to normal.

It was late in the afternoon before we reached the naval base in which Mussolini's fleet had sheltered for so long – and it was a depressing sight. Considerable damage had been done to the shore installations through shelling by the Royal Navy and aerial bombardment by Allied aircraft in diversionary attacks to make it look as if the invasion was planned for the mainland and not Sicily. To make things worse the docks reeked of urine.

There was no reception party to meet us, not surprisingly, because the ship was overdue by days. Darkness had fallen by the time all the troops had disembarked and in the meantime a movement-control officer appeared with the depressing news that our party was to move to a transit camp two miles away, and as no transport was available except for baggage, this meant marching. Moving five hundred men by road through unlit streets in a strange country is not the easiest of exercises, but the danger of the troops being mown down by a poorly lit lorry was lessened when a dozen or so hurricane lamps were provided – enough to indicate the head and tail of the column and a few for the flanks. By the Grace of God the procession reached the temporary accommodation without injury, and by this time everyone was ready to bed down.

A further change of plan was announced on the following morning when we learnt that the unit was being moved to a permanent camp near to the port of Bari, and the sceptics thought that this was an odd way of returning to the UK via the Mediterranean Sea. We were transported back to Taranto and had a lengthy wait before a train was provided to take us to our new destination.

It was not a pleasant journey, there were constant hold-ups for long periods, the carriages were unheated and although southern Italy is generally warm, it was now mid-January. One of Mussolini's boasts was that he succeeded in making the trains run on time, but the driver of this one let him down.

We arrived in the camp on the following day and there was clearly uncertainty about the unit's future. It was resolved when the CO was summoned to the area HQ at Naples. He returned with the news that his unit was to remain there until it could join a large convoy forming up at Bari. The change of plan had been made because although the Mediterranean was free of enemy submarines, some still lurked in the Western Approaches and a naval escort would be provided at Gibraltar to see it safely home.

A further change of plan involved individuals. One of

the company commanders, Major Kelly, whom I remembered from Catterick Camp as a lance-corporal drill instructor, CSM 'Topper' Brown, who joined us as a reservist at Bulford, and I were all to report to No. 2 Air Formations serving in Italy. No explanation was given, except in my case and I was told that I was relieving an RSM no longer fit for duty. It took a few days before transport could be spared to take us to our new unit, and in the meantime I explored the countryside.

There is a saying that south of Rome Africa begins, and indeed the area surrounding us was barren and the local inhabitants poverty-stricken. The messing-officer of every military unit is obliged to negotiate a local contract for the sale of kitchen waste and by-products. This is known as a 'swill contract'; the swill is fed to pigs and the cash received from the sale credited to the messing-account for extras not normally issued as rations. With the purchase of a piglet in mind, I followed the swill contractor to his piggery. I never reached it because within a mile of the camp I saw his vehicle stationary, with a crowd of Italians formed up beside it. The sight shocked me; he was delving into the swill barrels and selling our kitchen left-overs to human beings at so many lire per can.

The day dawned when a driver reported to convey us to a place called Macerata, just over two hundred miles from Bari. We travelled along the coast road, passing through Barletta, Cerignola, Foggia and Termoli. There were signs of fierce fighting having taken place along this route, with damaged buildings and bridges destroyed by the retreating Germans in their effort to delay the advancing Eighth Army. Burnt-out tanks and damaged guns littered some areas, and where bridges had been blown up we had to cross the rivers over Bailey Bridges hastily erected by the Royal Engineers.

There was little traffic on the road, most of the serviceable transport having been commandeered by the retreating Germans to replace their damaged trucks, and after five hours' motoring we arrived at the small town of Civitanova and turned inland to our destination.

The unit was commanded by Lieutenant-Colonel F. K. 'Ginger' Morton, who was much older than me. He had been commissioned shortly after the Great War and had served at regimental level with distinction. He was assisted by a major with a name sounding like Lovejoy, and a young captain as adjutant. The unit consisted of a regimental HQ and a company HQ based at Macerata, with its three companies deployed at Ancona and Leghorn and in the South of France. The Macerata company consisted of skeleton staff, and Major Kelly, to his digust, was given command of it. He was so incensed with being diverted to Macerata that he had confided to me he was finished with work until his repatriation. With a staff of ten NCOs and men, it was unlikely that he would find anything to do, especially as CSM Topper Brown was posted as his sergeant-major.

The role of an air formation unit was to provide internal communication for the RAF on their airfields in forward locations and to their rear formations. Wireless was unsuitable for this because speech was insecure and almost certain to be overheard by enemy intelligence, and land lines, temporary or permanent, were the only practical means of linking the switchboards to their extensions. The maintenance of these lines depended on the linemen, many of them GPO-trained, who had to work in open country and were often subjected to ground strafing by enemy planes, and the efficiency of a unit depended upon their skill.

Topper Brown recounted that when he was serving in Egypt his company was partially overrun by a German column. Hearing of this incident, their colonel, Burgess Winn, who had spent some time at Trimulgherry in India, paid a visit to assess the damage. The OC, in an effort to play down the extent of his casualties, reported no officers lost and only two linemen. 'Officers,' stormed Burgess Winn, 'I can get half a dozen officers from Cairo tomorrow, but linemen, they are gold, they're gold.'

When the CO interviewed me he confessed that there was not a great deal to do there. The company commanders of the detached companies were operationally responsible to their own RAF HQ and, apart from sending casualty reports and other documentary returns to Macerata, they were independent. It looked as if my job in life was to keep thirty or so men in order and to accompany the CO on his Saturday morning inspections of MT and the men's bed spaces. There was a further duty, he went on to explain. The current policy was to be nice to the Italians, and to encourage this friendship unaccompanied girls were invited each Sunday afternoon to dance with the soldiers in their common-room. It was one of my jobs to act as MC and see that the proprieties were observed!

The orderly room of a unit is where all records are kept and documentation takes place. It is normally supervised by the chief clerk, usually holding the rank of sergeant, and for some reason unknown my new unit carried two of them on its establishment. When I handed in my documents to the senior one, he noted my length of service in the Middle East and said that I was the next one in line for LIAP. Seeing my puzzlement he explained that a new system of leave to the UK had been introduced and that the longest-serving men in the Middle East or Central Mediterranean Forces were being granted two months' leave to the UK. LIAP was an abbreviation for Leave In Advance of Python, the latter being the code-name for repatriation. Once again I was to be deprived of this concession, for in the very month that I arrived in Italy it was withdrawn.

Although 2 Air Formation Signals was the only military unit living in the town itself, one or two others were sited on its outskirts. I learnt that an officer referred to as 'the Town Major' had a small office nearby, so I paid him a visit. His job was to act as a liaison officer between the military and the local authorities and to requisition any land or property needed for accommodation purposes. He was effectively the military governor of the allied military government. The Town Major told me that there were two large units encamped within his area, one being a South African field ambulance and the other the rear division of 1st Armoured. I wasted no time in visiting the latter and was delighted to find that my friend Tim Cole and the talented chef Paul Gaultier had survived the bloody battles they encountered on the long march from El Alamein to Macerata. One of the first things that I spotted was the wireless receiver brought out from England which I had given to Tim in the Nile Delta and which still worked. Paul Gaultier, the chef who could provide an appetising meal out of Army rations, was in good spirits now that he had access to wine rather than the occasional bottle of gin that I had provided him with. He had strong views on mixing drinks and was contemptuous of the gin and lime favoured by ladies of that era. 'Gin,' he pronounced, 'is an enlivener but lime juice is a depressant, so why mix the two.'

I little realised that he was to rise to the top of gastronomy and to have a chapter included in *The Scallop*, published by the Shell Transport and Trading Company in 1957 to celebrate its diamond jubilee. The chapter was headed 'The Scallop at the Table' and described the innumerable ways of preparing succulent dishes out of shellfish. By this time Paul had been elevated to membership of the Institute of France and was President of the Academy of Gastronomes.

Macerata was built on high ground and renowned throughout Italy as a seat of learning. The university buildings were constructed of stone and its walls were almost completely surrounded by a broad carriageway best described as a promenade. It was the practice for the inhabitants to dress up in their finery every Sunday evening and parade in an endless stream up and down this 'promenade'.

Our HQ was located in a very old building, said to have been the municipal offices, which stood in a cobbled square within the town walls. It was secured by massive iron gates and guarded by one of our soldiers until midnight, when the sentry locked the gates and was allowed to rest but remained on stand-by in case of an emergency. Above this entrance door stood a large balcony from which Mussolini had addressed the throng below, when his words were still being taken seriously.

The soldiers' accommodation was generous and our mess comfortable. The kitchen was on the ground floor and meals were sent up to the dining-area by dumb waiters. The room used for Sunday afternoon dancing must have been where the municipal council deliberated.

The offices were no less lavishly furnished and mine was spacious and next door to the CO, who shared his with the second-in-command, Major Lovejoy, with whom I was to cross swords a few times. The first clash happened when I had occasion to march an NCO before the CO for some minor disciplinary hearing. A private soldier when marched in on a charge is deprived of his headdress and his belt to prevent him using them as missiles if found guilty and sentenced. This ruling does not apply to non-commissioned officers, so I marched in the defendant, properly escorted and wearing his beret. The case was dealt with and, after the hearing was over and 'CO's orders' dismissed, I entered their office to retrieve the charge sheet, whereupon the second-in-command said, 'That was very good, Mr Thomas, but you marched him in with his cap on.' I replied with some asperity that an NCO always wore his headdress when arraigned before his CO on a charge. As I spoke to him I saw Colonel Morton hiding a grin behind his hand. After this incident I wondered where the previous RSM had learnt his military law – and also where the second-in-command had gained his regimental experience.

Within a month of my arrival the CO departed to take up another appointment, but before leaving he expressed his satisfaction at the improvement in the turn-out and deportment of the soldiers.

I learnt that the Quarter-Master – a captain who had served during the last war and subsequently joined the Territorial Army, only to be called up on mobilisation – was paying a visit to one of the detached companies at Leghorn, and I expressed a wish to travel with him.

It was not his first visit and he knew the way. We followed the route over the backbone of Italy and passed through some mountainous country with snow glistening on the distant peaks, and after skirting Lake Trasimeno in Tuscany reached the west coast and travelled north to Leghorn. As far as the QM was concerned it was a courtesy visit, but in the two days spent there I was able to make an assessment of their qualities.

Their CSM told me that the Leaning Tower of Pisa was quite near and on the road to Florence, so I suggested to the QM that we returned by another route and he readily agreed. I had learnt at school that the Leaning Tower was one of the Seven Wonders of the World, and I had photographs of it – but these did not capture the size and grandeur of the edifice. It was immense, and as we climbed to the top the effort tested our fitness to the full. It was well worth the exercise; the view, extending as far as Leghorn on the coast and the ancient City of Florence inland, was superb. It was thought at the time that it was leaning over too far and that it would soon topple over, and yet fifty years later it is still standing.

From Pisa we travelled east to Florence, skirting the River Arno, which had proved such an impediment to the Allied advance, and eventually reached that beautiful city known worldwide for its art treasures. Both the Quarter-Master and I were pleased that we had made the detour and added to our knowledge of historical places.

I arrived at my office one morning to find the previous night's sentry waiting to report an unusual occurrence. He said that there had been a disturbance in the square during the early hours involving the local residents, and when I enquired into it later a grim story unfolded itself.

It appears that one of their number collaborated with the Germans and had informed them of the whereabouts of Italian partisans operating from the region. As he had no means of sustenance he decided to return home and beg for forgiveness from his family. The family did not show any mercy and denounced him to the neighbours, some of whose sons were harassing German positions to the north. Aided by the priest, they tied him with a rope to the tow-hook of a car, then drove around the cobbled streets, dragging the collaborator behind until life was extinct.

Two well-dressed Italians called one morning and I was asked to help them with their problem. They introduced themselves as the Count and Countess de Costa and explained that they wanted to retrieve some of their property stored in a building belonging to them which had been requisitioned by the military for use as offices. I told them that I would obtain authorisation from the Town Major for its release and suggested that they return within a few days to hear the result.

The Countess was delighted when told that she was free to arrange the collection of her goods, and invited me to their villa for tea. Although nearing middle age, the Countess was vivacious, cultured and spoke excellent English. The Count was much older than her and seemed to resent her high spirits, but he welcomed me to their villa with its well-tended garden decorated by goldfish ponds and with peacocks strutting on the lawns. As we sipped tea out of delicate Meissen cups, it occurred to me that the Countess would have welcomed the attentions of a younger and more virile man.

Encouraging news was being broadcast by the BBC on the progress of the war. The Russians were now fighting on German soil; the Americans and British, with the setback of the Ardennes behind them, were crossing the Rhine; and the Free French under General de Gaulle had liberated Paris. Even in Burma the tide had turned against the Japanese and they were on the retreat. Rumania, facing the threat from Russian Forces in the Ukraine, had also defected from the German cause.

Plans were now in hand at the War Office to repatriate the longest-serving members of the Army, and the method adopted was the 'age and service group' system. Our Quarter-Master, whose age and service group was assessed as No. 3, was the first to leave us. He was replaced by Major (QM) Michael James Noonan, known throughout the Corps as 'Jimmy', and I was pleased to see him. The rumour spread that he had been involved in an argument with an American officer whom he had struck on the head with a field telephone, but I doubted this as a man of his physique would not have needed a telephone, even to fell an ox. Major Noonan, of course, had been my RSM at Quetta and I had also served on his staff at Bulford.

I was beginning to feel guilty at not visiting the South Africans who were camped so near to us and decided to call on them. They were a fine bunch who came from the Cape Province and were longing to return there. The Italian winter did not suit them, and to lessen its effects their people had spent hours knitting Balaclava helmets, woollen gloves and scarves – which they did not now need as they hoped to return home soon. They had originally volunteered to serve on the continent of Africa only, and now felt that they had done their share. I was given a carton of canvas 'comfort' bags, each of them containing such useful items as razor-blades, bars of soap, face-towels, packs of playing-cards and darning-wool to take back and share among my men. One of their warrant-officers gave me a Sam Browne belt and another one a pair of *Veldt-Schoen,* brown African field boots. They were so generous that I was prompted to return their kindness by inviting them to a dance at Macerata.

The Town Major arranged for the use of a local school, we hired an impromptu orchestra made up of local instrumentalists and our mess provided cold drinks and pastries for the Italian lady guests. The dance was due to end at midnight, but long before then I was beginning to feel sleepy, possibly because of the number of spiked drinks I had been given, and I cannot remember bidding our guests goodnight.

The twittering and chirping of birds awoke me at sunrise on the following morning and I found myself perched on a high shelf, fully dressed in my blue patrol suit. Worse was to come when I prepared to leave and found myself locked in. There was only one option and that was to open a window and drop to the ground. I now faced another dilemma because the main gate to our building was locked at midnight, and although the sentry slept nearby for emergencies it would not have been tactful of me to disturb him at 6 a.m. to gain entry. The solution was to climb the wall at the rear of the building, tap on the corridor window outside the dormitory and hopefully attract the attention of one of the sergeants.

When I arrived at Macerata I had noticed the tall flagstaff above the balcony with no flag flying. With the end of the war not too far away, I thought it would be an excellent idea to procure a Union Flag, often referred to by newsreaders and press reporters as the Union Jack, so that it could be flown from the mast-head on VE Day.

The only success I had met with so far was to be lent a small silk flag which formed part of the kit of one of our amateur conjurors, but this would have looked insignificant on a high pole. When I tried the Ordnance depot I was told that Union Flags were only issued to drape coffins at military funerals. It appeared that the only option left was to report a fictitious death and stage a mock funeral.

I had by now spent four months in Italy and, although not fluent in the language, understood it fairly well and was able to converse with the local people on simple subjects. The children were very friendly, mainly because any self-respecting soldier did not eat his chocolate ration, preferring to give it away to the *bambinos*. The shops were re-opening and manufactured goods started to reach them from the factories. Some of the shoes displayed on the shelves made us envious but were far beyond our means because of the prohibitive rate of exchange, which at that time stood at 400 lire to the pound.

A bronzed Italian gentleman paid us a visit one morning and introduced himself as Colonel Giuseppi. He said that he was so disgusted by the wanton destruction caused by the Germans in their retreat that he formed a unit of partisans which spent its time disrupting their supplies in Tuscany. His group was well supplied with arms, ammunition, emergency food and medical aid dropped by air and were often given money by the Special Operations agents so that they could buy fresh produce from the hill farmers. The colonel invited me to his elegant villa, where I was welcomed by his charming wife and young daughter, and from then on I became a frequent visitor to his home.

The Russians had crossed the River Oder and their heavy guns were pounding the outskirts of Berlin. The Western Alliance had devastated great cities such as Cologne, Hamburg, Hanover and Dresden by aerial bombardment and the people were demoralised.

The situation was not lost on the German commanders in Italy and 29th April saw the unconditional surrender of all German forces in that theatre of war. By early May Berlin was in the hands of the Russians, and Hitler, in consultation with his chiefs of staff, declared that Germany wished to capitulate unconditionally.

Our first priority once the news was confirmed was to raise the Union Flag to the top of the flagstaff, and when the local people saw it hoisted there was rejoicing in the streets of Macerata. I wasted no time in breaking the news to the partisan colonel, and he was so elated that the wine was brought out and we drank toasts late into the night.

Because the unit was so low in manpower it had been agreed that a victory march through the town was out of the question, but the defeat of the Germans had to be celebrated in some way. The solution arrived at was to hold a football match on the town's sports ground in which the opposing players would wear fancy dress. The problem was how to get hold of costumes, but the Italian domestic staff were let into the secret and by midday they had produced a motley collection of skirts, bodices and other items of female attire which the teams donned on arrival at the ground. The match was not played in accordance with FA rules, and to avoid damage to their opponents' shins ammunition boots were discarded in favour of canvas gymnasium shoes. After forty minutes of play the result was inconclusive, so our uniforms were packed into a truck and to the merriment of the townspeople we paraded through their streets back to barracks.

The question on everyone's lips was 'What happens now?' and it was not many weeks before we knew the answer. As 2 Air Formation Signals were now surplus to requirements in the CMF, the High Command ordered it to an area in the south of Italy pending a decision by the War Office on its future role.

The venue chosen for our concentration was Viesta on the Adriatic coast, and the intention was for the HQ and No. 2 Company to take over a standing camp soon to be evacuated by a unit returning to the UK. The detached companies would join as soon as their commitments to the RAF were ended.

The major had been holding the fort since the departure of the commanding officer, and when he told me of the new plans he said that in deference to the wishes of a new CO he would like our webbing equipment to be coated with buff-coloured blanco instead of our traditional colour of khaki-green. Blanco came in the form of a cake of dried paste which when moistened and applied to canvas with a nail-brush produced the required shade and enhanced the finish of the webbing. The shade favoured by the Infantry was a light brown, possibly in memory of that famous Kent regiment 'The Buffs'. The Corps Committee of the Royal Corps of Signals had from its inception in 1920 stipulated that all canvas equipment should be treated with blanco khaki-green. Perhaps the new CO did not know this, so I told him that I could not support this change as I did not wish to go down in Corps history as a senior warrant-officer who acquiesced in flouting dress regulations. There was another aspect to the matter: man-management. We were not dealing with raw recruits who could be drilled to accept most things; ours were long-serving soldiers, many of whom had volunteered for service in 1939 and were looking forward to returning home. They would not take kindly to the messy chore of removing one colour of blanco and substituting it with another. That kind of provocation was usually reserved for soldiers sentenced to detention in military corrective centres, one of whose nightly tasks was to polish a rusty can until it gleamed, only to have it thrown into a tank of water to rust, in readiness for a repeat performance on the following day.

The new CO, not wishing to lose face, was unmoved by my objections; so I had to resort to subterfuge to circumvent an unnecessary change dreamt up by a passing temporary lieutenant-colonel. All I had to do was persuade the local NAAFI manager that he was out of stock of buff-coloured blanco and that now that the Infantry units had moved out of his area he was not expecting further supplies.

In due course the advance party travelled south to Viesta and the QM and I took over from the outgoing unit. Their RSM warned me that there had been a high incidence of theft in the area, resulting in numerous courts of inquiry. As soon as the main body arrived I instituted a sound method of patrolling the camp, using twelve men as piquets to cover the area in shifts of four. This proved so effective that during our two months there no losses or thefts were recorded.

Our camp was sited in the grounds of a prosperous landowner who was married to an Englishwoman. His chief source of income was derived from the sale of olives grown on his property and at the time of our arrival the fruit was ready for harvesting. Naturally at this time of the year the grass was tinder-dry and harboured midges, which were troublesome but not as harmful as mosquitoes. The CO's next edict was to have the undergrowth burnt to dispel the insects. When I mentioned this to the landowner he was aghast as he could visualise olive trees which had taken generations to grow being destroyed by fire. I told the CO that I would organise the clearing of the ground provided the QM obtained fifty fire buckets and I was given fifty men to organise a fire patrol.

He also had a bee in his bonnet about dust. The road skirting our camp was unmetalled and the occasional passing vehicle raised a little dust, which was soon cleared away by the sea breeze. However, the little amount of dust annoyed him and his solution was to pour barrels of lubricating oil on to the surface to allay it. Throughout the war we had been exhorted to avoid wasting fuel and material goods, because they all had to be carried in ships and seamen's lives were always at risk. Fortunately, Jimmy Noonan came to my aid in this instance and said that he could not countenance wasting valuable engine-oil in order to allay a few specks of dust.

Soon after our move to Viesta we were joined by a chaplain to the forces. He did not impress me; when we met, his handshake, to use a cliché, was like clutching a piece of fish.

I was sitting on my camp-stool one evening reflecting on the events of the day, when the peace was disturbed by the arrival of a small group marching at the double. It stopped at my tent and one of the soldiers reported, 'One padre, under arrest, sir.' I told the men to release him, and in answer to my questioning they said that while visiting the men's latrine the padre had tried to solicit one of them and they decided to carry out a citizen's arrest. I told the padre to return to his tent and reported the incident to the CO. It was a delicate situation which had to be handled discreetly, and in the morning I arranged for the entire area surrounding the CO's office to be cleared. Rather than have two soldiers testify against him, the padre confessed to his importuning and he was despatched that day to Naples to answer to his ecclesiastical superiors.

Marsala is considered to be a Sicilian wine but the grapes from which it is made were also grown in our region. Because the transportation system in Italy had broken down, the wine-growers could find no outlet for it and were prepared to sell it at very low prices. The mess took advantage of this and collected large wooden barrels of wine from the vineyards. The Army ration of spirits and beer had not been increased since Eighth Army days, and although heavy and sweet to the palate, the wine made a good substitute for beer if not drunk to excess.

Load-carrying vehicles were subjected to rigorous security precautions against theft because anyone possessing a three-ton lorry could have collected a cargo of olives and wine at Viesta and sold it at Naples, where there was a dire shortage of cooking-material, at an enhanced price. With the proceeds he could have filled the truck with manufactured items and obtained an astronomical sum for them on the Adriatic coast, where they were unobtainable.

There was further danger from the many bandits operating in the region, and vehicles were not allowed to leave the camp without an armed escort. An appreciable number of Italian-speaking American soldiers had deserted from the forces, some of whom were in possession of automatic weapons. They constructed rough shelters for themselves or occupied damaged cottages near to the coastal road and preyed on individual vehicles using the supply route to the north. They would observe the approach of a lorry from their concealed positions by the road side and if the driver was not vigilant erect a road block and help themselves to the cargo. RASC drivers carrying rations were the most vulnerable victims. Not only did the food supplies sustain the looters but they were a source of income when sold to the local population, who were in need of proteins as most of their dairy cattle and pigs had been slaughtered by the retreating Germans.

By now there was a steady trickle of older men returning home each month under the age and service group system. What concerned the authorities most was that a high proportion of these were commissioned Quarter-Masters category and it was envisaged that twenty-five of them would be repatriated within the next two months. Applications were invited from regimental sergeant-majors to apply for these posts, and my CO urged me to do so. I asked Major Jimmy Noonan, our own QM, for his advice. He advised me against applying, saying that I was young enough and sufficiently senior to be commissioned as a regular Quarter-Master in due course. He recalled that at the end of the 1914-18 War scores of officers holding wartime emergency commissions were demobilised and found it difficult to attune to peacetime conditions. I took his advice and declined the invitation, a decision I was to regret later. However well-meaning, he had failed to visualise the changed circumstances between the 1918 situation and post-1945. The Great War had been very largely a European conflict, and once the Armistice had been signed there was no further part to play for those who had fought on the Western Front, apart from deploying a peacetime force on the Rhine and settling the dispute in Russia. On the other hand the 1939-45 War had been a global war; our military forces were heavily committed overseas and could not be withdrawn easily.

The strength of the Royal Corps of Signals had expanded fourfold from the time hostilities began to its peak in 1945, and with its worldwide commitments it would take years for it to contract to its former establishment. Another aspect was that nearly all the officers and men who had served in the Great War would have reached the compulsory retirement age.

Throughout the war the country had been led by a coalition government headed by Winston Churchill with Clement Attlee as his deputy. Now that the main object of defeating Hitler had been achieved, a political decision was reached to dissolve Parliament and hold a general election, with Churchill heading a caretaker government.

Because so many of the electorate were serving their country overseas, it was decided that the poll should reflect the views of the services. All units were instructed to arrange for polling stations to be set up in their own locations, and ballot papers were distributed to all eligible voters. Suitable instructions were issued on procedures to be adopted and ballot-boxes were manufactured locally.

It took several weeks for the result to be announced but when it did come through we learnt that the Labour Party had won a majority of seats in the House of Commons and that Clement Attlee was to be the next Prime Minister. The analysts of the day attributed the Labour victory to the 'service vote', which had been influenced by the promise of a new Welfare State and the Beveridge plan to provide a free social service for everyone.

Within a few days of the change of government our next commitment was announced. The unit headquarters was to be disbanded but all line companies were to embark for further service in the South-East Asia Command. This came as a blow to some who thought that with the war in Europe over they would be returning home. What they had overlooked was that the Japanese were still holding out in many of our colonies and it was difficult to dislodge them.

Some encouragement was gained when the news reached us of the American atom-bomb attack on Hiroshima on 6th August, when 91,000 Japanese were reported dead. This was followed by an attack on Nagasaki a few days later, resulting in further casualties to the civilian population.

It was now felt that these events would have the effect of shortening the war with Japan, but despite this plans for the movement of the companies to the Far East remained unaltered. They proceeded to the port of Bari for embarkation to India and it was a long time before they were repatriated. The Japanese capitulated on the 15th August 1945 but they had to be cleared from a vast area of South-East Asia, including the Dutch East Indies. Dr Soekarno, with the connivance of the Japanese, declared the independence of Indonesia, which upset the Dutch, and 2 Air Formation were part of an Allied force sent there to disarm and concentrate the defeated Japanese, recover and rehabilitate Allied prisoners of war, and restore order. My late unit was earmarked to restore communications in Sumatra and then went on to Java, where it disembarked at Batavia during October 1946.

The two orderly-room sergeants and I were told that we were being posted to an LOB (left out of battle) camp near Klagenfürt in Austria. The CO had a friend in Venice and he arranged for us to spend two weeks' leave there before reporting to the camp.

As we travelled along the five hundred miles of roadway between Viesta and Mestre we reflected on the difficulties that General Alexander and the forces under his command had encountered on their drive northwards. They had met formidable opposition from the Germans, who could choose the ground on which to fight and whose main aim was to defend themselves from Allied river crossings. They had established the Gustav Line, the Caesar Line, the Gothic Line and the Venetian Line, but despite their determined resistance at Cassino they had been driven back inexorably by the Americans, Australians, British, Indians, New Zealanders and Poles. So much for Churchill's prediction that the second front would take place in the 'soft underbelly of Europe' – or was that to bluff the Germans? As we passed through the towns of Pescara, Ancona, Pesario, Rimini, Ravenna, Ferrara and Padua there were signs that things were slowly returning to normal and whenever we stopped there were vociferous demands for chocolate from the children.

We met some military police at Padua who directed us to Mestre, which was the railway terminal for Venice. The driver carried on to the waterfront and we were met and escorted on to a gondola with porters trailing behind with our baggage. The gondolier, who was hired by the Army, knew our destination and propelled his craft along the Grand Canal to the pier serving our hotel, which was in a *calle* close to the Rialto Bridge.

Our escort, a sergeant in the Intelligence Corps, explained that his CO was the officer in charge of port security and that the modest but comfortable hotel had been taken over to accommodate his staff and guests. The manager was courteous and showed us to our rooms, suggesting that if we cared to take a bath a maid would take away our soiled clothing and have it laundered. The food was exotic after the rough and ready fare at Viesta, and wine was served with every meal.

The Intelligence Corps sergeant briefed us on places of interest and said that an exhibition of old paintings was being held at a nearby academy – and entrance was free to servicemen. As we entered the building we saw notices displayed signed by General Alexander warning that he had guaranteed to the Italians the safety of all works of art. The title of the exhibition was '1000 years of Venetian art', and it depicted some of the earlier history of the island when the inhabitants of the original city fled from the barbarians to swampy land and built houses supported by piles driven into the sea bed. More attractive paintings were portrayals of Venice in the fifteenth century. We were lucky to have seen the Venetian School masterpieces under one roof because until 1945 they had been dispersed widely all over Venice. Many of the priceless ones had been concealed from the Germans because it was well known that Hermann Goering was an avid collector of looted works of art.

The millions of tourists who have visited St Mark's since mass tourism began will have seen the four prancing horses mounted on the terrace above St Mark's Square but these were not in evidence at the time of our visit and for a very good reason. Napoleon Bonaparte captured the copper-gilded statues during the Napoleonic Wars and removed them to Paris. Knowing this, Mussolini, not trusting his German Allies, had them removed and hidden for the duration of the war.

We had been in Venice for two days when I was awakened at 3 a.m. by a terrific din which seemed to come from the harbour. Ships' sirens sounded off and flares and rockets lit the sky. It was the morning of 14th August and the commotion was to signal that the Japanese had surrendered.

Unlike today, St Mark's Square was never crowded. Some of the more enterprising café-owners placed tables and chairs outside their premises, more in hope than expectation of custom, and it was pleasant to sit down to drink a glass of beer. Inevitably our presence attracted the attention of some females whose motives were obvious, but we bought them a drink and chatted to them in our indifferent Italian. There was a marked absence of males, which was understandable, and perhaps that was the reason for the friendliness of the women. Many thousands of Italian men of military age had been held as prisoners of war in England, where they helped out on the farms; in East Africa, where they exercised their skills at road building; in Palestine, where they served as domestics; and in Egypt, where their presence was useful in guarding military depots against the attentions of Egyptian thieves. Although the Italian Government had surrendered a long time ago, there was insufficient transport to return these POWs to their homeland and in the meantime their womenfolk had to remain unsatisfied.

(I revisited Venice with my family twenty-two years later and was amazed at the transformation. St Mark's Square was thronged with people. Children were pestered to buy peanuts and biscuits at exorbitant prices to feed the already overfed pigeons. The square was splattered with bird droppings, and humans were lucky to escape unmarked. I recalled that in 1945 there were few pigeons to be seen and the reason was clear: there was no food to spare and many Venetians snared the birds and ate them.)

Sergeant Barry, one of the Intelligence Corps staff, asked me one evening if I would like to visit a Venetian home. He explained that a young couple who had no entry permit to the island had imparted valuable information to the British regarding documents which the Germans had failed to destroy when they withdrew. They lived in a small apartment on the waterfront and hoped that they would now be allowed to remain. Because the conversation was desultory, we left after accepting a glass of wine and a biscuit.

By the time we crossed the Rialto Bridge it was already dusk. My two sergeants were approaching so I asked them where they were going. Their reply was startling but at the same time it appealed to me. It was their intention to swim across the Grand Canal! It was well known that some of our Commandos had resorted to swimming when capturing the city, but that, as the Americans would say, was 'in the line of duty'. When I said I would join them they were taken aback. We recrossed the bridge, walked to the bank and stripped completely, leaving our host in charge of the garments, and struck out to the other side. When half-way across, a Royal Navy launch came racing up the canal and I alerted the coxswain by shouting 'Ship ahoy'. Clearly recognising an English voice, the reply was terse and to the point: 'You bloody fools'. But he did slow down and we reached the other bank safely. The only problem now was that our clothing was on the distant side, so rather than cross the bridge completely naked we had no option but to swim the canal again to retrieve our kit.

The enormity of what we had done sank in on the way to the hotel. Venice does not possess an underground sewage system and all waste finds its way to the sea. In fact, the canals are the sewers of Venice. I recalled that when in Syria we had been forbidden to swim in the River Euphrates because of the danger of contracting bilharzia, but that river was reasonably clear of human excrement. My first action on returning to the hotel was to drink a tumblerful of whisky to counter any ill effects.

As soon as the news of our stupid exploit circulated around the hotel, someone suggested that there were better places to swim in than the Grand Canal. We learnt that the Royal Navy organised a free launch trip to the Lido each afternoon, leaving the jetty at St Mark's Square at 2 p.m. The Lido is the summer resort for Venice, and within fifteen minutes of leaving the quay we were basking on beautiful beaches in clear sea water as yet unadulterated by industrial waste.

The days passed by quickly and, thinking of buying some souvenirs to take home, I visited the main market area, the *Mercerie*, where goods were displayed on stalls. Apart from exorbitantly priced leather goods, the only attractive items were made of glass, hand-blown on the nearby island of Murano. But most of them were either fragile and intricate and would not stand up to rough handling, or massive vases and ashtrays too heavy to carry in a soldier's kitbag. I had met this problem in Deir ez Zore, where fifty miles away on the Iraq border genuine Persian carpets could be bought for a pound.

My instructions were to proceed to Villach at the end of the leave period, and when we asked for the bill we were told there was nothing to pay apart from settling our bar bill. We thanked our hosts and left a generous gratuity for the hotel staff.

As we proceeded towards Austria the scenery changed and, unlike the flat coastal regions of southern Italy, the mountain peaks of the Dolomites came into view. The air was fresher, animals grazing in the fields were well nourished and the villages were better designed. Our journey was not a long one; only 150 miles separated Mestre and Villach. The first sizeable town we reached was Treviso, followed a little later by Udine, a city boasting a population nearing 100,000 and situated in the region of Fruili-Venezia Giulia. With its good railway system and ready access to Trieste, it had been a prime target for the Allied bombers.

Despite the damage caused to much of the city, many of the buildings designed by the world-famous sixteenth century architect Palladio were still standing. My memories of it are a huge square containing an impressive fountain and a massive clock tower, surrounded by Gothic and Baroque style buildings with beautiful façades.

After a short break at Udine, the driver headed for our destination, skirting Mount Triglav (9,400 feet) as we neared the Austrian border separating Carinthia from Italy, and we came upon road signs directing us to the transit camp, a large complex of wooden huts formerly used by frontier guards and Austrian ski-troops.

The camp seemed to be casually organised and our instructions were to attend the 9 a.m. parade and keep an eye on the notice-board, otherwise we were free to do as we pleased.

My hope was that I should be posted to another unit in Italy or Trieste in my present rank, and for a very good reason. At that time I was an acting warrant-officer I, and to become established in the rank one had to retain it for a year. Having already served nearly nine months as an

RSM, I had no wish to be posted out of the theatre for that would mean reversion to my war substantive rank of warrant-officer II. With this in mind I wrote to a former commanding officer in Naples who thought well of me, and whose RSM had left recently to return to the UK, saying that I was available.

It did not take me long to guess that the camp was designed as a transit base for the sizeable number of men serving at Klagenfurt and Trieste who were time-expired and awaiting transfer home over the recently established 'overland route'. Quite a number were Royal Signals personnel, and I was put in charge of them.

To overcome the boredom of the camp, a group of us decided to exercise ourselves by exploring the area. While out on one of these rambles we met an elderly Austrian gentleman accompanied by two ladies. He was eager to talk to us. He introduced his wife and sister-in-law and explained that he was a baron and had served as a colonel in the Austrian Army. His English was excellent and he invited us to his home. The baron lived in a villa nearby and his wife offered us tea and cakes. We accepted a cup of tea but declined the pastries because we knew that there was a food shortage in that region. He apologised for not offering us a drink and went on to complain bitterly about the behaviour of some American troops who had taken over his villa as a billet and, not content with sleeping in comfortable beds, had raided his cellar and drunk all of his Hennessy brandy. They were so friendly that I asked if we could call on them again, and we did so on the following afternoon. On my return to the camp I told the cook sergeant that four of us would not be in for lunch on the following day and asked him to prepare haversack rations. Carrying a generous supply of food, we descended on the baron's villa. Their eyes lit up when we handed over our rations and asked them to share a meal with us.

The camp had no bar facilities but the Army had taken over a tavern in the town for use as a canteen. Four of us walked there one evening in time to see a barrel of beer delivered and a queue form up. Grasping a half-litre glass each we joined it, and one of us paid for a round. The light Austrian lager tasted like nectar compared with the heavy Marsala we were accustomed to at Viesta, and we drank it slowly – which was to prove a mistake because by the time we were ready for the second round the barrel had run dry. This was a lesson learnt, and every succeeding evening we were there at opening time and each of us held four tumblers by their handles to be filled up.

Villach lies in the Karnische Alps, with a fast-flowing river surmounted by a high bridge dividing the town. Its main tourist attraction was a funicular railway running to the top of a high peak overlooking the town and surrounding countryside. No one was interested in accepting the Italian lire which we offered, so we boarded the cabin along with many local people. The view from the top was breath-taking; in the distance the Gross-Glockner, standing at 12,641 feet, could be seen clearly. Noticing some chalets at the top of the cable railway, we asked their purpose. Fellow passengers told us they were rented out to people wishing to spend a few days there. All they had to do was to take up their provisions and portable cookers, or they could buy snacks from the cafè. We found that on the downward trip there were insufficient seats, so as good ambassadors of our country we gave ours up to the ladies. A breeze had sprung up and the cabin began to sway. I noticed an overhead handle resembling the straps fitted to the London Underground system and reached up to steady myself – until I noticed the looks of fear on the faces of the women. I hastily withdrew my hand, at which they relaxed. Not knowing any German, I had failed to grasp that the red-painted handle was some sort of control which should not be interfered with. It was dusk by the time we reached the ground station, and as the fresh air on the peak had whetted our appetites we decided to return for our evening meal.

As we crossed the bridge I passed a young woman standing on the narrow pavement. My three companions who were following were sure that she spoke, and in English. One of them lingered to speak to her, and told us later that she was a refugee from southern France making her way to Yugoslavia. He was a fast worker and on his return to camp said he had arranged to meet her in the morning after collecting some rations, and that they were spending the day on the peak. I warned him not to miss the 9 a.m. check parade, and for the next three days he returned to camp shortly before 9 a.m. to check in, collect his rations and rejoin the lady at the chalet he had rented on top of the hill.

The camp staff were active on the Saturday morning and it was announced that a large draft would be leaving on Monday to return to England by road. My name headed the list, so I wrote an air letter to my wife telling her to expect me on the following weekend.

Before leaving we were briefed by the convoy commander, who told us that our route was to be via Innsbruck, Ulm, Mainz, Luxembourg and Calais. He explained that we would not be following the shortest connecting roads between these cities because many of the bridges linking them had been destroyed by the Germans in order to hinder the Allied advance.

The three-ton vehicles were fitted with seats and I was fortunate enough to secure one next to the driver, giving me a good view. Normal convoy discipline was maintained and we stopped for a twenty-minute break at twenty minutes to each even hour. After passing through Bressanone, we commenced the steady climb up the Brenner Pass and at 4,500 feet began the gradual descent into Innsbruck, the capital of the Tyrol.

We left Innsbruck quite early on Tuesday because the convoy had to deviate almost to the Swiss border to avoid having to travel through Munich, and after a pause to eat our packed lunches near Lichtenstein we carried on to Ulm in Baden-Württemberg. As we approached it the devastation wrought by the Allied bombers was plain to see. My lasting impression of Ulm was the cathedral standing in the middle of bombed out buildings. It was a tribute to the accuracy of the bombing crews that the cathedral had escaped permanent damage.

The convoy was now travelling through industrialised Germany and for part of the way drove on the autobahns which linked the great manufacturing areas and centres of communication. Because of the damage caused to

German airfields, long stretches of the autobahns had been used as airstrips for their planes to take off and alight, and there was plenty of evidence of aircraft which had been shot down or crashed. The convoy leader skirted Stuttgart and Mannheim and we reached Mainz in the late afternoon.

After a bath and a meal I suggested to some of the men that after sitting for three days in a lorry it was time to stretch our legs. A dozen or so of us left the transit camp, but we had gone less than half a mile before we encountered an unusual smell. Our first thoughts were that it came from blocked sewers but then realised that the sweet and sickly odour came from the houses and noticed that their windows were all bricked up. On returning to the transit camp we learnt the truth from the camp permanent staff, and it was gruesome. The German civil defence workers had not yet been able to dispose of the bodies killed by bomb blast – and had left them where they died until they could raze the buildings to the ground. The reek was decomposing bodies left in their temporary tombs.

None of us was sorry to leave Mainz, and the convoy passed through the small Principality of Luxembourg on its way to the Channel port of Calais.

17

UNITED KINGDOM 1945-47

On the last day of August 1945 a vessel on charter to the Ministry of Shipping left Calais for Dover carrying several hundred soldiers who had taken part in the Western Desert, North African and Italian campaigns, and others who had served in Northern Europe and helped to drive the Germans back within their own frontier. Some of those travelling on the ship wore five medal ribbons and a few sported a ribbon denoting that they had been decorated for an act of bravery.

On arriving at Dover there was no military band to greet us and the WVS ladies appeared to be off duty for the weekend. The British public had long since celebrated VE Day and VJ Day and we felt like members of General Slim's forgotten Fourteenth Army. There were no HM Customs officials to be seen, so it was assumed that they too were enjoying a long weekend. The movement-control staff directed us to a large open space near the dockside, and there we stayed until late afternoon.

When they reappeared I was detailed to take a party of Royal Signals to a holding depot in Yorkshire. It was not until midnight that we boarded and the guard announced that the train was due at York at 3.30 a.m.. It was on time and I had some trouble in rousing the sleepy ones. We were met by a major whose face appeared familiar – Bill Paget, whom I had last seen at Meerut in 1936.

Our destination was Thirsk racecourse, which had been taken over by the military for the duration of the war. A reception party was on hand when we arrived, and it carried out its drill with practised ease. Within an hour of arriving, each of us had been issued with a leave pass, ration cards, return travel warrant and four weeks' pay and ration allowance. We were given a hearty breakfast, issued with packed lunches and conveyed to York station to catch a train to our various destinations. I hoped to be met at King's Cross railway station and, heavily laden with my kitbag and equipment, kept glancing towards the barrier. There was a small crowd awaiting the arrival of passengers, and when I realised that my wife was not amongst them I was in a quandary. I knew that her firm had moved back to London from Milton Court at Dorking and that she was living in a maisonette at Streatham Hill, but I had not thought of asking her its precise location. The ticket-collector advised me to travel on the Underground to Victoria Station, where I could board a tramcar which ran through Brixton to Streatham.

I alighted at Streatham Hill and asked several passers-by if they could direct me to Criffel Avenue. In earlier times the saying was 'If you want to know the time or the way ask a bobby' – but there was none in sight. Eventually someone said he thought Criffel Avenue was half a mile away, but he did not seem to be too sure.

Rather than do a reconnaissance with a sixty-pound kitbag on my shoulder I dumped it on the pavement and went in search of number twenty-six. It was not difficult to find, but when I rang the doorbell repeatedly no one answered, so I decided to retrieve my baggage. When I returned to the tramcar stop I found it guarded by a solid-looking Metropolitan Policeman, who gave me a friendly warning about leaving one's possessions unguarded in that part of London.

Reconciled with my personal kit, I returned to the flat and met another obstacle in the way of a six-foot-high side-entrance gate bolted on the inside. My effort to climb over this attracted the attention of the lady living above, who asked me my business. When I explained, she said: 'The young lady has gone away to Margate for the weekend.' She noticed my disappointment and offered me a cup of tea.

Scaling the wooden side-gate was no problem, and having unbolted it I carried my kit inside and looked around the likely places in which the back-door key might have been hidden. Not finding it and not wishing to spend a night under the stars, I broke a small window-pane and clambered into what turned out to be the kitchen. It did not help when I discovered that the kitchen door was locked and the key was on the other side. It was unfortunate that the larder was on the other side of the locked connecting door, but at least the electricity had not been turned off and the cold-water tap functioned. I had not slept since leaving Calais, so I made a makeshift bed out of my equipment and greatcoat and dozed off until I was awakened by the chirping of the sparrows.

My mother-in-law lived at Upney, and having washed and shaved in cold water I decided to call on her. Naturally, she was surprised at my sudden arrival. Her first action was to telephone Edith at the office and she was released for the day. When she unlocked the front door of the flat the aerogram I had sent from Villach was lying on the mat. She had spent the weekend with her cousin Kathleen at Cliftonville and had not returned to the flat since leaving it on Saturday morning. The ground floor was roomy and not very well designed but my wife had gone to a lot of trouble to furnish it. Household goods were in short supply at the time and people setting up home for the first time were issued with coupons for the purchase of furniture and the like.

Our reunion passed all too quickly and it was time for me to return to Thirsk until my next posting was received. The sergeants' mess was full of long-serving people like myself without a job, but many of us had served together before the war and it was interesting to hear of their experiences. The process of demobilisation proceeded steadily, but up to then only a trickle of time-expired men had passed through the depot and a flood was expected later in the year. The authorities realised that the facilities at Thirsk were insufficient to cope with the numbers involved so it was decided to open up a number of satellite depots nearby, and a selection board was appointed to seek out suitable candidates to form a cadre for the new sub-units. This procedure was dubbed 'the slave market'. I was interviewed by an officer with the unusual name of Goby, who asked for a thumb-nail sketch of my previous experience, and when I told him that I had to drop a rank on returning home he showed interest.

The result was that I was offered a job as company sergeant-major in a new establishment being opened at Kirklevington near Yarm in North Yorkshire. It so happened that Lieutenant Goby was earmarked as administrative officer of this new set-up and he had a few months to serve. We were billeted in a large mansion standing in its own grounds, with Nissen huts dotted around the park for the use of the troops.

Our purpose was to accommodate the men due for release in the near future, relieve them of their arms and equipment, prepare travel warrants for them to travel to Guildford, where they would be issued with a complete set of civilian clothing, and keep them occupied until authorised to release them in accordance with their age and service group.

We were too few in number to form a sergeants' mess, so anyone wishing for a drink had to walk to a nearby tavern. The evenings were dull and I was attracted to a small pub in Yarm whose landlord was on good terms with the brewer's agent and kept him well supplied with beer – unlike the public houses in Thirsk, where their weekly delivery lasted only two days. Mine host had a wooden leg and the loss of his limb caused him to be cantankerous at times. However, his wife made up for his ill humour. The customers were mainly agricultural workers on low wages. As they started work early in the day they did not keep late hours, and for this reason the bar was closed at 9.30 p.m. The favoured ones, myself included, then moved into the private parlour, where business was resumed as usual.

At the stroke of 10 p.m. the local police sergeant would appear. He supervised a quiet 'patch' and his main preoccupation was to track down poachers snaring rabbits, which fetched a good price in those days of strict food rationing. He would remain with us for at least an hour, fortifying himself against the rigours of the hours ahead. Now and again we were disturbed by a loud banging coming from overhead but soon realised that it was caused by the landlord thumping the floor-boards with his wooden leg, a signal for his wife to join him in bed.

The transitees now began to arrive in larger numbers. Many were senior NCOs, so we reviewed our decision not to open a mess. The weather was becoming colder and with the winter ahead the thought of walking a mile to the local pub for a drink settled the matter. The problem was how to acquire a bar, but this was resolved when we heard that Lend-Lease material was being destroyed at a nearby disused airfield. I sent a sergeant there to see if he could find anything useful, and he returned with a truck-load of valuable timber which was to have been burnt. One of our number was good at carpentry and he constructed a magnificent mahogany-topped bar and several stools from the scrounged material.

With the approach of Christmas the Army decided that there was to be no movement of troops from overseas for a ten-day period, and all except a small rear party were granted leave for a week. My wife had written to say that we were invited to her parents' home over the holiday period and I arranged to meet her at Victoria Station.

As we travelled on the District Line to Upney, the devastation caused by Hitler's bombers and V2 rockets was plain to see. Vast areas where houses or factories had once stood had been flattened, and because of the housing shortage many homes had two or more families living in them. However, plans were afoot to provide prefabricated houses with a lifetime of ten years to serve as temporary homes until more substantial buildings could be erected.

Mr and Mrs Clarkson lived with their son Arthur in a modern house in Westrow Drive. It was just a short walk along Upney Lane to the Royal Oak, a well-run pub sometimes patronised by Vera Lynn and Tessie O'Shea.

Edith's mother produced good meals out of the meagre rations that could be bought. Many of the voters at the recent General Election hoped that with a new government all restrictions would be set aside, but if anything the position had worsened. Bread, potatoes and jam were still rationed, and each adult was allowed eight pence worth of meat per week. To discourage caterers from buying food on the black market, restaurant meal prices were limited to five shillings, and coupons had to be surrendered when purchases of clothing, boots and shoes were made. Petrol rationing was still in force, restricting the movement of motorists and traders.

As time went on I became disenchanted with my job, which was routine and did not provide a challenge. Each day dozens of soldiers reported in to be processed for their release, only to stay for a few days and be replaced by others. The only consolation was that I was stationed in England and entitled to three travel warrants a year. On the other hand, the strength of the Corps reached a peak of nearly 150,000 officers and men in 1945, compared with the Regular Army total strength of 160,000 in 1939. Although by March 1946 several thousand of the surplus had been released, the end was not yet in sight and I had no wish to serve for much longer in a non-productive unit.

I delayed asking for a move until May, when I applied to be sent to the Home Counties. A replacement was found for me, and I was instructed to report to a special communications unit stationed on the outskirts of Leatherhead. This suited me admirably because Edith had lodged at Westcott while working at Milton Court, and Leatherhead was only nine miles distant. We agreed to sublet the maisonette and she moved into a cottage owned by an eccentric spinster named Florrie. It did not take me long to be granted a 'sleeping-out pass', which was conditional on not using public transport between workplace and home. This restriction was easily overcome because my wife had been a keen club cyclist before the war and lent me her machine.

There was less to do operationally at Leatherhead than there had been at Kirklevington. The sub-unit was commanded by a captain aided by a subaltern, and they spent their time in the office. They were assisted by a quartermaster sergeant, a section sergeant and a dozen or so storemen, drivers, clerks and batmen. The headquarters was at Bletchley Park, where the country's experts worked on decrypting German secret wireless traffic, aided by an Enigma machine which, unknown to the Germans, had found its way into Allied hands. It was at Bletchley that the special operators, many of them linguists, were trained, and most of them were deployed behind enemy lines intercepting coded messages. On becoming proficient in their trade they were sent to Leatherhead to learn the secret of survival in hostile country and trained in the use of firearms and unarmed combat. Now that the war was ended the sub-unit was used solely to debrief the special operators returning from their overseas assignments.

I had not been long at Leatherhead when I read an Army Council Instruction stipulating that peacetime qualifications for promotion were to be reintroduced in 1947, and that anyone holding the rank of warrant-officer II would need a 1st Class Certificate of Education and a first-class trade rating to be eligible for promotion to WOI. I had passed the former but my trade rating remained as electrician/fitter class 2. With the growth of mechanisation my earlier trade was now designated as vehicle mechanic, which was less skilled than the former one because it did not need electrical knowledge.

When I applied to be trade-tested as a VM class 1, it came as a shock to learn that my first trade was obsolete and that I would have to qualify as a mechanic. I protested to the officer in charge of records, but he was adamant. In due course I joined a class of recruits at an MT school run by the Royal Electrical and Mechanical Engineers at Bordon Camp in Hampshire.

It was while I was attending this course, learning afresh the mysteries of the Otto cycle, double-declutching and carving bits of metal, that news reached me of the birth of my daughter Patricia. I asked the OC for a day's leave to visit her and received the set answer: 'No leave permitted whilst attending a course', so I mounted Edith's cycle and rode to the Dorking nursing home where she was confined. She was well, and when visiting hours were over I cycled back to Bordon in order to attend class in the morning.

The only new thing I learnt on the course was how to drive a tracked vehicle as opposed to a four- or six-wheel truck. When the result of the trade testing board was forwarded to my CO at Bletchley Park, he learnt that I had achieved the highest marks ever awarded on a course and was graded as class 2. He promptly wrote to the commandant of the REME school saying that in view of the excellence of the report he failed to understand why I had not been graded class 1. The reply was that class 1 was only awarded to those with long practical experience. I had passed my class 2 rating at Meerut twelve years previously and had spent eight years on the maintenance of transport!

On my return to Leatherhead I learnt that the sub-unit was to be disbanded, news that did not surprise me because its *raison d'être* no longer existed, and I was asked to combine my duties with those of the CQMS, already released. My additional responsibility was simply to arrange for the return of our technical stores to Bletchley Park and the accommodation stores to Ordnance. Ultimate responsibility for stores was vested in the QM, who held an emergency commission and did not appear to me to be very bright. On one of his visits he confessed to being worried about a shortfall of 900 blankets which had gone astray through laxity on the part of his staff in allowing released soldiers to take their blankets home instead of handing them in. At the very least the loss of such a quantity would have resulted in a court of inquiry to determine who was responsible, so he had good cause to be concerned. He cheered up when I suggested a possible way to cover up the discrepancy and took my advice. On the next occasion that he returned stores to the depot he should include 100 blankets in the consignment but show the figure of 1,100 on the issue and receipt vouchers. If the discrepancy was noticed by the Ordnance staff his representative was to apologise saying that it must have been a typist's error which had passed unnoticed. He got away with it because on the afternoon the stores were returned, the Ordnance crew was engrossed in the radio commentary of an important race meeting and could not bother to check the items. One of their number indicated where the stores should be unloaded, signed the receipt voucher and hurried back to the radio, so instead of a deficiency of 900 he ended up with a surplus of 100 to meet further contingencies.

Gradually the personnel departed and I was left with a storeman and two drivers. For the sake of security we moved the remaining stores into one Nissen hut. One of the items that caught my eye was an easy chair which would have fitted in well at our Streatham Hill flat. It bore no resemblance to the standard Army issue, and I asked the RAOC accountant if he could overlook its disappearance only to receive an emphatic 'No'. The piece of furniture was registered as Lend-Lease and not only had President Truman stopped shipping aid immediately the war ended but the Americans insisted that all stores in situ in the UK supplied under the Act were to be destroyed.

The winding-up continued without a hitch and it came as no surprise when I was asked to remain with the special communications unit but in a different location at High Barnet. Edith and I discussed our next move, and as my post was at the end of the Northern Line we agreed to return to Streatham Hill. When we told our landlady Florrie of our intentions she was upset. She had become very fond of Edith and had lavished care on her during the wartime years. She was well known locally and on good terms with the small village shopkeepers and farmers, from whom she could wheedle a few extras to provide appetising meals, and before leaving I assured her that she would be welcome if she cared to visit us once we had settled in.

My new place of work was a large country house standing in an extensive orchard bordering a quiet road leading to the film studios at Borehamwood and ten minutes' brisk walk from High Barnet Station. If I left home at 7 a.m. and walked a mile to Balham Underground Station, it was possible to reach my office before 9 a.m., and it was rare for me to return before 7 p.m. The fares were expensive but there were concessions for servicemen travelling in uniform. Even so, the cost of travelling to work reduced the amount of housekeeping money I was able to hand over and Edith found it difficult to manage, so in order to make life more comfortable she rented the largest of the the three bedrooms to a lady who became a lifelong friend.

Here again the work was routine and dealt with the reception, debriefing and release of the special operators, and the atmosphere was decidedly non-military. I felt that

I was filling a vacancy rather than doing a job, but fortunately the inevitable happened and we were earmarked for closure.

Shortly before we were disbanded the officer in charge of records wrote to say that my next posting was to be War Office Signals. This news raised my morale, which had slumped because of the insecurity brought about by serving short periods in units that had no prospects. War Office Signals provide the communications for what is now known as the Ministry of Defence, and its long-term future was assured. The location also suited me because it occupied several large requisitioned houses in Eaton Square and Eaton Place, so less time would be taken up in travelling to and from work, with the added bonus of less expenditure on fares.

The unit's main attraction as far as I was concerned was that it was staffed by a large proportion of regular officers and NCOs but, like everywhere else in the Army, these were supplemented by National Servicemen, some of whom were very proficient at their trade. My initial interview was with Lieutenant-Colonel Tozer, the CO, who welcomed me and stressed the importance of maintaining a high standard of discipline and deportment, before assigning me to No. 1 Company. My new OC, Major C. D. 'Daddy' Hinds, was an elderly officer born at the turn of the century who had spent most of his service in remote places like Mesopotamia and India. My brief was to relieve CSM Lee, and by a remarkable coincidence the name of the RSM was Lea. Jack Lea and I knew each other well from the days we spent at Bulford barracks in 1939, and he told me that he had recently returned from Nairobi after spending most of the war years there.

Because of the shortage of barracks in London and the limited number of private houses that could be requisitioned, most of the rank and file were encouraged to live in private accommodation. Even so, my company occupied two very large town houses in Eaton Square, with the HQ taking up a third and the sergeants' mess a fourth.

The role of No. 1 Company was to provide switchboard and teleprinter operators to enable the War Office to keep in touch with all its subordinate formations both at home

A camel train in the north west frontier of India.

The Indian frontier.

A herd of rhinoceros on the slopes of Mount Kilimanjaro (courtesy Juanita Carberry).

Buffs cholera grave at Meerut, India.

The Taj Mahal, Agra.

The band of the Royal Corps of Signals at a Blandford function (courtesy Royal Signals Museum).

The guard at Buckingham Palace provided by the Royal Signals (courtesy Royal Signals Museum).

The 'White Helmets' display team (courtesy Royal Signals Museum).

Iced-up radio masts at Mount Olympus in Cyprus
(courtesy Royal Signals Museum).

The MV *Geestport* leaving for South Georgia in the Falklands (courtesy Geest plc).

QUETTA EARTHQUAKE 1935.

The ruins of a mosque in the city area.

An RAF biplane torn from its anchorage by the force of the quake.

The late Brigadier Henry Crawford jumping over a bar drawn between two motorcycle despatch riders of the Royal Signals (courtesy Royal Signals Museum).

and overseas. The communications centre where they operated was deep underground in a building which we called 'the Citadel'. It was in this complex that Churchill's War Cabinet met because of its immunity from German bombs. The Citadel also housed a large cipher section responsible for encoding and decoding messages of high security classification. The cipher operators were no longer dependent on the code-books and one-time pads in universal use in the early days of the war, because the boffins had developed sophisticated machines capable of defying enemy cryptoanalysts. Lord Haw Haw had been aware of this during the later stages of the war, and his propaganda broadcasts apparently warned the ATS operators that they risked becoming sterile by using them. His effort to disrupt communications failed and it was said that the more free and easy female operators exposed themselves before the machines as an added safeguard against pregnancy.

Army rations were issued to the messes only for those members 'living in', so no meals were provided for ration-card holders and we had to manage on snacks served at a nearby club for senior ranks or a pork pie in a pub. Uniform was still being worn by service personnel, and most of us preferred to patronise the club, where we had the opportunity of conversing with colleagues employed in the War Office. When it was announced that Field-Marshal Montgomery was to take over the post of Chief of the Imperial General Staff, it caused some worry to the garrison commandant because the standard of dress had deteriorated. He took immediate steps to order six hundred new suits of battledress. The thought that crossed everyone's minds was how the field-marshal and Emmanuel Shinwell, the Labour Government's War Minister, would get on. This topic was discussed years later when Lord Shinwell was interviewed on BBC television on his hundredth birthday, and he said that they had enjoyed a good working arrangement.

One of the topics they must have been concerned about was the long-term future of the Army because at that time many of the experienced NCOs were electing for de-mobilisation rather than extending their service. As a sop to the uncommitted, a scheme was devised to retain their services. In return for a guarantee that they would serve a further three years beyond their current engagement, they were given a bounty of twenty-five pounds and a free outfit of civilian clothing.

Having already served fourteen years, I saw no point in leaving the Army until I had completed twenty-one and qualified for a pension, so I had nothing to lose by signing an undertaking to continue for a further term. The money was paid into my account and I was given a railway warrant to travel to the Demobilisation Clothing Centre at Guildford. The mistake I made was not to hand over the usual ten-shilling bribe to the usher, so instead of being escorted to the stands displaying garments tailored by Aquascutum and Moss Brothers I was pointed to the area where the Fifty Shilling Tailors' suits were on offer.

One of the problems of soldiering in a residential area was the lack of facilities for military training. Although formal parades were discouraged, it was necessary to find space for weapon training as every soldier was required to qualify on the rifle or pistol range annually. The solution was to use the extensive gardens separating the two sides of the square to go through the drill associated with range practice, to the amusement of some and the annoyance of other civilian residents. The actual firing-range was a 25-yard miniature one at Wormwood Scrubs Prison; as live ammunition was used, great care had to be taken that shots were directed at the target and not into the air.

Queen Mary sometimes visited one of her friends who lived a short distance from our office, and I had an arrangement with her personal detective to warn me of any impending visit so that I could keep the troops away. The last thing that the CO would want was a complaint from Buckingham Palace that Her Majesty had not been recognised and saluted by one of his soldiers.

An important ritual of Army life is 'commanding officer's orders', usually held at twelve noon, when the CO conducts interviews with new arrivals, those about to depart, those wishing to air a grievance and those appearing before him on a disciplinary hearing. RSM Lea, as the CO's disciplinary adjutant, was always present on these occasions, but when the procedure was over he took it for granted that his office work for the morning was over and we both went for a stroll before lunch. Jack Lea introduced me to a new arrival who had joined us as the CSM of No. 2 Company. Guy Symonds had joined the Army as a National Serviceman and spent a few years in Burma. He was to gain notoriety in the 1960s when accused of the murder of his wife Phyllis, but the prosecution failed to prove its case and he was acquitted. More details of the case will appear later.

The winter of 1946-47 was a very severe one and many unemployed gained temporary work by clearing snow from the streets of London. At a time when German women helped in rebuilding their houses by cleaning up old bricks for reuse, most people in England were apathetic and waiting for something to happen. The position was aggravated by the shortage of coal available for factory and domestic use, and because it was not being mined in sufficient quantity nearly two million people were out of work and power cuts were the order of the day. Ernest Bevin had served as Minister of Labour in the Churchill National Government and, mindful of the need to produce coal for feeding the workshop furnaces and ships' boilers, he had solved the problem of the shortage of miners by offering National Servicemen the option of working in the coal mines instead of the armed services. Ten per cent of those liable for conscription took advantage of this offer, but many of those were now being released from their commitment. These 'Bevin boys' had spent the wartime years working underground in arduous conditions. Not for them the modern coal-cutting machinery, underground railways and lifts; they had to be content with winning coal by using picks and shovels in cramped conditions where imported wooden pit-props were used to support the roof and pit ponies pulled the coal waggons along the track.

My wife shared in the hardship caused by the coal shortage and it was not unusual for her to push the perambulator to the gasworks and queue for a ration of coke, coal being unavailable.

The irony was that there were thousands of Polish

servicemen who did not wish to return to Communist Poland, many of them with mining experience, all too eager to work in our pits – but the mining unions vetoed the idea. The appeal made by Ernest Bevin, now Foreign Secretary, went unheard. He had said that two million tons of coal, then readily exportable, would be worth more to him than two Army divisions when it came to negotiations with other nations.

In the late summer of 1947 we were visited by a representative of the Postings Office who was seeking volunteers to serve in some of our colonial stations. Jack Lea had been loud in his praise of Kenya, and when I saw that they needed a WO II at Nairobi my hand shot up. When I told Edith of my decision she showed great interest, not having been overseas before except for Paris, Ostend and Jersey.

Now that I was committed to serving abroad again, the time passed very quickly. We were anxious not to miss the pageantry associated with the wedding of the year. Princess Elizabeth's engagement to Prince Philip had been announced in July, and the marriage was to take place at Westminster Abbey on 20th November 1947. Philip, the son of Lord Louis Mountbatten, had served as a lieutenant in the Royal Navy and the young Princess had volunteered to serve in the ATS and had been granted a commission.

Television was still in its infancy, so the only way to view this spectacular event was from the pavement on the procession route. We left home early, and with young Pat on my shoulders managed to find standing room near the entrance to Buckingham Palace and had a good view of the royal couple as they passed by. As the day drew to a close they appeared and reappeared on the Palace balcony to the cheers and enjoyment of thousands of well-wishers. No sooner was the royal wedding over than I received instructions to report to an Army camp at Pocklington near York for documentation and fitting-out with tropical kit – in addition to numerous inoculations, including yellow fever, which was endemic in East Africa.

The railway journey north was torture as the coaches were unheated, and there were frequent stops along the route because good South Wales steam coal was in short supply and the engine had to be coaxed along. At these stops the passengers would alight and do some quick stamping of feet to restore the circulation, until the stoker raised enough steam to blow the whistle signalling the train's departure.

The camp was cheerless and no fires were allowed to be lit before 5 p.m. This rule was enforced and piquets were on duty to report the number of any hut where smoke was seen belching out of the chimney before the permitted time. The only good thing about it was the cheerfulness of its commanding officer, Lieutenant-Colonel Harry Worth, an ex-ranker who had enlisted as a boy soldier in 1919. (I sat next to him at a Corps luncheon held at Blandford in 1992.)

Despite its remoteness, the mess was visited by several females, one of whom was the daughter of a small-time farmer who kept a few pigs. Under wartime restrictions the birth of all farm animals had to be registered with the Food Ministry, but its officials could not cover a vast area and so false returns were often submitted. The daughter worked at the camp laundry and told me that she had served with the WRNS as a writer and had spent some time in Australian waters.

She also told me that her father was about to kill one of the surplus pigs and promised that I could buy a leg of pork when the animal was slaughtered. On the strength of this, I bought her dinner in an old-fashioned tavern in Pocklington. As far as I know the pig was not killed, and because the occupants of the camp spent only a week or so in transit I wondered how many others had been deceived by her promise of a leg of pork.

As soon as the formalities of preparing for overseas were over we were granted embarkation leave and told reporting instructions would be sent by letter to our home address. Edith and I had discussed our future plans, and as I expected to be out of England for three years we decided to give up the Streatham Hill flat and that she would stay with her parents for a few months then join me in Kenya. We arranged for the removal of the furniture needed at Upney and posted a notice in the front window that we would be selling the surplus in a house sale. The neighbours flocked along and we had no trouble in selling the utility furniture at a higher price than we had paid for it.

Jack Lea had promised that Edith would be invited to all the Christmas functions being held in the sergeants' mess as I was due to leave in mid-December. At Upney I was given a domestic job to do which helped to relieve the boredom of living in someone else's home. It involved the removal of the Anderson air raid shelter erected at the bottom of the garden, in which they had spent many hours during the aerial bombardment of London. The shelter had been in position for eight years and was settled in, but after two days' laborious work the metal framework was removed, the cavity filled in and Edith's father could carry on with his hobby of growing flowers and vegetables.

Instructions reached me from Pocklington that I was to proceed to Southampton, where I would be placed in charge of the Royal Signals draft posted to various stations in East Africa. On the Saturday before I was due to report, Edith's father drove us around on a farewell visit to her many relatives who lived in the London area. The capital was always referred to by the soldiery as 'the Smoke' because of the prevalence of fog and smog in those days of coal fires, and it lived up to its name on the last weekend before I left. By the time we reached Barking it had become progressively thicker, and I had to walk along the pavement with a white handkerchief in my hand to guide the driver along. It was no wonder that I longed for sunnier climates!

18

EAST AFRICA 1948-51

The reinforcements for East Africa Command sailed from Southampton in mid-December on the *Empress of Australia,* a large passenger liner formerly known as the *Empress of Japan.* There was only a small military contingent on board, the vast majority of the passengers being connected with the ill-fated ground-nuts scheme. Some joker at the Ministry of Food had conjured up the idea of sending a small army of civilians to Africa to set up an organisation for supplementing our deficiency of oils – at the same time providing employment for the Africans who had served with the British Army during the war years. The originator of the idea had believed the hoary old joke that Africa was so fertile that if one's finger was poked into the soil it would take root.

John Strachey, the Food Minister, was so taken with the idea that he persuaded the Government that the scheme was in the best interests of the taxpayer. The idea was to clear the jungle, set up agricultural areas for growing the nuts, organise townships and medical centres for the African workers, build storage facilities to prevent the monkeys from eating the crops, and finally erect processing plants for the manufacture of margarine – or alternatively ship the harvest to the ports for freighting to the UK. In the event not one pound of margarine was produced and in 1949 the scheme was abandoned at a cost to the British taxpayer of £36·5 million, a vast sum of money in those days. The term 'ground-nuts scheme' became a national joke, and if anyone made a silly remark it was greeted with the rejoinder, 'Peanuts'. Apart from a few technicians who travelled third class, the majority of the executives of the project were officers of the three services who had been granted short service commissions during the war. Not only did they travel first class as temporary civil servants but they were accompanied by their wives, whose accommodation costs at the coastal hotels were met out of public funds. Many colonial businessmen, farmers and other settlers visiting the UK before war was declared had been trapped into spending the war years away from home, and those with influence in high places managed to procure a berth on the vessel. One such person was a Miss Williamson, the daughter of a diamond-mining magnate living in Rhodesia. She had been sent to finishing school in Europe and had been unable to secure a passage home.

Certain changes had taken place in the Corps during 1946, one of them being the designation of units. Companies and sections were now known as squadrons and troops, and the rank of a CSM now became SSM. Another change was the design of our cap badge, which had formerly had an oval band surrounding the figure of Jimmy, and this was now discarded. My cabin-mate was SSM 'Tim' Trimbrell, who because of the war had been trapped in India for eight years, several of them spent in the outstations of the Zhob, Loralai, Fort Sandeman and Hindubagh, where he gained the reputation of being an excellent wireless operator. His next posting was to Nanyuki, a station straddling the equator. The ship also carried a number of service wives whose husbands had either preceded them or been transferred to Kenya from nearby stations. They looked a haggard and dispirited lot, having had to endure years of food rationing at home, and their clothes were drab and uninteresting. But as we approached the warmer waters of the Mediterranean they were transformed and quite friendly.

There were no shipboard romances on this vessel because in those days a wedding-ring was respected and, after all, a bird does not foul its own nest. The nearest approach to a romance involved Miss Williamson, who became very friendly with a young Irish warrant-officer named Paddy O'Byrne, and she spent more time with us in the second-class lounge than she did in the first, for which she had paid.

The *Empress of Australia* was a fast vessel and apart from encountering heavy weather in the Bay of Biscay there were no hitches. Within eight days we had reached Port Said and not long afterwards arrived at the infamous bunkering-station of Aden. Having taken on stocks of oil and water, which was always brackish there, we rounded the Horn of Africa to commence the 1,600-mile final stretch to Mombasa. As we approached Kismayu in Somalia, the passengers who had never crossed the equator were looking forward to the crossing-the-line ceremony, and there was some disappointment when the bridge announced that King Neptune would not be coming aboard because we were overdue at Mombasa.

Later that day orders for disembarkation were issued and passengers proceeding to Kenya were warned to be ready to leave the ship early on the following morning. The ground-nuts crowd would remain on board until they reached their destination of Dar es Salaam in Tanganyika (now known as Tanzania), which boasted a good railway network ending at Kigoma on the banks of Lake Tanganyika, the 700-mile stretch of water which separated the country from Uganda and Kenya. One of the last places of interest which we passed that day was the mouth of the Tana River, which provided irrigation and powered the plants supplying the colony with electricity.

When we disembarked in the steamy atmosphere of Mombasa it was to hear gloomy news. The railway had been severely damaged by the collapse of an embankment further up the line, and movement by train was cancelled until repairs were carried out. Road transport awaited to convey the draft to a disused transit camp at Nyali on the outskirts of the port, and the wives to a hotel in Mombasa.

Meanwhile, hundreds of Africans using picks and shovels were loading rocks on to wheelbarrows to fill in the breach to the embankment, but it was a long-drawn-out process. After eight days spent in the camp, word reached us that the damage had been repaired and a train was on its way from Nairobi to resume the normal service and would arrive at Mombasa station on the following day. It was not a troop-train, but sleeping-berths had been reserved for the service wives and the military. The train left Mombasa in the late afternoon and commenced the 300-mile gradual climb to Nairobi, which was 6,000 feet above sea level. There was a prolonged stop at the rail junction of Voi to enable a party travelling to Moshi in Tanganyika to exchange trains, and by this time darkness had fallen. It was midnight before the journey was resumed, by which time most of the passengers had settled down for the night. Although we did not know it at the time, we passed within 50 miles of Mount Kilimanjaro, at a height of 19,340 feet the highest mountain in Africa.

Anyone who has passed through or lived in the tropics will be aware that the twilight and the dawn are short-lived, and true to form the rim of the rising sun could be seen from the east shortly after 6 a.m. The air was now fresher, and most of us had regained our appetites and ate a hearty breakfast in the dining-car.

Paddy O'Byrne, on secondment to the King's African Rifles and rejoining his battalion after UK leave, had travelled this route before and gave a running commentary on places that we passed through and the warriors in their war-paint who greeted us at the main railway stations. When the train reached Konza, he announced that we had now arrived in lion country. Progress from now on was slow as the train approached the area where the embankment had collapsed, and it was not until 4 p.m. that we arrived at Nairobi Station.

Timbrell and his small party travelling on to Nanyuki remained on board, and two of the sergeants joining the unit and I were met and escorted to our new home, which was named Killarney Camp. I was pleased to have two experienced senior NCOs to join the team; both had served throughout the war and one of them, a Glaswegian named Spike Hughes, had spent some years in India. The other, Smudger Smith, was an ex-Infantry man who had elected for discharge and found work with the AA as a patrolman. It was the custom in those days for uniformed AA men to salute the drivers of all cars displaying the Automobile Association badge. Smith became disillusioned because he did more saluting than he had ever done in his days in the Army, and so he applied for re-enlistment.

It was dark soon after 6 p.m., and after a meal and two pints of Tusker beer I felt weary and opted for bed.

My first visitor on Sunday morning was Njeroge, the boy assigned to be my personal servant, who arrived with a mug of tea and took away my soiled clothing. Conversation was difficult because I had no Swahili and he knew no English, but it was not the first time that I got by through the use of sign language. Shortly afterwards there was a knock on the door and a European wearing a white shirt and shorts appeared. Recognition was instant and mutual. The visitor was Bertie Hollingshead, whom I had left behind at Meerut in 1936. He was now a major in charge of the East Africa Command Signal Squadron. We chatted for a while and I was pleased that he had taken the trouble to pay me an informal visit rather than wait for the official interview on the Monday.

On returning after lunch to my *banda*, the Swahili word for a room, it was to find that Njeroge had polished all my footwear and brassware, and my KD tunic and shorts had been washed and starched ready to wear for work in the morning. I was not impressed by what I had seen so far, and the reason for the neglected state of the camp was revealed to me by Major Hollingshead on my initial interview. He had inherited a run-down unit from an officer whose sole preoccupation was running an amateur radio network. His SSM was a National Serviceman who had gained rapid promotion because those senior to him had completed their service. SSM Rowden, who was reputed to be a useful boxer, had been demobilised before I arrived and had taken his discharge in East Africa, where his ability to handle horses earned him a good living.

Bertie told me that shortly after taking over, he had been visited by his formation commander, who was so unimpressed with the state of the unit that he gave him six months to get it up to standard or lose his command. I assured him of my support and accepted the challenge of smartening up the squadron. Before leaving his office, he briefed me on the Signals set-up in East Africa, and it was the most unorthodox that I had ever encountered. Our own squadron was commanded by a major who was assisted by a Quarter-Master and RQMS, appointments normally held by those serving in a regiment. Northern Area Signal Troop was commanded by Major Eric Buirski, assisted by SSM Timbrell, the usual establishment being a captain and a sergeant, whereas Southern Area Signal Troop at Moshi had a captain and staff sergeant. East Africa Command was subordinate to GHQ Middle East at Cairo but was responsible for a large detachment stationed at Mogadishu and another at Hargeisa, in Somalia.

Our squadron was responsible for the communications between GHQ and the outstations in East Africa, Somalia and Eritrea, all of which were radio-operated except for the Signals Despatch Service, which carried classified mail and packages within the colony. It was a mixed squadron consisting of one-third British ranks and two-thirds Africans. SSM Mwambile, who belonged to the Kamba tribe of the Machakos area, shared my office, and I asked him to conduct me around the camp. It occupied a large area on high ground and was divided into three main areas of accommodation; the British single men's quarters, the African askari area, and the African married quarters, which consisted of forty rooms in two large wooden blocks. Fortunately, he had a good command of English and was able to explain how his African askari (soldiers) were deployed.

It was a requirement that all new arrivals from the UK learnt the local language of Swahili within six weeks of joining, but many of the senior Africans had received a good education at mission schools and spoke better English than the average British soldier.

My first task was to learn the names of the soldiers so that when they greeted me with the words '*Jambo, Bwana*' or '*Jambo, Effendi*' I could return the greeting with the word '*Jambo*' followed by their name. The office records had been neglected, so I produced a new roll showing every detail of a man's personal record, and this was always referred to as 'the Bible'. I had also to study the intricacies of the King's African Rifles Ordinance, which differed in most respects from the *Manual of Military Law* in force in the British Army.

It took a week to organise the office records, after which I was free to carry out inspections of the living-quarters and messes. As the sergeants' mess was to be my home until my wife arrived, a start was made to smarten it up. The building was constructed of wood and consisted of a dining-room, a large lounge and a lock-up bar with a servery. The ceiling was covered with hessian and it sagged with the weight of feral cats which had made their homes above it. The cats posed a health hazard because they emerged at night and raided the waste-bins, strewing left-over food on the outside kitchen floor. Anyone entering the hut from the fresh air could not help noticing the reek of cat's urine coming from above, and a reluctant decision was made to eradicate the nuisance. The ceiling had no trapdoor and was inaccessible, so the only solution was to fire rounds of small-bore rifle cartridges into the sagging hessian and dispose of any wounded ones that escaped from the roof.

We next tackled the garden fronting the mess and removed masses of canna bulbs which had taken over the ground, and had the soil cultivated in readiness for planting flowers which would flourish when the long rains arrived in March. Finally, we had both the dining-room and lounge redecorated, and the smell of fresh paint neutralised the lingering odour of cat's urine.

The most pressing thing to be done was to find somewhere for my wife and daughter to live as there was a shortage of married quarters – and families were not called forward to join their husbands until private accommodation was found for them. I prevailed on Mr Slapak, a European Jew who had started life in Nairobi as a rag-and-bone merchant and now owned a third-rate hotel in a reasonable location, to guarantee me a room.

Whatever shortcomings Jimmy Rowden had in maintaining military standards, it must be said that he presided over a popular and hospitable sergeants' mess, although at the time when I arrived most of our visitors were civilian settlers.

One of our most colourful and interesting guests was Juanita Carberry, the daughter of Lord Carbery – who dropped his title on his arrival in Kenya and changed his name by deed poll to John Evans Carberry, adding a second R to his surname.

Maia, his second wife, was an accomplished aviator who met a tragic end in an aeroplane accident at the Ngong Aerodrome while instructing a learner. Juanita was then three years old. The Maia Carberry Nursing Home was built by her brothers as a lasting memorial, and this building provided medical and nursing treatment by qualified European staff to those suffering from severe illness or convalescing after major operations.

John Carberry ventured into marriage for the third time in 1930 and his new wife was an English girl named June Weir-Mosely, whom he had brought to Nyeri and passed off as 'Cousin Juney' to cover up the deception.

After the death of her mother, Juanita spent most of her childhood in the care of ayahs, nannies and relatives, and it was not until she became a teenager that she was admitted into the household to be brought up by a governess in the nursery wing. Those who have watched the BBC drama *The Happy Valley* will have seen how badly she was treated by her father, and the cruel punishment meted out to her by the governess Isabel Rutt on John Carberry's orders. Juanita rode on her pony Springbok to Nyeri police station to show the duty officer the weals on her body caused by Rutt's whipping, and asked for her injuries to be recorded in the log-book.

Juanita never returned to the family home and lived with her uncle, Gerald Anderson, in Nairobi until enlisting in the Women's Territorial Service, an offshoot of the Females Auxiliary Nursing Yeomanry (FANYS), at the age of seventeen and a half. Because of her decision to live with her mother's brother, John Carberry renounced her and cut her off without a penny.

About the time of her enlistment, the Royal Signals manning the communication centre at command HQ were in dire need of reinforcements and asked for volunteers from other services to undergo training as telephone switchboard operators and despatch riders. Juanita qualified in both trades, in addition to learning how signal messages were processed in the signal centre.

Not only were Royal Signals short of personnel but they

were having difficulty in replacing their 350cc motor cycles. They were fortunate in having a competent vehicle mechanic named Jack Green who was adept at keeping the machines on the road by cannibalising serviceable parts from otherwise defective motor cycles.

After Juanita's spell of carrying despatches to the outstations, the signal master realised her potential as an operator and she was promoted to supervisor of the command telephone switchboard, a seven position affair handling many hundreds of calls a day, and after demobilisation she retained this post as a female civilian employee – a rather stilted term then in use by the Army.

With the cessation of hostilities, the Army were auctioning surplus equipment and machinery, so Juanita prevailed upon Jack Green to bid for a 500cc BSA motor cycle, which he was able to restore. Much of her subsequent leisure time was spent riding her white pony Raschid, or on the saddle of the BSA – in her own words, 'I loved it to bits even though it kicked like a mule and I always had a struggle to start it. It was a heavy brute.'

When I arrived at Nairobi, the Women's Territorial Service (East Africa) had been disbanded and Juanita missed the comradeship of service life she had enjoyed in the FANY mess at the Loretto Convent. Knowing this, we always made her welcome at the sergeants' mess.

Little did I think then that we would meet again in London more than forty years later.

Arthur Dodsworth, our SQMS, had become friendly with the Fletcher family who lived near the camp. He had met Duncan, one of the sons of an eminent engineer who had settled in Kenya in 1902, and was often invited to his home. Duncan then lived with his mother, who had emigrated to East Africa in 1914 and was invariably referred to as 'Ma' Fletcher. He was a frequent visitor to our mess and returned our hospitality at his mother's home. 'Ma' was of Yorkshire stock and told us of the hardships and privations suffered by the earlier settlers, and the danger to life and limb the wild animals posed to settlers and construction engineers building the railway from Mombase to the White Highlands. It is recorded that in East Africa nine settlers were killed or badly mauled by lions, four by elephants, two by buffaloes and one by a rhinoceros.

Many fiction writers have spoken disparagingly of the life-style of the Kenya residents. General Sir George Erskine, who commanded the Mau Mau operations in 1953, went so far as to say that it was 'a sunny place for shady people' and caused a storm when he described the white women as 'middle-class sluts'. These sentiments did not go down well with the pioneers, many of them widows whose husbands had lost their lives at Longido, fighting the Germans under General Von Lutlow in World War I when Tanganyika was part of German East Africa. Nor did it impress those who had survived the war and rallied to the flag by serving in the East Africa Mounted Rifles, the King's African Rifles and many of the British services fighting the war in Europe.

Killarney Camp was on the Ngong road, four miles out of Nairobi and within eight miles of the Ngong Hills lying to the west of the town. They ran roughly north to south and were eight thousand feet above sea level, with the highest of the four peaks rising two thousand feet above the surrounding area. The elders of the Kikuyu tribe could remember when they were roamed by buffalo, rhinoceros and eland, and the oldest of them could recall seeing herds of elephants there. BOAC pilots, relaxing in the Norfolk Hotel over a gin and tonic, asserted that the Ngong Hills' proximity to the airstrip posed a navigational hazard to the slow-climbing piston-engined aircraft in use at the time, but during my five years there not one of them came to grief.

It was beneath this long range of hills that Baron von Blixen-Finecke purchased land and cultivated coffee on a large scale shortly after his arrival in 1911. He was later joined by his wife, but they did not lead a happy life. The long rains failed one year, resulting in crop failure and consequent bankruptcy. Their marriage ended in divorce and the Baroness returned to her native Denmark, where under the pen-name of Isak Dinesen, she wrote a book entitled *Out of Africa,* which was made into a film of the same name.

Between the wars parasites flocked to Kenya to satisfy

their lust for big-game hunting, gambling, drinking and fornicating. The older settlers, who by dint of hard work had developed the colony, referred to them as the 'Happy Valley set', and it was no doubt these people General Erskine had in mind. They were also the subject of the film *White Mischief,* produced from James Fox's book of the same name. Foremost of these was Joselyn Hay, who arrived in Kenya in the mid-1920s. He married soon after his arrival but divorced his wife on succeeding to the title of the Earl of Erroll in 1928. His next adventure was with the wife of Major Ramsey-Hill. He was cited in the divorce case and married Molly Ramsey-Hill. From all accounts 'Joss' was a handsome fellow and had no difficulty in seducing women single or married. His philandering did not go unnoticed by the Countess, who took to drink and then to drugs and died in 1939.

Joselyn's next target was Diana, the young second wife of Sir Jock Delves Broughton. Within a fortnight of her arrival at Nairobi she fell under his spell, and their affair soon became common knowledge.

The announcement made on the radio on 24th January stirred the whole of East Africa and reverberated overseas. The body of the Earl of Erroll had been found in his car on the Ngong road in the early hours of the morning with a bullet wound in his head.

Sir Jock was suspected of committing the crime and arrested. After some months spent in Nairobi Prison, he was tried for murder. The trial dragged on for longer than a month, then a verdict of 'Not Guilty' was reached by the all-white jury.

It is no wonder that the pioneers and settlers who had worked so hard in developing the land to produce crops of coffee, tea, pyrethrum, flax and maize, and the ranchers who introduced pedigree cattle, horses and sheep to stock their farms, resented these aristocrats, the wife-swoppers, playboys, drunkards, drug addicts and remittance men of the Happy Valley set.

The appearance of the camp improved gradually and I was able to persuade the soldiers to smarten up their surroundings. Their sleeping-quarters were bordered by small plots and I organised a competition for the best garden. The soil was fertile and also had an ample water supply, so in no time we had a show of geraniums, fuchsias, sweet-scented stocks and many other species grown from seed. They had no success with zinnias, which do not like to be transplanted, and yet these colourful flowers sprang up like weeds after the rains.

Not long after settling in the camp I was visited by the chaplain, whose wish was to start a weekly session of 'padre's hour' so that soldiers could discuss their problems with him. We had no formal church parades because, as a working unit, a third of the operating staff were either on duty or resting from a strenuous eight-hour stretch at the Communication Centre. Attendance at church was sparse and the chaplains found it expedient to visit the troops in their barracks or through the medium of the local radio station. I always insisted on our padre joining us in the sergeants' mess for coffee prior to his chat, and he had an amusing experience to relate.

He had gone home on leave and was asked to take a casket holding the ashes of a deceased resident to hand over to a relative in England. He also took a sporting rifle left behind by a serviceman who had left the colony at short notice. On arrival at Southampton, the Customs official asked if he had anything to declare and was told that he was carrying the mortal remains of the dearly departed Mr Blank. This was a new situation for the Customs man, who referred it to his superior, and after much thumbing of the regulations book it was agreed that the casket should be admitted. The discussion took so long and he was so relieved to know that the ashes would not be consigned to the bond room that he forgot to declare the rifle – nor was it noticed by HM Customs and Excise.

When he asked me if I attended Sunday morning service, I made the usual excuse of lack of transport and he retorted that surely then I listened in to *Padre's Half-Hour* every Wednesday evening on Nairobi Radio. To salve my conscience I resolved to do so, and some weeks later I was surprised to hear the senior chaplain come to a sudden halt while reciting the Lord's Prayer. In the hiatus the announcer apologised for a technical hitch and the service had to be abandoned. When next our padre visited us he was very indignant when I mentioned the matter. He drew me aside and explained that Padre Good (who later christened my second daughter, Linda) had played a round of golf in the afternoon, imbibed a gin and tonic or two after sundown, then suffered a lapse of memory, and when half-way through the Lord's Prayer forgot the words. And that is the Gospel truth!

Most of our askari were of the Christian faith, having been educated in mission schools which competed with each other in teaching their own brand of Christianity. When compiling my records I had included their tribes and religious beliefs and found that there were as many as sixteen representatives of tribal groups but the great preponderance came from the Wakamba, Kikuyu and Jaluo. We had also a number of Sudanese, Somalis, Ethiopians and men from the coastal area who were followers of Mohammed, and I was surprised to learn that we had one self-professed pagan on our strength. His home was in the Congo, and whereas the normal leave entitlement was one month in the year, a special concession had to be made in his case because it took two weeks for him to travel to his village, and another two to get back. He travelled by train to Kilembe, skirting Lake Victoria, and from then on caught native buses between centres of civilisation before trekking through the bush for days before reaching home. The journey was so hazardous and lengthy that he was allowed three months' leave every three years and, according to SSM Mwambile, he had never failed to return before his furlough expired.

The peace of the officers' married quarters at Kenton was shattered one day by the sound of a pistol-shot, and the body of Major Brown lay slumped on his doorstep. A sergeant of the Intelligence Corps stationed at MacKinnon Road near Mombasa had become too friendly with Major Brown's daughter and was forbidden to call on her. Despite this he travelled up, rang the doorbell and asked to see the daughter. When his request was refused he drew his revolver and murdered the major in cold blood. He was tried at Nairobi and sentenced to death by hanging. The padre confided in me that whenever he visited the sergeant in his condemned cell he was indifferent to his fate and showed no signs of remorse. He was subsequently hanged at Nairobi Prison by Hoppy Marshall, the official hangman.

Killarney Camp occupied a large area and because of its size was difficult to patrol. As the incidence of theft by residents of the nearby Kibera Village increased, it was decided to construct a perimeter fence to keep out the intruders. Once completed, the barbed wire enclosure was patrolled daily by Corporal Jumna, the provost NCO. Jumna was a huge Ethiopian as beefy as a eunuch and as thick as a plank of wood, but for all that a dedicated policeman; he reported every breach found in the fencing so that it could be repaired. The alarm was sounded late one evening when Africans were seen running away from the area carrying bundles of clothing, and we rushed out to investigate – only to find that the sergeants' rooms had been raided. We made a search of the boundary nearest to their huts and found a gaping hole in the fence, through which, aided by the moonlight, the robbers had made their escape.

We had an unexpected visit one Friday evening from a lady named Mavis, a widow who managed a hairdressing salon in the town and lived in a bungalow at a place called Langata. She seemed depressed and we tried to revive her spirits with gin and tonic. Mavis seemed loth to go home, and gradually the mess members drifted away because there was a parade to attend in the morning, followed by the Saturday inspection.

The weekly caterer was Spike Hughes. He was responsible for closing the bar at 11 p.m., and he offered to escort her home. One of Spike's failings was that he was unable to hold his drink. Knowing this, Mavis declined his offer – at the same time making a visual appeal to me which Hughes resented. We reached a compromise and agreed that her escort should be the winner of a game of darts. I was an accomplished darts player but on this occasion lost the game, much to Mavis's distress, and in an aside I told her to drive herself home whilst Spike was locking up his bar. He was furious, and rushed like a bull towards me with his head down and arms flaying the air. It was not difficult to step out of the way of his onrush, at the same time delivering a short blow to his head, and he measured his length on the car-park. I now had an injury case on my hands. I lifted him up and told him to reopen his bar so that I could clean him up. His face was contused by the murrum (clay) surface, and as I washed away the blood and the soil I told him that he should be grateful that his anti-tetanus injections were up to date.

In a close community an incident like this does not pass unnoticed. When his boy saw his bloodied shirt and my boy Njeroge saw a smear of blood on my bush jacket, they compared notes and the whole camp knew of it. It had even reached Major Bertie's ears and his first remark to me in the morning was, 'Good for you.'

The incidence of thefts from the camp increased. We were concerned lest a large gang made a concerted raid on the vehicle spare parts or clothing stores, so a security conference was convened. I knew that a dog section of the Royal Military Police had arrived from Egypt and that their animals were kept in kennels at Waterworks Camp, so it was decided that I should invite their sergeant-major over for a discussion.

The CSM said that he would prefer to see his dogs doing the work that they had been trained for rather than sitting in kennels. He further explained that the dogs were either 'killers' or 'barkers'. The barkers were intended to stay indoors and arouse the storeman in the event of a break-in, whereas the killers were given freedom to roam within a secure compound such as the MT car-park. He readily agreed to lend us three dogs which would be transported to the camp by dusk and taken away by his handlers shortly after dawn. We were warned not to approach the killers, because they had earned the reputation in Egypt of savaging or killing intruders approaching their territory. When I asked him if they were to be fed, he said that their food was handled by British cooks for obvious reasons, whereas we humans had our meals prepared by Africans.

The arrival of the guard dogs gave us peace of mind. We were no longer troubled by sneak raiders, so could relax. The weekends were dull, as those of us who had left our wives behind waited anxiously for news that they would be rejoining us. To dispel the boredom we sometimes took part in a 'dawn session', and on these occasions I allowed the bar to remain open until daybreak. As Spike and I returned one morning from an all-night sitting, we noticed that rain had fallen and the ground was soggy. On reaching the MT compound, we saw the guard dog looking unkempt and miserable and felt sorry for him. Spike was a tough man but loved animals. Even so, I was surprised by his next action – which was to unlock the padlock of the enclosure and lead the dog by the collar to his *banda*. The sight of the inviting bed with its white sheets was too much for the animal, who leapt upon it. In no time the colour of the sheets turned from white to red ochre from its paw-marks. Spike's idea was to give the dog shelter from the rain, not to occupy his bed, and with a cuff he made him settle on the floor. At noon, having slept for six hours, I was called to the telephone to hear an anxious RMP sergeant-major bemoaning the loss of a valuable dog. He was very relieved – and red-faced – when I told him it was asleep in Spike Hughes *banda*.

One of our members proposed at a monthly mess meeting that we hold a dance, but in view of the shortage of lady partners I doubted the wisdom of this and said so. He then explained that a number of English nurses working at the Maia Carberry Nursing Home would be delighted to attend, so I sent an invitation to the matron. Ten of the off-duty nurses came along, and I like to think that they enjoyed the party.

East Africa Command had been without a GOC for several months but news reached us that a new commander was to join us soon. Every general officer shows an interest in the unit which enables him to keep in contact with the rest of the world, so we expected him to inspect us soon after he settled in. The area commander, who had given Major Hollingshead six months to sort out his unit, must have thought on these lines and announced that he would visit us before the GOC arrived and, his inspection over, said that he was very pleased at the improvement.

We had seven days' notice of an official inspection by Lieutenant-General Sir Arthur A. B. Dowler, our new GOC, and a great effort was made to impress him by the turn-out of the soldiers and the tidiness of the camp. I had the quarter guard paraded half an hour before his arrival and their equipment shone. The major made a serious *faux pas* in not introducing me to the general, so instead of leading the way to the transmitting station at Kenton I followed in the rear. We had not walked very far before General Dowler paused and asked who was marching behind him, and when told he chided Bertie with the words, 'I must always meet the sergeant-major.' The inspection of the station having been completed, we toured the domestic area, after which he said, 'Let's rally around the sergeant-major,' and went on to express satisfaction at what he had seen. I then knew that the threat of Bertie losing his command had receded.

It was now late March and the long rains were due. The vegetation had dried up after four months of drought, and to avoid the danger of bush fires all scrub had been cut down by fatigue parties wielding pangas.

The rain reached us early one afternoon, accompanied by an electrical storm. It was not torrential like the monsoons of India, but within two hours of its arrival the sunburnt plateau had been transformed into an area of green shoots of grass. The air, too, was easier to breathe and lacked the humidity associated with the Indian rainy season.

By this time I had a reasonable command of Swahili, which, like the Urdu of India, was the common language that most of the tribal people had learnt to speak. OC's orders, where interviews took place and justice was meted out to offenders, was conducted in both English and Swahili, and I was always present. There was also an interpreter in attendance, a Sudanese named Muhammed whom I suspected of misinterpreting the evidence in favour of the accused – and possibly being bribed. I made a point of becoming sufficiently proficient in the language to intervene should Muhammed misrepresent the facts.

Welcome news reached me in April that Edith and my daughter Pat had been warned to be ready to embark for East Africa. In the event, they sailed from Southampton on the troop-ship *Empire Ken* in mid-May and were expected in Mombasa in the first week of June. All went well until they reached Port Said, where a number of Mauritian soldiers were taken on board for repatriation. This deviation caused them to spend a further week at sea but enabled them to visit the Indian Ocean island.

Mombasa was then a small and straggly town with few hotels. Its main attractions were the seafront, the docks and the railway station. Apart from the numerous vessels at anchor in the harbour, there were dozens of dhows whose crews braved the Persian Sea to bring their cargoes of oriental goods to sell to the Indian traders in their bazaars.

The room which Mr Slapak had promised me was sparsely furnished and badly carpeted, so I bought a very large Indian rug and had it delivered to the station. When Edith saw it she questioned the need for it, but it proved useful to enhance the drab room and travelled with us twice to Germany, once to Singapore and then to Cyprus, where we presented it to our Greek servant on our departure.

I had forgotten that it was against the rules to travel to Mombasa to meet newly arrived families because of the limited number of sleeping-berths on the train. Rather shamefacedly I asked the RTO if he had spare seats. As he was an understanding man, he pointed to a two-berth coupé, which I shared with an RASC corporal whose wife and Edith slept in a ladies' four-berth compartment with the two children. The corporal, a dull and unimpressive fellow, was to figure in another murder case some time later.

Edith was appalled when she was shown our room. The double bedroom was one of four in an annexe of Parklands Hotel. There was a shared bathroom with hand-basin, and the lavatory was primitive – consisting of four cubicles containing a metal bucket covered by a wooden seat, and generally referred to as the 'thunder-box'. To make matters worse, the dining-room was in a separate complex eight minutes' walk away; but fortunately the long rains had ended.

We decided that we must have an outlet from our surroundings and discussed purchasing a car. Throughout the war years Edith had managed without her marriage allowance, which had been saved and was being transferred to Nairobi through the Post Office Savings Bank. I too had managed to save in my few months in Kenya, so we decided to visit the Ford showrooms of Hughes and Co. Ltd, who were pleased to sell me a Ford Prefect (pre-war model) in return for a ten per cent deposit. We would have preferred a large car, but British industry was slumbering and had not woken up to the fact that there was a vast potential market for cars and agricultural machinery in the colonies.

Edith's initial disappointment was offset by the wonderful climate, the well-stocked shops and the colour of the hibiscus and bougainvillaea trees that graced the avenues. The tropical fruit also appealed to her and she was able to buy bananas, pineapples, mangoes and pawpaws, which were seldom seen in England.

When we visited the post office to withdraw her transferred money, she was asked to produce her passport for identity purposes. It was then that I noticed the pompous language used by the Labour Government's Foreign Secretary. The message commenced:

We,
    Ernest Bevin, a Member of His Britannic Majesty's Most
    Honourable Privy Council, a Member of Parliament . . .
    His Majesty's Principal Secretary of State for Foreign
    Affairs . . .

and went on to request and require the holder to pass without let or hindrance, and ended up with his signature beneath. I was amused by the royal 'We'! Later passports are couched in less flamboyant language, possibly because the habit of sending gunboats to threaten those who do not toe the line has stopped.

Now that we owned a car the next step was to teach Edith to drive, and what better place than the Nairobi Game Park. It was within easy reach of the town and was relatively free of traffic. There were well-defined tracks which led to the haunts of different species of wild animals, and the African game-warden would also advise where they were likely to be found. At that time the park was not fenced in and the animals were free to roam, often ending up in residents' gardens. Several salt-licks had been established to discourage them from wandering further afield. The general rule was keep off the grass, to avoid damage to the grazing on which the non-carnivorous animals were dependent. A more important one was to remain in the car with windows closed, except in certain safe areas like the small lake in which the hippos wallowed.

The main attraction was the lions, and whole prides of them would stroll around the area where visitors parked their cars. There was a profusion of gentler beasts, including zebra, wildebeest, eland, ant-eaters, Thomson's gazelle, and occasionally a small herd of giraffe could be seen. These were the animals on which the lions preyed before those scavengers the hyenas and jackals appeared at night to pick the bones. There was bird-life in the park as well, brightly plummaged beauties, guinea-fowl and spur-fowl, but the most amusing was the strutting secretary-bird. One had to travel much further afield to see the really aggressive rhinoceros and buffalo and further still to encounter the elephants.

Driving-instruction continued apace in these pleasant surroundings, and as Edith became more proficient we ventured on to the roads. I arranged for her to take a driving test and was so confident that she would pass that I left her with the car in the Kenya police compound before going to work. (The Colonials were touchy about their driving tests, and although I had held a UK licence since 1934 I have had to take further tests in Kenya, Singapore and Cyprus, as well as Germany.) Edith passed at the first attempt, and we decided to join the AA to take advantage of their cheaper insurance rates. Annual membership of the association then cost two guineas but overseas membership was only 10s 6d.

The Colonial Secretary, Mr Creech-Jones, was becoming increasingly involved in the affairs of the colony, and to the annoyance of the Legislative Council sent out officials to persuade the African workers to interest themselves in trade-unionism. The average pay for a houseboy was then 35s a month, with his quarters and food supplied. The union demand was for a minimum of £5 a month, and this was laughed out of court, with many settlers saying that they would dispense with their services.

One service that could not be dispensed with was the clearance of human waste from the 'thunder boxes', which was done at night by hygiene crews manning what was known as the night-soil carts, and the union organisers thought that they held a trump card in withdrawing the crews. This development worried the municipal authorities, who feared an epidemic of fly-borne diseases if the excreta was not disposed of, and they appealed to the European residents to man the lorries. The settlers responded magnificently and, dressed in the shabbiest of their clothes, met at selected venues to carry out this unpleasant task. No less a personage than the Bishop of Nairobi was one of the many who volunteered to drive the carts.

We were becoming frustrated at the way Mr Slapak managed his hotel, and when I was offered accommodation in the families hostel we were both delighted because it was run by the Army and the sanitary arrangements were modern. We had two bedrooms, meals were served in a communal dining-room, and a large lounge was set aside for social functions. Edith had obtained a secretarial job with the East African Land Office, and we employed a Seychellese nanny to look after Pat. Because she was classified as a European she did no household chores, but with help from one of my African sergeants I had found an excellent houseboy named Lolo.

In order to compensate for the extra cost of living abroad, we were given an overseas allowance which some considered to be inadequate. General Dowler was concerned lest the standard of living of his soldiers and their families fell below that of civilians of similar status, and he made representations to the War Office that the amount should be increased. The general was keenly interested in the welfare of the families and had expressed a desire to visit the hostel, so this was arranged.

He arrived with Lady Dowler and his daughter a little early, to find that our senior member had not yet made an appearance. Having met the general and as the next senior resident present, I went forward to greet him. When asked what he would like to drink, he replied, 'A pint of Tusker,' and added, to my surprise, that 'she [Lady Dowler] will drink a pint of Tusker too.' We chatted until the senior member appeared. The general told me that he had recently returned from London, where he had been pressing for an increase in the local overseas allowance. He also discovered that prior to 1939 British forces serving in East Africa had drawn Colonial Inducement Pay, and he was arguing for it to be restored. His vigorous presentation of the case resulted in it being agreed, and we were all better off financially.

Kenya was now a very attractive place in which to live, with its wonderful climate, no food rationing, duty-free tobacco and drinks from the NAAFI, colourful dress material on sale without coupons in the Indian bazaar and money in our pockets.

Edith received a letter one day from an ex-colleague in England announcing that Doris and Dick Hoyle were on their way to Nairobi. Dick had served in the Kent police force and was being seconded to the Kenya police in the rank of senior superintendent in order to administrate its fast-growing traffic division. We welcomed the new arrivals at the railway station and offered any help we could give them in settling in.

Dick's first brief from the commissioner was to sort out the chaos in Nairobi itself and in particular the notorious 'Ainsworth crawl'. Residents from the surrounding residential areas drove into the town in time to reach their place of work between 8.30 and 9 a.m. and they invariably travelled home to lunch. Most of them had to traverse the Ainsworth Bridge over the Nairobi River, a traffic bottleneck because it was narrower than the roadway approaching it. By the simple expedient of removing twelve inches from each footpath, it was possible for three lanes of traffic to cross it, two into town during the morning rush-hour and after lunch, and two out of town at lunch-time and after work. All that was needed were two police askari to guide motorists into their lanes. Another of his innovations was to introduce angle parking in the town centre, which enabled twice the number of cars to be parked.

Meanwhile, back at Killarney Camp the standard continued to improve. As more wives arrived to join their husbands we were able to hold monthly social evenings in the sergeants' mess, with dance music provided by Radio Nairobi or gramophone records. Ladies foam-filled brassieres were the vogue in England for the flat-chested and there were titters of laughter when it became known that some of the new arrivals wore 'falsies'.

The peace of the camp was often shattered by the noise of commercial aircraft taking off from Nairobi West Airport. (It is now called Jomo Kenyatta International Airport and handles thousands of passengers each day, but was then little more than an airstrip.) The age of jet aircraft, apart from a few in use by the military, had not arrived and the Comet was yet to be designed. Although the runways were level they were unmetalled and graded by bulldozers from time to time. As these piston-engined propeller aircraft warmed up, huge clouds of soil were raised and followed them on their take-off run. It was reliably estimated that when a large passenger aircraft took off, two tons of earth was lifted into the air.

Up to now we had not travelled far out of Nairobi, and so we were pleased to receive an invitation from Tim and Agatha Timbrell to spend a weekend with them at their Nanyuki home. We drove through the coffee-growing areas of Kiambu, Thika and Fort Hall before reaching Nyeri. The Signals had a training-school here for African radio operators and despatch riders, and we paid a courtesy call on them; I was amazed at the aptitude shown by the recruits in handling a Morse key. We had set out early and were now ready for lunch, so we called at the now world-famous Outspan Hotel for an appetising meal.

The Timbrells were luckier than we were in that they had been granted a spacious quarter from the time of Agatha's arrival, but the outpost of Nanyuki was not so heavily populated as Nairobi. We visited a local hotel in the evening and I noticed a narrow metal strip running along the length of the bar. When asked the significance of this the barman replied that it represented the exact line of the equator – a drink served in the northern hemisphere was drunk in the southern.

After a convivial weekend at the Timbrells' we decided

to tour part of the Aberdare Mountains. Our first stop was Thompson's Falls (since renamed), where water cascaded from high levels and flowed into a river leading to Lake Naivasha. On reaching Nakuru in the Western Rift Valley we experienced some trouble with the suspension of the car and decided to return via Gilgil, where we could stop for a meal. As we neared the hotel entrance a short, sturdily built European emerged who looked familiar, and I recognized him as Jimmy Rowden.

We greeted each other with the Swahili word *Jambo*, universally used by all Kenya Europeans, and I persuaded him to join us for a drink. When he heard that we were staying for lunch, he suggested that we forgo the meal and have dinner with him, so we were content with a few drinks. Jimmy told us that he was acting as caretaker manager for a farmer who owned a string of valuable racehorses. The farmer had returned to England for a holiday and had given him permission to entertain any of his friends visiting the area. After a sumptuous meal we sat besides a blazing log fire and chatted over a bottle of whisky until bedtime.

He was up early organising the morning exercises of the horses, and when we appeared he invited Edith to a ride. She had never ridden a horse before and was rather nervous when a white gelding was led out and we helped her into the saddle. She was frightened of the animal bolting and after riding for a hundred yards she tried to halt the horse by calling out 'whoa', a command he didn't understand.

On returning home I made a point of investigating the suspension problem on the car. The Ford Prefect had been designed to travel on well-surfaced roads and the shock-absorbers were inadequate to cope with the corrugated tracks met with in Kenya.

The wily Indian traders were aware of the weakness and had bought up all available supplies, which they were selling for £25 per set of four, an extortionate amount of money in those days. I wrote to Armstrong Bros – the manufacturers – explaining the difficulty and asking for replacements to be sent out COD. They were unhelpful, so I wrote back to say that I had removed the shock-absorbers and the car ran just as smoothly without them. Within days I received an air-mail letter saying that they were despatching a set by fast parcel post and to ignore the invoice which gave their cost as 1s 11½d each.

From a military point of view the squadron was entering the 'silly season' leading to the annual administrative inspections. Experts from the medical profession arrived to report on our health and hygiene record, the fire inspector came to test our preparedness in coping with barrack-room or bush fires, a representative of the Ordnance Corps checked on the technical and clothing stores, where they made a point of looking for 'woolly bears' – parasites which fed on socks and woollen garments. Military transport was tested for serviceability, and particular attention was paid to the safeguarding of arms held in the armoury. Their reports were collated and presented to the formation commander and his staff officers when they arrived to inspect the guard, the messes and canteens, the barrack rooms, the cookhouses, the ration stores, the latrines and the general area which included the gardens. His report when it arrived was more than satisfactory and rewarded us for the hard work put in by all ranks. Our squadron was graded 'very good', and beneath his signature on the typed report the commander wrote in his own handwriting: 'This unit would have been graded "Excellent" had it not been setting a precedent and causing it to become complacent!'

Our second daughter, Linda, was born at the British Military Hospital in August 1949, and this addition to the family enabled me to qualify for a quarter. Four new warrant-officers' married quarters had been constructed within a compound of an ordnance vehicle depot on the Athi River Road leading to Mombasa. They were well designed and the sanitary arrangements were excellent, but the most pleasing aspect was that we now had our own kitchen and were not dependent on hotel or hostel food. Edith could buy whatever she pleased in Nairobi and received the help of a good native cook. The quarters were located in a compound within the main complex and entry to it could only be gained by giving the gate sentry the password, which was changed weekly.

We had not lived in the camp for long before I was awakened by a single shot ringing out. Thinking that the sentry had let off a round accidentally, I paid no heed to it; but on arriving for duty at Killarney Camp I was asked if my sleep had been disturbed. A shooting incident had been reported on Radio Nairobi and it seemed that the sentry had noticed a raider climbing the perimeter wire and alerted the guard commander, a British corporal, who gave the intruder an opportunity to surrender. This was not taken, so he shot him dead. The corporal was taken to Nairobi police station to make a statement and was detained in custody. His CO, an RAOC officer who had lost a limb in the war, travelled to the station and asked for him to be released into military custody. When his request was refused, he said: 'If you will not release him I will march a thousand men to your police station and they will release him, on my orders.' He was freed within minutes of the ultimatum being uttered!

It had been known for some time that King George VI had agreed to confer a Royal Charter on Nairobi early in 1950 to celebrate its half-centenary, and as February drew near many rehearsals were held by those chosen to take part in the ceremony.

The King had nominated his brother, HRH The Duke of Gloucester, to bestow the honour on the town, and he arrived accompanied by the Duchess. Dick Hoyle had secured Edith and me a good vantage-point on the steps leading up to the municipal buildings, where the Duke and Duchess were to meet the city fathers after taking the salute as the parade marched past them. The ceremonial was intended to depict the growth of the town since 1900 and the procession was led by the band of the King's African Rifles, followed by the resident battalion and the Kenya Regiment – a territorial unit manned by European nationals. The Kenya police were next in line, displaying their mobile division and foot police. A great cheer erupted as Colonel John Boyes led his Legion of Frontiersmen on horseback; some of the original bullock carts which had survived the long trek from the coast were drawn by a team of twelve oxen. Mule carts used by Baroness von Blixen at her Ngong farm came next, followed by camels from the Northern Area Region, the offspring of those who had helped in the construction of the railway, and after them came floats advertising the great trading emporia that had been established in the colony, bearing names such as Bousted and Clarke, Bullows and Roy, Gailey and Roberts, Torrs the Confectioners and many others founded by the earlier settlers. A great cheer went up as Sergeant George Ellis RE appeared at the rear of the procession, being pushed along in a wheelchair. He had trekked up from South Africa at the end of the Boer War, and was reputed to be the first white man to make his home in Nairobi. He helped to build the road which ran from Kibwezi through Nairobi to the White Highlands.

With the march past over, the Royal Duke and Duchess passed between Edith and me to hand over the Royal Charter. The Mayor of Nairobi emerged a few minutes later to say that Nairobi was now a city and he had been honoured by the King, who had appointed him its first lord mayor.

There was much revelry in the city that evening. Crowds flocked to the Norfolk, Torr's and the New Stanley Hotels, the Muthaiga Club and the Travellers Club, where excitable lady members drew their handguns and fired shots into the ceiling, as was their custom.

Soon after the celebrations were over another tragedy occurred. The RASC corporal who had shared a couchette with me when we met our wives at Mombasa disliked socialising, but his wife was lively and enjoyed dancing, much to his annoyance. Things came to a head late one night, and on her return from a dance they quarrelled and he clubbed her to death with a hammer, this being the second time in three years that Hoppy had executed a British soldier.

The spell of Africa was growing on me and the thought of returning to England, still in the grip of food rationing, did not appeal, so I applied for a further tour of duty. This was granted on condition that my family and I took at least one month's leave in the UK, but that would not start until January 1951. Apart from taking a few days' local leave when we visited the Aberdares, neither Edith nor I had enjoyed a decent break since our arrival in the colony, so we decided to spend two weeks on the beach at Nyali.

Except for a twenty-mile stretch from Nairobi to Athi River and another from MacKinnon Road to Mombasa, the road was unmetalled and rutted, although efforts were made to regrade it after the seasonal rains. It was only the intrepid, who risked coming face to face with a herd of elephants, that preferred the road to the railway, so we travelled by train.

The Army had taken over Nyali Beach Hotel for use as a leave and transit centre. It stood in idyllic surroundings; the beach was fringed by palm trees and the bathing area was protected from sharks by a natural coral reef. I swam to the reef one day and trod lightly on the coral, looking for the exquisite shells which could be found there. Unfortunately, I had neglected to wear some form of foot protection. After a few steps I felt an agonising pain in one foot and had to hop on the sound one to reach the sea. I had trodden on a sea-urchin! It is not easy to walk along coral in bare feet and more painful to hop on it on one foot, and my greatest fear was treading on another sea-urchin with my good one. Edith spent hours extracting the spines with a darning needle as she applied copious amounts of Dettol to guard against infection.

We had by now become quite friendly with the Hoyles, and Dick invited me to the annual police sports day. We watched the various track and field events until it was announced that the competitors in the five-mile cross-country race would arrive shortly and run two laps of the track. When the winner's time was made known Dick remarked that it compared well with the AAA record. It was then that he realised the potential of the Africans, whose staple diet was maize. Thereafter he took a keen interest in athletics, persuaded the Kenya Olympic Committee to enter for the 1956 Olympics due to be held in Rome, and managed the first-ever Kenyan team to participate in the Games.

While visiting the city one day I met an ex-corporal who had been my chief clerk in a previous unit. His name was Adams and he was employed in a supervisory capacity at

Gailey and Roberts store. Adams had heard that the Royal Navy, one of whose ships was paying a courtesy visit to Mombasa, had been invited to send a large contingent to Nairobi to be entertained by its citizens. The officers and chief petty officers were to be the guests of the Travellers Club, originally known as the 400 Club. Saturday night was usually gala night and members from as far as fifty miles away often flocked in. Adams and I, although not members, decided to attend, and as it was a dressy affair I put on my blue patrol suit and he wore a dinner jacket. Our formal dress foxed the usher, a huge Swede, who mistook us for official guests and we circulated freely amongst the members.

Fortunately for us there was no bar-chit system in operation that evening, so we were able to pay our way for drinks. Some ladies invited us to sit at their table and one noticed my row of five medal ribbons and asked where I had earned them, so I told her that I had seen service in India, France, the Western Desert, the Lebanon, Syria, Palestine and Italy – which puzzled her because she thought she was talking to a naval man. She had either been widowed early in life or her husband was away up-country and I was asked to spend the remainder of the night at her house, but I said that we had to check in by 1 a.m. A friend of hers told me afterwards that she lived alone in a bungalow not more than three hundred yards from the entrance to Killarney Camp!

One of the male members of the club recognised me and said 'You are Mrs Thomas's husband, are you not?' He worked in the Lands Office and he proposed and arranged for me to be seconded for membership.

We had lived at Athi River for some months when I heard that a quarter was becoming vacant nearer to my place of work. I applied for it on the grounds of being able to share transport with our adjutant, whose house was in Spring Valley. This stratagem worked because there was a current drive to economise on petrol, and we moved to a block of wooden buildings near to the old wartime airfield of the Royal Naval Air Station. Our new accommodation had another advantage in that a track leading from it was only ten minutes' walk from Killarney Camp. Shortly after moving in, my son Bryan was born at the BMH Nairobi, and when Major Bertie heard the news his comment was: 'A son for the Regiment.'

Our mess was a lively place on Sunday mornings, when members could invite their male friends to foregather for a chat and pre-lunch drinks. Duncan Fletcher was a popular guest. After a few glasses of gassy Tusker beer he often demonstrated one of his party tricks. Methane is a highly inflammable hydrocarbon gas, the product of decomposition of organic substances, and Duncan proved how explosive it could be. During a lull in the conversation he would raise his knee, strike a match, and when the time was right position the lighted lucifer below his shorts, when a vivid blue flame would ignite.

Our children had not been ill until Linda became sickly and was admitted to hospital in a feverish state. The doctors seemed puzzled and were unable to diagnose the complaint. Edith and I were worried and asked Phyllis, the Seychellese nanny, who always bathed her, if she had noticed anything unusual. She admitted seeing an insect on Linda's body, which she had brushed off. It then dawned upon me that it may have been a tic, those loathsome blood-sucking insects which attach themselves to dogs and have to be scraped away. I remembered, too, that in India one of our British soldiers had been diagnosed as suffering from tic-typhus. We lost no time in driving to the hospital and telling the duty MO of our fears. It was a timely visit and the information we were able to give resulted in a speedy recovery.

The short rains arrived in November and were welcomed, if only to allay the dust and to nourish the garden plants, but the parade-ground and paths became squelchy because they were hard and the rain did not soak in.

The Saturday morning routine of OC's inspection always ended by visiting the African married quarters, where the soldiers' wives and *totos* gathered outside their huts in their best clothes. We arrived early one morning to see the women clapping their hands in the air and Sergeant-Major Mwambile explained what they were up to. Dragonflies laid their eggs on the ground after the long rains and these hatched into larvae, often known as leather-jackets, which fed on the roots of green vegetation. When further heavy rain fell they emerged from the ground as dragonflies, and it was the appearance of these that excited the wives. They caught them in their hands, and when they had collected a bowl of dead insects cooked and ate them with their maize.

Notice had been served on me that we were to sail from Mombasa in January for our leave in England and I had many arrangements to make, the most pressing of which was organising the Christmas festivities. On the personal side the Ford Prefect car had to be disposed of because it was now too small to carry a baby and two youngsters on the rear seat. The local car agents were advertising a post-war Standard Vanguard, and I ordered one to be collected from the London showrooms upon my arrival.

One more problem had to be solved before we left and that concerned our quarters. Because I was returning to the same duty station, the rule was that I could retain it; but to do this meant paying rent for it during our absence. Fortunately, I found a friend prepared to rent it from me while we were away, and because of this I left many of our possessions *in situ*. He also agreed to employ Lola, the cook-houseboy, on my recommendation.

My family and I sailed from Mombasa on the HMT *Orduna*, which had left Singapore with a large contingent of RAF personnel and their families and been diverted to East Africa to collect leave and duty people – so relations between the services were rather strained. Apart from experiencing foul weather in the Bay of Biscay, the voyage was completed without any complications. The ship berthed at Liverpool on a miserable day in January and my wife, with assistance from the WVS, coped with the children – leaving me to clear the baggage through HM Customs and Excise.

I collected the Standard Vanguard from the showrooms and paid for it in pound notes because at that stage I had not opened up a bank account. It cost me about £400, which included the cost of shipping it back to Kenya. The salesman said that if I drove it a block away the wide boys would gladly hand over £1,000 for an export model.

It was still austerity time in England with food rationing

in force, and the climate and dark evenings compared badly with the wonderful weather we had enjoyed in Kenya. To make things worse the children sickened and young Bryan developed whooping cough; Edith and I took turns to nurse him throughout the night. The London smog did not help matters and the laws making smokeless fuel obligatory had not yet been enacted.

The appearance of a new export-model car caused envy and friction amongst some of the neighbours, who were unable to buy even a utility model because of the export drive to improve our balance of payments deficit. When Bryan had recovered from his attack of whooping cough we decided to visit my family in Anglesey. We found accommodation in Government House, formerly the grace and favour residence of Admiral Sir Percy Grant, by that time converted into an hotel. My father had retired from work, sold his house, moved into lodgings and, not caring for the life, had decided to remarry. His new wife was about ten years older than I was. The fresh breezes coming from the Irish Sea brought colour into our cheeks and gave us an appetite – amply satisfied by the generous portions provided by the landlady, who had good contacts with the seamen manning the mail-boats to Ireland, where food was plentiful.

In a small town with a population of ten thousand, news travels quickly. Most of the shopkeepers had heard that a Holyhead boy was in town, and I was offered provisions 'off the ration' to take back to London.

Edith's home was not spacious, so the children slept in the front room. This meant that four adults spent their evenings in the dining-room watching black and white television or playing bridge. The outlet to the chimney had been blocked off to conserve heat and we were dependent for warmth on a two-bar electric fire. After an hour or two the atmosphere became stifling with the door firmly closed. I often left the room on the pretext of visiting the lavatory, leaving the door slightly ajar to admit fresh air, only to hear it clicked firmly behind me.

During my stay in England I was very much aware that I had served as a warrant-officer class II for longer than nine years and was nearing the top of the seniority roll.

My fear was that if a vacancy for WO I occurred while I was on leave, my return to Nairobi could be blocked. That would be disastrous, as most of our belongings had been left there and the increase in pay for the higher rank would not compensate for the loss of overseas allowances and colonial pay. The car was another complication because it had been supplied out of the export quota and could not be retained in the UK. There was also the climate to consider.

It was with some relief that I received orders to proceed with my family to Southampton and embark on the HMT *Multan*. My last job in England was to hand back the Standard Vanguard to the agents so that it would be in Nairobi when I returned there.

19

EAST AFRICA 1951-52

The outward voyage proved uneventful. The only departure from a direct course through the Red Sea was to call at Port Sudan and Massawa to disembark families whose husbands were serving in the Sudan and Ethiopia. The sight of the fully armed soldiers and escorts was a welcome change from the boredom of life on board a ship and brought us back to reality. As we neared Mombasa I noticed that the sea ahead of us was discoloured and asked a ship's officer the reason for it. He explained that we were approaching the mouth of the Tana River, which was in flood after the recent long rains, and the river carried eroded soil as far as twenty miles into the Indian Ocean. We disembarked on 3rd May 1951 and the train to Nairobi awaited us at the dock railway sidings, ready to carry us on the all-night climb to the capital city.

The friend to whom I had lent my quarter was as good as his word and had moved out the day before we returned. I found out that Lolo had not got on with him and had left to go to his village. Despite that, he had heard that I was returning on the fourth and was there with his big grin to greet us. It is remarkable how news travels quickly in Africa, some say it is done by 'bush telegraph' or the beating of tom-toms, but in this case I guessed that Sergeant Boaz had seen a message in the communication centre advising our arrival and passed it on.

The news that greeted me on reporting for duty was that we were being visited by Major-General C. M. F. 'Slap' White, our CSO from Cairo, and that I had been awarded the Long Service and Good Conduct Medal. The cynics averred that it was awarded for eighteen years of undetected crime, whereas others described it as 'the mark of the beast'. The medal was made of silver – unlike those issued for service in the war, which were made of baser metal – and showed the head of King George VI on the obverse. It is the main qualification for admission to the Royal Hospital Chelsea, the home of that august body of men known as the Chelsea Pensioners, and it was the custom for the recipient to proceed to the mess, 'christen' it in a mug of beer, and buy a round of drinks.

Our friends soon learnt that we were back and many of them visited us in the evenings. It was pleasant to sit on the verandah drinking sundowners and listening to the roar of lions as they got ready to stalk their prey in the game park, which was only a mile away. We spent the weekends sharing picnic lunches with the Hoyles or the Lawrence-Browns, and sometimes organised a mess outing on Sunday afternoons, when the living-in members helped out by bringing along a hamper of food and an icebox full of drinks.

Dick Hoyle had rewritten the Traffic Ordinance for Kenya and the motorists had learnt to comply with the Highway Code. John Lawrence-Brown was Edith's former boss at the Lands Office and lived with his wife Bid and young family some miles out of the city in an area frequented by game, and lions could often be found in his grounds. They lived in primitive surroundings without electricity, and water had to be carried in a fifty-gallon drum to supplement the rain-water stored in the butts, but they enjoyed the life.

Edith had resigned from the Lands Office when we left to go on leave but soon found another job as secretary to the East African Airways, whose aircraft provided an internal service as far as Zanzibar, Tanganyika and Eritrea. It was based at the old Royal Naval Air Station, and at that time was the only airfield in Nairobi with tarmac runways.

Our sergeants' mess was as popular as ever and many members of other units in the garrison whom I had met at the hostel and the Athi River quarters were welcomed to attend our social functions, as well as our own officers and their ladies. Major Bertie asked me one day if he could bring a friend along, and when they arrived he introduced her as Mrs Markham.

Beryl Markham was at home with horses and she was a well-known trainer winning many top awards for her skill. She was also an ex-professional light aircraft pilot who made headlines in 1936 when she flew solo across the Atlantic from Abingdon to Nova Scotia in adverse weather conditions and without the aid of radio in less than twenty-four hours. We chatted for a little while during refreshment time and when she saw me nibbling a stick of celery remarked with a mischievous grin, 'That will put lead into your pencil.'

The day dawned when Major-General White was due to visit us and things started off badly. He and the CSO East Africa Command were due to start their tour at 9.30 a.m., and while I was making a preliminary inspection of the guard at 8.30 a.m. I noticed a staff car approaching the guard room along the murrum track. We were prepared for them to arrive a few minutes early but this was going too far, and it was my unpleasant duty to explain that they had arrived an hour too soon, so they returned to the HQ at Waterworks Camp – no doubt to deliver a 'rocket' to the unfortunate staff officer who had wrongly briefed them. The inspection went well, he was pleased with the turn-out and drill of the quarter guard, and we then walked to the transmitting station at Kenton, from which signal traffic was passed to his HQ at Cairo.

Next on the list was the barrack-room accommodation and messes, canteens and cookhouses. As we passed the tidy gardens outside the sleeping-quarters he noticed the flowers and with a twinkle in his eye said, 'I can see that these were not planted yesterday for my benefit.' The tour of inspection ended in the sergeants' mess, and as he looked out of the windows at the shrubs and verdant banks surrounding us he remarked that it was a pity that Hollingshead could not enjoy the beauty of it. Noticing my lack of comprehension he added, 'Didn't you know that he is colour-blind?'

Major Hollingshead called me to his office one afternoon to say that a sergeant who was due to join us from Eritrea had caused trouble on the plane and an escort was required to meet him at the airfield. I decided to go in person and apologise to the airways staff. On my arrival I was told that he had drunk too much of the duty-free drink supplied on board and when told that no more was forthcoming he became abusive. On our return to camp I ordered him to remain in his room until the morning and detailed another sergeant to make sure that he did. His name was Laurie Hitchcock, and I remembered serving with him earlier in another theatre of operations. He did not fit in well with his fellow sergeants and in order to understand him better I invited him home for dinner, after which I offered him a bed for the night. When he emerged rather bleary-eyed in the morning, Edith asked what he would like for breakfast and was surprised to hear him say, 'A gin and Andrews Liver Salts, please.'

Dick Hoyle suggested one day that we make a trip round the Ngong Hills to see if there was any game about, and we decided to travel along the track nearest to the Rift Valley, which most travellers avoided. The soil at this end was known as 'black cotton' and consisted of volcanic ash formed out of lava which had flowed down the Rift from now extinct volcanoes. During the rainy seasons the surface of the plain becomes a glutinous mass impossible to traverse by wheeled transport and avoided by hoofed animals, who tended to sink into it. After we descended two thousand feet the atmosphere became humid but the trees and vegetation flourished, and we came upon hundreds of giraffe feeding off the tree-leaves that only they could reach. It was a wonderful sight to see so many together and it was apparent that man was a strange animal to them. Alerted by the sound of the car engines, they looked at us with an arrogant gaze and then made off, using a curious but graceful lope peculiar to their kind. We saw no more game that day and after a picnic lunch started to climb and it was not long before we reached the firmer murrum tracks which are immune to all but torrential rain.

John Lawrence-Brown surprised us one day by saying that he and a blue-stocking colleague from the office intended to climb Mount Kilimanjaro. We thought he was joking until they both set off in his truck filled with equipment and provisions, heading for Moshi in Tanganyika. They returned two weeks later, claiming that they had climbed the 19,340-foot peak without suffering any mishaps. John was mildly teased about his relationship with his companion, with whom he shared a tent, but retorted that after climbing 3,000 feet a day they were in no mood for other activities at night.

Now that we had a larger and more powerful car than the Ford Prefect we decided to spend a week 'up-country' before the arrival of the short rains. The Standard Vanguard had a spacious passenger seat and a roomy boot, which contained a portable cooker and sufficient emergency food for our needs. As we drove towards the Rift Valley it was noticeable that the trees in the nearby forest were being felled to provide *kuni* (firewood) for the fireplaces and kitchen stoves of the Europeans, and there was speculation about a dust bowl being created around the city.

The Great Rift Valley starts at what is now Malawi and extends through Kenya and surrounding territories until it reaches the Red Sea. It is between thirty and forty miles wide and its floor is between two and three thousand feet lower than the surrounding high ground. The climb up to the escarpment was gradual and the ride smooth, thanks to the efforts of Italian prisoners of war captured in Eritrea and Ethiopia. These troops, sent by Mussolini to defend his 'empire' in the 1930s, were no match for the British, East African and Indian Divisions, which captured their strongholds and shipped them back to Kenya for the duration of the war. The Italians are clever engineers who excel at road-making, and the metalled highway leading up to the escarpment was a tribute to their skill.

As we moved nearer the top we were surprised to see dozens of snakes wriggling across the road on their way to lower ground, and they squirmed because they disliked the heat of the tar macadam surface. At the base of the escarpment stood a small church built of stone by the Italian construction workers, where they could worship. The metalled road ended at the bottom of the escarpment and we continued towards Gilgil on tracks composed mainly of volcanic soil.

Our aim was to stop at Nakuru for lunch, and we arrived at the Stag's Head Hotel in time to drink a glass of beer first. The bill of fare suited every taste and Edith did justice to it, sampling every dish – to the amazement of the bearers, who were more used to serving hungry men.

When John Lawrence-Brown, who was Kenya born, heard that we were travelling up-country, he told us not to miss Eldoret, which had started off as a farm and grown into a sizeable township. He also related that one of the pioneers had trekked up by ox-waggon early in the twentieth century and, helped by his brother, built the first stone house on the plateau. The Cripps brothers called their farm Curraghmore and it was well known because its grounds contained a full-sized tennis court.

As we approached Eldoret we saw an unusual sight, a team of twelve oxen drawing a huge waggon loaded with maize. The animals were approaching the road from a side-track, and I stopped the car so that the team could maintain its momentum. Unaccountably the white farmer in charge halted, and I waved to him to proceed. He ignored my signal, so I drove slowly past and waved to him in thanks but was ignored. He was a big man, standing well over six feet in height, and I could not understand his reluctance to return a friendly greeting. It was not until we returned to Nairobi that I related the incident to John and was saddened to hear that the farmer had volunteered for service in the British Army and been drafted to the Far East. He was taken prisoner by the Japanese, and because he would not kowtow they had gouged out his eyes. He must have been an understanding man and realised that his waggon would hold us up on the narrow roadway, which is why he had halted his oxen.

We booked into a colonial-type hotel in Eldoret, and after putting the children in charge of an ayah Edith and I repaired to the long bar, where some of the local residents assembled for their sundowners. The settlers who lived in the White Highlands were disdainful of those living in Nairobi, considering them all to be Government employees, bureaucrats or traders; however, when I told them that I was serving in the British Army but seconded to the East African forces, showing them my slouch hat to prove it, they became quite friendly.

We had intended to visit Kisumu on the shores of Lake Victoria but the children were becoming bored and tended to suffer from car sickness. After taking a last look at the 14,000-foot Mount Elgon with its surrounding forests we decided to make a leisurely journey home. Schooling did not start in Kenya until a child was seven years of age, so to relieve their boredom when travelling we used to teach them the alphabet, simple spelling and mental arithmetic.

Now and again we encountered young Masai boys guarding their cattle, and although they had not reached the warrior stage they carried a spear and were always willing to be photographed. The Masai are a nomadic race and travel vast distances to find grazing for their herds, and because of their roaming way of life they were not considered to be suitable material for the Kenya Army. The settlers told us that many of the Masai women were barren, and it was not uncommon for the warriors to raid Kikuyu reserves and take away their women for mating purposes.

We reached Naivasha in the late afternoon and stayed at the Rift Valley Hotel. Our friends had told us that Lake Naivasha must be seen at all costs. The locals said that this area had been the stamping-ground of the Happy Valley set, and described the huge villa, bordering the lake, which had once been the home of Molly, the Countess of Erroll, and was known as the 'gin palace'.

We were all eager to see the wildlife and bird-life that Lake Naivasha sustained. We found a spot which, judging from the tyre tracks, was a popular viewing-point. Back in the Nairobi Game Park the hippo pool was one of the few areas where visitors were permitted to get out of their cars, and in my naivety I thought that the hippos were harmless creatures. We watched them, from within the car, with their young calves cavorting in the water, surrounded by thousands of flamingoes, egrets, ducks, herons and many other species of birds.

I have learnt since that hippos can be very dangerous and unpredictable animals. They are very large hoofed creatures with thick hides, susceptible to sunburn, and feed on vegetation bordering the lakes or rivers in which they live. Because the sun's rays affect them, they are almost totally immersed in water by day and do their grazing at night. It happens sometimes that they do emerge from the water in the day, and woe betide the human who comes between them and their natural habitat or their young. Juanita once told me that she was chased by a hippo at Tsavo, and it was only clambering over a fallen tree trunk that saved her from being trampled to death. Because of their weight they tend to shuffle and are unable to climb over an obstacle, and knowing this fact proved to be her salvation.

When we reached home we were greeted by Doris and Dick Hoyle, who told us that they had a house guest who was visiting Nairobi to advise the Kenya police on modern fingerprinting techniques. He was a police superintendent serving with the Special Branch at New Scotland Yard, named Sydney Barnes. When his wife joined him a few weeks later, I knew that this was no fleeting visit and it crossed my mind that his advisory visit was a pretext. The Kenya police were well versed in identification procedures, every African carried a fingerprinted ID card, and why should the Colonial Office spend money on sending a senior Special Branch officer to Kenya on a prolonged stay when a local man could have been sent to London and brought up to date with modern methods? The real aim of his visit was to arrange for the security of Princess Elizabeth and the Duke of Edinburgh, who were due to visit Kenya in 1952, and in order to fulfil his brief he had to investigate the activities of the Kenya African Union and other dissidents who were clamouring for independence.

I had now served in East Africa for four years and knew the characteristics of the askari. They had been trained to perform their routine tasks well, but what irritated me most was their insistence on holding a *baraza* if they were required to depart from the normal drill. A *baraza* is a meeting convened to discuss the new orders and is time-consuming because each askari present is entitled to his say. Its origin sprang from their tribal traditions, when the headman summoned his followers from time to time, to lay down the law, but seemed inappropriate when dealing with trained soldiers.

Dick Hoyle surprised me by saying that Doris and he had been invited to Kibera Village and asked if we would join them. The village was barely a mile from our camp and was home to the thieves who raided our bungalows before the arrival of the guard dogs. It was peopled by Nubians and Somalis who had been allocated a reserve in recognition of their war service, and it was a den of iniquity. Its inhabitants were responsible for law and order within the community and it was off limits to the Kenya police. They brewed their own pombe (native beer), produced a drug called bhang and paid no poll-tax. Our own pay clerk Muhammed lived there, as did another African RSM who was stationed at Waterworks Camp. I often saw him as he skirted our camp on his way to work on foot and he was as smart as anyone I had seen wearing uniform, but late one afternoon he returned to the village dishevelled and inebriated. As he passed by he noticed me observing him, and his face assumed an expression of animal hatred. What upset him was that he had been seen by a *bwana* in an intoxicated state.

The elders of the village made us very welcome, and after a tour of the area produced cups of tea and cakes which we were assured had been bought in Torr's confectionery shop that morning. Dick was puzzled at being invited and asked the reason. The reply was that he was the senior superintendent of the traffic division and not an ordinary policeman, but no doubt they knew that he had the ear of the commissioner and would report favourably on his visit.

Christmas was now approaching and with it the retirement of our adjutant, Bill Savage. He was a popular figure in the Corps which he had served so long, and the hospitality he and his wife May had shown to his men when he was a section sergeant at Rawalpindi was legendary. We gave him a good send-off before he retired to settle in his house at Spring Valley, and made him an honorary member of our mess.

With Christmas over, preparations were made for a gala dance on New Year's Eve. I read a piece of poetry in the

East African Standard entitled 'Ring Out Wild Bells' and memorised it so that I could do it as my party piece. We then installed a microphone in the bar and Smudger Smith and I entered it shortly before midnight. The timing was crucial; at the stroke of twelve I concluded my rendering of the poem with the words:

> *Ring out the old, ring in the new,*
> *Ring out the false, ring in the true,*
> *Ring out the thousand years of war,*
> *Ring in the thousand years of peace.*

It was well received, and to the strains of 'Auld Lang Syne' and kisses all round we continued to celebrate the New Year well into the early hours of the morning.

Princess Elizabeth left London in January 1952 with her husband, the Duke of Edinburgh, on a Commonwealth tour. King George VI, who was now ailing, travelled with them to the London airport, where they emplaned for Nairobi. Although it was deemed to be an official visit, the royal couple had expressed their wish that it should be regarded as a holiday rather than a ceremonial affair, so the Governor, Sir Philip Mitchell, arranged to dispense with pomp and formality. Dick Hoyle alerted us that the Princess and her husband were to visit a school in the city, and Edith and I were among the few Europeans who stood at the school entrance when they arrived. We all clapped politely and were rewarded with a gracious smile.

Plans had been made for a trip to the Nairobi Game Park on the following morning, this being the time of day that the lions rested after gorging themselves on the previous night's kill. The chief game warden and his scouts were aware of the roaming habits of the beasts and were at pains to locate a small pride close to the route taken by the escorting party. Lions, unless seen in silhouette, can be difficult to spot because their skins blend with the surrounding vegetation, but this pride was so close to the track as to be clearly visible.

Tree Tops was within the grounds of the Outspan Hotel at Nyeri, a settlement in the Aberdares from which the twin peaks of Mount Kenya could be seen. It was constructed as a restaurant high up in the trees, supported by massive tree trunks, and it also served as a hide from which the movement of big game prowling below could be observed.

Customers lunching at the hotel could obtain admission to the grounds using the proprietor's transport for a small fee and were allowed to dismount, provided they did not stray far afield. During the heat of the afternoon the animals usually rested, but precautions existed for visitors to escape an attack by means of ladders attached to trees; for the less nimble, there were solid redoubts which would withstand the charge of a rhino.

Access to Tree Tops was by means of a long wooden staircase and the grounds had been floodlit. It was only the wealthy who could afford to spend a night there, and those who did usually lunched at the hotel, rested at Tree Tops in the afternoon, and after tea and sundowners spent the night spotting the game below them.

It was on 5th February 1952 that the royal party, which included Lady Mountbatten, climbed the steps leading to Tree Tops, where the Princess was able to see elephants, rhinos and waterbuck, but on the sixth news was received that her father had died, and she and her husband returned to England forthwith. She was proclaimed Queen on 8th February. Out of respect for the late King, a period of court mourning was announced, and black armbands were worn by warrant-officers and above.

The British soldiers posted to East Africa were hand picked and the African askari retained to serve as regulars were chosen for their ability and loyalty, and because of this we had few defaulters. On one occasion a British other rank was charged with an offence and at the hearing he appeared to be confused. The OC suspended proceedings and said to me that the defendant looked guilty but asked my opinion. I remembered a saying of Victor Hugo's and quoted, 'Nothing looks more guilty than innocence unjustly accused.' Bertie took the point and the case was dismissed.

In 1952 some of the Africans were becoming truculent and the incidence of robberies increased. The practice of 'fish poling' came into being – thieves poked long hooked bamboo sticks through open windows, hoping to fish out handbags or clothing. If disturbed by these intrusions, one avoided grabbing the pole; many of them had razor-blades fitted to them.

Press reports were coming in of atrocities committed by those members of the Kenya Africa Union who were demanding independence. The Europeans most at risk were the farmers living in remote areas whose servants had been coerced by the extremists to commit acts of treachery. The district commissioners and district officers were aware of the situation but their reports were not taken too seriously at Government House. The *East African Standard* quoted cases of European-owned cattle having their teats severed and their limbs hacked off. As the year progressed it became apparent that African servants had been persuaded into committing atrocities against their employers; many settlers in the remoter districts were hacked to death by their own houseboys and their farms razed to the ground. Many African chiefs who spoke out against violence were themselves murdered, and the member of the Legislative Council for Kiambu, a Kikuyu, was done to death by his own tribe. It was soon clear that these were not isolated cases of terrorism carried out by disaffected workers or agitators, and district commissioners' reports to the Governor suggested that the trouble was being master-minded into a full-scale insurrection.

The new Governor and Commander-in-Chief, Sir Evelyn Baring, realised the seriousness of the situation and declared a state of emergency in October 1952. Before the state of emergency ended in 1956, Jomo Kenyatta had been imprisoned as a suspected Mau Mau manager, the Kenya Regiment, of which John Lawrence-Brown was a member, had been mobilised, a British Army brigade and four British Infantry regiments were sent out to reinforce the King's African Rifles and they received air support from two squadrons of the RAF.

Thousand of African rebels were killed in the campaign, over 100 Europeans lost their lives and an estimated 2,000 Africans loyal to the Government of Kenya had been murdered by the insurgents. It is open to question how many of the rebels were summarily executed by the Kenya Regiment, but for years after the state of emergency ended Edith and I received a gruesome Christmas card from the regiment depicting an African hanging from a gallows erected in the bush. Sadly Tree Tops was burnt to the ground by guerillas in 1953, but it was rebuilt after the emergency ended.

My promotion to RSM was promulgated in March and this, unlike my previous appointment during the war, was of a permanent nature and entitled me to serve on in a rank carrying a lucrative rate of pay. But it was debatable whether I could remain in East Africa because the rank of warrant-officer class I was surplus to the Signals establishment. This question was resolved a few weeks later when a signal reached us asking if I wished to attend a conversion course in England, leading to commissioning as a cipher officer.

Two cipher officers were already held on our strength, Captains Harry Gilmore (who had defended me at my court martial in the desert) and Jack Leggett, married to a charming Greek lady of classical beauty named Cleo. Their advice was to accept, otherwise I might have to wait for several months before being commissioned as a Quarter-Master. At the same time an approach was made to me by the Kenya police to take over the post of transport officer for their expanding fleet of vehicles in the rank of superintendent. Many of the forces' senior officers had transferred to Kenya from the Indian police service after independence was declared in 1946 and were nearing retirement age. What they needed was a military man with extensive knowledge of the care and maintenance of vehicles who was well versed in workshop practice. The salary was attractive but the conditions of service did not match my prospects in the Army, which was always considered to be a good employer, and I declined the offer.

SSM Mwambile came to the office one day in a state of excitement and told me that Colonel Ellis was visiting us. Jim Ellis had joined the Army in 1919, before the Corps was formed, and had spent the war years in Kenya, where he became Chief Signal Officer East Africa Command. He was well liked by the askari and was paying a private visit after his retirement in 1951. The spell of Africa is difficult to shrug off!

Prior to 1952, the squadron had not suffered any serious casualties, but during that year we had two deaths involving members of a unit attached to us which had arrived recently from the Canal Zone in Egypt. One of its younger members had decided that the drinks served in the canteen lacked punch, so he visited the New Stanley Hotel and had too much to drink. When the taxi bringing him back to camp arrived, the driver discovered that he had a corpse lying on his rear seat. The post-mortem report revealed that he had died as a result of choking on his own vomit.

The second case was sad in that it involved Sergeant Bob Adams, whom I had known since we were recruits at Catterick Camp and whose wife had joined him a few months earlier. Bob was in charge of despatch riders and took part in a training exercise to acquaint his men with the area. When riding from one point to another, he noticed on his map a disused railway bridge – and to shorten his journey decided to cross it on foot, pushing his motor cycle along beside him. Unfortunately he stumbled, and both he and the machine crashed to the river bed below. We all did our best to comfort his widow, who now had to face the three-week voyage home alone with her grief.

In May 1952 Edith was admitted to hospital for what was then referred to as a 'tidy-up operation' to clear up a condition brought about by childbirth. The Army was finding difficulty in replacing the skilled medical officers leaving the service and found it necessary to engage CMPs (civilian medical practitioners) in lieu of RAMC doctors. The civilian surgeon who operated on her was Mr E. R. Ormerod, who later in life took silk and became a high court judge.

She did not respond readily to the post-operation treatment and spent weeks in hospital before being discharged. John Lawrence-Brown paid us a visit to wish her well. John, a non-smoker who had a good nose for scents, expressed misgivings about her physical condition. He must have passed them on to the BMH staff, because shortly after leaving us a serving medical officer appeared and ordered a bed to be made available for her forthwith, and his prompt action saved her life.

At the subsequent inquiry it was disclosed that there had been gross negligence on the part of the medical team because not all of the swabs used in the operation had been removed, and after the incision was stitched up one of these foreign bodies remained within her and was beginning to putrefy.

An emergency operation was carried out that day and my OC was instructed by the medical people to grant me leave in order to look after the children. Edith's immediate reaction when the effects of the anaesthetic had worn off was to discharge herself from hospital, and after boarding a taxi at the car-park she arrived home in a distressed state. Fortunately, Joan Perrin, the wife of one of my sergeants, lived nearby and I asked her to do what she could to comfort her.

It was now less than a week before we were due to leave for home, there was no certainty that Edith was medically fit to travel, and I was angry. My last official action was to write a complaint to the medical authorities stating that on my return to the UK I intended to complain to the Army Council, since at that time it was not possible to sue the Crown for damages caused through the negligence of one of its servants. I handed the letter to Major Dicky Brett, who had replaced Bertie Hollingshead, paid a quick visit to the mess to apologise for not throwing a farewell party, and stayed at home to await further instructions.

The incident had caused some consternation in the medical branch of East Africa Command, who made every effort to smooth our passage home. A nursing sister paid twice-daily visits to our quarter to renew dressings, and we were assured that a nurse would be made available to accompany Edith on the train journey to Mombasa, then she would be escorted on to the ship by the nursing staff.

The surgeon, as head of the operating team, could not be absolved from responsibility, and before we left he told Edith that he had arranged for Mr Lack, an eminent London consultant, to check on her progress when we reached home. In a follow-up letter sent from his private consulting room at Corner House, Hardinge Street, Nairobi, on 2nd September 1952, written in his own hand, he expressed his sorrow at the complications that arose following the operation.

Instructions were passed to the ship's staff that two cabins and a bathroom were to be put at our disposal for the voyage home, and for a week or two I became a children's nanny, bathing them and taking them to the dining-room for meals at the special sitting.

When I climbed the companion-way to the deck on the morning after we sailed, I noticed that instead of steaming north-east towards the Horn of Africa the ship was heading due east. The reason for this was announced from the bridge at noon. The vessel was being diverted to Mahé in the Seychelles, where we were taking on board a contingent of local technicians and labourers for work at our base in Egypt – to replace British soldiers who were being withdrawn gradually to other defence zones following the Egyptians' abrogation of a 1936 Anglo-Egyptian Treaty. (It was just a few weeks later that Colonel Nasser headed a military junta which deposed King Farouk and appointed General Neguib as head of state.)

It was a very rare event then for a passenger vessel of any sizeable tonnage to visit Mahé, which lacked docking facilities. Because of its draught, our vessel 'stood to' some distance from the shore and the contract labour bound for Egypt was transported to it by tender. The Seychelles Islanders are a people of mixed race and vary from Creoles to near-European. For the whole of the time we remained in the bay the local people flocked to see us, using dinghies, rowing-boats and launches, until the ship's siren signalled that it was time to depart.

The Seychelles lie five degrees south of the equator, and as we were not scheduled to call at any port before refuelling at Aden, the captain had time to organise the crossing-of-the-line ceremony – and King Neptune, to the delight of the children on board and amidst much hilarity, boarded the vessel. The chosen victims sat in the barber's chair, their faces were smeared with soft soap and using a massive wooden razor, the King of the Ocean removed it, before tipping them backwards into a large canvas bath filled with sea-water.

After a few days at sea Edith's health improved and colour was restored to her cheeks. By the time we reached the Great Bitter Lakes she was back to normal. The Seychellese passengers were disembarked in tenders while we queued up to take our place in the westbound convoy. Because national pride was running high in Egypt, we were cautioned not to taunt the local people by calling them wogs when we reached Port Said. The vessel tied up for a short while quite close to Ferdinand de Lesseps' bust and the bum-boat owners tried to sell us 'feelthy pictures', Spanish fly (an aphrodisiac) and garish trinkets which all of us had seen before. One saw the usual leering Arab undo his fly buttons and flash his penis before the women passengers; some of them averted their eyes, while others exclaimed, 'What a whopper!'

We were not sorry to leave Port Said behind us. Our trip through the Mediterranean was uneventful, and for once the Bay of Biscay was placid. Our ship docked at Southampton in late June and from there it was only a short journey to our temporary home.

20

MUMBO-JUMBO

After the customary disembarkation leave I joined 4th Training Regiment at Catterick Camp and met for the first time seven other RSMs who were to be my fellow pupils on the cipher conversion course. A remarkable change had taken place in this North Yorkshire garrison since I had left it eighteen years ago. A few of the old huts built to house German prisoners of war still stood in Baghdad lines, but elsewhere modern brick-built barrack rooms and messes had replaced them. In an effort to neutralise the wind-swept moors, and to commemorate those members of the Corps who lost their lives in World War II, saplings had been planted, one for each soldier of the Corps who did not return. The hope was that when they grew up into mature trees, the camp would lose its barren appearance.

Our class was welcomed by Colonel Tozer, the CO, who summarised the training programme and was at pains to stress that anyone wishing to withdraw from the course should do so sooner than later, reminding us that most of us were used to an active outdoor life and might not relish working in an office for the remainder of our service.

The first requirement was to learn to touch-type and achieve a speed of thirty words per minute on a manual typewriter before being taught the mysteries of ciphers – no easy task for men whose average age was forty and whose fingers were not so nimble as a young female learning to become a stenographer. Through perseverance we all attained the standard required and then graduated from the Olympia typewriter to the Creed teleprinter then in use by the Army. For some reason we were taught to press the carriage-return key twice at the end of a line, followed by double spacing. At the end of six weeks we were all proficient touch-typists, albeit at lower speeds than a trained stenographer.

After a day in the class-room some of us were in need of fresh air and exercise, and spent the evenings walking to the delightful local taverns that abounded in that part of Yorkshire. Television was coming into its own, but in some remote parts of the country reception was poor. North Yorkshire was no exception, so consequently very few thrifty Yorkshire folk bought a set. A few enterprising pub landlords spent money on expensive aerial equipment, hoping to attract customers and boost their profits by installing TV sets in their saloon bars. This ploy did not work, because the viewers were content to gape at the screen and did not trouble to walk to the bar to replenish their drinks. Those of us who patronised pubs to enjoy a drink, a chat and an occasional game of darts or shove-halfpenny resented being told to hush if we spoke louder than in a whisper, and transferred our custom; so the publicans enticing drinkers through the lure of TV lost out.

As the coverage of television improved some householders got rid of pianos to make room for the new monster. 'Piano-smashing' events were held – encouraged by the TV manufacturers – and that was the beginning of vandalism in England.

The provisions of the Official Secrets Act preclude mention of the methods used to train cipher operators, but anyone who has read fictional tales about espionage will know of the existence of one-time pads. Similarly, the public will now be aware of how German secret wireless traffic, encrypted by the Enigma machines, was decrypted by our cryptographers through the use of identical apparatus which the Poles had captured in the early days of the war and handed over to us. We were now in an era of technological development, and it would be naive to believe that our scientists had not designed better devices than Enigma to protect our communication security.

Our training was now coming to an end. In the last week we were sent to the War Office Signal Centre to gain an insight into how a large communication network functioned, and it was in a coach on the way to the Embankment that we saw a trendy group of young men out walking. They seemed out of place until it dawned on us that they were the Teddy boys we had heard about but never seen.

We had all qualified on the course, and on returning from the Signal Centre we had an opportunity to visit Moss Bros at Covent Garden to be measured for our dress uniform, and to Herbert Johnson, the Corps hatters, to ensure that our headgear fitted.

On our return to Catterick the colonel gave us a talk on the problems we were likely to meet in the transformation from warrant-officer status to commissioned rank. Because of our length of service we would be given the rank of lieutenant, and a third of the time served after twelve years would count towards promotion to the rank of captain. The daily rate of pay would increase marginally, involving in my case a rise of 1s 6d above the highest skilled trade rate of 27s 6d for an RSM.

He suggested that before joining our next regiment we gave thought to the name by which we wished to be known. I had been christened William John Thomas, and inevitably my Christian name was abbreviated to 'Willy', which I disliked because that was the word used to describe a little boy's appendage. John Thomas was worse because it was the term applied by music-hall comedians to describe an adult male's pride and joy, so I settled for 'Tommy'.

Finally, the colonel advised us to open a bank account before we left, as in future we would be paid monthly in arrears instead of weekly at the pay table. The talk over, Colonel Tozer wished us all good luck in our new units. The president of the Catterick sergeants' mess threw a farewell party for us that evening, at which a brother warrant-officer, Guy Symonds, with whom I had served at Eaton Square, was present; I was to meet him again many times before he became involved in that notorious murder trial.

Our party left by train on the following evening, our destination being Newton Abbot in Devonshire, where we were to complete our documentation for commissioning.

Each of us was handed a Regular Army Certificate of Service listing our personal particulars and service history, including a Certificate of Discharge certifying that we were being discharged on 3rd November 1952 for the purpose of being appointed to a short-service commission in Royal Signals. My total service on that date was shown as 19 years and 363 days, of which 7 years and 250 days were spent in the ranks, 11 years and 73 days as warrant-officer class II and 1 year 39 days as warrant-officer class I.

When the formalities were over, we removed our badges of rank and fitted two stars to each of our epaulettes. We were now what is known as 'two-pippers'. Lunch followed in the depot officers' mess, after which we were free to travel home on leave.

In due course I received my commission, printed on parchment, which commenced:

> *Elizabeth the Second by the Grace of God, of the United Kingdom of Great Britain and Northern Ireland and of Her other Realms and Territories Queen, Head of the Commonwealth, Defender of the Faith.*
> *To our trusty and well beloved William John Thomas Greetings.*

It went on to say what was expected of me and ended as follows:

> *Given at Our Court at Saint James's the Eighth Day of December 1952 in the First Year of Our Reign.*
> *By Her Majesty's Command.*

We considered it unfair to foist ourselves once more on Edith's parents, and while I was away at Catterick my wife found accommodation in a flat at Cliftonville in Kent which was close to a sandy beach. The thing we missed most was the car. I had had to sell it in Kenya because I had not used it abroad for the full two-year term that would have absolved me from paying purchase tax. Fortunately, I had found a buyer for it, thanks to a prolonged strike at the Ford factory at Dagenham which resulted in a shortage of export cars.

Before my two weeks' leave had expired, I received instructions to report to Harwich en route to join the British Army of the Rhine, leaving my family behind until quarters could be found for us in Germany.

21

POSTWAR GERMANY

Five of us recently commissioned cipher officers met again at Harwich for a night crossing to the Hook of Holland. Then we joined a special train to take us to HQ BAOR, then stationed at Bad Oeynhausen – a town just south of the Minden Gap, which throughout history had formed a natural defence barrier against hostile forces attempting to overrun the plains of Saxony. We were interviewed by Colonel Paul Gambier, who told me that I was being posted to a Signals squadron located at Hanover in Lower Saxony, the main reason being that the shortage of families' accommodation was less acute there than elsewhere.

When I arrived at Hanover a heavy layer of snow covered the ground, although it was only mid-November, and remained on the surface until it thawed in late spring of the following year.

Our squadron HQ was in Sterling House, an imposing building on the outskirts of the city, which was also home to elements of the Control Commission Germany – an organisation created to serve as a form of government covering the transition period between the chaotic state of affairs when the Germans surrendered and the restoration of good democratic government.

My new OC was Major 'Dickie' Dirs – great character – a corpulent man who had spent most of his life as a sergeant on the North-West Frontier of India before moving with his division to Burma, where his ability was recognised with the grant of a short-service commission.

We were insufficient in number to form our own mess and were attached to 'B' Mess, with members of other branches of the service and the numerous transitees who passed through the garrison. Field-Marshal Montgomery, in his capacity as CIGS, had decreed that bars should be removed from Army officers' messes, but because of the number of temporary members we had been granted dispensation and 'Willie', our elderly Silesian barman, was quite happy to serve anyone who signed a chit.

The field-marshal had received a lot of publicity in November when he reached the age of sixty-five and thus qualified for the state pension. When he emerged from the local post office clutching his pension book, there was no lack of press photographers to keep him in the limelight that he so dearly loved, and this did little to improve the image of the Welfare State.

One of our members, known as 'Monty', had played an interesting deception role when the then General Montgomery was pursuing his North African offensive. 'Monty' had a striking resemblance to the general and from time to time acted as his double in visits to places far away from the front, where he was photographed by the press, and Pathé Gazette for the cinemas, giving the fifth-columnists and informers the impression that he was relaxing, whereas the real Monty was in his forward HQ planning the next move.

Hanover District was responsible for administrating the greater part of the British Zone, and it was the task of our squadron to provide communications back to Rhine Army HQ independent formations and individual units within our area, and to Hamburg and Rhine Districts. This was achieved by means of formal teleprinter messages, the Signals Despatch Service and numerous telephone switchboards. The German economy was slow in recovering and we were fortunate in having access to qualified and well-educated German staff who would otherwise be unemployed.

The job was interesting because, apart from controlling my own small cipher office and signal centre staff, it enabled me to supervise our far-flung exchanges and at the same time meet the Army units for whom the operators provided a service. One of our largest detached switchboards was at Hohne on Lünenburg Heath, where the bulk of our armoured forces had taken over an immense barracks, formerly occupied by German troops and close to the village of Bergen-Belsen. Belsen was one of the many concentration camps set up by the Germans to eliminate the Jewish population by means of gas chambers and furnaces, and although the infamous buildings had been razed to the ground no one ever heard birds singing there. It has since been converted into a permanent memorial site for those who were murdered in the Holocaust because of their race, and attracts millions of visitors each year.

The earliest Allied occupation troops to arrive in Germany had not endeared themselves to the local people, who were desperately short of food, fuel, clothing and the small necessities which make life bearable. It was not uncommon for a woman to sell herself for a packet of cigarettes, a tablet of soap or a bar of chocolate. The Allied commanders imposed a non-fraternisation order, which was generally observed, but a black market sprang up in small luxuries such as cigarettes. It was not helped by UK tobacco manufacturers advertising parcels of duty-free tobacco and cigarettes – which could be posted from England to serving personnel in BAOR and sold by the unscrupulous to German Nationals for twenty times their price. In an attempt to stop illegal trafficking, the authorities arranged for this export of tobacco to be curbed and for cigarettes sold by the NAAFI to be individually stamped, so that any German found in possession of them would have some explaining to do to the police. As a result of their black-market activities, many of the wide boys had acquired large sums of Deutsche Marks which they hoped to exchange for English currency later, but to thwart them occupation money was introduced in the form of BAFSVs (British Armed Forces Salary Vouchers) which became legal tender at any service establishment. From then onwards anyone found in possession of a large amount of German currency had some explaining to do.

Hanover, the state capital of Lower Saxony, was an important communication centre, and its marshalling yards provided facilities for rail traffic to be routed to

Berlin, the ports of Hamburg, Bremerhaven and Wilhelmshaven, Denmark and the industrial cities of the Ruhr. Because of this it was a legitimate military target and was pounded by the Allied bombers, but sadly many blocks of dwelling-houses suffered damage or demolition in the process, leaving people homeless. By 1953 most of the damage had been repaired and the Germans to whom I spoke bore no ill will. They said they had an affinity with the British, reminding us that King George IV was King of England and Hanover and their *Burgomeisters* had named the principal shopping avenue *Georg Strasse* in his memory. Many of them also maintained that it was American, not British, bombers which had brought so much devastation to their city.

One of the first priorities given to the Royal Engineers when the British Zone was established was to restore a brewery with sufficient capacity to meet the demands of the thirsty soldiery; and the one chosen was at Dortmund in North Rhine-Westphalia. Their product was named Dortmünder Pils and it became a popular drink in the clubs and messes. Dickie Dirs once told me that such was its nutritional qualities that a man could sustain himself on four pints a day without eating solid food.

Dickie's tipple was gin and tonic at lunch-time and beer in the evening, so he was overweight. He arrived at the office one morning and related that he had visited the doctor for his annual fitness test and been told that if he persisted in his drinking habits he was unlikely to live another year. Dickie was so shaken that he accepted medical advice to restrict his drinking to two double whiskies a day, and by keeping to this prescription he lived long into his eighties!

Christmas was approaching and as part of the festivities the members of 'B' mess were invited to a cocktail party in the district commander's mess. Dickie introduced me to Brigadier Shacklock and his wife. During the course of a brief conversation he suggested to the brigadier that because of the sensitive nature of my job a married quarter should be found for me as soon as possible. The commander, no doubt with other things on his mind, nodded his agreement, and this was Dickie's cue to approach the garrison commander with his tongue in cheek and tell him that the brigadier wished me to be housed quickly. The ploy worked, and Colonel 'Curly' Moore, who was leaving the station soon, allocated me his quarter and invited me to look over it.

The colonel, nicknamed Curly because he was completely bald, had a problem because his car was snowbound in a garage beneath the house and he could not find a buyer for it. I offered him a hundred pounds for it. It was a foolish thing to do, and on reflection I should have told him to leave it behind and when the thaw came I would arrange for its removal to a dump.

My family joined me in January and we moved into our quarter at Brandmeier Strasse on the outskirts of the city. It was a huge house, the former home of a Nazi sympathiser, with a very large garden containing numerous fruit trees. The colonel's wife, by virtue of his appointment, was required to spend much of her time on social matters, not the least being easing the lot of displaced persons housed in a camp nearby, and because of this he had been granted the services of a housekeeper instead of the usual daily help. We took her on, together with the boilerman, whose services were free, because their pay was charged to occupation costs, and retained a laundress, which cost me 1s 6d per day. It was an ideal arrangement because the boilerman did not spend much of his time stoking the central-heating furnace and so was able to keep the grounds tidy. Frau Faust, the housekeeper, was a typical domineering Prussian who had been allowed too much freedom; I envisioned a clash of personalities before very long, and it was not long in coming. On my return from a few days detached duty, Edith told me that some rations delivered the previous day were missing, so I told her to tackle Frau Faust and ask for an explanation. When Edith confronted her she became insolent, whereupon I appeared from the bedroom and sacked her on the spot.

Our next-door neighbour was Bill Fawley, an ex-captain now re-employed on liaison duties with the German Bundespost, who maintained our switchboards and provided us with any telephone circuits we needed. Bill had married a German lady but was not often at home as much of his time was spent visiting our numerous detachments, which stretched almost as far as Hamburg.

The belief was that he was having an affair with one of our operators whose husband had been killed on the Russian front. It must be remembered that millions of Germans had either lost their lives in the war or remained captive in Russian labour camps, consequently there was a surplus of German women – and many of them were not averse to having a relationship with a well-paid British officer.

The weather was improving and I thought it timely to take a look at the car reposing in the garage. It was a large American cabriolet of unknown vintage and it lacked a hood. Apart from some rotted floor-boards, which I was able to replace, and a flat battery, it was sound, so I applied for a road licence and had it insured. The fact that we were now mobile gave me a sense of reassurance because relations with the Soviets stationed on the border between East and West Germany were sometimes strained and we were in a state of readiness to evacuate our families, 'should the balloon go up'. To this end each household was required to have a suitcase ready packed with sufficient clothing and necessities to complete the journey to the Channel ports. My private advice to Edith was to keep the petrol tank filled and if the evacuation order was given to drive as quickly as possible to Ostend or Calais.

At least our families had a reasonable chance of reaching the UK safely, but those living in Berlin were in an invidious position, being completely surrounded by a potentially hostile force, and it was accepted that the entire Allied garrison would be prisoners if trouble broke out.

In order to provide training and recreational facilities for skiing, the Army had taken over a large complex of buildings at Bad Harzberg, including the principal hotel, which was converted into an officers' club where families could spend a weekend at little cost. The hotel was less than fifty miles from Hanover and we spent a few days there. It was approached by a winding road which climbed from Goslar until reaching its peak of 3,000 feet. The road was fringed by pine trees and the air was crisp and fresh to breathe.

As we approached Bad Harzberg we saw a number of cars parked off the road, so we stopped too and found that it was a popular picnic spot. Close by, an attractive waterfall cascaded down the rock-face and its sound was like music, but marred by the noise of quarrying opposite. The Germans were removing a great chunk of mountainside so that the road could be straightened, and the rocks were being broken to provide hard core for yet more of their autobahns.

My children were too young to ski and Edith and I were too old to learn, so we contented ourselves with walking along the forest paths that meandered through the pine trees. Each of these walks led to somewhere; there was no danger of becoming lost, because every route was signposted in different coloured paint, a necessary precaution as the border was not far away.

We drove up to Braunlage later, this being the highest point of the Harz Mountains in the British Zone, and from here we looked over a valley to Brocken, 3,750 feet high, which served as an observation post for the East German militia and Soviet troops. Its commanding height was also ideal for siting radio listening posts for intercepting our signal traffic.

We also had a club nearer home quite close to the Masche See, a large artificial lake not far from the middle of Hanover. It had been constructed on the orders of Hitler to provide recreational facilities for the citizens and to create work for the masses of unemployed Germans. The labour gangs were conscripted to carry out this mammoth task, for which they received no pay, the Führer having decreed that it was for the good of the Fatherland and their labour was in return for the state benefits they were receiving. The lake was a popular venue for sportsmen and sightseers; sailing-dinghies and rowing-skiffs could be hired and the more athletic formed crews of eights to compete against each other. There was also a large motor-propelled ferry-boat to take passengers along its banks. Angling was not permitted although it was stocked with carp, a fish that Germans considered a delicacy at Eastertide.

The officers' club was in an ideal position for providing meals and drinks for those residing in Hanover, and for visitors from outside the garrison. It boasted a large aquarium that ran the whole length of the restaurant, filled with exotic tropical fish. There was consternation one morning when the caretaker went to feed them, only to find that they were all dead. At the subsequent inquiry it was revealed that a bunch of subalterns on a visit from an outstation had decided to get the fish tiddly. In their ignorance, they had tipped several glasses of wine into their water tanks, causing the fish to die from alcoholic poisoning. The brigadier was furious and ordered that all steps were to be taken to discover the culprits.

For the Coronation of Queen Elizabeth II, our commander decided not to hold a formal military march past because the Germans were used to seeing massive bodies of troops on the move, and Hanover district soldiers were thin on the ground. A token force of Gunners and Infantry soldiers paraded at the football stadium on 2nd June, and every available serviceman attended to hear the Royal Artillery fire the Royal Salute and the Rifle Brigade ripping off a *feu de joie*, after which the parade commander called for all to remove their head-dress and three cheers were given for Her Majesty.

The main event of the afternoon was a garden party held in the grounds of the British consulate general, to which all British officers in the garrison and their wives were invited, together with many distinguished consular officers from other countries and a number of German dignitaries, including Prince Ernst August of Niedersachsen. The consul general hosted the garden party in his capacity as the Queen's representative and greeted the guests as they arrived. He had an important announcement to make later in the afternoon when he walked to the public-address microphone to say that belated news had come through of Hillary and Sherpa Tensing's success in conquering Mount Everest on 29th May.

Two of the VIP guests whom we met were the Canadian consul general and his wife, who had an official role to play because they represented a Canadian brigade still serving in Germany as a token force. Earlier that afternoon I had an embarrassing experience when driving the open cabriolet at a sedate speed towards the consulate. Suddenly there was a loud horn-blast from behind and I edged over to allow a chauffeur-driven car to overtake me. It was a large flagged vehicle bearing the maple leaf insignia of Canada, and as the consul general sped by wearing his full diplomatic regalia he gave the impression that the hooter was sounded more in amusement than impatience.

He told us that the Canadian Infantry brigade was being moved shortly to barracks on the outskirts of the city. The Canadians were not provided with married quarters, but if they found accommodation privately their wives could join them. We British were often asked if we could help by sharing our homes with them. I met a young subaltern serving with Princess Patricia's Regiment of Canada, who told me that his wife had booked a passage on the newly constructed *United States*, which was about to make its maiden voyage across the Atlantic. (It won the Blue Riband for the fastest crossing.)

I took pity on him and asked if he and his wife would be content to live in the study, which was the size of a large drawing-room, and sleep in the maids' quarters, which had its own bathroom. He was delighted and cabled his wife, telling her to pay the passage money. At that time the Canadian Army was the highest paid in the world, and it was no hardship for him to give me £4 4s per week, which covered my rent. Kathy and Jim Richardson settled in and stayed with us until his regiment moved to Soest. They were very grateful to us for having them and we were often invited as guests to their mess at the Tiergarten.

Kathy's one dislike was the German-manufactured toilet-paper with which we were issued, and on one occasion she complained that it had bits of wood in it. Toilet-paper was not on sale in the Canadian PX or the NAAFI, so she ordered a continuous supply to be despatched to her from a firm in Ontario.

Guard services for the garrison were provided by the MSO (Mixed Services Organisation), which had been recruited from foreign nationals who had fought on our side during the war. Most of them were Yugoslavs, preponderantly royalists and political refugees from the Communist regime that had taken over the country. Their officers had their own mess, to which we were invited from time to time, and one of their captains, who spoke excellent English, had served in the personal bodyguard of King Peter of Yugoslavia before he was ousted. I likened them to the White Russians who fled their country when the Bolsheviks seized power and murdered the Czar.

High summer was now with us and we spent most of the weekends at the lakeside. Unlike the man-made *Masche See*, there were two large natural lakes within reasonable distance of Hanover, the Blauer See on the outskirts, adjacent to the autobahn, and Steinhuder Meer, more of an inland sea than a lake; both provided safe swimming.

We preferred Steinhuder because of its size and facilities for sailing and boating. The lake surrounded a small island in its midst, where storks, ducks and geese nested. It was said that the more foolhardy young Germans drove their cars over the icy surface to reach the island in midwinter, when the temperature rarely rose above zero Fahrenheit and the thickness of ice was capable of carrying a heavy weight.

Thanks to Marshall Aid and the correct German attitude to work, their economy was starting to boom and they had eyes on the export market. To this end they organised a great annual trade fair and built massive exhibition halls in which to display their products. Such was their enthusiasm for the project that they constructed a new highway, called the Messe Schnellweg which bypassed Hanover and led to the exhibition site on the Hildesheim road. Overseas buyers flocked there and some enterprising British salesmen exhibited their products.

Some of the goods on display were sold off at half-price on the last day of the exhibition and I bought a set of table-mats produced by a manufacturer from Newcastle. The design was taken from paintings by Canaletto and depicted scenes of the waterways of Dresden, London, Nymphenburg, Vienna, Venice and the centre of Warsaw.

I showed them with some pride to my Dutch brother-in-law, who was visiting, explaining that they were the paintings of the great Venetian artist – but he tried to correct me by saying that they were scenes of canals. He must have thought that Canaletto was the Italian plural for a canal!

Bill Fawley was a cricket enthusiast and he arranged for our squadron team to play a match against a side from Altona one weekend. We went along and booked into a large lakeside hotel requisitioned by the Army as an officers' club, near the centre of Hamburg. The cricket match was a dull limited-overs affair and we looked forward to some night-life – and who better than Bill to show us around?

Our venue was the Reeperbahn, which had a reputation almost as unsavoury as Port Said. It was well known to sailors as the red-light district of Hamburg, but it also had other attractions, and gaudily dressed touts did their utmost to persuade visitors to enter their establishment. The main event in the one we called at was a wrestling match between two beefy German women who wore only a pair of stout bloomers. They covered their bodies with slimy black mud from a container in a corner of the ring. After the winner was announced, they were applauded as they stuffed each others' bloomers with handfuls of mud. The other innovation at this place was the provision of a telephone at each table, with its extension number displayed boldly on a card. There was no way of knowing who was calling a particular number, so liberties were taken by those wishing to make advances or pass lewd remarks. Towards midnight the MC announced that donkey races were about to begin in the basement, which had been converted for use as a sporting arena. Gisela Fawley and Edith went down to investigate, while Bill and I got down to the serious business of drinking some Pilsener beer which had found its way to Hamburg from Pilsen in Czechoslovakia, noted for the purity of its water.

With the approach of autumn I looked into the possibility of buying a new car as we did not relish driving around in the cold weather in an open automobile, and was shocked to hear from my bank manager that the cost would have to be met from the foreign currency I had saved from my earnings in Germany. However, the agent of the Ford subsidiary at Cologne turned up one day with a British soldier who, because of his length of stay, had amassed a large number of Deutsche marks. We struck a deal and a week later I collected a coffin-shaped pre-war Ford Prefect identical with the model I bought in Kenya in 1948. A month later Ford UK announced that post-war models were rolling off the production lines!

The owner of the house in which we lived appeared to be a friendly old man, so I gave him permission to collect as much fruit as he wished to from his own garden. His next request was permission for his wife and himself to move into the cellar, but when I raised the matter with the housing staff I was told that in no way could this be permitted because of a quirk of German law. Some months later I learnt that he had applied for the derequisitioning of his house on the grounds that he was terminally ill. I agreed to vacate it if a suitable alternative became available.

Hitherto the nursing sisters attached to the British military hospital had occupied rooms in a very large house in Lenbach Strasse, but a new wing had been built for them in the grounds of the hospital. I was asked to view their previous mess and agreed to take it over, provided it was redecorated and a number of partitions put up to serve as cubicles were removed. The drawing-room was vast: it was fitted with twenty-four wall lights, and two large settees and several lounge chairs seemed lost in it. We had recently employed a young woman named Trudy, whose home was in the East Zone, and she was delighted when she was given her own bedroom suite. She was pretty and soon attracted the attention of a young German policeman. He sometimes called, gave a smart salute, clicked his heels and asked if he might speak to the *Fräulein*.

The German police were very formal and I often watched them as they went through the charade of relieving each other on traffic duties. The relief would salute, shake hands, report, shake hands, salute and take up position, all these movements being reciprocated by the officer going off duty.

Christmas was a time for celebration, commencing with a round of cocktail parties, and each family vied with its friends to put on the best show. After a few drinks the chatter from the guests rose in a crescendo before the carpets were rolled back and dancing began. Party-giving was not expensive, with gin at six shillings per bottle and whisky not much more. These parties were usually held from 6 p.m. to 8 p.m., and two hours was long enough because they were held in overheated drawing-rooms and the air thickened with the fug caused by cigarette-smoking.

The children were not forgotten, and they looked forward to the arrival of Father Christmas riding in a tastefully decorated Jeep laden with presents, or sometimes in a sleigh made by the local REME workshops. There were shrieks of delight when the parcels were opened and they found a present to their liking, but these shouts diminished as tea was served and the jellies and cakes were wolfed down.

It was obligatory for us to visit the sergeants' mess so that they had an opportunity to achieve their ambition of 'drinking the officers under the table', but what some of the younger ones did not realise was that I had spent thirteen years as a member of the sergeants' mess! All messes have their favourite party game: some favour arm-wrestling, while others prefer the boat race, in which everyone who participated had qualified by drinking a pint of beer in less than five seconds. The test in the Hanover district mess was more difficult: it involved competitors 'toeing a line' and, by lowering the palms of their hands over the necks of two empty beer bottles, moving by easy stages towards an empty glass some six feet away, using the bottles as an acrobat would manoeuvre his stilts. The trick was to reach the glass, pick it up with one's teeth, reverse the process and stand up on one's feet without assistance and without releasing the glass. This exercise imposed a great strain on the shoulder muscles and some discomfort to the hands, but I was adjudged the winner by stretching out further than anyone else.

The New Year's ball held at the Masche See Club was

the last military function to be held there. The Burgomeister of Hanover had formally requested the return of the building, and as the policy was to foster good relations with the local community his request was acceded to and a hand-over date of 1st May agreed. The senior Royal Engineers officer, Colonel Beech – who ended up his career as the Army Chief Engineer – had spare funds, and constructed a large club in the grounds of Sterling House by joining two Nissen huts together. It was scheduled to be completed by the middle of May, and we attended the opening ceremony. Many German guests were invited, and we spoke to a charming lady who related that she and her sister had run a flourishing car business before the war. It had been flattened by the bombers, but, nothing daunted, they set to and cleaned up the bricks for use in rebuilding the premises. Carriages were ordered for 3 a.m., and as we drove home we passed workers lining up at the tram-stops ready to commence work for the day.

Bill Fawley was friendly with the camp commandant in Hamburg, who rather than draw up a contract with German farmers for the sale of swill (kitchen waste), set up a piggery and fed it to his own pigs to fatten them up for Christmas. Bill, who never missed a trick, bought a piglet at Hanover market and transported it to Hamburg on the rear seat of a VW Beetle, hoping to make a killing at Christmas. Unfortunately for Bill, his friend was posted to another job and his replacement made a head count of the pigs, found that one was surplus, and promptly took it on his books.

High summer was now upon us and we decided to visit Hamelin, where a monthly festival in remembrance of the Pied Piper was a tourist attraction. Hamelin, on the banks of the River Weser, was an extremely picturesque town which had escaped serious war damage. The Piper, dressed in medieval costume, and surrounded by a score of small children dressed up as rats, narrated the tale of the plague of rodents that had invaded the town. His story over, he played tunes on his flute and, with the 'rats' scampering all around him, led the way from the river bank to a school adjacent to the Rathaus, the municipal offices. There was no charge for the entertainment, for the show attracted many visitors who spent freely at the hostelries and confectionery shops. For our part, we bought a souvenir made of dough shaped into a rat and hardened off. Forty years later it has retained its shape and is an object of interest to our visitors.

Fundamental changes were now being made in handling the volume of signal traffic passing through our communication centres, and the practice of a radio or teleprinter operator tapping out messages at thirty words per minute was no longer acceptable. What was known as tape relay was introduced, and this enabled the text to be processed on a perforator utilising the Murray code, and the resulting tape was fed into an autohead enabling the message to be transmitted to its destination at sixty-six groups per minute – a considerable saving in transmission time. Another innovation was the world-wide routing system, which by the judicious use of indicators enabled a message to be despatched to its final destination with a minimum of handling. Up to 1950 the senior Signals officer on duty had been known as the signal master, but this title was changed to duty signals officer, a timely change to avoid embarrassment to the female officers employed on signal office duties, who did not wish to be known as mistresses!

In 1954 a fresh look was taken at the role of the cipher officer. It was decided that his duties should be broadened to include the management of the communication centre as a whole, and his new appointment became traffic officer. The new term caused confusion outside the Corps, as some thought it referred to the Military Police, while others thought it was to do with the railways branch of the Royal Engineers.

Those qualifying as traffic officers were considered suitable candidates for regular commissions, and Dickie Dirs suggested that I should apply, so I thought it over. Under the rules in force, if retrenchment occurred I could claim a pension covering my twenty-two years' service, but if I was granted a regular service commission my previous service would not count for retirement pay. I grasped the nettle, was accepted and some months later was handed a second commission as a regular officer, this one bearing the Queen's signature and given at the Court of Saint James's 'in the third year of our reign'.

Dickie's term of office with the squadron was coming to an end and I accompanied him on his farewell visit to our detachments and 7th Armoured Division 'The Desert Rats', then stationed at Verden. The Signal Regiment was commanded by Lieutenant-Colonel Charles Nettleship, a recalled officer who retired with the rank of brigadier in 1958 and became a clergyman. During lunch at the mess, I sat next to the station staff officer who was also the official hangman for Rhine Army, although he was not often called upon to perform this macabre duty.

Soon afterwards Dickie departed to take up a staff appointment with the RAF at Moenchen Gladbach, and a little later I received a warning notice that I was being drafted to Singapore early in 1955. This was not welcome news as it meant parting with the car at a loss because import restrictions stipulated that a vehicle had to be used abroad by its owner for two years to avoid payment of UK duty. I considered importing the car and shipping it out to the Far East and wrote to HM Customs for guidance. The reply, couched in officialese, was signed by someone named Evans and unhelpful, so I wrote again asking for answers to specific questions, adding that the HM Customs letter appeared to have been written by the office-boy. This did bring a response in the form of a letter signed by 'H. Evans, Head of Department' advising me that if I wished to re-export the car it would be a matter for the Board of Trade. Impasse!

The movements staff told me that it was possible to have our heavy baggage shipped directly to Singapore, so the children's toys and other non-essentials were crated and despatched. Edith and I had decided that she would travel home by train and ferry-boat with the two girls, and because Bryan was at an awkward age he should accompany me in the car. Fortunately, by this time the two-year rule had been modified to one year, and one problem had been overcome.

Tempus fugit, and we prepared to hand over our quarter and prepare for the trip home.

In 1954 there was a group of armed bandits operating

on the Hanover-Cologne autobahn. Using fast stolen cars, they would block the highway, divert motorists into a parking-area, and rob them. Car telephones were non-existent and the police VW Beetles were no match for the fast Mercedes Benz and Borgwards used by the bandits, who were seldom caught.

My intention had been to cover the 440 miles from Hanover to Calais at night, but because of the banditry and the atrocious state of the Belgian roads I was prevailed upon to break my journey and spend a night with Jessie and Dickie Dirs at Moenchen Gladbach. Bryan and I left early on the following morning and crossed the border at Aachen, before encountering badly maintained roads leading to Brussels and the ports of Ostend and Calais, from where we were due to cross the English Channel to Dover. The five motor cars waiting to be ferried across were pushed over a net and lifted by derrick before being consigned to the ship's hold, and we relaxed in the restaurant until the white cliffs of Dover loomed into sight.

The disembarkation of passengers took little time, but it was a different matter for the car-owners, who had to wait on the quayside and glance anxiously at their vehicles being hoisted out of the hold and deposited on dry land. By this time it was quite dark, the rear seat was packed with luggage, and I set off along Watling Street for the tedious journey to Barking. Long before we reached there Bryan had curled up in the well of the car and was fast asleep when we reached Westrow Drive.

Edith had a relative in the employ of a shipping-agent. We had made tentative arrangements for the Ford to be freighted to Singapore for the modest sum of £45, but such was the demand for shipping-space that he pressed me for a final decision. As the Ford Motor Company was just a few miles away at Dagenham, I visited their retail department hoping to trade in the car for an export version of the latest model and was surprised at the generous deal they offered me. All that remained for me to do was to pay HM Customs the import duty, and a visit to their London head office resulted in an amicable arrangement being made. The clearance papers reached me on the following morning and by midday a new export model was parked outside 59 Westrow Drive.

Preparations for our departure continued smoothly until one morning I received a telephone call from a War Office department called A.G.11(O), which was responsible for the posting of officers to wherever a vacancy occurred. The caller was Colonel Patrick, an elderly officer promoted from the ranks who had spent his entire service in the same department, starting off as a clerk and eventually running it. What he had to say startled me: my move to Singapore had been reconsidered and it was now proposed to send me to Eastern Command at Hounslow.

I protested that our worldly goods were on the high seas, that my wife had discarded much of the children's winter clothing, that I had bought my tropical uniforms, and that I had a motor car ready to be shipped out. His reply was: 'If your preparations are so well advanced, you had better proceed to Singapore.'

I think the colonel took the point that my preference was for overseas service and annotated my personal file accordingly, because for the next ten years my movements were restricted to overseas stations.

22

BOUND FOR SINGAPORE

When we arrived at Lime Street Station in Liverpool at the end of February the sky was overcast and the gloom was reflected by the run-down appearance of the city. My father, now in his seventy-second year and ailing, was standing at the platform to greet us, as were the Bennetts, friends from Hanover who had left there before us and whose house guests we were to be until embarking on the following morning.

On our arrival at the dockside my father appeared to be ill at ease. The thought must have crossed his mind that we would be away from England for three years, a long time for someone of his advanced age. All partings are painful and it was obvious that he was emotionally upset as we neared the gangway, but he put a brave face on it and kept his voice level as he bade us *bon voyage*.

I glanced at the large vessel moored to the quayside bollards and saw that it was the *Empire Fowey*. Before long an embarkation officer told us we were free to board the ship, saying that our cabin baggage had already been loaded. We were early arrivals and soon settled down in a five-berth cabin on the boat deck, before emerging to gaze at our fellow passengers now trudging up the gangway. Most of the ladies wore fur coats, which gave the impression that they were voyaging to the Arctic and not the tropics.

Below decks, one of the first to greet us was a major wearing the badges of the Ordnance Corps who introduced himself as Ted Macey. He seemed to be a man of immense physical power, built like a tank, and his appearance suggested a Mediterranean background. Ted told us that his last unit was stationed at Gloucestershire, and because he was an expert in unarmed combat his services were much in demand by the county police force in training their young constables. He did not say this boastfully, and later in the voyage we saw how he put young subalterns through their paces in a makeshift ring erected on the sports deck.

High tide at Liverpool was at 3 p.m. and an hour before then the ship's bell was rung and the familiar cry of *All ashore that's going ashore* was heard. The tugboats appeared, mooring-ropes were cast and the vessel was gradually eased out of her berth and commenced the voyage down the River Mersey on the ebb-tide.

Shipboard life after our previous voyages to Africa was now becoming routine, and we were not surprised to hear the alarm bells ring to order the passengers and crew to their lifeboat stations. Meticulous attention was paid by the ship's officers to the way life-jackets were attached firmly to the chest because loosely tied straps could result in a broken neck if the wearer had to jump into the sea in an emergency.

As we emerged from the estuary the signal was passed to the engine-room for full speed ahead and the ship headed towards the Irish Sea. It was not long before we steamed past Moelfra, a village on the coast of Anglesey, off which the wartime convoys formed up before commencing their hazardous voyages to the United States when the Battle of the Atlantic was at a critical stage. The ships were well protected here from enemy attack, relying on air support from RAF Valley and minesweepers and destroyers from the naval base at Holyhead to guard them from submarine attacks. By the morning we were well into St George's Channel and would soon be passing the Scilly Isles on our port bow, to meet the swell of the Atlantic Ocean.

We had travelled this route before and were familiar with the ports of call, but we had never been ashore at Aden and it came as a pleasant surprise to be allowed shore leave for eight hours. Our group paid a cursory visit to the bazaar but were not tempted to buy any of the duty-free goods, so we found a pleasant bay protected from the sharks by a stout steel net and enjoyed a swim.

Our next port of call was announced as Colombo in Ceylon, now called Sri Lanka, 2,092 nautical miles away and within seven degrees of the equator. Awnings were put up on the decks and passengers warned to avoid excessive exposure to the sun and to drink plenty of fluid to minimise the danger of heat-exhaustion resulting from dehydration.

Our stay at Colombo was short, but long enough for us to take a taxi to one of its sandy beaches before returning to the ship for the final leg of our voyage to Singapore, now only 1,500 sea miles distant. In a few days we were sailing through the Straits of Malacca, separating Malaya from the island of Sumatra, *en route* to the colony of Singapore.

We passed through the Immigration Department on 30th March 1955, and Edith was directed to apply for a national registration identity card within thirty days. Temporary accommodation had been reserved for us in a small residential hotel in Orchard Road until we were able to find somewhere more suitable. The colony was full of service and civil service families for whom no quarters were provided, and as a result many sub-standard hostels and houses were hired out by their enterprising Chinese owners.

The Signal Regiment to which I was posted was stationed at Tyersall Park, not far from GHQ FARELF at Tanglin. When I reported for duty I was told that my job was to take charge of one of three shifts manning the communications centre. I was responsible for passing and receiving signals traffic between us and the War Office, GHQ Middle East at Cyprus, Accra, Nairobi, Hong Kong, Malaya Command at Kuala Lumpur, Melbourne, Delhi, Ottawa and many other subsidiary HQs.

The three shifts covered a twenty-four hour period, which meant that each one was on duty for fifty-six hours per week, the most gruelling spell being one of fourteen hours' continuous duty from 6 p.m. to 8 a.m. the following morning twice weekly. It was no joke trying to snatch a few hours' sleep after breakfast, only to be awakened by the boarding-house domestics entering the bedroom to do their cleaning, or being disturbed by noisy infants quarrelling in the corridors, so I made a habit of driving to the Singapore Swimming Club, where it was peaceful in the mornings, and then rested in the afternoons.

We had not been there very long when I was called to the office and told that the War Office had granted me compassionate leave to travel home to visit my father, who was dying of cancer. Urgent preparations were made for me to join a BOAC flight leaving that day, and after a hurried visit to the medical centre to be inoculated against cholera, I packed some belongings and left for the airport, wearing a civilian suit.

By a remarkable coincidence the passenger sitting next to me was a Merchant Navy officer travelling home on leave from Australia who had served as chief officer with my uncle Ebenezer Evans, now retired. They were the only two British navigation officers on a ship crewed by Lascars, Mauritians and Chinese, and he spoke of the strained relationship between the master of the vessel and himself. Ebenezer was a martinet, respected but disliked by the crew, and he had a fear of being poisoned by the Chinese cook. One of his beliefs was that if a man swallowed a human hair it would clog his digestive system and cause his death, so he inspected his food closely before eating.

The pilot followed a course over the jungles of Malaya. Our first stop was at Bangkok, where we were served with a meal before resting in a club in readiness for an early take-off. Our flight plan from there was to Delhi, where a party of Indians joined us. Meals were not served on the plane then; they were eaten in airport restaurants whilst the aircraft was refuelled and serviced. On arrival at Karachi, we were led to a clean and spacious club for food. The Indian passengers distanced themselves from the Europeans, and we were the first to be served by immaculately dressed Pakistani waiters who still addressed us as 'sahib'. When half-way through our meal I heard muttering from the Indians, I noticed that no effort had been made to attend to them. They were completely ignored by the Pakistanis, and it crossed my mind that the bitterness following the partition of India in August 1947 should not be directed at the Indian clients of BOAC.

My next recollection after leaving Karachi was our flight over the Italian and Swiss Alps – and to one who had never flown before this was an unnerving experience. The plane appeared to be heading straight for a peak but miraculously skimmed over it, and at other times the pilot guided his aircraft between them. We touched down at Zurich in the early morning to find the air chilly and bracing after the warmth and humidity of Karachi. Our stay at Zurich was short, and after refuelling the pilot took off for our final destination.

Air travel was in its infancy and the airport in London consisted of a makeshift arrangement of buildings intended to cater for the needs of immigration and HM Customs, with little heed paid to passenger comfort, so I was pleased when the military representative handed me my leave and travel documents.

I travelled to Holyhead on the Irish Mail train, and it then dawned upon me that I had nowhere to stay. However, a helpful taxi-driver drove me to Soldiers Point, now converted into a guest-house, and less than a mile from where my father lived. When I visited him he was emaciated and bedridden but reasonably cheerful, and he told me that because of his terminal illness his doctor had taken the initiative to write to the War Office asking if I could be granted leave.

It was over twenty-two years since I had left home to join the Army and I was out of touch with my former friends, so I spent hours at my father's bedside. As the weeks dragged on, my thoughts were with my family in Singapore. The newspapers reported student unrest and demonstrations in Singapore, and because of the withdrawal of my overseas allowance my cash was dwindling. I explained the position to my father in a tactful way, saying that having seen him my duty now was to my family. He understood, and I wrote to my CO, asking to be recalled. Events moved quickly. I was instructed to report to the movements centre within two days, and I bade my father a sad farewell before returning to London. When I reported to the commandant he told me that I had been appointed OC flight of a passenger aircraft carrying a contingent of families and service personnel due to leave on the following day.

During the course of a short briefing ceremony I was identified to the passengers, who were told that I was serving in Singapore and would be pleased to help if any problems occurred on the flight. The aircraft was a converted bomber flown by an RAF crew, and the first thing I noticed was that the seats faced the tail of the plane, presumably for safety considerations.

Our first stop was at Rome for refuelling, and the passengers were required to disembark because of the risk of fire – aeroplane engines at that time ran on high-octane fuel. Many of the younger wives about to be reunited with their husbands had never been abroad, and I was asked countless questions about the life-style and climate of Singapore and Malaya.

The date was Wednesday, 3rd August 1955, and it was on this day, I learnt later, that my father died; it would appear that after my departure he had given up the will to live.

The pilot had instructions to land at Nicosia Airport in Cyprus in order to take on board fresh fruit and soft drinks to supplement the food supplies stored in the refrigerators, and I was allowed to alight from the plane to savour the balmy air of that delightful Mediterranean island, at the same time taking the opportunity of buying a bottle of Cypriot brandy from the Greek contractor. Not very long afterwards we left for Bahrein. Our short stay at the airport gave the passengers an opportunity to stretch their legs and wander around the shaded duty-free area to examine the exquisite curios and rugs on sale there. Although it was a Muslim country and the drinking of alcohol was taboo, special dispensation had been granted for the sale of spirits because of the revenue it engendered.

Our respite over, it was time to board the plane once again. The pilot guided it to the runway, and it was while preparing for take-off that a serious incident occurred which I had to include in my flight report. It appears that an incoming aircraft had requested emergency landing precautions to be taken, and we were denied the right to take off. The plane was unpressurised, and after standing for several hours on the ground the temperature in the cabin rose alarmingly. Babies were distressed and screamed, perspiration stood in globules on exposed parts of the body and clothing was covered with sweat patches. Fortunately, the suspect plane landed safely, and within a few minutes we were airborne and the electric fans circulated cooler air around the cabins.

The cabin steward told me that our next stop was Karachi, where we would stay overnight, and I reflected that this rate of progress was like travelling on a slow boat to China. The plane was 'dry' and the Pakistani laws on the consumption of alcohol were puritanic, so I looked forward to a night-stop at Delhi, where at least a bottle of wine could be bought with a meal at any reasonable hotel.

Delhi had not changed since I had last seen it in 1934, more than twenty years earlier, and what amazed me was that traffic signs erected long before partition were still worded in English – not that it made any difference to the bullock-cart drivers, tonga-wallahs and cab-drivers, who had learnt to treat them as symbols. We were booked into a good hotel and given a curry meal. There was a wine waiter in attendance, so I ordered a bottle of hock – which set me back seven pounds, a punitive amount of money at the time – but it helped the conversation at the dinner-table.

The bad news was that we were due to depart on a flight leaving Delhi at 3 a.m. in order to refuel at Dum Dum Airport near Calcutta, before flying on to Bangkok. Some of the passengers questioned the wisdom of going to bed for such a short time but common sense prevailed. In due course we arrived in Thailand for breakfast, which consisted of a huge beefsteak, and from there we followed a route to the RAF airfield at Changi, where I submitted my report and was driven home.

The English newspapers had not exaggerated the seriousness of the student unrest, and all military personnel were on a state of alert. The colony had been promised self-government, but until that was granted it was controlled by a legislative council. The chief secretary was a lawyer named Marshall whose reputation was considered unsavoury by some local businessmen. The Chinese students wanted self-government now, and in their ignorance thought themselves capable of running the colony. Because of the weakness of the chief secretary, the Commander-in-Chief thought it prudent to proclaim a state of readiness. There were few combat troops serving on Singapore Island as most of the British regiments were fighting Communist terrorists in the jungles of Malaya, so a Gurkha battalion was brought in from Johore Bahru to deal with the situation.

At a conference to discuss tactics it was suggested to their brigade officer that warning shots should be fired over the heads of the demonstrators, a questionable exercise as shots fired into the air were likely to wound innocent people when they dropped to the ground. The major curtly dismissed this suggestion, saying that his Gurkhas were trained to kill the enemy and in this instance he considered that the leaders of the dissidents were the enemy.

His decision was accepted and the students were ordered to disperse. When they ignored this and surged towards the Gurkhas, an order was given, five shots rang out and five of the ringleaders dropped to the ground. Within minutes of this action taking place the troublemakers broke up into small groups before returning to their campus or lodging houses, and law and order was restored.

Most of our leisure time was spent at the Singapore swimming-club, a select establishment whose membership was restricted to Europeans. This rule was strictly enforced to the extent of applicants and their wives having to meet the club committee by appointment before being admitted. The pool was one of the few in the Far East which measured up to Olympic Games standards: the water sparkled and the filtration system drained off surplus surface water into the sea. The club amenities were excellent, the catering facilities second to none – all profits being ploughed back into refurbishing and replacing sunshades, deck-chairs and other property as it deteriorated. A special attraction was the one-armed bandits, which netted thousands of dollars each week. In one year alone the proceeds were sufficient to meet the cost of a new visitors' car-park.

On special occasions, gala dances were held in its magnificent ballroom, where black ties for men and long dresses for ladies were *de rigueur*. One of the most popular annual events was the New Year's Ball, part of the fun being the game of lotto or housey-housey, known now as bingo, where the winner of the last house could expect to win 1,000 Singapore dollars, equivalent to £125. The game ended before the orchestra played the last waltz, and as soon as 'Auld Lang Syne' was sung, the more adventurous hurried to the swimming-pool and dived fully-clothed into the water.

Safe sea-bathing was also available at other places along the coast, the most popular being the RAF beach at Changi, a few miles beyond the notorious Changi Prison used to intern British and Allied civilians from the fall of Singapore until their release after the surrender of Japan. Guy Symonds, then an RSM attached to the RAF, and his wife Phyllis had the use of a beach hut on the coast at Seleter and often invited us to join them.

Soon after my return from leave, Edith secured a secretarial job with the Shell Company of Singapore and met an Australian expatriate who was friendly with Walter Wearne. Walter's father had come to Singapore from Sydney and founded a motor-dealing business in the colony. On the death of his father he expanded the venture, and by the time I met him he had become an entrepreneur holding the franchise for all British cars and several makes of German cars for the whole of South-East Asia. Margaret, who later married him, drove Edith back from work one day and was shocked when she saw our accommodation. As a result, we were offered a vacant Wearne Brothers manager's house in Cornwall Gardens, a select residential area, at a peppercorn rent, and I accepted with gratitude. Walter asked me to meet him there, and a Chinese contractor arrived, driving a Jaguar car, who was given precise instructions to redecorate the house, carry out any repairs needed and complete the work within a week.

The chief cipher officer, Andy King, was due for

repatriation, and I was appointed to the post, which involved managing a large office responsible for handling highly classified information of a sensitive nature. I was assisted by several WOs and NCOs who were expert at encrypting and deciphering messages. The highly graded ones were dealt with by the WOs; but I had to be available twenty-four hours a day to deal with those endorsed 'officer only', and to cover this contingency I was authorised a residential telephone. As the CCO of GHQ Far East, I also had direct access to the CCO at the War Office in a system limited to us alone, so that I could report any breaches of transmission security directly to London.

I made a point of checking all incoming and outgoing traffic for accuracy, and through doing this learnt the views and thoughts of generals. One exchange of signals threw up the War Office in a poor light and reinforced the general opinion that too much responsibility was being delegated to junior civil servants.

Our Commander-in-Chief, General Sir Charles Loewen, was born in Canada, attended the Canadian Military College at Kingston and was commissioned into the Royal Artillery in 1918. He was nearing retirement and had expressed the wish to travel back to England by air via Canada. His request was passed to the War Office, but in a lengthy signal it was rejected on the grounds that this concession was granted only to senior officers wishing to travel to the country of their birth before retirement. The reply to this was succinct: *But General Loewen is Canadian.*

This must have caused embarrassment: a distinguished general honoured with the K.C.B. and K.B.E., awarded the Distinguished Service Order, twice mentioned in despatches and a Commander of the Legion of Merit, USA, denied his right by an underling in Whitehall!

Confusion was often caused at the distant end by writers sending unduly abbreviated texts in the mistaken belief that they were saving transmission time. One such signal sent from Malaya Command to the War Office comes to mind and the text simply read: *Confidential. Can you please send vital statistics of Miss Tessie O'Shea.*

The recipient was nettled and signalled back: *Why*

confidential and why the interest in Miss Tessie O'Shea?

The reply to this was a lengthy message to the effect that Tessie O'Shea, the entertainer, was fulfilling a number of engagements in Malaya and her programme included visits to remote areas of the jungle where British troops were flushing out the terrorists. These parts were not accessible by road and the only aircraft capable of landing on the improvised airstrips were Tiger Moths. Their query was whether Miss O'Shea, who was ponderously built and known as 'Two-Ton Tessie', could be fitted into such a small plane.

The most ineptly written signal that I ever saw was from the South Wales Borderers in Germany to the Royal Welch Fusiliers at Wrexham, exchanging greetings on St David's Day. The text simply read: *A Dewi Sant.* When it arrived at the War Office it was thought to be garbled and a rerun was requested, but by that time it was 2nd March and the whole point of it was lost. Had the originator written *Quote A Dewi Sant Unquote,* it would have stood a chance of reaching its destination, although messages sent in foreign languages were rarely accepted.

Royal Signals soldiers were not lacking when it came to using their initiative, and often had to improvise when their radio equipment suffered damage. Many pack sets were carried on the backs of mules, and these unpredictable beasts often ran amuck, shedding their loads and it took a skilled radio mechanic to repair the damage. Others were dropped by parachute into inaccessible areas with a similar result. In one instance the set was recovered by an NCO operator, who got it working and maintained contact with his base station; his detachment would have been isolated but for his skills. When news of this reached the brigadier, he received a signal message on his own set which read: *5361 Corporal Nale J. to be mentioned in despatches,* and the corporal had added *and to be appointed Lance Sergeant.* (I have changed his name. Before he retired he rose through the ranks to become a major.)

The management of the Shell Company were good employers and entertained their staff to lavish Chinese dinner-parties on festive occasions such as the Chinese

New Year and appropriate English holidays, and the husbands of the English employees were invariably invited as well. The food was a gourmet's delight. It was usually contained in a communal dish sufficient for up to sixteen people, who helped themselves with chopsticks – and some were so adept at using them that they could pick up a single grain of rice. Brandy was freely available and every few minutes one of the diners stood up and toasted his fellow guests with the words *'Yam Sin'* and a chorus of *'Yam Sins'* echoed around the restaurant.

The Shell Company also had an option on a few government bungalows on Penang Island to the north of Malaya, and Edith was fortunate in being allotted one for her two weeks' annual holiday. I applied for leave, and we travelled up through Malaya, keeping to the coast road and thus avoiding the danger of running into bandits, who preferred to hide in thickly wooded country near to the rubber estates. There were several government rest-houses on this route and the beaches were ideal for swimming. My one complaint was the number of sand-flies in evidence; I knew from my days in India that sand-fly fever, although not as dangerous as malaria, could be very painful. All our meals were taken in the rest-house, where sleeping-berths were available, and at the end of the second day we had reached Port Dickson, having visited Batu Pahat, Muar and Malacca. A leave-camp had been set up at Port Dickson so that families and single men could spend weekends or longer away from the capital, Kuala Lumpur, and its heat, to swim or rest beneath the palms and enjoy the cool breezes. It also contained an information-room where individuals travelling privately up-country were required to report, and learn of the precautions to be taken when travelling through 'bandit country'. We were told to join an armed convoy at Kuala Lumpur which would escort us as far as Ipoh, but there had been no sightings of Communists beyond it and we were free to travel the remaining hundred miles to Butterworth unescorted.

Butterworth was the port where the ferry left for the mile-long trip to Penang Island, and on arriving there we drove to the railway station serving Penang Hill – where our holiday bungalow was located 1,000 feet above sea level. The car was unpacked by porters and then left behind on the station car-park, for the only access to the government bungalows was by a cable railway or a long climb on foot.

Before we left Singapore the thought had crossed my mind that we were fortunate in being offered a well-staffed and appointed bungalow at a nominal cost, so I was not surprised when we woke up to find that we were enshrouded in cloud and the sun never appeared to break through. After two days the children were longing for the beach, and this meant travelling by cable train to see the sea and the sand, which was clean and powdery and the water warm and clear. But we were warned not to swim too far from the shore because of the presence of poisonous sea snakes that claimed the lives of several Malay fisherfolk each year.

Too long a time spent on the beach can be boring, so we decided to see more of the island before returning to Singapore and took a trip along the coastal road surrounding Penang Island. It was known that sixteen Communist terrorists were still in hiding there, but they kept to the forests and high ground, living off the land and seldom venturing down to the coastal villages. The possibility of encountering them was remote, and we enjoyed a picnic in a quiet cove.

Sadly, the time came for us to leave Penang and begin to retrace our steps. As we headed for Ipoh the car developed symptoms of transmission trouble which, although not serious, reminded me of our times in Kenya, and I resolved that on our return the Ford Prefect would have to go.

Our CO, Colonel Eraut, had purchased an MG Magnette, which, because of its crimson colour, had been dubbed 'the Fire-Engine', and I decided to trade in the Prefect for an MG of a more sober colour. Walter Wearne's second-hand car manager, Sharkey, drove a hard bargain, but we finished up with a sleek black Magnette, which was paid for with the help of a twelve-month interest-free loan advanced to Edith by the Shell Company of Singapore.

One of the extra duties that came up twice in a tour of duty was that of officer commanding the Singapore to Kuala Lumpur night train carrying military personnel, local civilians and stores to the Malayan capital. The officer appointed was there to organise the defence of the train and its passengers and cargo if it was attacked by terrorists lying in wait in the jungle. This duty involved staying in Kuala Lumpur for longer than twenty-four hours and qualified one for the award of the General Service Medal (Malaya), one of the easiest means of earning a medal I had come across. I was detailed for this duty, and as I waited at the railway station for the train to be loaded I heard squealing sounds emerging from a stack of gunny sacks piled ten deep on the platform. Curiosity overtook me and I stepped closer, only to be shocked by what I heard and saw. The cargo consigned to the capital comprised live pigs trussed up tightly in sacking and stacked above each other to reduce the amount of platform space they took up. I dared not think how long it had been since they were trussed up by the Chinese merchants at the pig farm and carried by lorry to the railway station, only to face a twelve-hour train journey to Kuala Lumpur without water, food or the means of stretching their legs.

The train journey passed without incident. On arrival I had the option of staying in the transit camp or making private arrangements, so I chose to spend the day with a colleague named Jack Lea and his wife. My return trip took place on a Friday, a day detested by young subalterns because it was leave weekend for soldiers visiting Singapore and many of them had imbibed too well in the canteens, but I experienced no trouble. Perhaps the sight of a middle-aged captain wearing the Long Service Medal ribbon had a calming effect on the more recalcitrant ones.

The *Straits Times*, an English-language newspaper, one day quoted an article in an English Sunday newspaper about some of the wives of servicemen fighting in the jungle. The article, denounced by the editor of the *Straits Times*, alleged that the wives were part of a call-girl racket pandering to the appetites of wealthy Chinese clients. It transpired later that there was some truth in the scandal unearthed by the overseas correspondent, because I met a retired Royal Navy captain in Germany who had been in administrative control of Serangoon Garden Estate, where many families lived in hostels, and he confirmed part of the story. He quoted the case of a soldier, on weekend leave from Malaya and wanting 'a bit on the side', telephoning a number he had been given and being answered by his wife.

This sort of behaviour caused concern at the War Office, as the personnel branch was at pains to maintain the good image of the Army amongst politicians and the public. We were living in the 1950s, when couples did not hop into bed with each other at their first meeting and it was considered a stigma for a woman to give birth to an illegitimate child. To safeguard against a soldier on embarkation leave seducing a girl and leaving her with child, the Army had introduced what was known as 'The Pregnant Fiancée Scheme', which enabled him to proceed home on compassionate leave and marry the girl if he so wished, provided there was medical evidence to prove her pregnancy. One of my cipher WOs decrypted such a message and found that the soldier's number had been corrupted in transmission, so instead of asking the War Office for a repeat he telephoned the local personnel duty officer for the soldier's correct regimental number before relaying the signal to his regiment in Malaya. By a remarkable coincidence there were two soldiers, both corporals and both with the same initials, serving in the same regiment – and my office had quoted the incorrect personal number. The wrong corporal was summoned to his orderly room and professed his indignation at being accused of ditching a pregnant woman – and then the error came to light.

The sequel to this was that my warrant-officer and I were summoned by the staff officer concerned, to be told that he had a procedure for checking on these cases and our gratuitous action had almost caused the wrong corporal to be flown home on leave at public expense.

Tyersall Park contained two officers' messes, our own GHQ Signals and HQ Singapore District, and we always met on the verandah after work on Saturday mornings for a lunch-time drink. On one of these occasions we saw an unusual sight – two tiger cubs gambolling in the grounds of the district mess. Their scent attracted the attention of our German shepherd guard dog, who stood quivering in the background and could not be soothed. Their history was interesting. A British patrol had discovered the body of their mother in the jungle, killed by a terrorist booby trap which she had triggered off, and the two cubs were rescued to prevent a lingering death through starvation. The local commander suggested that they should be presented to Sir Winston Churchill, and steps were taken to air-freight them to London. Many years afterwards we visited Regent's Park Zoo and saw the tigers, now fully grown, caged side by side and named Romulus and Remus.

There was no lack of social life on the island, although much of it was restricted to service activities. We had three major Royal Signals units stationed within miles of each other, and our mess was the focal point for Corps functions such as dinner nights and balls. There was competition amongst the subalterns to see who excelled at deeds of daring. Black ties were discarded after a regimental dinner, monkey-jackets removed, trestle-tables set up and mattresses laid down – so that the intrepid could dive over the length of a long table, and whoever propelled himself the furthest was adjudged the winner. Another prank, but not performed in the presence of senior officers because of the risk involved, was to form a human pyramid so that the uppermost man could reach up to the very high ceiling ad chalk his signature on it, but this practice was stopped when Paddy Burke fell to the floor and broke his arm.

The frivolities were not confined to the Army. A young flight lieutenant hid a tape recorder in the ladies' powder-room prior to an RAF grand ball, and after the show was over had the temerity to play it back in the presence of his seniors. Not surprisingly, he was summoned to the station commander's office early the next morning, told to pack his bags, and flown out of Changi two hours later.

Des Woudstra, who worked for Shell, was the wife of a Dutch sea captain who spent most of his time sailing the

China Seas. She threw lavish parties at their house in Collyer's Quay, but despite her friendliness she was possessed of a sadistic streak. Normally male guests at informal drinks-parties wore shirts and slacks because of the humidity, but Des insisted that they arrive wearing linen or shark-skin jackets. The men would leave home with their jackets folded neatly on the back seat of the car, drive to her house, struggle into their top garment and climb the steep staircase to her home, by which time they were bathed in perspiration, and only then were they invited to remove their jackets.

When there was nothing pressing to do on Wednesday afternoons, we went down to the quayside, where Chinatown began, and looked for bargains in 'Change Alley'. But we avoided this like the plague when passenger ships were in port, because then prices shot up. It was here that construction workers using massive pile-drivers were fighting a losing battle trying to secure foundations for the new Shell building.

At other times we visited Tangs, that world-famous departmental store, which stocked a range of goods from massive, delicately carved camphor chests to intricate pieces of ivory. Most of the carved wooden items were made by Indian craftsmen and expertly finished, and many of them were inlaid with opals. Cultured pearls of great lustre were sold for a tenth of the price they would fetch in England, and Edith bought a necklace of Miki Moto pearls strung in Japan for a mere song. Another innovation introduced by the Chinese was the sale of two oysters sealed in a tin can, for a Singapore dollar (12½p), which when opened were as likely as not to produce a pair of pearls large enough to adorn a set of cuff links.

We bought a magnificent 74-piece set of A1 cutlery, housed in a handsome oak cabinet and made by Harrison Bros and Howson, cutlers to HM King George V, and wondered why they had not been looted by the Japanese invaders – until I remembered that they ate rice with their fingers.

Paddy and Johnny were frequent visitors to our house to share a meal with us. Paddy was Irish and a confirmed bachelor; we knew that Johnny was married, but no one could recall meeting his wife, and because he had served in India we suspected that she was of mixed race. We often saw them in the company of cheongsam-clad Chinese girls, and as there was a widespread belief amongst men that oriental women were made differently from their western sisters – something to do with lateral rather than vertical – I sounded our friends out about this but they refused to be drawn!

Singapore was well endowed with sports facilities, and Gilman Park provided race-tracks, tennis-courts, cricket-pitches, rugby union and soccer playing-fields. Although the daytime temperature rarely varied by more than a few degrees throughout the year, it surprised me that they had separate sports seasons as they then did in England, until it was explained that this was done to rest the grounds.

I arrived home early one afternoon and was shocked to see the girls poking a stick at a large green snake quite near to the house, but was relieved to see that it held a rat in its mouth. A passing motorist noticed us, told me to stay, and then went into his house and emerged with a samurai sword. He slew the snake with one swipe, before telling me that snakes living in the nearby marshland often interbred with cobras and could be quite deadly.

We became friendly with the Wearnes', our mutual interest being bridge, and found Walter to be an exceptionally talented player. He told me that during his incarceration in Changi prison four of the inmates had made their own playing-cards from the bark of trees, and it was only the satisfaction derived from playing bridge that had enabled him to keep his reason. He invited us to a grand ball organised by the Singapore Chamber of Commerce. It was being held at Raffles Hotel, built in memory of that great adventurer who discovered the island and realised its potential as a trading-centre and strategic defence position. Raffles was then a colonial-type hotel situated at the edge of the sea and quite unlike the huge complex it has now become, surrounded as it is by acres of reclaimed land, with its pink roof and tropical gardens, where the cost of a single room is £346 a day.

Leslie Bainbridge had been nominated as my relief, and

he arrived with his wife Betty long before I was due to return home. I met them at Changi RAF Station and helped them to settle in, before arranging the customary cocktail-party so that they could be introduced to fellow members of the regiment and their wives. The CO wanted him to assume my duties as quickly as possible because he had other plans for me.

Every document in a cipher office is classified and serially numbered, and stringent precautions are taken to prevent its loss. Superseded paperwork had then to be destroyed by fire, as shredding-machines had not been introduced, and destruction certificates, countersigned by two witnesses, rendered to the issuing authority. So tight was the control that a document rarely went astray; if by ill chance it did, the outcome was at best a board of inquiry or at worst the court-martial of the custodian. Things went well until we looked for the 'cases wood packing outer', which could not be traced. Normally we ignored these when handing over, but Bainbridge was a stickler and an answer had to be found. War Office policy was to double-envelope any message or package graded 'Top Secret', but no indication was given on the outer envelope of its contents. The same principle was adopted when classified equipment was consigned by ship; the item was enclosed in an inner plywood case, which itself was carried in a stout wooden crate. Because of their size, storage space could not be found for these outer cases, so they were left in the open to be damaged by sun and rain or eaten by termites. There was not the remotest chance of the equipment in question being returned to England, and when I reported to the War Office that the cases had been damaged by white ants they accepted the position.

Reorganisation was now taking place, and the communication network formerly known as the Army Wireless Chain was renamed the Commonwealth Communications Army Network (COMCAN). My new job was to manage the operating side of it, under the command of Bill Renton, and from the moment I joined his squadron we developed a close rapport. We worked in ideal conditions and our complex was one of the few in GHQ that was fully air-conditioned. The plant was installed for the efficiency of the equipment rather than the comfort of the operators, because limp transmitting-tapes could not be perforated cleanly and resulted in corrupted messages, so it was essential for them to be crisp and moisture-free.

One of the semi-official duties that went with this job was giving away the bride, and many of my Saturday afternoons were spent supporting the arm of a WRAC servicewoman as I walked her down the aisle of St Thomas's Church in Tanglin. Very often my daughters Pat and Linda were co-opted as bridesmaids for these happy events. Sometimes things went wrong, and on one occasion the best man forgot to order the cars to take the couple to the church, so Edith drove the bride and me in our MG to the church, and afterwards I took over and drove the bride and bridegroom to the reception, but in the confusion Edith found herself left high and dry without any transport to take her there.

The Corps suffered a loss in 1957 when Brigadier Derek Good, our Chief Signal Officer, sustained an eye injury while playing polo. Because he could no longer meet the exacting medical standards for overseas service, he had to be evacuated to the UK. His replacement was Brigadier Leonard Lewis, who at the age of fifty was still capable of playing a good game of tennis. My partner and I had the misfortune to meet a pair led by the brigadier in the first round of the GHQ tournament, and although it was customary to allow one's senior officer to win, the case did not arise and we were soundly defeated.

At about the same time, a late Royal Signals officer joined the GHQ staff to fill an administrative and quartering post and soon made his mark. Before his arrival the married quarters had been equipped with evil-smelling cooking-stoves using kerosine as fuel, which no self-respecting memsahib would deign to use on the Chinese cook's day off. Colonel Mickey Whistler, the new AQ, was aware of this; he also knew that six hundred new electric stoves were held in store but not installed because the REs considered that the mains electric cables could not cope with the extra load. Whistler's solution was to have them installed, and if the mains blew up to have new cables laid. The stoves were fitted, the mains carried the current to feed them, and the families were happy!

Christmas 1957 was almost upon us, so we and the Bainbridges booked a table at the Singapore Swimming Club. The highlight of the evening was the game of bingo, when the jackpot was won on the last house of the night. Play was at first desultory, punctuated by rounds on the dance floor, but when the final session of bingo was announced dancing was forgotten. When I was three numbers away from a full house I glanced at Leslie's card and noticed that he needed only one, and seconds later there was a roar of 'House'. He had won over 1,000 Singapore dollars when the stake for each hand was a mere 50 cents!

The New Year came and went and my thoughts dwelt on where my next posting would be when my three-year tour of duty ended in April. After life in duty-free Singapore the prospect of returning to England was daunting. Because of this I had resolved to give up smoking, and as a result my intake of food had increased and I was in danger of growing out of my uniforms, so it came as a relief to hear that my next post was to be in Germany, where NAAFI supplies were free of duty, so I resumed the smoking habit.

We had barely two months in which to make plans for our departure and my biggest concern was the disposal of the MG. The Suez Canal had been blocked by Nasser, and although it was now partially reopened, large freight vessels still used the Cape route to England, which was expensive. The Royal Navy operated an 'indulgence scheme' and allowed service personnel's cars to be carried on the decks of aircraft-carriers travelling back to England. The snag was that in the event of vessels being needed for operational duties the decks were liable to be cleared and the cars dumped into the sea. Another risk was for a temperamental captain to take a dislike to his deck cargo and order it to be consigned to Davy Jones's locker. I was fortunate in finding a buyer for the car, and before leaving Singapore ordered a new Wolseley on home delivery.

Another heart-breaking decision that had to be made was the disposal of children's toys, accumulated over three years, because of the limitation on our heavy baggage allowance. Bryan had a fine collection of Dinky Toys ranging from Jeeps to howitzers, all made of metal and therefore weighty, and these had to be sold in the local thrift shop. Today the collection would have raised hundreds of pounds, some of them being collector's pieces.

A few days before we embarked we noticed a set of Noritake porcelain on display in the bazaar and asked the Chinese vendor if he could have it packed and despatched to the ship. 'No problem,' said the man, 'I have cases unopened,' so we bought a twelve setting dinner and tea service unexamined. It was twelve years before the packing-case was opened; the pieces were packed in sawdust and miraculously not one item was broken.

Air-trooping was now in full swing and we were fortunate in being able to travel home by sea, although this entailed dressing up for dinner each night. I had not worn my UK evening uniform since leaving Suez, so I removed it from its camphor chest to have it let out because of my increased girth and took Edith to the Singapore Cold Storage Company to retrieve her fur coat, which had lain in their vaults for three years.

I was appointed to the ship's staff as a supernumerary baggage officer and was allotted a huge cabin on the boat deck. Unfortunately, we embarked on a Monday morning which coincided with the Chinese New Year, so the coolies demanded triple pay. This was turned down by the shore authorities, and the ship's baggage officer had no option but to carry the wanted-on-voyage baggage of a family of five from the dockside to the upper deck of the ship. I had a quick shower and change of clothing before going on deck and waving goodbye to Singapore and the well-wishers who came to bid us *bon voyage*.

23

GERMANY – SECOND TIME ROUND

HMT *Nevasa*, a commodious ship which had replaced the pre-war troop-ship of the same name, had sailed from Hong Kong *en route* to Southampton on her last voyage before being consigned to the ship-breaker's yard because the era of air-trooping had now arrived.

The first days at sea passed uneventfully, and as no one needed to visit the 'wanted on voyage' hold I was not troubled with any ship's duties. In any case, a member of the ship's complement was responsible for the stowage of passengers' suitcases and my presence was only needed in a liaison capacity. It was not an onerous or time-consuming job as access to luggage was restricted to two hours following the captain's daily inspection.

Our first port of call was Colombo, and once again we spent an hour on the beach before visiting the local zoo to admire the gaily plummaged birds and other wildlife. During our stay there we witnessed an unusual sight, that of a P and O liner filled with passengers emigrating from England to start a new life in Australia. Because so many Australian servicemen had lost their lives in the war, the country had initiated a subsidised scheme to encourage suitable immigrants to enter at a cost of £10 passage money per individual.

During the balmy days and evenings at sea, I had time to reflect on the last three years spent at Singapore, the island discovered by Sir Stamford Raffles in 1819 and established by the East India Trading Company as a trading-post. Initially it had formed part of the Straits Settlement of Penang, Malaya and Singapore, until becoming an independent colony in 1946 after the ousting of the Japanese, and the people elected their own legislature in 1955. To commemorate this, they introduced their own postage stamps with 'Singapura' imprinted on them, and I had bought a set of first-day covers at the Army post office in Tanglin on the Sunday they were issued. I was the only customer that day, and had the collection remained intact Stanley Gibbons would doubtless have paid me a good price for a unique set.

I remember, too, the son of Ramsay MacDonald arriving in the colony as Governor, and the eyebrows raised by the establishment at his unorthodox behaviour in fraternising with the locals on the beaches and in boats.

I had been given notice that I was being posted to Bünde, and when I mentioned this to a German diplomat at one of Des Woudstra's parties his comment was: 'Bünde is in North Rhine-Westphalia. You won't like them and they won't like you. In fact, they don't like each other.' I also reflected on the folly of wives taking fur coats to Singapore so that their husbands could pay storage charges for them for three years.

Another memory of that voyage was the variety of curry dishes served at lunch, and for the whole of the six weeks' trip a different spicy dish was provided each day.

I had taken the precaution of taking aboard my own deck-chair, with my name stencilled on it, so that Edith could claim a seat when she wished. The German tourists have earned a reputation for 'booking' seats at holiday resorts by placing towels on them; but long before the days of mass tourism, ship's deck-chairs were reserved by the selfish by resting books from the library on them.

We steamed leisurely through the Indian Ocean and our stay at Aden was brief, so we looked forward to passing through the Red Sea and reaching the more temperate climate of the Mediterranean. We spent two days in the Great Bitter Lakes, waiting for a westbound convoy to form up, and were reminded that relations between the British and Egyptians were strained and cautioned not to antagonise them. Johnnie Walker's advertisement for Scotch whisky still stood there, but I looked in vain for the bust of Ferdinand de Lesseps. Soon we were out of Port Said and experiencing once again the ground swell peculiar to that area before reaching deeper water.

At last the Needles hove into sight, and we berthed at Southampton in the late afternoon ready for disembarkation in the morning. After clearing HM Customs I spotted a movements officer whom I knew, and he asked me if I would like a reserved compartment for the family in return for carrying out the nominal duty of officer i/c train to Waterloo Station.

I reported my return to the UK in writing to our personnel branch at Stanmore and was not surprised to receive a telephone call from John Brown, the major who had replaced Colonel Patrick. The gist of it was that because of reorganisation in Germany I was no longer to join 6th Armoured Division at Bünde but to proceed to Herford instead.

A few days before I was due to join the unit I was told that married quarters were available and, having given them the registration number of my car, that we would be met at the Herford Ost exit to the autobahn. We caught an early ferry and reached Herford by mid-afternoon. Seeing no one in uniform at the exit, we drove into the town hoping to see a Military Policeman to direct us; but it was Wednesday afternoon, sports half-day, and not a soldier could be seen. Some passers-by came to our aid, and when I asked to be directed to the *kaserne*, they sent me to a barracks formerly occupied by Signals but now used by the Life Guards. From there I was shunted to Wentworth Barracks, and redirected to Maresfield Camp some two miles further on.

The orderly officer was apologetic, saying that the reception party was still out, and eventually Bill Stagg turned up with egg on his face explaining that a GB car had passed him but it was being driven so confidently that he was deceived. We were taken to his house for tea and afterwards settled into our new quarter in An der None.

My new unit was 1 (Br) Corps Signal Regiment and I reported to the CO's office in Bradley Block, named after a former CO who later achieved high office in the Corps and became our second Master of Signals, an eminent appointment held by only four major-generals since Royal

Signals was founded in 1920. The CO, Lieutenant-Colonel Basil Barnes, told me that he had held a senior appointment at HQ BAOR and was sent to Herford charged with the task of providing efficient communication for 1 (Br) Corps, which was part of NATO. He realised that the system he had inherited was intrinsically faulted, and suggested that after a few weeks I report my findings to him to confirm what he already suspected. The colonel also mentioned that an appointment which went with the job was that of unit security officer, and that caused me to raise a wry smile because in the corridor outside reposed a tea chest full of top-secret files in full view of the German clerks and cleaners. He confessed that he was not happy with the operating standard of his unit, saying that 'they think they are busy if they pass fifty messages a day, and yet they lose a half of them'. I realised that I was facing a challenge.

My first brief after checking the cipher equipment and classified documents was to analyse the contents of the tea chest, and I was given considerable latitude in the task. My only instructions were to retain documents likely to be of use as historical records and to destroy the rest. It did not take me long to realise that they related to Operation Musketeer, Anthony Eden's Suez adventure, which would have put paid to Nasser's plans for domination of the Middle East – but for the intervention of the Americans.

To fulfil my brief, every piece of paper had to be scrutinised, and although it was a boring job it gave me a good insight into the UK-French-Israeli conduct of the campaign. The number of breaches of security that came to light was unbelievable. Top-secret documents which had been copy-numbered for limited distribution had been circulated indiscriminately, and scores of operation orders for which destruction certificates had been rendered were found unscorched by fire. It took ten days to complete, and all that was left for me to do was bag the unwanted documents, carry them to the incinerator, have their destruction witnessed by another board member and hand over the retained documents to the adjutant for safe keeping in his archives.

The non-technical reader must bear with me in my

attempt to describe how communications were handled in the late 1950s; because of the vast technological strides made since then, our procedures bore no relation to modern-day practice.

Apart from its radio element, 1 (Br) Corps Signal Regiment was attempting to operate 'tape relay in the field' and to emulate the functions of the static Commonwealth Network; but, unlike COMCAN, it was trying to do so as a mobile field force, with its attendant difficulties. COMCAN equipment was permanently located in dust-free or air-conditioned buildings, but ours was fitted into vehicles which had to traverse farm tracks or other uneven ground, raising dust as they travelled, and the equipment was powered by mobile electric generators, which were temperamental and could not be relied upon to give a steady output.

Because of the nuclear threat, elements of Corps HQ were widely dispersed and separated into groups known as Diamond, Triangle and Square. These groups were subdivided into working and resting groups, each having their own equipment so that in the event of a working group being put out of action by nuclear attack it could be replaced by the resting group. The worst feature of the organisation was the separation of the Signals operational side from Corps HQ by a distance of up to five miles to reduce the threat of aerial bombardment. This was a nonsense, as any incoming signals to the HQ from its three divisions, rear corps and its higher command Northern Army group had to be transmitted by teleprinter to our one permitted terminal at Corps HQ or by despatch rider.

On our first field exercise, the Colonel General Staff visited us at Square to complain that incoming traffic was not being received, and with a twinkle in his eye Colonel Basil said to me, 'Go along with him, Tommy, and tell him what is wrong.' On arriving there, we found that both the teleprinters fitted into the vehicle were defective and there was no mechanic available to repair them. I wasted no time in telling him that we were manning an unnecessary extra link, and our proper place was with the HQ so that messages could be delivered by orderly or runner. He took the point; on the next exercise we were located in the vicinity of Corps HQ, and the staff had learnt that the Signals had to be part and parcel of their HQ.

Our next problem was the antiquated Creed teleprinters, perforators and reperforators with which we were equipped. In simple terms, a perforated tape was received from a distant terminal and had to be relayed to other stations in tape form, but with a print-out copy for local delivery. Our equipment was incapable of doing this without further processing, and after consulting with Trevor Reece, an excellent technical officer, I told Colonel Barnes that what we needed were teleprinters capable of producing a tape and three page copies simultaneously.

The idea was accepted at local level and the many observers from the War Office who attended our exercises thought it was sound. I was told that UK manufacturers could not supply such machines but the German firm of Siemens would meet our needs. It took over three years for the War Office procurement agency to arrange their supply, but on my last exercise in Germany the machines were delivered and, furthermore, adopted by the War Office as standard equipment.

When I arrived at Herford the Chief Signal Officer at Corps HQ was Brigadier Charles Nettleship, who was nearing his retirement, and he invited all Royal Signal officers to his farewell party. Because of the numbers involved, he could not invite them all at once so he thoughtfully invited all ex-rankers, comprising Quarter-Masters, traffic officers and technical officers telecommunication, known collectively as 'Quarter-Masters and analgous categories', to one function. It was an ideal arrangement which enabled me to get to know my opposite numbers in the formations which made up the Corps. It was known that the brigadier was seeking to be ordained as a priest, but I could not visualise Mrs Nettleship as a vicar's wife, because at times she swore like a trooper.

Ours was not a working unit and the only time the operators were able to practice their skills was when we were out on exercise; but I had an arrangement with George Cowshill, my opposite number at Wentworth

Barracks, to lend him some of my cipher clerks from time to time so that they gained practical experience of their trade.

Exercises took us far and wide. One time it was within hailing distance of the East German border, and another to the low-lying area of Ostfriesland, bordering the Netherlands, where the Dutch were ready to flood their land in the event of a Soviet attack. Some of them were prolonged, and we would enter a forest in late winter and emerge two weeks later to find the landscape totally changed because the trees were in leaf.

The technique of leap-frogging was tried out. This involved setting up a forward communication centre with its radio and switchboard facilities ready to commence operation when the code-words 'command has passed' were given. The colonel and I would then move to the new location, carrying all uncleared messages with us to be transmitted at the next site. Road congestion often caused delay, so a new drill was tried out. This involved travelling to a nearby airstrip and boarding a light aircraft to the new location.

On one occasion the Auster on which we flew had been parked in a field and aroused the curiosity of some cows, one of which gored the fuselage. The pilot was patching it up with Elastoplast from his first-aid kit when we arrived. I felt a bit queasy on the flight, and more so when I saw the muddy state of the ground below, criss-crossed by vehicle tracks, but we made a safe landing.

One of our young subalterns, Second-Lieutenant Tony Willcox (now a retired brigadier) showed considerable initiative on an exercise near Hamelin. He was in charge of a line party detailed to connect cables to a pick-up point on the other side of the River Weser, and the promised raft had not appeared. Without further ado, Tony slung a loop of cable over his shoulder and swam the icy river. The Weser is fast-flowing, and he was praised for his action in getting the circuits through.

We slept where we could, but usually a large barn was provided for the soldiers, although these could be cold and draughty in winter. The German farmers kept their cattle indoors during the cold weather, and we discovered that the warmest barns were those above the cattle byres, centrally heated by the body warmth of the beasts.

I had looked in vain for the bust of Ferdinand de Lesseps when we passed through Port Said, but it was not until I joined 1 (Br) Corps Signals Regiment that I learnt the full story. The Sappers had found it lying on its side but undamaged, and intended to have it crated and shipped home. They were forestalled by a party of Signallers, who removed the bust from its crate and transferred it to one of their own consigned to Maresfield Camp in Germany. It reposed in the Corps Signals mess for a time, until it was returned to the Sappers as an act of contrition.

Towards the end of my first year at Herford, all Signal units were redesignated and from then on we became 7th Signal Regiment. At the same time it was decided that National Servicemen were to be phased out, and 7th was earmarked as the first postwar all-regular Signal unit. My National Service cipher staff were hand-picked and their loss would be felt for some time.

The regiment occupied two large complexes divided by the Herford-Bad Salzuflen road. Crossing from one to the other proved hazardous for marching troops, so the CO persuaded the Royal Engineers to span it with a bridge. Naturally, it became known as 'Barnes Bridge'.

The 7th, like Topsy, 'just growed' – to such an extent that it became unwieldy to administer. It was decided to split it into two, and 22nd Signal Regiment came into being under the command of Lieutenant-Colonel Curly Spence, our former second-in-command.

Basil Barnes was a boffin. The holder of science and engineering degrees and a winner of the coveted Agar prize, he not unnaturally had contacts in the Institution of Electrical Engineers, so it was no surprise when that august body asked for a group of its members to be invited to assess modern signalling techniques.

Considerable advances in technology had been made since the war ended. Major John Newman was pioneering satellite communication in the Far East; and fax, considered to be a recent innovation, was in use by the Army in 1958 and proved invaluable in passing air-reconnaissance photographs between the various HQs. These facsimile machines were fitted into Army vehicles, powered by mobile generators and connected by land lines laid by Army linesmen. Computers, suitably primed, were in use for transmitting classified messages, and these were operated by specially vetted personnel, thus relieving the pressure of work in the cipher offices. The visitors were impressed, and a demonstration was laid on for their benefit. This involved passing messages by radio relay from our base at Herford to Rheindahlen, 125 miles away. This exercise had unforeseen consequences: the railway marshalling yards at Moenchen Gladbach were operated by radio and the frequencies we were using triggered off the railway shunting system, causing consternation as unmanned freight trains travelled willy-nilly along the tracks.

My daughter Pat attended an Army boarding-school at Hamm and carried her own passport. We were invited to spend the weekend with my sister, who lived near Utrecht in Holland, and decided to collect Pat from school and take her with us. As we approached the Dutch border control post, I asked for her passport – and to my dismay was told that she had left it at school. The Dutch, mindful of their treatment by the Germans during the war, always scrutinised their passports; but we were in luck because our car bore BZ registration plates, and after a perfunctory glance at our documents we were waved on. The border guard had assumed that Pat, a female aged thirteen, was the male child Bryan, aged nine, included in Edith's passport! The problem now was, having entered Holland, how did we get out?

We often travelled to Hamm on school visiting weekends and camped on the banks of the River Lippe. On one of these occasions it rained continuously and I watched with envy from our tent the parents who sat in comfort in their caravans, so I resolved to invest in one. We travelled to the Sprite Musketeer agency near Utrecht on the following weekend, hitched a four-berth caravan to the tow-bar and drove back.

I had some leave due and decided to visit the South of France during the school holidays, stopping in the Black

Forest *en route*. Our base camp was at Friedrichshafen, on the shores of what the Germans called the Bodensee and others Lake Constance, which separates Switzerland from Germany. There was a ferry service from Friedrichshafen to Constance, and we decided to spend a day on the Swiss side of the lake. We took some exercise propelling the hired paddle-boats, but we were not conversant with the warning signs and felt ourselves being drawn by the current. I made frantic signs to Edith to paddle her boat nearer the quayside and eventually turned mine around to reach calmer water. I had forgotten what every schoolboy knows, that Lake Constance is the source of the Rhine, and we had been in danger of being swept down-river.

Our route to the south was via Zurich and Geneva, and down the Rhone Valley to Lyon and Avignon, where we branched off to Sète on the coastal road to Spain. I calculated that the laden weight of the trailer was twenty hundredweight, and the sturdy Wolseley towed it up gradients effortlessly.

Once established at Sète, I fitted the canopy made specially by the Dutch dealer, and it drew admiration from fellow campers. We soon tired of this campsite because the main road separated us from the beach, and so we packed up and meandered along the coast through Marseille and the French naval base of Toulon before setting up camp near St Raphael.

We spent a pleasant week on the Côte d'Azur, and the idea of returning to Germany through the Alps appealed to me so we retraced our journey along the coast and joined a road leading to Aix. The scenery in this part of Provence was superb, and we were soon in wooded country as we followed the course of the River Durance with the Maritime Alps on our right. We passed through Manosque, Sisteron and Serres, and motored a further ten miles before encountering a problem. My road-map covered the whole of France and showed the main roads and centres of population. Minor roads were not clearly defined, so that when we reached a signpost marked Gap, I turned right, thinking that it was on the route to Grenoble. The road climbed fairly steeply from this point and after a further twenty miles we arrived at Gap, and followed the signs to the camping-site. It was on wet, sloping ground and I found difficulty in steering the car into a parking-plot, but as usual there were many helpers to lend a hand. The campers stared at the small British car and the large caravan. They looked at me in disbelief when I said I had left Aix that morning, and they were dumbfounded when told that I was following the route to Grenoble. All this should have made me suspicious, but I still did not realise that we ought to have carried straight on at the signpost.

Gap lies on the approaches to the Cottiennes Alps, which separate France from Italy, and is on the road known as the 'Route Napoléon', where the Emperor and his troops, like Hannibal and his elephants before him, crossed the border to conquer Italy and defeat the armies of Rome and proclaim himself king.

I decided to reconnoitre the route ahead and unhitched the caravan, taking my son Bryan with me in the car. We came upon some fearful bends, but I had faith in the ability of the car to draw the trailer; the main danger was if the tow-bar broke, in which case the caravan would roll backwards and be lost. On returning to the camp, I managed to buy a wooden chock and briefed Bryan to jump out and place it behind a road wheel should the engine stall, to avoid the caravan dragging us backwards over the mountainside.

As we set off on the following morning, the campers wished us luck – but I noticed one or two of them making the sign of the cross. Nothing untoward happened, and an hour later we reached Embrun. The scenery was breath-taking, with the 12,600 feet Mount Visc ahead of us and the 13,400 feet Mount Pelvoux to our left. By midday we reached Briançon – and it was here that the road ended!

We found a small café in the village and over a coffee and cognac learnt that we were within two miles of the Italian border and the track leading to Grenoble was passable now that the snow had melted.

We had now reached a plateau between the mountain peaks. If there ever had been a road, its surface was broken up by snow and ice, but the track was fairly level and free from boulders. Eventually we saw a rough roadsign indicating that Grenoble was fifteen kilometres away and we were all relieved when we joined a metalled road leading to the city. Only one car had passed us on the whole journey and as the occupants waved it reminded me of Stanley meeting up with Dr Livingstone in darkest Africa.

One difficulty had been overcome only to be replaced by another. As I looked down at Grenoble 2,000 feet below, my fears were for the brake linings of the car because although forward pressure of a trailer on the car actuates its own braking system, it also adds to the effort needed to slow the vehicles down. Overloaded and underpowered small cars travelling south were negotiating the steep gradient, and sometimes passengers vacated their cars and walked behind them carrying their baggage.

Mont Blanc and the Matterhorn were two of the magnificent sights that we passed as we neared the Swiss border. We knew that the worst of the journey was behind us, but by the time we reached Geneva Edith was suffering from raging toothache. After paying the dentist's fee my cash resources were dwindling. Once inside the British Zone I could ask for a cash advance at any area pay office, or at the worst I could ask a petrol station attendant to buy some of my petrol coupon vouchers at half their face value, although this was illegal.

Two days later we were back at Herford fully recovered from our Alpine adventure. On their return to school the children heard that NAAFI were hiring out television sets and begged me to get one, and it was installed within a few days. The programmes were on the heavy side, with an emphasis on education and enlightenment rather than entertainment – although many imported films were shown, with voices dubbed into guttural German, which did not deceive anyone. Perry Mason could be seen propelling his wheelchair around the court rooms of America, the Eurovision competition made its yearly round and we were regaled with performances of *Holiday on Ice*. Dostoyevsky's *The Idiot* had been televised and was shown on Sunday afternoons for months on end. A variety show was broadcast from Hamburg and an earthy comedian was seen bemoaning – in German – the fact that 'his apparatus did not work', meaning that he was impotent. Competitions were held on stage and the winner received a small gold bar. An English visitor entered one of these and was successful, but forces viewers were not impressed when the compère presenting it to him said, 'Take this home and give it to your Chancellor' – at a time when the Treasury could not pay its overseas debts.

Guy Symonds arrived from Singapore on being commissioned as Quarter-Master and we welcomed him and his wife Phyllis with a small party. They had not been with us very long before she announced that she was pregnant. The arrival of a baby after so long a marriage raised a barrier between them and the couple slept in separate beds. It was not long before Guy started to cultivate the NAAFI manageress. She spent hours in his office, which did not go unnoticed.

Colonel Basil's term of office was up and he left us on promotion to a staff appointment, being replaced by Colonel Peter Pentreath, an officer who had been involved in the Suez operation as a major, and had earned promotion to brevet lieutenant-colonel. Under his command 7th Signal Regiment earned a fine reputation and many officers whose future prospects were in doubt joined us for what can only be described as a probationary period.

One that fell into this category was a major who, because of his seniority, was appointed second-in-command. By virtue of his appointment he carried out the duties of president of the officers' mess committee – until an incident occurred which doomed his chances of further advancement.

The Royal Signals had been born out of the Royal Engineers, and traditionally each corps entertained the other to dinner every year. It was our turn to host the Sappers in 1959 but unfortunately the CO could not be present and arrangements were left in the hands of his deputy. The waiters served an hors d'oeuvre followed by trout, and to our consternation and the surprise of our guests no main course was forthcoming. Naturally Colonel

Pentreath heard of this on his return to duty and the second-in-command's prospects of further promotion vanished.

Because of our static role I had insufficient work to occupy me and I gradually undertook extra duties, starting with running the small-bore shooting team. An annual postal competition was held under the auspices of the International Rifle Association, and my duties as captain included selecting the team, arranging for an invigilator to witness the targets, mustering the competitors at our 25-yard miniature range and forwarding the certified targets for evaluation by the association. Our one success was in winning the team award for young soldiers, which was encouraging considering that we were competing against trained Infantry marksmen. Colonel Peter was interested in producing a boxing team, and although I knew nothing of the noble art I was pressed into service to form one. Two of my team were talented, and qualified for the BAOR finals taking place at Berlin. As their captain, I was able to secure a room for Edith and me at Edinburgh House, a requisitioned hotel intended for use by visiting forces to the old capital but invariably filled by NAAFI officials, who used it as a closed shop.

The tournament was held at the Olympic Stadium, where Hitler had offended many competing nations in 1936 by uttering remarks about the superiority of the Aryan race, and my nominees were adjudged BAOR champions.

During our stay there I met Major Max Sawyers, who commanded the Berlin Signal Squadron and had served in the Far East during the war. He had arrived in East Bengal with a Signals squadron of the 81st West African Division and they marched from Bengal to the Burmese Arakan. Initially mules had been used to carry the equipment but they could not cope with the terrain and were replaced by bullocks. Because of their colour, the bullocks were easily spotted, so they were painted jungle-green to blend with their surroundings. But as they proved to be lazy and unable to cope with their loads, they were shot and their carcases provided the only fresh meat the soldiers had eaten in weeks. Thereafter the men carried the equipment in head-loads weighing up to forty pounds, in addition to their own arms and equipment.

We were taking part in an autumn exercise in 1959 when we were surprised to see a small group of senior officers approaching our communication centre. Our distinguished visitor was General Sir Francis Festing, who had recently relinquished command of GHQ Far East and was about to take up a Field-Marshal's baton as Chief of the General Staff. He showed great interest in the complex and asked questions about its defence. When told that in wartime it would be defended by a platoon of Infantry, he was not impressed, remarking that a well-lobbed hand-grenade would paralyse the nerve-centre of the Corps HQ.

An airmail letter addressed to Edith arrived from Nairobi announcing that a friend of hers, June Hall, was marrying a Dane in Copenhagen and asking for her moral support as her parents were unable to travel. June was a fresh-complexioned girl with blonde naturally wavy hair. Her mother owned a flourishing hotel at Kampala on the shores of Lake Victoria, while her father panned for gold in a worked-out mine, hoping to come across an undiscovered nugget or two. She had spent her entire lifetime in Uganda and Kenya, and like all Europeans who elected to remain in Kenya after Kenyatta was appointed President, had suffered the indignity of being fingerprinted as a condition of residence.

June had met her fiancé, Svend Knudson, when he visited the Kenya capital on a trade mission organised by the Danish Government. As we had not travelled to Scandinavia we decided to explore the small kingdom before ending up in Copenhagen for the wedding ceremony.

Our route took us to Hamburg and Rendsburg, where we crossed the Kiel Canal, after which we made for Sylt in the North Frisian Islands and spent a day on the unspoilt sands before driving to Kolding for a night-stop at a caravan site. My image of Denmark had been of one country and not a group of islands, and it was with some surprise that we boarded a ferry to carry us to the island of Fyn. The capital, Odense, is well known as the birthplace of Hans Christian Andersen. Unlike in the Hollywood film, its streets were not made of cobblestones, and its residents were deeply hurt by the way their town had been portrayed by the film producer.

We still had a channel to cross. We embarked at Nyborg to cross the Store Baelt and landed at Korsor on the island of Sjaelland, on which Copenhagen stands. The terrain was flat and we met little traffic as we drove along roads fringed by verdant fields in which contented-looking cattle browsed. Svend had booked us into an hotel in the heart of Copenhagen. It was not difficult to find as it faced the Carlsberg lager brewery, an imposing building covering many acres.

It was considerate of Svend to book us into an hotel as it enabled us to have our clothes laundered, but the wedding was some days ahead so we drove the caravan to a seaside town up the coast to make the most of the beaches. Denmark is renowned for the quality of its pork, but try as we did we could not find any edible bacon; to describe what we saw as 'streaky' was flattery – it resembled large chunks of fat. We also failed to find any fishmongers until someone told us that fish was sold from refrigerators at the dockside. We had to agree a price with the trawlerman which we thought was extortionate. I passed this information on to a fellow service camper, who smiled knowingly and said that his custom was to lay a packet of John Players cigarettes in the bottom of his plastic bucket, and at a nod from the deckhand he would lower it down and haul it up full of fish.

Cigarettes were very expensive, and many residents of Copenhagen found it rewarding to pay the return ferry fare to Malmo in Sweden in order to buy a carton of duty-free smokes.

On returning to Copenhagen we did the tourist rounds of the Tivoli Gardens and the harbour. Most visitors there have seen the statue of 'The Little Mermaid', *Langelinie*, resting on a huge spherical boulder, but when we spotted it the tide was out and it looked insignificant perched on a veritable mountain of rocks.

The wedding ceremony was simple and followed by a reception which was anything but. The bride and bridegroom were toasted, and so was the bridegroom's parents, absent friends, English guests, distant relatives and all and sundry. Svend delivered a speech with many passages in English for our benefit – and to the annoyance of those who did not understand the Anglo-Saxon tongue – and afterwards the dance orchestra struck up and the guests took to the floor. June appeared to be petrified when the women pounced on her as she was about to leave and started to pluck pieces of material from her wedding veil, but soon regained her composure when her husband reassured her.

Non-resident visitors to the Carlsberg brewery were allowed to drink as much as they wished in order to promote the sale of their product, and it was becoming very popular in service messes in Germany. But I could never understand the penchant for members of the sergeants' mess to top it up with a tot of lime juice, a custom which found its way to many English public houses.

We returned to Germany by a different route, travelling south to Naestved and boarding another ferry, before connecting up with a causeway that ran for miles. Finally we reached the port of Gedser and embarked on a train-carrying ferry to the ancient town of Lübeck with its quaint half-timbered houses. It was on this ferry trip that we discovered *smorrbrod*, those delightful open sandwiches so popular with the Scandinavians, and for a nominal sum we could have eaten for the whole length of the sea crossing.

Our Colonel-in-Chief, Princess Mary the Princess Royal, had indicated that she wished to visit her Corps in Germany in 1960, and she was due at Maresfield Barracks in October. We all hoped that the weather would be kind on 14th October but were prepared for the worst, and as usual for these VIP visits 'fine weather' and 'wet weather' programmes were arranged. In the event the sun shone and HRH was able to inspect the regiment on the parade ground. My role, as security officer, was to conduct the press around agreed areas of the camp and prevent them prying into matters which did not concern them. Edith and I were honoured with a short audience with HRH, who was very concerned with the welfare of the families – despite worries about her prize herd of cattle, threatened by an outbreak of foot-and-mouth disease on her estate at Harewood House.

With the approach of Christmas came the party season, and this took the form of private house entertainment, usually 6-8 p.m. cocktail-parties, or the more formal mess functions when local dignatories and representatives of other messes were invited. One of these went off to a bad start when some influential Germans were invited and someone suggested that the host ladies wear a single red rose to identify them to the lady guests. There were titters when the Germans arrived, because the chosen emblem was the trade mark of high-grade prostitutes. Clearly someone had blundered!

Another mess function to which we were invited was at Bünde, the HQ of 2nd British Division, to commemorate Kohima Day, when General Slim's Fourteenth Army inflicted a punishing defeat on the Japanese.

Towards the middle of 1961 I received the usual three months' notice of my future posting – and learnt that I should be proceeding to Cyprus in November.

24

APHRODITE'S ISLAND

I left for Stansted Airport on a dull November morning without my family, who were to follow when I had taken over suitable accommodation. Travel arrangements were in the hands of RAF Movements. There was little delay in boarding the aircraft, but after taking our seats and listening to the air-safety drill there was a slight hiatus. A group captain of the RAF Medical Branch was reluctant to fasten his seat-belt, giving the impression that he was going to Cyprus against his will, but eventually the persuasive cabin crew brought him round to their way of thinking. The passenger sitting next to me was a WAAF officer whose first action after take-off was to swallow two sleeping-tablets, which made communication difficult for the remainder of the flight, and a few hours later we landed at Nicosia Airport.

Marmy Turner, whom I was relieving, met me and pointed out places of interest on the way to Episkopi. The first major town we came to was Limassol, which also served as the island's second seaport, but we avoided the busy town centre and skirted it on a bypass built to relieve the congestion. The inevitable happened and shops sprang up on both sides of it, which caused the cynical to say that soon a bypass would have to be built to bypass the bypass.

As we neared the Sovereign Base area of Episkopi, we traversed a new stretch of road about a mile in length, dubbed the M1 after the newly constructed motorway from the outskirts of London to the north of England. Road signs indicated that we were nearing the RAF base at Akrotiri, and soon afterwards we reached the domestic area of 15th Signal Regiment and I was dropped off at the officers' mess to meet Keith White, with whom I was to share a room. Keith and I had served together in Germany and got on well. I suggested one Sunday that we went for a swim after the church service, and was surprised when he said that the swimming season was over. Despite that, we drove down to Tunnel Beach and spent an exhilarating half-hour in the sea.

My new appointment was OC the Cipher Equipment Troop, and this involved distributing and accounting for all military cryptographic material in use by Signals units deployed throughout the Near East, which at the time was a major military command, some areas of which were unstable.

A case in point was Libya, where ambitious Army officers were secretly planning to remove King Idris from his throne. From a communication point of view this raised some difficulties because it was his habit to spend the summer months at Benghazi and the winter at Tripoli, thus the British Army Signal squadron responsible for his security had to be mobile and operate two separate communication centres.

The history of Cyprus has been turbulent. It was annexed from Turkey in 1914 when the Turks sided with Germany in the Great War and became a Crown Colony in 1925. After Makarios was appointed Archbishop in 1950, a movement now known as *enosis* (Union with Greece) came into being, resulting in clashes between the Turkish and Greek communities.

Because of the British forces' withdrawal from the Suez Canal Zone and their subsequent transfer to Cyprus in 1954, the patriotic feelings of *enosis* supporters were inflamed and the more militant of them set up a force known as Eoka, commanded by Colonel Grivas, a fanatical Greek-Cypriot army officer.

This resulted in bitter guerilla warfare. A state of emergency was declared in 1955, resulting in the trouble-maker Makarios being deported to the Seychelles. Years of guerilla fighting continued. A measure of peace was eventually restored and under the Zurich-London Agreement a new republic came into being in 1960.

In drawing up the constitution, account was taken of the size of the Greek-speaking population, amounting to eighty per cent of the total 600,000, the remainder being Turkish-speaking Muslims. It was decreed that the President should be Greek, with a Turkish Vice-President. Makarios and Kutchuck filled these roles. Under the Zurich-London Agreement, the United Kingdom retained areas of land at Episkopi, Akrotiri and Dhekelia, with enclaves at Nicosia and Ayios Nicolaos for the use of its forces, and these were known as Sovereign Base Areas.

The security of these bases was the responsibility of the British authorities, who were mindful of the sabotage carried out in the Grivas era. All sensitive areas were enclosed and patrolled, and in the case of my equipment stores it was installed in a compound within a compound.

The hand-over was painstaking and took a week to complete: every piece of paper was copy-numbered and destruction certificates had to be checked for all documents that had been burnt since the last annual return was rendered to the War Office. Eventually it was over, and Marmy Turner and his family were free to emplane for England.

Like all large military HQs, Episkopi was overflowing with senior staff officers and had a shortage of families' accommodation. Quarters were allocated on a points basis, consideration being given to rank, length of service and periods of separation. Many Greeks hired out their flats to the Army and were prepared to live in shacks in the grounds in order to raise the dowry price for their sisters and daughters. A large complex named Beregaria Village had also been erected on the outskirts of Limassol to house those having sufficient points to qualify for admission, but the ultimate aim was to acquire a quarter in Episkopi itself. I had amassed enough points for a hiring and was due for promotion to major in February, so I arranged for my family to be called forward and took over a spacious flat in Limassol.

From the moment that she arrived Edith detested it. She was used to a busy life, and after the Greek maid had done the housework she had little to occupy herself with. The position was aggravated because working hours were from 7 a.m. to 1 p.m. to allow time for recreation in the afternoons, which meant that I left at 6.30 a.m. and did not return until 1.30 p.m.

My promotion was duly promulgated in the *London Gazette,* and when the next waiting-list for quarters was published I headed it and did not have long to wait for a house in Episkopi.

My car had been shipped out and collected from Famagusta, so we were mobile. As soon as we settled in, we decided to tour the island. Cyprus is the third-largest island in the Mediterranean and can be likened to a frying-pan with its handle extending north-east to Cape Andreas, fifty miles from the coast of Turkey. It is an island of plains and mountains, dominated by Mount Olympus (6,400 feet high), which lies in the Troodos Mountains in the south-west, and the Kyrenia range in the north. At that time it was unspoilt and almost unheard of by the tourists who flocked to the Balearic Islands and the Canaries, and the partition of the island, although mooted as a solution to the Greek-Turkish problem, was a thing of the future. Because of its short length – 138 miles from Cape Andreas to Paphos – and a width of only 60 miles from Larnaca to Kyrenia, it was possible to drive to any part of the island for a picnic and be home by early evening. It was also possible to swim at the Episkopi beach and ski on the slopes of Mount Olympus within the hour. One of our favourite outings was to the 'Pan Handle', driving across the fertile plains to Nicosia and descending through olive groves, where Turkish boys tended their goats, to the idyllic pinafore-sized harbour of Kyrenia. It was in this area that we came across the ruins of three medieval castles and the abbey of Bellapaïs, said to have been occupied by King Richard's crusaders when they conquered the island.

Further north the fields surrounding the coast road were a mass of wild flowers, with cyclamen and anemonies providing great splashes of colour, and it was here that we found a quiet cove and shared a bottle of wine and some sandwiches before returning via Famagusta.

Our next-door neighbour had completed one career in the seagoing branch of the Royal Navy and taken up a second one in medicine. He surprised me one day by asking if I could visit him in his surgery. On my arrival he said that he had been treating Edith with antidepressant pills and it was time that she was weaned of them. The doctor then asked me what was wrong with her and I told him that she was a worrier and had insufficient to occupy her, so he suggested that she found herself a job. She obtained work as an FCE through the PCLU (officialese for a woman worker employed through a procurement agency) and started work typing up tabulated ration returns. This was not her forte, and after lining up for her pay she left at the end of the week.

Her next post was more in keeping with her professional skills and involved working for the SBA chief of police as his secretary. It was not demanding work and she found time now and again to come home for coffee. The deputy chief, Bill Williams, was based at Dhekelia and often visited the HQ. Bill was a fine man who had served in the Palestine police until its disbandment and was in receipt of a disability pension as a result of losing a leg in a Jewish terrorist ambush.

The climate of Cyprus favours agriculture, and the central plain of the Mesaoria is suited to producing wheat, carobs, potatoes and barley. Nearer the coasts, citrus fruits and bananas are grown. Many retired servicemen settled in the north of the island, where they made a comfortable living from growing oranges and lemons in addition to poultry-farming.

The slopes of the mountains were particularly suited to grape production, the early morning mists helping to swell the fruit which festooned the vines. The grapes were gathered in late summer and conveyed to the wine factory in open lorries. Several of these lorries passed through Episkopi daily, making the Tarmac roads hazardous as the juice spilt on to the surface, and notices set up by the SBA police cautioned military drivers of the danger.

Carob trees, which had existed in biblical days, were a main source of revenue. By government decree there was a set date for harvesting the crop to ensure that immature beans were not cut down for early sale.

Wine production made a large contribution to the

economy of the country and provided a livelihood for thousands of small grape-growers whose land was unsuitable for crops such as wheat and barley. The grapes were taken to a large factory near Limassol, where they were processed, and we were given a conducted tour of the huge presses and vats where it fermented. Our guide told us that there was a growing export market for bottled wines but much of their produce was sold to other countries for blending purposes in the form of concentrated grape juice. It is said that the Knights of St John of Jerusalem, who built the Castle of Kolossi seven miles away, introduced a special blend of wine, known to this day as Commandaria, from grapes grown in this region. Every type of wine or spirit could be sampled free of charge at the annual Limassol wine festival, at the risk of a hangover in the morning.

We sometimes made trips of historic value for the benefit of the children. It was not far to go to see the excavations at Curium, with its two ruined temples said to have been dedicated to Apollo, and a colonnaded portico built by the Romans. The work of discovery was still going on and the team from Pennsylvania had unearthed a Roman theatre with an auditorium capable of seating two thousand.

Legend has it that Aphrodite, the goddess of love, was born near a group of rocks, close to Koukla (old Paphos), where an inscription reads: *Aphrodite, Goddess of Love, was born of the foam, off the coast of Paphos.*

We visited Limassol for shopping and the odd meal, our favourite being the skewered kebabs, until Edith heard from her SBA police contacts that a café-owner had been convicted of selling food unfit for human consumption. It transpired that he had paid street urchins to collect the bodies of feral cats run over by speeding taxi-drivers, skinned them and barbequed the flesh with other meat before serving it up as kebab.

The main shopping centre was at Nicosia and boasted some fine Greek restaurants and jeweller's shops. Most of them were situated in Ledra Street, which had acquired an unsavoury reputation during the earlier troubles, when it was known as 'murder mile' and shootings and stabbings took place hourly.

There were two brothers of the same name serving in our Corps, David and Jim, and it was our luck to have David, a confirmed bachelor, as our CO. I was attached to his unit for administrative but not operational purposes and was a member of his officers' mess. As such I was expected to bear a fair share of mess duties. Currently I was the house member, responsible for overseeing that furnishings and equipment were properly maintained.

Our Colonel-in-Chief was visiting Cyprus in the autumn and arrangements had been made for her to take lunch with us, so painstaking efforts were made to spruce up the camp. An imposing, detached ladies' powder-room was constructed in the grounds on the off chance that it would be needed, and the pathway leading to it was lined with decorative lime-washed stones.

To minimise the chances of a hitch, it was decreed that a full-dress rehearsal be held a week before the visit. There then followed an extraordinary sequence of events. Husbands were instructed to bring their wives to a 'practice' lunch and were lined up on the right of their husbands in the ante-room to meet the Princess Royal. HRH's place was taken by Colonel David, and my hackles rose as Edith and the other ladies were expected to bestow a practice curtsy on him; as he passed he could not fail to notice my glower. The charade was followed by the arrival of Lieutenant-Colonel The Hon. Mary Anderson, the local chief of the WRAC and daughter of the designer of the wartime air-raid shelter, to receive her practice curtsy, after which we took our seats for lunch.

The waitress service was provided by off-duty members of the WRAC, all of whom received extra-duty pay chargeable to mess members' bills, and there was one waitress for every four diners. The menu was precisely the same as the one arranged for the royal visit, and after the meal a photograph was taken of the members of the Regiment with Mary Anderson standing in for HRH and another for her lady-in-waiting.

The 15th Signal Regiment mess was impoverished, having little to offer the Colonel-in-Chief except sherry or coffee. Fortunately, I had an eighteen-inch A1 plated tray bought in Singapore, and this was pressed into service.

The day of the visit dawned, and as house member I looked in to see how preparations were proceeding. We had an experienced mess supervisor and, not wishing to be too intrusive, I made a cursory inspection of the dining-tables and could not fault the layout. I was astonished when some time later Second-in-Command Dunkley, no doubt acting under orders, appeared and made a thorough inspection of not only the head table but every other place-setting. One staff-sergeant and two majors to supervise the work of the mess staff: over-insurance perhaps!

The Army establishment in Cyprus was top-heavy and had very few formations to administer on the island and the remainder of the Near East. General Sir Dudley Ward, the Commander-in-Chief, had relinquished his command in BAOR and was approaching retirement, so the day-to-day running of the HQ was in the capable hands of Lieutenant-General Sir John Anderson, and the largest military formation under command was 3rd Brigade at Dhekelia, ably commanded by the highly decorated ex-Irish Guardsman Brigadier Basil Eugster.

It came as no surprise therefore that the HQ was to be cut down to size and reduced to the status of a District. The Army general officers were to leave, and command of Cyprus was to be taken over by Air Vice-Marshal Barnett within six months. The 3rd British Infantry Brigade was to be dismantled, leaving the Army with only one Infantry battalion of the Greenjackets. I had instructions from my branch at the War Office to run down the Cipher Equipment Troop as all future requirements would be distributed by courier. The District HQ was to be located at Dhekelia and a large building programme was set in motion for the redeployment. Major Paddy Mclauchlan was serving on the staff of Brigadier Honeybourne, the Chief Signal Officer, as communication security officer, and he invited us to lunch one Sunday. After an excellent meal we adjourned to the nine-hole golf-course, and in between drives he told me what was on his mind. For family reasons he wished to return to England three months before his tour of duty expired, and the CSO had agreed to this provided I took over his duties – in addition to my own! After such a wonderful lunch how could I refuse? So I found myself, to use the Army expression, 'wearing two hats'.

One of my duties was to attend committee meetings with the RAF to discuss inter-service matters. A committee has been described as an arrangement enabling one to share the blame with others. Another saying is, 'If you wish to shirk making a decision, pass it on to a committee.' I found the meetings trying and indecisive. My fellow members ranked as Squadron Leaders, and when pressed for an opinion or a decision resorted to the phrase: 'We do not know what is in the minds of the Wing Commanders'; so very often I had no constructive views to report to my CSO.

The run-down of the headquarters continued throughout 1962 and I was hard-pressed to reduce the mountain of reserve documents held in my store, all of which had to be burnt in an incinerator within the compound and their serial numbers recorded. Much of the machinery was obsolete but still of security value, and it had to be disposed of locally. My instructions from London were to break it up and dump it at sea at a depth of more than six hundred fathoms. This precaution was necessary because at the time Soviet trawlers were patrolling outside territorial waters, allegedly fishing (in an area notoriously devoid of fish) but in reality eavesdropping on our radio networks.

The dumping necessitated my staff and me making several trips to sea in a requisitioned RAF launch to areas beyond the three-mile limit where it was known that there was an abundance of deep water.

The reorganisation involved the disbandment of 15th Signal Regiment and the formation of three independent squadrons, each commanded by a major. These were: 259, which was to remain in Episkopi as the Operating Squadron; 261, remaining in Episkopi as the COMCAN Squadron; and 262, which was being formed in Dhekelia as the Cyprus District Signal Squadron, to which I was to be posted as soon as my commitments at the HQ were over.

The OC 262 was John McKellar, a down-to-earth Scot born in Rothesay on the Isle of Bute and a long-serving and experienced officer. John was anxious for me to join his squadron to manage the new communication centre opened recently by the Princess Royal, and he was impatient at the delay caused by the need to finalise the closure of my Episkopi set-up.

A serious incident occurred early in 1963 involving some WRAC operators attached to our unit. It had long been suspected that some of them were practising lesbianism, but that was a matter for their own officers until it came to light that they had involved a young Greek girl in their orgies. The Greeks were jealous of the chastity of their women, and if the affair came to the knowledge of their menfolk retribution would follow; they would have an unmarriageable woman on their hands and the lives of the WRAC lesbians would have been at risk. So the servicewomen involved were given an hour to pack their kit and driven straight to Nicosia Airport to board an aircraft for home.

I moved to Dhekelia in the spring of 1963 to take over a new quarter and spent two days helping my daughter Pat to clean up the mess left behind by the decorators, leaving Edith to hand over the house at Episkopi. Blenheim Village consisted of houses which blended into the coastal surroundings and were of excellent design. Stress was laid on privacy, so no one was overlooked. The new communication centre was compact and well laid out, and it did not take long for me to assume my new duties.

Our new GOC was Major-General Peter Young, who had been commissioned into the Oxfordshire and Buckinghamshire Light Infantry in 1932, two months before I enlisted, and he was two months my senior in age. He had served with the Royal West Africa Frontier Force and commanded 44 Paratroop Brigade, besides holding many senior staff appointments including that of Grade I Instructor at the Staff College. General Young was to remain at Episkopi with a small staff so that he was available for consultation with the Air Vice-Marshal Commander-in-Chief (Cyprus).

Our local commander at Dhekelia was Brigadier

Douglas Parker, late of The Royal Scots (Pontius Pilate's Bodyguard) whose decorations included the Chevalier of the Order of Leopold II with Palm and Croix de Guerre 1940 with Palm, Belgium. He, too, had held numerous staff appointments and had qualified at the Joint Services Staff College.

One of the first actions of the GOC was to plan an exercise to see how well his services could cope in an emergency, and one of his aims was to test the capability of the Signal Service to its utmost limit. Normally the communication centre was staffed on a three-shift basis, but this was not *de rigueur* and allowance had always to be made for situations leading to heavy traffic loads. My solution was to dispense with the third shift and split it between the remaining two, thus ensuring that the off-duty shift had adequate rest. The outgoing traffic generated incoming replies and most of the signals were of very high precedence, ranging from Flash to Operational Immediate, which had replaced the old wartime Most Immediate so often quoted in works of fiction. The new order of priority was: Flash, Emergency, Operational Immediate, Priority, Routine and Deferred.

General Young presided over a conference at the end of the exercise and I was able to report that all messages were processed promptly and no delays were experienced.

There was a general tendency amongst staff officers to attach a higher precedence to messages than their texts justified, and they did not realise that if each one was graded Priority they all were treated as Deferred. Eventually the nettle was grasped and the Army Council instructed that on receipt of a Priority signal, the duty clerk would contact the addressee – who had to deal with it immediately even though it meant him leaving his bed. This stopped the abuse, and the drafters of signals finally 'got the message'.

I had reason to visit 9th Signal Regiment, an intelligence-gathering organisation, one day and bumped into Ted Macey, with whom we had travelled out to Singapore, and visited several times as guests in his mess. He was now wearing a Royal Pioneer Corps cap badge, which I thought odd but he brushed it off by saying that he was employed as Civil Labour Officer.

Our new CSO was a colonel whose arrival in Cyprus had been delayed because of some difficulty in replacing him at Saighton Camp in Chester. He asked me to visit the Military Attaché seconded to HM High Commissioner at Nicosia. Together with one of his officers and Len Stone, who was in charge of the Foreign Office communications set-up in Cyprus, I drove to the High Commission building in Alexander Pallis. The attaché told us that HE was concerned at the worsening political situation and, although he had adequate secure communication to the outside world by radio, he felt vulnerable to any mob violence which might isolate his office from the protection of the security services. In short, he wished to be in contact with the GOC at Episkopi should he wish to call for help.

There were two items of equipment suited for this purpose; the one recommended was as temperamental as a prima donna but was readily available. I asked Len Stone, who would be responsible for its maintenance, where his nearest technician was based, and he replied 'Cairo'. Not very convenient in the event of a breakdown, and I envisaged one of my hard-pressed mechanics being called out to the rescue. A decision was made to install it, and I briefed the Head of Chancellery on its capability before giving the High Commission cipher clerks instruction in its use. I now had a foot in the doorway because from time to time my sergeant or I would have to deliver to HE's office the means to make the equipment function. Having signed the visitors' book, I could look forward to the next garden party.

Because of the disbandment of 15th Signal Regiment, a home had to be found for the Albacore dinghy presented to the unit by the Nuffield Trust, which was very generous in providing the forces with leisure equipment. What better home for it than the Dhekelia Sailing Club? They had a well-appointed clubhouse and a small sheltered cove where the boats could be launched by means of a trailer. The club was an all-ranks affair whose commodore was Brigadier Parker. Many of its members were senior specialists from the nearby BMH, and the commandant of the REME workshops, Colonel Day, was always ready to help with minor repairs.

My introduction to dinghy-sailing was through the tutelage of Jimmy Webber, who allowed me to take the helm from Larnaca harbour to our jetty. I became hooked, and did not take long to qualify as a helmsman. The members of the squadron showed no interest in sailing, so I trained my son Bryan and Edith to act as crew.

The club owned a variety of dinghies, including Albacores, Fireflies and GPs, and races were held on Wednesday afternoons and Sunday mornings on a handicap basis. As soon as I felt competent I entered a race, and to my surprise was the first to pass the finishing-line – largely due to the splendid condition of the boat. One of my assets was excellent eyesight, and I could see a distant marker buoy long before my rivals. We were often first home – but not the winners, because of our heavy handicap.

We entered a race one Sunday morning when there was a fresh force three breeze blowing and my daughter Pat volunteered to act as second crew member. As we manoeuvred for position near the starting-line, Edith became nervous and asked me to abandon the race. When I refused, she dived overboard and swam ashore. Seconds later Pat followed suit and I was left without a crew. One can manage a dinghy single-handed but not in a race in a force three so I had to opt out. Having entered for the race in the logbook, I had to justify withdrawing. The reason I gave was mutiny on the part of my crew, which raised howls of laughter but which took a long time to live down.

The summer and winter proved to be tranquil and we enjoyed swimming, sailing and the occasional trips to Kyrenia and the medieval castles, unaware of the difficulties that lay ahead.

Tension between the Greek and Turkish populations appeared to be rising, and we sensed this from the attitude of our two domestic servants. One was a Greek named Maria, the other was a Turk named Emily, whom we had engaged privately because she came from a nearby village and was desperately poor. She was so undomesticated that she once picked up an electric toaster still switched on and suffered electrical burns to her fingers.

In mid-December the usual round of cocktail-parties began and preparations for the soldiers' Christmas dinner and New Year's Eve party were made. These were preceded by a comic football match in which there were no clear rules, with the opposing sides wearing fancy dress. When the match was over, I called at the office to find the district chief clerk organising one of the spare rooms for use by a team of orderlies. He told me that trouble was expected and that we had been put on a state of alert.

For the past few months President Makarios had tried to make a unilateral change to the constitution to reduce the number of Turks in the public services and modify the number of Turks in the forces of the republic. The Turkish Vice-President felt humiliated by these moves, and on 20th December the Foreign Ministers of Cyprus, Greece and Turkey met in Paris to discuss the situation. That day, shooting broke out in Nicosia and in Hermes Street an incident took place in which a Greek policeman was shot, a young Turk was killed and a Turkish woman wounded.

What has never been disclosed is that the Greek and Turkish police and gendarmerie were in the habit of taking over each other's duties on their respective religious holidays. Christmas, being a Christian holiday, it was the turn of the Turks. This would have left them in charge of all the police stations and posts, the armouries, the police vehicles and patrol boats – giving them control of the country. The plot was foiled, and tension between the communities was at its height.

The BBC had a relay station located in a large compound near Larnaca from which its World Service was relayed to all countries of the Near East, and its engineer in charge was worried by the turn of events. Because of its remoteness he considered it to be vulnerable to terrorist attack and asked for military protection, but there were insufficient troops available to provide him with a 24-hour guard, and I was asked to visit him to proffer advice. One of my corporals and I took a one-time pad along and told him that this could provide secure communication to our cipher office should the need arise, and that we could relay any appeal for help. His staff were given instruction in its use, and after a few practice messages were enciphered and deciphered his fears of isolation were set at rest.

By midday on 22nd December all Turkish policemen and government employees had left their posts. The Turks fortified themselves in their own areas in prepared defensive positions and thousands of Turkish peasants abandoned their farms and moved into overcrowded quarters in Nicosia. The United States Ambassador and the High Commissioner called on the President to express their misgivings at the turn of events. The position worsened, and on 23rd December Turkish-Cypriot extremists moved into the Armenian quarter, looting and displacing the residents from their shops, clubs, churches, schools and houses. Nor was this trouble confined to Nicosia; British servicemen and civilians were sniped at in Lefka and Larnaca. John McKellar and a small party of armed soldiers had to escort Greek linesmen to repair faults in the telephone system at Larnaca. Major Alec Isaacs' family lived in a hiring on the outskirts of the town, and on 23rd December their house was in the line of fire between opposing gunmen and three of his children were hastily evacuated and billeted on us – at a time when the NAAFI had closed for the holiday and further provisions could not be bought.

During this time I was confined to the office. Meals were brought to me from the mess, I slept fitfully on an easy chair and did not go home for three days. Information was received from the High Commissioner's office that two battalions of Turkish troops had marched out of their base camp and were patrolling the streets of Nicosia. They took up positions on its northern outskirts and the Nicosia-Kyrenia road leading to the coast, giving rise to rumours that the Turks were about to invade.

On Christmas Day Turkish jets flew over the rooftops of Nicosia, and Turkish naval units were observed manoeuvring off the coast, reinforcing the view that a Turkish invasion was imminent. General Peter Young then took the initiative and, with the agreement of the Greek and Turkish army commanders, established a joint peace-keeping force, with British troops patrolling the streets of Nicosia and Larnaca. The patrols were light and were found from the Royal Greenjackets, our only effective military force on the island.

This was a sad time for their commanding officer, Lieutenant-Colonel Hew Butler, who learnt of his father's death and had a signal sent to the War Office the text of which read:

> Regret unable to attend General Butler's funeral for operational reasons. Please advise Lady Butler.

There was a slight lull after Christmas and my family were invited to a party by Superintendent Bill Williams. I decided to join them and relax for a few hours. I returned after midnight, only to learn that a search had been made for me without success. I had been needed to produce lists of address groups and daily-changing call-signs for elements of a force moving to Nicosia at short notice, but my duty cipher staff had been able to cope.

It was that night that the GOC moved all available Infantry soldiers at his command and established the famous 'Green Line' to separate the opposing factions. The outbreaks of violence had not passed unnoticed by the world powers: Cyprus was of direct strategic interest to NATO, which was concerned with the safety of the British bases, and the leaders of the local communities feared an attack from either Greece or Turkey. The Cyprus government requested the intervention of the Security Council, on the grounds that Turkey had committed aggression and intervened in the internal affairs of Cyprus by violating the island's airspace and territorial waters.

At 12 p.m. on 28th December 1963 I decrypted a delayed Top Secret message announcing that Duncan Sandys, the Secretary of State for the Colonies and Commonwealth Relations, was due to land at Nicosia Airport at 12.15 p.m. that day. We were faced with a dilemma because the message had been misrouted to Dhekelia, we did not have time to re-encrypt it, and the security rules forbade any part of the text of a Top Secret message being sent in clear by telephone or radio, so I trusted that the reception party expected him.

Mr Sandys must have been aware of the inadequacy of the peace-keeping force. Within hours of his return to London reinforcements were flown out, and their equipment followed in huge Hercules transport planes. At the same time a decision was reached to move service families living in Limassol and Larnaca into the safety of the SBA, and to make room for them a large number of wives and children were evacuated to the UK on the returning aircraft.

Edith's father was a remarkable man who had survived a fall from the deck of a ship on to the floor of a dry dock, and contracted pneumonia and tuberculosis in his early seventies. His latest misfortune was to fall downstairs and break his neck, and I had no difficulty in securing her a seat on one of the returning planes so that she could comfort him and her ageing mother.

Frenzied efforts were made by the district quartering staff to provide tentage for the influx of troops. By New Year's Eve they were sheltered from the elements, and warmth was provided by means of kerosine stoves.

The Dhekelia Officers' Club was filled to overflowing on the night of 31st December, and I renewed my acquaintanceship with many whom I had served with earlier – notably two Quarter-Master types of the Life Guards from our Herford days. The earliest arrivals were a battalion of the Royal Irish Fusiliers, a Parachute battalion and the Life Guards, and they were followed closely by the HQ of the 4th Paratroop Brigade, who assumed command over them.

It is unusual and a signal honour for a Royal Signals officer to be given command of a brigade, and this distinction had been bestowed on Brigadier Anthony Deane-Drummond, M.C., whose first action as soon as they were organised was to invite the garrison officers and their wives for drinks. Although I had not met him, he spotted my Corps tie and had a few friendly words to say.

Cyprus has an annual rainfall of only fourteen inches on the plains and one of the points made by the authorities was that the expansion of Dhekelia would draw too heavily on its meagre water supplies, so the British agreed to install a water desalination plant on the coast. I heard that before any of the huge Hercules transports took off it was necessary to use forty water trucks, each carrying 230 gallons of water, to allay the dust on its take-off path. A wartime RAF bomber pilot had scoffed when I told him that passengers planes took off from Nairobi on a murrum surface, so I went along to witness a Hercules departing. The 'airfield' on which it had alighted with a full cargo of armoured cars was literally a field, and it was a tribute to the skill of the pilot and the versatility of the plane that landing it in such a confined area was possible. Had it not been for the wetted runway, the dust raised by the mighty engines would have blinded the pilot and made take-off impossible.

At about this time there was speculation in the *Cyprus Mail,* an English-language newspaper, on the whereabouts of Major Ted Macey. Some reports suggested that he had gone underground to assist the Turkish independence movement, which was patently absurd. Yet others suggested that he was an undercover agent working for the Intelligence Service and that he had been held by the Greeks. It was several weeks later that a lurid report was published suggesting that he had been abducted by Greek guerillas, tortured, his body dismembered and his limbs thrown into a disused well, and I trembled to think of the agonies such a strong and muscular man had suffered were that the case. It was a further two weeks before a Top Secret message reporting his disappearance passed through my office on its way to London. In accordance with the regulations, a copy was kept for three days before being destroyed.

Shortly after our arrival at Dhekelia, the Sailors, Soldiers and Airmen's Families Association (SSAFA) representative in Cyprus was due home. Because there was no relief available, an interim replacement to carry out welfare work on behalf of service families had to be found. Applications were invited and Edith's name was included on a short list submitted to Lady Pamela Barnett, the SSAFA patron for the Near East. The welfare of the families is given high priority in any well-run regiment, and as she had helped Colonel Pentreath's wife Elizabeth in problem cases she was experienced. She was appointed acting deputy director, and Lady Barnett told her that if ever she needed help not to hesitate to contact her at Episkopi.

Mrs Wikner, the new deputy, arrived some months later. She expressed concern at the plight of some Turkish-Cypriot ex-servicemen living in remote areas, and sought an audience with Vice-President Kutchuk for authorisation to visit Turkish villages. Mrs Wikner and Edith were invited to the Presidential Palace, and on meeting the Vice-President were dismayed to find that he did not speak English. They were about to leave when Kutchuk asked them to wait, and to their surprise President Makarios himself entered the office and acted as their interpreter.

With the arrival of the reinforcements the situation became easier and we settled down to normal routine. This was upset by an incident involving my cipher sergeant. Sergeant Parrish had joined us from NATO, where, we learnt, he had begun a liaison with the wife of a Swedish lieutenant-colonel. The lady must have been besotted because she followed him to Cyprus and rented a private house in Larnaca, where they continued their adulterous relationship. He was seen emerging from her home one evening, his future movements were observed, and at 4 p.m. one afternoon I received orders to relieve him of all duties and despatch him on the next aircraft to the UK – and that was the end of his career in ciphers.

A tragic accident befell some men of the Parachute Regiment late one night after they returned from a visit to the NAAFI canteen. They were accommodated in EP/IP tents, each large enough to contain six camp-beds. The cause of the accident was obscure but the subsequent inquiry concluded that the kerosine stove was knocked over during the night, setting bedding ablaze, which in turn set the tinder-dry grass and tentage alight.

The soldiers, suffering from severe burns, were rushed to the nearby BMH, where Captain Adrian Boyd, RAMC, devoted days to help ease their suffering. Skin damage does not heal readily in Cyprus, and a high-level decision was made to evacuate them by air to the specialised burns unit of the BMH at Woolwich. Sadly, most of them did not survive the flight.

A peace-keeping force had taken over operational duties by late March 1964 and the build-up continued gradually until early June, when its strength had risen to six thousand – provided mainly by Canada, Finland, Sweden, the Republic of Ireland and the UK – with Lieutenant-General Gyani of India in command. There was speculation about possible clashes between the Irish troops and the Royal Irish Fusiliers recruited mainly from Northern Ireland, but this was discounted by their CO, who said it would give the two battalions an opportunity to collect each other's deserters!

Our son Bryan spent his Easter holidays with us. The previous year he had been sent to boarding-school at Chard in Somerset after he was discovered conducting slanging-matches with his schoolmates on my official telephone.

I had applied for a flight to accompany him to his new school and was disconcerted to be told that two seats were available on an aircraft leaving Akrotiri in two hours' time. So while Edith packed Bryan's suitcase, I flung a change of clothing into a small weekend case. The RAF transport plane was flying to the UK via Malta, from where it was airlifting casualties, and after a night-stop at Valetta we were soon airborne and landed at RAF Lyneham in the early afternoon.

On reaching Chard I apologised to the headmaster for arriving without notice, and went about kitting up my son at the school outfitters before booking into a large rambling hotel once used as a staging-post for horse-drawn coaches. My presence there appeared to arouse the interest of several well-dressed dark-suited men carrying black attaché cases, and I wondered why so many commercial travellers should descend on Chard on a Thursday evening.

After seeing Bryan settled in, I sampled the local beer and returned to the hotel. As I climbed the creaky stairs I heard strange sounds coming from the end of the corridor leading to a balcony overlooking a stage, and on glancing down witnessed some grotesque actions taking place. It then dawned upon me that I was unintentionally witnessing the ritual swearing-in of Freemasons.

I left for London on the following morning, travelling on Isambard Kingdom Brunel's God's Wonderful Railway, which was now equipped with the new diesel engines. These were experiencing teething troubles, and sure enough as we approached Reading the train slowed down and came to a halt. It took two hours for a replacement to arrive and we reached London in the middle of the rush hour.

Edith's parents were unaware of my arrival, and when I reached their house it was to find that they were away for the weekend. However, Edith had a friend who lived at nearby Ilford, so I bought a bottle of wine as a peace-offering, hoping that she would allow me to sleep on her settee. She was not cooperative, her attitude being 'What would my landlady and the neighbours think!' As a last resort I telephoned the Nuffield Club in Eaton Square, but they were fully booked, so rather than compromise the lady I left and sat down in a bus shelter on the main Tilbury road and watched police cars speeding by.

Waiting passengers were eyeing my attaché case suspiciously and I wondered why. It was only after glancing at a discarded copy of the *Evening Standard* that I realised the reason. Unknown to me, an armed gang had held up a Royal Mail train by faking an emergency stop signal. When it came to a halt they coshed the driver, threatened the fireman, uncoupled the engine and a few carriages, and drove it to a rendezvous where a lorry awaited them. The train was carrying mailbags containing currency notes to the value of two and a half million pounds – a vast sum in those days.

Some of the thieves, including their ringleader, were arrested quickly; the remainder escaped, and the police were hot on their trail. Airports and seaports had been alerted – hence the frenzied activity of the Essex police patrolling the Tilbury road.

I felt too conspicuous where I was and decided to take a train to the anonymity of London, where I spent the hours of darkness in an all-night café. It was not the most salubrious of places and envious eyes were being cast at my case. One of the most nauseating sights was a couple who persisted in delousing each other's hair. I was pleased when the dawn appeared, and I emerged into the fresh air to notice the inquisitive glances of the taxi-drivers and railway staff.

The Clarksons arrived back on Sunday evening and I was very pleased to have a bath and a change of underwear before returning to Cyprus on Monday.

Despite the presence of the UN peace-keeping force, sporadic fighting continued, some of it centred around the Saint Hilarion fortress. U Thant, the UN Secretary-General, reported that there had been 126 outbursts of shooting within the past month and, unless all the irregulars were disarmed, violations were likely to continue. The situation was not helped by the arrival of Grivas in June, and within a few months he was appointed commander of the Cypriot national guard.

There was a lull in the fighting during July, but this was short-lived and I was summoned to the operations room at District HQ, where I learnt that several Greek patrol boats had been damaged by Turkish jets off the northern coast and that a Turkish invasion force had left the port of Mersin, less than a hundred miles from Kyrenia. Fortunately, the Turks responded to political pressure from the Americans, the attack was called off, and the fleet returned to base.

Because of the prolonged pressure imposed on his small staff, the CSO asked for an additional officer as an increment. This resulted in a signal from the War Office saying, 'What about Thomas?' – the reasoning being that I had opted for Cyprus as second choice for a retired officer post and could serve in uniform until qualifying for full retirement pay. The CSO's reaction was, 'If he asks me for the job he can have it.'

I did not ask for it, because I had no wish to remain in Cyprus while the country was in turmoil. Until the unrest began we had been free to explore the island without hindrance; now, if we left the safety of the SBA we were subjected to car searches and hold-ups at roadblocks by the Cypriot gendarmes.

I was due to return home in October, and a letter

arrived advising that my next posting was to be War Office Signal Squadron in Whitehall, commanded by Major Ian McAnsh, a New Zealander whom I knew well. I sent him the usual 'pleased to be joining you' letter and decided to make plans for our return.

My overseas membership of the AA had been kept up at an annual subscription of 10s 6d and I asked for a recommended route through Turkey and the Balkans. Its report on the state of the roads was discouraging, so I contemplated shipping the car home – then I learnt of another route.

Colonel Don Fairman from Famagusta was due home in October and told me that he had booked a passage through a local shipping-agent for a passage to Marseilles. The shipping-company was offering generous discounts to British servicemen and I lost no time in applying for a passage for ourselves and the car. On the whole we had enjoyed our time in Cyprus.

As our sailing date of 19th October approached, we were kept busy with farewell parties, packing our possessions and handing over the quarter. Pat had returned to England some months earlier to take a secretarial course, and Linda elected to remain behind for her GCE examination. Edith and I, together with the Fairmans, were invited to a farewell lunch at the Episkopi Club, hosted by Colonel Tommy Grigg, the CSO, and his officers. Inevitably, during the course of speeches the subject of 'mutiny by the crew' cropped up, to hilarious bursts of laughter.

Our ship rode at anchor in Limassol bay. After clearing Customs and Emigration, the cars were driven on to flat-bottomed barges and taken away to be loaded, and the passengers departed soon afterwards in tenders. The vessel paid for its keep by carrying cargo, but the icing on the cake was derived from the passengers. We sailed at dusk, and before dawn we had berthed at Haifa below the shadow of Mount Carmel.

It was nearly twenty years since I had last set foot in the Holy Land and sixteen since the British Mandate for Palestine ran out, leaving Ben-Gurion to lay the foundations for the new State of Israel. Terrific strides had been made in its development. Despite financial aid from America, the country was short of foreign currency, the inflation rate was high, and the tourist board strove to attract visitors. We joined a coach-load of people travelling on a conducted tour to the Sea of Galilee. Then we went on to a kibbutz near the Lebanese border, where mothers toiled in the fields by day, leaving their offspring to be looked after in crèches. Our lunch-time break was taken on the banks of the River Jordan, where we ate our sandwiches in calm and tranquil surroundings before returning to the ship for dinner.

Tel Aviv was close to Sarafand Camp, where I had spent many months during the war, and on the following day we travelled there by train. The transformation was remarkable but what struck me most forcefully was the number of men and women wearing uniform. At least every other adult was in the Israeli services and they all carried arms when out on the streets.

Haifa, like any seaport in the world, was not immune from pimps who lurked in sheltered places along the dockside, trying to trade their shekels for sterling, or better still American dollars, hoping to amass sufficient to pay for their passage across the Atlantic.

The ship's refrigerated holds had now been filled with citrus fruit, Israel's main export, and we were due to leave on the following morning. While the ship had been tied up in port we had appreciated the air-conditioning; unless a vessel is moving, its metal mass retains the heat of the sun, which makes for fitful sleeping. The French and some American tourists had boarded the ship at Marseilles and not unnaturally had secured the best seats in the dining-saloon, but we five Brits were quite happy to share a table and enjoy the fine wines and excellent cuisine while we steamed through the Eastern Mediterranean and the Dodecanese towards Piraeus, the port of Athens.

A coach waiting at the quayside took us to explore the wonders of the Acropolis and gaze at the goods on display in the shops. We looked around for souvenirs, but there was little choice except for statuettes of Adonis and Venus made to imitate marble but in reality moulded out of paste. Our last visit was to the entrance gate of King

Constantine's royal palace, where I took a snapshot of Edith standing beside a huge Greek sentry who was ever willing to pose for photographers.

The ship left Piraeus that night and by daybreak we had reached the Ionian Sea, not knowing if the vessel had passed through the Corinth Canal or steamed south around the Peloponnese coast because the navigation officer was uncommunicative. We continued on a westerly course until reaching the Straits of Messina, which separate Sicily from mainland Italy. Our only stop in Italy was at Leghorn, where many passengers would have liked a few hours ashore to see the Leaning Tower of Pisa, barely fifty miles away, but this was denied to us.

Within nine days of leaving Limassol we reached the Ligurian Sea, and as darkness fell we saw the lights of Italian towns on the Riviera di Ponente and later on the illuminations of the French Riviera with Nice, Cannes, Fréjus and St Tropez in the distance.

Disembarkation at Marseilles passed without incident and by noon we were clear of the port and heading through Provence towards Lyon, where we rested for the night before continuing our journey to Paris and the Channel ports. We had decided to board a ferry at Calais, but on arriving there were doomed to disappointment because the French harbourmen were on strike and no ships were able to put to sea without their cooperation. However, a helpful official told us that if we retraced our steps to Boulogne we might be lucky. We were, because the ferry's captain was able to manoeuvre his ship into deep water without the help of the French dockers and we sailed for Dover. Our troubles were not yet over. Dover at that time was not the developed port it is today and there was no berth available, but after spending hours within territorial waters the captain was given permission to proceed and we disembarked in the early hours of the morning.

25

RETIREMENT LOOMS

I rented a holiday cottage in the remote Cornish hamlet of Lamorna Cove so that we could spend Christmas together as a family. Less than six miles from Land's End as the seagulls flew, the cottage was designed as a summer residence and reasonably well furnished. But the kitchen was inadequate and now that November was with us the rooms lacked warmth. Edith's first discovery was that the kitchen stove was too small to contain a capon and she worried about how the Christmas turkey could be roasted.

The electricity meter was the 'pay as you use' variety, fed by half-crown coins, which it devoured, and when I asked for the meter to be checked the local electricity office admitted that it had been adjusted at the request of the landlady to give her a healthy rebate whenever it was emptied – a practice the staff assured me was quite legal.

I looked in vain for the central-heating radiators until I found that warmth was provided by underfloor cables, but the heat produced was barely sufficient to penetrate the carpets. We found the villagers to be extremely friendly and spent much of our time at the local pub, which went by the name of the Wink Inn, whose owner was slowly committing suicide by chain-smoking cheap cigarettes.

After some discussion we concluded that the cottage suited us in the short term but was too far from London, where I had to spend the remaining months of my service, so we went house-hunting in the Bath-Bristol-Cheltenham area. We had resolved never to live in a 'box', a term used to describe modern utility-built houses, but because thatched cottages were a rarity in that part of the world we settled for a modern four-bedroomed house in Charlton

Kings, near Cheltenham – said to be the largest village in England – and waited for the formalities to be completed.

Linda was the first to arrive for Christmas, and as I waited for her train to arrive at Penzance Station I noticed daffodils, planted in boxes on the station platform, in full bloom – a tribute to the mildness of the West Country climate. She was followed by Pat and Bryan, and with their help the cottage was soon festooned with Christmas decorations. The problem of roasting the turkey was overcome by an obliging neighbour, and all I had to do was transfer it from her kitchen to the cottage in the boot of the car.

Within a few days of my disembarkation and accumulated leave expiring, there was the usual nonsense and I was told that I would no longer be reporting to War Office Signal Squadron as it had been absorbed into 10th Signal Regiment. Two days later a letter reached me, signed by a young adjutant who sounded rather piqued that I had not written the customary 'pleased to be joining you' letter to his CO.

We moved into our new house on 1st Jaunary 1965 and managed to sort ourselves out before my reporting-date of 4th January.

We both drove to Hounslow, and Edith dropped me off at Cavalry Barracks before going on to spend a few days with her parents. My new CO was Lieutenant-Colonel John Ellis, whose first words when I reported to him were: 'I have no job for you,' which I thought rather unhelpful. He went on to say that a retired officer employed at HQ London District had died during the Christmas holidays and the CSO was anxious to find a replacement for him, so I agreed to be interviewed. The adjutant told me to whom I should report and where to find him at the Horse Guards, but the unit's staff work was not too efficient for when I arrived there I was informed by another retired officer, Norman Cleveley, that the CSO was away that day. Norman was an ex-ranker who had suffered at the hands of the Japanese, and somewhere along the line he had acquired the most affected accent I have ever heard.

I was luckier on the Tuesday but I was not impressed by the CSO, who shall be called Dupons. However, I agreed to help out for three months until a retired officer was found to take over. The appointment of CSO London District has been filled by many illustrious members of our Corps, including that superb horseman Brigadier Henry Crawford, whom I remember from my early days at Catterick Camp. His skill and understanding of horses was renowned, and together with Henry Firth and Wilfred Ponsonby (both of whom were to become brigadiers), was instrumental in forming the 'White Helmets' – the Royal Signals Display Team which thrilled spectators at Olympia and elsewhere by their feats of daring, including riding horses which jumped over approaching motor cycles. One of his acts was to leap in the air as a machine and its rider approached him at speed and passed between his legs, a performance which demanded split-second timing, athleticism and courage.

Sir Winston Churchill was ill, and his doctors feared for his life. Her Majesty The Queen had graciously agreed that on his demise he should be accorded a State funeral, and the military arrangements for this were the responsibility of the Major-General commanding the Household Cavalry. My first brief was to revise all aspects of Royal Signals' planning for this great State occasion, and many amendments had to be made to the original draft. The whole of the operation was graded Secret, and all copies were kept under lock and key in the cellars of the old Admiralty Building – with one exception. Richard Dimbleby of the BBC had been entrusted to comment on all aspects of the funeral, and so that he could compile his notes for the broadcast one copy of the voluminous document had been issued to him under an oath of secrecy. By 20th January Sir Winston was gravely ill and unlikely to survive the weekend. The plan was that if he died on the Saturday or Sunday, the State funeral would be held on the following Saturday; but if he survived until Monday it left twelve days to complete the arrangements.

I did not return to Charlton Kings that weekend and at 10 a.m. on Sunday received the code-word to report for duty. When I arrived at the office the entrance to the Major-General's office was thronged with Guards officers immaculate in uniform and carrying their swords, a rare sight because normal office dress for the HQ was dark suits and bowler hats. Our CSO attended the briefing, and from the time of his return it was action stations. Trestle-tables were erected end to end in a large conference hall and gangs of Guardsmen carried the operational orders from the cellars, to be laid out ready for collection by despatch riders and couriers from all over the kingdom. All telephone enquiries from every Signals unit were channelled to Norman Cleveley's and my desk. It was usually 7 p.m. before the day's work ended, after which I had to walk to Charing Cross Station to catch the tube to Hounslow West, hopefully to arrive at the mess before the supper-table was cleared. Lunch was no problem because I had joined the Junior Army and Navy Club at an annual subscription of £2 5s under the Corps block-membership scheme, and they provided a very good self-service menu.

HQ London District's role, in addition to organising the funeral order of march, was to accommodate and arrange transport for the British and Commonwealth service chiefs serving or living abroad; the reception arrangements for the Kings, Heads of State, Heads of the Commonwealth and Colonies, Ambassadors and other dignitaries were in Government department hands. London began to fill up with some very important people.

By Wednesday all the contingents taking part in the march had arrived, and in the small hours of Thursday morning the first practice parade was held while most Londoners slept. It is not generally known that the route to be taken by the cortège from Westminster Hall to St Paul's Cathedral was measured and timed by a Guards regimental sergeant-major using a pace stick (a device to measure the distance covered with each step taken).

Two rehearsals were held, commencing at 3 a.m., when London's streets were clear of traffic, and each time the Earl Marshal, The Duke of Norfolk, who was ageing, turned out to march at the head of the column. The timing taken by the cortège to reach St Paul's was crucial because the Queen had broken with precedent and elected to await the arrival of the body in the cathedral, and Her Majesty's dislike of being late was well known.

Thousands of people were queuing up outside Westminster Hall to pay their last respects to Sir Winston, whose coffin, covered with the Union Flag, rested on a dais. Guarding it were four senior officers from the three services, standing one at each corner with their swords reversed. Norman and I found time to witness the lying-in-state, but unlike the 300,000 of the general public we entered by a side gate reserved for those who were actively engaged in the funeral arrangements.

I answered my telephone on Friday afternoon to hear that the caller was the Lieutenant-General Commanding AFCENT, who explained that he was staying with General Sir Charles Jones, the Governor of the Royal Hospital Chelsea, and the car allotted to him was arriving five minutes later than that of the general. When he suggested that they both travelled in the same car to save on transport, I told him that this was up to the HQ staff and that my job was to deal with Signals problems, but I promised to pass on his message. He replied, 'That is why I am speaking to a clued up Signals officer. Have we met? What is your name?' Having told him my name, I knew that I had no option but to pass on his message! It was not my place to tell him that according to protocol, mourners arrived at St Paul's in order of seniority so that they could be ushered to their places smoothly.

When we left the office at 7 p.m. on Friday evening there was nothing else to be done, and we hoped for good weather on Saturday. As the time for the cortège to pass along Whitehall drew near, I sat by the window in a first-floor vacant office with an unimpeded view of the route; the spectators lining the pavements fell silent as the gun carriage approached. It was drawn by a phalanx of naval petty officers, each of them gripping a long white rope fixed to a harness which in turn was attached to the front hubs of the carriage. This was followed by another body of Royal Navy ratings, four of whom held restraining ropes to check its momentum on downward slopes of the route. The coffin was draped with the Union Flag, with Sir Winston's insignia and decorations laid on a velvet cushion above it. The Royal Navy POs and ratings were an inspiring sight, impregnable, indomitable, invincible, and it seemed as if no power on earth could stop their steady progress. Once the column had passed by, Normal Cleveley and I moved to Horse Guards Parade to salute the Queen as her car emerged from the Mall to Whitehall on its way to St Paul's by another route.

It was after 2 p.m. when I returned to the mess to find that lunch was over, so I watched the highlights of the ceremonial on television. I was in time to see the coffin, borne by four officers of the Queens Royal Irish Hussars, on its way to Tower Pier – to be taken by river to Waterloo Station and then by train to Bladon churchyard for burial within sight of Blenheim Palace, where the Churchill family had lived for longer than two centuries.

It was back to normal business on the Monday, and our pending-trays took longer than a week to clear. The London District telephone exchange was in the course of conversion from manual to automatic by GPO engineers, and I was required to liaise with them. The Command Secretariat looked after the interests of the Treasury and was concerned at the escalating cost of telephone calls once the users had access to direct dialling. Up to 1964 most of the clerical staff had been restricted to local calls only, and trunk calls were policed by the supervisor and operators to avoid abuse. With the introduction of direct dialling, the floodgates would be opened and the GPO bill for calls would soar unless proper control was kept. My brief was to visit every department and persuade them to accept as few trunk lines as possible, leaving local dialling telephones in the hands of the junior staff. Most of the heads of department cooperated, notably the regimental colonels of the Brigade of Guards, who were courteous and understanding; but I found great difficulty with the public relations people, who considered themselves to be more important than mere military men.

There was still no word of a replacement for the deceased Lieutenant-Colonel whose chair I was occupying, and I let this be known. A few days later Colonel Dupons told me that he had contacted the employing agency for retired officers and was told that the job was mine, that I could have it there and then or remain in the post until my retirement in September before carrying on as a civilian. As I had no wish to work in London I declined.

Unknown to him, I had been accepted to attend a business training course at Ealing Technical College commencing in April, and when I told him this he said that he could always have it cancelled. I said, 'Try it,' and he retorted: 'If you talk to me like that I'll put you where the crows can't shit on you.' In less crude language that meant he would have me confined in the Tower of London, where I would be safe from the ravens' droppings.

Needless to say I reported to the college at St Mary Road on 26th April, together with eight others from all branches of the services. The hours of attendance were congenial, Monday to Friday from 9.15 a.m. to 4.30 p.m., and we attended lectures, visited progressive industrial establishments such as BP, A C Pumps, Cadbury's chocolate factory and Hoover, and were given talks by captains of industry. I was most impressed by a trade union official, a member of the Transport and General Workers Union, who must have been hand-picked for his ability and tact, given the service attitude towards trade-unionism.

The course ended on 4th June and I was not required to return to London District. Apart from the monotony of the tube journey from Hounslow West to Charing Cross, I was relieved to be freed from the duty officer's roster. This tedious duty commenced at 9 a.m. on Saturday through to 9 a.m. on Monday followed by a day's work at one's own desk. There was no provision made for meals, the club was closed on Saturdays and Sundays, and the pubs which provided bar meals for the Ministry of Defence and London District staff served only drinks at the weekend because of lack of demand; the only source of sustenance was a run-down Joe Lyons café near Northumberland Avenue. The duty was boring and the most frequent enquiry related to the timing of the Changing of the Guard routine. On one occasion an RAF duty officer, calling from RAF Valley at 10 p.m., announced that two guard dogs and their handlers were arriving at Euston shortly after midnight and needed transport to cross London, to which I replied: 'If they ring you back, tell them to hire a cab.'

My request to spend the remainder of my time with 14th Signal Regiment at Gloucester, ten miles from my home, had been turned down, so I spent the last months of my service at Beavers Lane Camp, relieving officers so that they could enjoy their leave. The usual letters advising me of my impending retirement started to arrive. One was from the Military Secretary's Branch of the Ministry of Defence, and part of the text read:

> *I am to inform you that the Secretary of State for Defence has it in command from The Queen to convey to you, on your leaving the Active List of the Army, the thanks of Her Majesty for your valuable services.*

The Army Pensions Office wrote on 9th August to say that my retired pay under the 1964 code would be £965 per annum and that I had been awarded a terminal grant of £2,895. By comparison, a major with a similar amount of service would today be entitled to £15,865 retired pay and three times that amount as a terminal grant.

It is normal in most regiments for an officer who has given almost a third of a century of service to the Army to be recognised by being 'dined out', but my spies had told me that when the subject was broached the CO decided that I had not spent long enough with 10th Signal Regiment, so I proceeded on my terminal leave without being accorded the usual courtesy of a send-off by my brother officers.

In accordance with the custom of the service, I reported to Beavers Lane Camp on the expiry of my terminal leave to sign the Official Secrets Act declaration. I said goodbye to the CO, who asked me if I intended to stay for a lunchtime drink. I replied that my son Bryan was waiting for me in the car-park, and left his office to drive home.

In contrast to the attitude adopted at Hounslow it was refreshing to receive a letter from the Signal Officer in Chief, Major-General Peter Bradley, C.B.E., D.S.O., the text of which read:

> *Dear Thomas,*
> *I see you are shortly leaving the Active List and I am writing to express my appreciation of the long service you*

have given the Corps.

You may be assured of a welcome at future social functions of the Corps and I hope you will be able to maintain your ties with the Corps.

May I wish you a happy retirement.
Yours sincerely,
Peter Bradley

26

SEMI-RETIREMENT

Finding the money for the house we bought at Charlton Kings had not been difficult, thanks to the liberal overseas allowances that came my way through serving abroad and Edith's earnings, topped up with a loan of a thousand pounds from a life assurance company on the strength of an endowment policy taken out in 1952. Interest rates were low at that time and the return on National Savings Certificates was a meagre two per cent.

Our transition from service life was eased by the hospitality of our neighbours, mostly professional people, and the kindness of the CO and officers of 14th Signal Regiment, who accorded me honorary membership of their mess.

I was not rushing to find a job but had registered with the Professional and Executive roll of the Department of Employment, and as an insurance I applied to the Civil Service Commission for inclusion on its next open competition in the grade of executive officer.

The Officers Pension Society suggested that I applied for a post with Doughty, a local man who had made good and now headed a large industrial firm making hydraulic machinery for the National Coal Board, but I was insulted by his personnel manager, who offered me employment as a wage-earner.

While scanning the Situations Vacant columns of the local newspaper I read an invitation to ex-service personnel or retired policemen to apply for the post of 'Warden of Leckhampton Hill'. It aroused my curiosity, but I learnt that the incumbent was required to live in a lodge near Leckhampton which went with the job. The history of the appointment was interesting and dated back almost to feudal times. A large tract of land reaching almost to the Birdlip was owned by the Crown; its boundary was designated by drystone walls, which the commoners had been in the habit of moving to acquire more land for themselves. The sole duty of the warden was to patrol the area at least once daily to ensure that the boundary walls were intact, so it was an ideal retirement job for an active pensioner who wished to exercise his dog and liked fresh air.

A possible opening was GCHQ, a once 'hush-hush' establishment that shared its secrets with Washington, but because of media publicity is now over-exposed. Their man offered to take me on as a cipher operator, which was hardly my forte as I had been managing cipher supervisors for many years.

From time to time the labour exchange tried to entice me into manning the turnstiles at Cheltenham racecourse, but this sort of casual work did not appeal to me nor did I need it. My retired pay and savings provided a reasonable living standard, and until worthwhile employment turned up I was content to lay down a garden and improve the property.

Another irritant was the failure of the Government to repay Post War Credits unless the wage-earner of the family had been unemployed for longer than six months. This scheme had been devised by the wartime Coalition Government to withhold a substantial percentage of salaries to help pay for the war effort, and it had promised that repayment would be made when hostilities ceased. Twenty years later the bulk of it remained unpaid!

John Brown had himself retired and was now in an MOD department and responsible for placing retired officers in posts best suited to their experience. He contacted me early in November, saying that a vacancy would occur in Germany 'about mid-1966' and asking if I was interested.

Meanwhile I was in touch with Peter Pentreath, my former CO at 7th Signal Regiment, by this time a brigadier at HQ Northern Command in York.

On the last day of December I heard that I had been

selected for the appointment of Retired Officer Grade III with 225 Signal Squadron in Germany but cautioned that 'certain formalities', i.e. positive vetting, might well take some months. Brigadier Pentreath, by this time Chief Signal Officer at HQ, BAOR, wrote early in January confirming my selection. He said he was exercising pressure on his staff to have the formalities completed quickly, but any delay in my taking up the new job was not the fault of BAOR – the vetting people were vastly overloaded. He added: 'You will be worth your weight in gold and are needed now.'

In early March I was warned to expect a visit from one of the ministry's investigating officers. Out of the blue a chap called Dashwood telephoned from Cheltenham Station asking to be met, so I took him home for coffee and answered routine questions before driving him back. When we were within walking-distance of the railway station, he asked to be dropped off, and I saw him entering the police station – no doubt to check if I was known there.

Dashwood's investigation failed to reveal any skeletons in the cupboard and I received a firm offer of the RO III post, subject to clearance by a medical board, and was warned to be ready to move on 26th April. Someone in HQ, BAOR was becoming impatient at the delay, because within the week I was asked to contact Major Norman Baker of Defence Intelligence by telephone. Norman asked if I could attend a hospital at Tidworth on Friday of that week for medical examination and subsequently meet him on Saturday morning at Northumberland House for briefing. I was now certain that someone in BAOR was cracking the whip!

The 'medical board' consisted of a retired major-general RAMC whose main job was to examine recruits who had no stomach for Army life and were trying to 'work their ticket' – a term used by the soldiery for seeking medical discharge. He was noncommittal when I asked for his verdict, and said that his report would take several days to compile and submit to the MOD. He was unimpressed when I told him I was being interviewed at the MOD on the following morning.

I met Norman Baker, whom I knew in Cyprus, in the Metropole Building, and the medical officer's intransigence was short-lived. Within fifteen minutes of my arrival someone got him out of bed or off the golf-course and I had been pronounced fit. When asked how soon I could travel, I asked for ten days' grace to book a passage for my car and caravan as deck-space was limited at that time. He telephoned the ferry operators and secured me a passage on 3rd April, and arranged for the passport department at Petty France to have my travel documents brought up to date.

Back at home the main subject of conversation was the impending general election, and Prime Minister Harold Wilson could be seen on television, dressed in his Gannex trench coat, haranguing the electors. On Friday 1st April (All Fools' Day) it became clear that the Labour Party had won a landslide victory at the polls.

Edith had agreed to remain behind to arrange for the house to be rented, so my daughter Pat travelled with me. We left home on a Sunday morning, and arrived at Dover with time to spare for the night-crossing. To while away the time we called at a dockside pub where the landlord was chatty and asked if we were sailing to the Continent. He remarked that people had been leaving England in droves as soon as the election results were declared.

The crossing was uneventful. We followed the route to Antwerp and stopped at a large car-park on the outskirts of Ghent – hoping for a brief rest – but were moved on by the Belgian police, who told us it was not a camping-site. So we had no option but to head for the Dutch border. My sister and her husband lived at Bilthoven, near Utrecht, and we surprised them by arriving at their house in time for breakfast.

After a short rest, we left for Germany. We travelled east through Apeldoorn and Enschede, heading for Hamelin on the River Weser, and on to the military establishment at Scharfoldendorf, perched on top of a hill which formed part of the Ith range. I knew from a previous visit that the camp occupied a huge area of ground and was formerly an RAF monitoring base.

Pat and I were met at the gate by Captain Stokes, whom

I was relieving, and were told that Major Ian Rose, the OC, was away for the day. Stokes had served in public relations and was transferred to Royal Signals on the rundown of his old department. He said that my quarter was being redecorated and temporary accommodation was available in the officers' mess.

When I reported to the OC Station he asked me to assume my new duties as quickly as possible, so I surmised that Stokes was out of favour. Ian Rose was in his late thirties and I learnt that he had completed the demanding three-day ski trek held at the Norwegian School of Mountain Warfare, so there was no doubt about his physical fitness. He was also a man of letters and held a Master's degree in the arts. Ian had been aware of my military background and was happy to let me introduce any administrative changes I thought fit, provided he was kept informed of them as he was ultimately responsible for the management of the squadron.

The false but plausible role attributed to the squadron was to gather information from the Soviet and East German forces operating in the Eastern bloc. This surveillance was carried out at the static location and also by means of its mobile radio vehicles.

As far as Captain Stokes was concerned, my one aim was to ensure that the public and squadron funds were in order, after which I would tackle the remainder of the administration in my own time. I did ask him to introduce me to the local Commerzbank manager and show me round the area so that I could meet the senior NCOs supervising the squadron's departments.

The camp at Scharfoldendorf predated the 1939-45 War and had been used to train Luftwaffe pilots. Germany was denied the use of military aircraft under the Treaty of Versailles, and to circumvent this ban its future airmen were taught the rudiments of flying using gliders propelled into the air from the grassy slopes of the camp. It covered an area of seventy-five acres and was lavishly equipped with tennis courts, an outdoor swimming-pool, football and hockey pitches and a squash court. Its slopes were also ideal for the more active ones, who practised skiing in the winter months.

My quarter was ready for occupation by the weekend, but we did not move in immediately because of the pervading smell of fresh paint. The house was named 'The VIP Villa' and stood in its own grounds outside the security gates. It had four double bedrooms, one of which contained a huge bed formerly reserved for the use of Hermann Goering, the Nazi Luftwaffe chief, when he visited the camp so tht he could keep Hitler informed of the embryo pilots' progress.

What pleased me most was that the house was rent-free and there was no charge for fuel and light. I thought it proper for Edith to choose two domestic servants when she joined us, but this was not necessary as there was no shortage of part-time help. Whenever I visited the Commerzbank at nearby Eschershausen to draw pay for the soldiers, I enquired if my pay cheque had arrived, only to be told that no funds had yet been paid into my account. However, the manager was quite happy to give me advances to supplement the £80 I had withdrawn from my UK account under the Exchange Control Act of 1947 for conversion into foreign currency.

It did not take long for me to realise that things were in a sorry mess administratively, caused by Stokes' over-zealous passion to delegate his work to subordinates. Delegation is fine if properly supervised, but control must be maintained otherwise chaos ensues. I instructed the chief clerk to channel all incoming correspondence into my in-tray, and amongst other items I came across were fourth reminders from the RASC supply depot concerning overdrawn rations. The second case was more serious; it appeared that Stokes had been critical of the service provided by the Army Kinematograph Corporation, who hired out the films shown to families and troops in the unit cinema. Its director was touring units in Germany, and Major Rose was ordered to meet him at Hamelin to discuss the matter. I wrote to garrison HQ saying that the writer of the letter was no longer with us, that it was written without the OC's knowledge, that the views expressed were no longer held and that in my experience the AKC always provided an excellent service. Might the OC please be spared the journey to Hamelin? The director was mollified and that was the end of the matter.

Gradually everything fell into line and within four months I was certain that we would not be disgraced if faced with an administrative inspection. This was not long in coming, for Brigadier Pentreath decided to spend a week visiting all Royal Signals units in Germany, ending his visit at Scharfoldendorf, where he stayed the night.

Everything went well – except for one incident. Tony Fielding, one of the young captains, had cajoled the range warden into trapping a moufflon for use as a mascot, in the same way as Taffy the goat served as regimental mascot for the Royal Welch Fusiliers. Whereas goats can be trained up to a point, a moufflon is a wild mountain sheep and the rams have large recurving horns. The parade was drawn up for inspection, when suddenly the mascot took it into its head to butt his handler, knocking him over just as the brigadier arrived.

The CSO was pleased with what he saw and asked if the Master of Signals, Major-General Peter Bradley, and his wife Peggy could stay with us for a weekend in August during their visit to BAOR. Our late Colonel-in-Chief, Princess Mary the Princess Royal, had not been replaced, and the Master's role was that of titular head of the Corps, so we were all honoured to welcome such distinguished visitors.

The mess committee, of which I was president, after deciding on the mode of entertainment left the detailed arrangements to me.

The mess was a large one with several spare bedroom suites, and we found no difficulty in accommodating the Master and his wife – in addition to those guests who had travelled a long way to be with us – and before leaving they all expressed their thanks for an enjoyable weekend.

Those, like myself, serving abroad in a retired capacity were considered by the Inland Revenue to be non-resident in the UK and our income tax was assessed on a formula which took into account our UK earnings – such as retired pay, investment income or letting of property – and linked it with our foreign service pay, which was non-taxable. Someone suggested that if I commuted part of my retired pay my tax liability would be reduced, so I contacted the Pensions Commutation Board for details. The advice given to me was that I would be awarded approximately £11 50s for each pound commutated, provided I passed a medical board. The board was convened and the senior RAMC officer examining me remarked, 'I would love to be your insurer.' That is when I should have taken his cue and withdrawn my application by paying the statutory £2 fee, but I commuted £465, for which I received £5,320 10s 7d – not a princely sum. According to the actuaries, I had a life expectancy of 11½ years, which would take me beyond my 65th birthday; as I have passed my 82nd I lost on the deal.

Few Army people knew of the existence of 225 Signal Squadron because of its remoteness. Our camp was sited on a hill 1,000 feet above the surrounding countryside and was within 50 miles of the East German border. The operational and domestic areas were bisected by a public road which crossed the Ith range. From the security angle it was not a good choice of location as some of the 70 German civilians employed on domestic duties, all of whom were vetted, must have guessed its purpose. Included in the 70 were 12 dog-handlers patrolling in shifts, each with a fierce German shepherd dog held firmly on a stout leash. One of my responsibilities was to care for the welfare of the animals but whenever I entered their kennel they terrified me by hurling themselves against the side of their cage. The chief warden complained that one of them was too docile, so a replacement was sent from Sennelager. He proved so fierce that he bit his handler.

My entitlement to annual leave was three weeks and three days, so I decided to visit Austria before the longer evenings arrived. We left at an early hour on a Saturday morning and by lunch-time found ourselves in a well-organised camping-site at Bad Hersfeld, a small town to the south of Kassel. We intended to stay for the day because England was playing Germany in the football World Cup at Wembley and it was being broadcast by the British Forces Network at Hamburg. I tried in vain to tune in to the station before realising that we were out of range of the transmitter. At my suggestion Edith and the children took a stroll to the town whilst I listened to find if any German station would be relaying the match.

It was not long before they returned, saying that the Germans had installed a large-screen television set in a municipal hall and that we were invited to watch the match. The townsfolk were most courteous and insisted that we occupy seats in the front row. There were some nail-biting moments as we watched the game, and after ninety minutes it ended in a score of 2-2. Next came the replay and that disputed goal awarded to the English side. Tension was mounting amongst the watchers and I motioned to Edith to make for the door should trouble break out. The final whistle was blown and England were the World Cup holders by 4 goals to 2. Turmoil broke out behind us and we made a hurried departure as a police car arrived. We need not have worried, because the fighting broke out between the German viewers themselves and it was soon quelled.

Our route to the south took us through Würzburg and Nuremberg, the scene of the war trials and more recently a Grand Prix racing-circuit, before arriving at Augsburg and travelling on to Munich, the capital of Bavaria, where we stopped for the night. A visit to the Hofbrauhaus was called for, so we unhitched the caravan and sought the beer-cellar where Hitler and his henchmen once plotted to restore the Reich to its former glory. Strong German women were carrying huge litre mugs of beer, three in each hand, to the tables. I bought one of them as a souvenir, and it came with a certificate of authenticity.

We travelled through Upper Austria and stopped for lunch at Linz, now and again catching glimpses of the River Danube as it wound down to the Black Sea. What impressed us most about Austria was the inexpensiveness of the food and wine, although this was disguised by the favourable rate of exchange of 27 Austrian schillings to the pound.

We arrived at Vienna in the late afternoon but were unable to find a camping-site, so we spent an hour or two being shown the places of interest by the driver of a horse-drawn landau.

My tourist map listed the main caravan-parks and one

was sited near Bruck, on the edge of Lake Neusiedler, only twelve miles from Vienna and within sight of Hungary. As we approached it we passed through a hamlet where storks nested on the rooftops and I noticed a wine cellar housing vast vats of maturing grape juice. We found an idyllic plot on the water's edge and after settling in I returned to the cellar with a large plastic container. The cellarmen were drunk and insisted that I sampled their wine, exhorting me to drink glass after glass, before filling my flagon with free wine.

The next leg of our journey took us through Styria because I wanted to revisit Klagenfurt, with its beautiful lake and woodlands, before pressing on to Villach, where I spent a few weeks in 1945.

Judging from the number of stickers attached to the windscreens of German tourists, it was considered an achievement to climb the Gross-Glockner pass, over 12,000 feet in height. The sturdy British Wolseley coped quite well on our climb to Mallnitz, where I was surprised to find a railway station. The electrically-powered train carried cars and vans – it appeared that the timorous, not having the stomach for heights and hairpin bends, preferred to travel on the flat-bottomed carriages and view the scenery from their car seats.

It had always been our wish to visit Berchtesgaden, Hitler's fortified redoubt in the Bavarian Alps where he hoped to defy the Allied forces bent on capturing him. We found it had been converted into a tourist attraction with an aerial lift carrying visitors to the Eagle's Nest. Edith and the children took the lift to the summit, while I spent an hour carrying out maintenance on the car in preparation for our return to Scharfoldendorf.

During the autumn of 1966 we had a number of VIP visitors, including the First Secretary of the British Embassy at Bonn and Major-General Tuzo, Chief of Staff at Rhine Army, who later commanded the security forces in Northern Ireland. Some of them arrived in helicopters which landed on our own helipad, thus sparing them the tedious journey from their HQ.

These visits culminated in an inspection by the Director of Intelligence at the Ministry of Defence, a post held in rotation by members of the three services. On this occasion the incumbent was an admiral, who arrived resplendent in naval uniform much embellished by gold braid. His visit caused speculation amongst the civilian employees; Albert, our barman, who was very astute, queried the connection between the Royal Navy and the Army signallers. My guess was that the station was under consideration for closure and a top-level decision had to be made. Why else should the Head of Intelligence spare the time to visit a minor Signals establishment?

The autumn weather closed in around us. The hill was often shrouded in mist and in November the snow started to fall, encouraging the skiers to use the gentle slopes and the children to bring out their sledges. With the approach of winter the usual social festivities began, starting with a party for the German civilian staff, who professed eternal friendship with their hosts. There followed parties in the sergeants' mess, the children's Christmas party, attended by Father Christmas riding in a Land Rover carrying presents, the officers' mess party and the usual cocktail-parties held in private houses.

Our spirits were dampened when news came through that Scharfoldendorf was to be closed down in 1967 and handed back to the Germans. This did not surprise me, knowing the enormous cost of maintaining it. The squadron was being moved to Langeleben, a tiny hamlet situated on high ground not too far from the town of Helmstedt and very near to the border with East Germany. The move was phased as we were taking over the role of 226 Signal Squadron, which was being transferred to England.

The change-over posed many administrative problems as there was a surfeit of married accommodation at Scharfoldendorf and a deficiency at Brunswick, the garrison town responsible for housing the families, which had once been the home of the South Wales Borderers and since then occupied by a battalion of the German Army.

Hamelin also suffered from a shortage of quarters, and a number of Royal Engineers working there had been found dormitory accommodation with us and were reluctant to move. Several subterfuges were thought up to retain the station for military use, one of them by a Royal Engineers major commanding an amphibious squadron camped on the banks of the River Weser. I watched in amazement as he led his squadron up the hill to see if the car-park was large enough to accommodate his vehicles and, like the grand old Duke of York, led them down again to the water's edge. Who ever dreamt that an amphibious unit which spends its active life in water would be dry-docked on a hill one thousand feet above its natural habitat?

The Queen's Royal Irish Hussars was the regiment responsible for allocating quarters. It had been formed out of two distinguished regiments with battle honours going back to the Crimean War and beyond, the 8th King's Royal Irish Hussars and an English regiment known affectionately as 'the Cherry Pickers' with which Winston Churchill had been associated – hence the presence of the QRIH pallbearers at his funeral.

A story was told of its commanding officer, who had reason to complain of the muffled tones sounded by his instrumentalists on band practice. 'Bugles sound a little woolly this morning, Buglemaster,' he remarked. The buglemaster apologised, saying that the buglers' hands were a little cold, only to hear the rejoinder: 'But the bugles blew at Balaclava' – a reference to the Charge of the Light Brigade.

One of the most distressing aspects of the closure was the need to break the news to the civilian staff. They lived in small villages some miles from the camp and they had served the British forces faithfully. To make matters worse, it was a rural area, remote from large towns, and industry was non-existent in the locality. Their severance terms were a matter for the German Government, and all we could do was to wish them well and thank them for their loyal services.

My time was spent mostly at Scharfoldendorf, with occasional visits to Langeleben, and until most of the service people remaining there were repatriated I retained my office and the VIP villa. Gradually the position changed and when 226 Squadron relinquished control I moved to Langeleben.

The officers' mess was tiny compared with the one we had vacated, and as there were no spare rooms I moved into a hotel at Helmstedt until a house became available. I strolled into the lounge one evening after dinner and saw a group of residents watching television in awe. Well might they be, because they were witnessing the oil-tanker *Torrey Canyon* shipwrecked on the rocks of Cornwall and being pounded by the heavy seas.

Judging from our enhanced officer strength, our new squadron, although retaining its identity, had a far greater role to play than formerly. One of the newcomers was a British officer on loan from a Gurkha battalion who was fluent in Russian – apart from his command of Gurkhali, which was a prerequisite for those seconded to Gurkha troops. Another was a captain from a crack Cavalry regiment whose father was a general. In addition, we had an American wearing the uniform and the badges of rank of a captain who I suspected was a member of the CIA.

I was given the quarter of Major Hayes, the former OC, in Bolsche Strasse in a terrace of houses built for the British Occupation Forces and by this time shared with members of our NATO Allies. My next-door neighbour on one side was a friendly German major from Bremen and on the other by a taciturn *Oberst* (colonel) who commanded the resident German battalion.

The camp was twelve miles away, with two routes leading to it. After two trial runs I settled for a minor road which led to little better than a track that skirted a remote village where intermarriage had produced a population of halfwits.

With unfailing regularity on my approach to the village I met a float loaded with milk churns and drawn by six of the villagers, heading for the nearest collecting depot. As I passed the crew their leader always gave a cheery wave; but it was a sorry reflection on their mental state that they could not be entrusted with a horse let alone a mechanical vehicle.

Whoever designed the buildings at Langeleben had little regard for the German climate. Unlike the usual structures with their steep roofs to encourage the snow to slide down, every one had a flat roof – which meant that it had to support a huge weight of packed snow in the winter months, and water seeped into the ceilings when it thawed.

The Commerzbank had no branch in Helmstedt, so I was obliged to open the squadron pay account with the Deutschebank. While waiting to draw the cash one day, I noticed several gold coins in a display case. On enquiring the price of gold sovereigns, I found that they could be bought for as little as £5, compared with the present price of £56; but at that time the price of gold was fixed at $35 per ounce, which bears no relation to its present price of $369, albeit a fluctuating rate.

An invitation reached us from Berlin to visit the Sudells, old friends from Hanover, and instead of driving there on the deteriorating autobahn we decided to join the Berlin train which left from Hanover. The major in charge of the Royal Military Police suggested that we leave the car in his compound: his clerk would complete the necessary documentation and his driver take us to the checkpoint at Helmstedt Station. Inevitably, the Soviet clerk who examined our travel papers at length while we waited beneath a portrait of Lenin found a minor typing error which meant that the documents were invalid, and this involved returning to the provost office to have them retyped.

Berlin had changed a lot since our last visit and looked more prosperous. Large numbers of East German professional people were finding their way to the Allied sectors of the city, and there was talk of a wall being built to separate East from West.

Hitherto the demarcation line between the zones had been simply a ploughed strip fifty yards wide in open country, with notices which read:

HIER IST DEUTSCHLAND NOCH GETEILT
AUCH DRUBEN IST DEUTSCHLAND!

(Germany is still divided here. Beyond, it is also Germany.) Clearly, the ploughs could not be driven through hilly or wooded country such as the Hartz Mountains, in which case recourse was taken to notices nailed to trees reading:

HIER IST DIE GRENZ

These areas were patrolled by uniformed members of the Frontier Service based at Hanover – who were always willing to escort organised parties such as wives' clubs to the very edge of the border. Members of the forces were prohibited from approaching within three kilometres of the Deutsche Democratic Republic lest they stray to the other side and be apprehended and accused of spying.

Nor were the East Germans stupid enough to demolish houses in the middle of villages; they simply erected a checkpoint in the main street which relatives and neighbours were forbidden to pass. To prevent the police posts being bypassed, fences were erected enclosing savage guard dogs, each linked by a swivelled lead to cables a hundred yards in length, which gave them freedom of movement to attack anyone foolish enough to stray into their area.

Jeff and Edith Sudell knew that this was not our first visit to Berlin and that we had seen most of the landmarks such as the Brandenburg Gate, the old Reichstag building and the impressive Russian War Memorial erected to commemorate those who lost their lives between 1941 and 1945. Although this stood in the British sector, it was guarded by a detachment of Soviet soldiers who turned out each day to pay homage to the fallen beneath the shadow of a Russian tank and a solitary field gun.

Although Edith had visited East Berlin on an outing arranged by the WRVS, the nearest I had been to the famous Checkpoint Charlie was seventy yards away because I was forbidden under the Official Secrets Act to cross the threshold or to visit any Iron Curtain countries. Knowing this, Jeff took us to an area on the very edge of West Berlin where a swath of dwelling-houses had been bulldozed to give a clear line of vision to the East German marksmen in their watch-towers, ever ready to shoot down those bold enough to attempt to escape to the West. We saw grim reminders of the fate that befell many who slithered down ropes from upper-storey windows, only to be spotted and shot before reaching refuge: their sacrifice was remembered by wreaths or vases of flowers left there by their fellow Germans living in the West.

We were shown Spandau prison, where Rudolf Hess, found guilty by the War Crimes Tribunal at Nuremberg, languished. Repeated efforts had been made to have him released as an act of clemency but the Russians were adamant that imprisonment for life meant just that.

The Sudells took us out for a picnic in the lake area of the city, an idyllic spot where wealthy German industrialists lived in villas, some of which had landing-stages to enable them to walk dry-shod on to the decks of their yachts or dinghies.

Jeff was in charge of the Telecommunications Branch of the British sector and had many useful contacts amongst the Allied forces, with access to their clubs and duty-free shops. He took us to the French establishment and we marvelled at the selection of fine brandies and wines for sale there. The French people were kind to their soldiers and we were told that all alcoholic drinks sold there were donated by the vintners of the wine-growing regions of France. The prices charged at the shop were so low that we regretted not having travelled to Berlin by car – I could have returned with my boot full of vintage wines.

So far we had seen no night-life and on our last Saturday there we were driven along the Kurfursterdamm and saw throngs of locals promenading on the pavements under garish street lights. Many young women found positions close to hotel entrances where they openly accosted likely clients. We also saw a sprinkling of transvestites, some bewigged and wearing costume jewellery, but most of them confined themselves to the homosexual clubs.

Some yards further along we came upon a commotion in a side-street, which Jeff thought was caused by militant student protestors claiming their democratic rights and likely to turn into a riot. In no time at all police whistles were blown and reinforcements arrived in the shape of paramilitary police with dogs.

This force existed as a second line of defence in the event of internal disorder. The men carried heavy wooden staffs, which they were not afraid to use, and very soon the recalcitrant students stampeded into alleys and the demonstration was broken up.

The last place we visited during our stay in Berlin was Tempelhof Airport, where Jeff was meeting a colleague on his return from Hanover. Tempelhof – now a military airfield – formed part of the air corridor to the old capital from West Germany and was used extensively during the Berlin airlift. Landing and taking off from there was a pilot's nightmare because it was surrounded by tall tenement buildings, and there was no room for navigational error if the pilot and his passengers were to survive.

Shortly after this, Major Rose and his wife Brenda left us, Ian to take command of a Signal regiment in England on his way to becoming a brigadier. His place was taken by a well-qualified technical officer who had spent the past two years in Belgium setting up the communications for the new NATO location – after General de Gaulle decreed that it was beneath the dignity of Frenchmen to have foreign soldiers serving on French soil at Fontainebleau.

The new major was keen and remained in his office long after normal working hours in order to read into the job, but he tended to concern himself with administrative matters which Ian Rose had left entirely to me.

Langeleben was isolated, and with the approach of winter I was not looking forward to the road journey between my home and office. So when I heard that the Telecommunications Group in Hanover had a vacancy for a Signals Works Services Officer I made discreet enquiries about the nature of the job. Their liaison officer swallowed the bait and reported my interest to his head of department. This led to the senior tels officer visiting Langeleben on some pretext, to 'look me over'.

I did not apply officially for a transfer, preferring to be 'poached', but the intrigue reached the ears of the CSO. He asked me how many knew about it, and when I told him only the Hanover people, he said, 'Leave it with me.' In due course I received a letter from the MOD saying that it was proposed to transfer me to the appointment of RO Grade 3 Telecommunications Group on 21st September, but as it was a voluntary transfer no allowances would be payable.

Before I left Langeleben the squadron was visited by the Intelligence brigadier from HQ BAOR, to whom we owed some allegiance. George Cox and I had served together as corporals in Mobile Divisional Signals at Bulford before his departure to Poland with a team of expert wireless operators to augment the staff of General Carton de Wiart, V.C. Over a drink before lunch he drew me aside and asked, 'Why are you leaving us?' When I gave him a noncommittal answer he pressed his point: 'You are an old soldier. I am an old soldier. Tell me.' There was only one honest answer and that was the remoteness of the station and its distance from the married quarters.

On my departure from Langeleben I took a trophy with me which I had inherited at Scharfoldendorf. It was a chunk of shrapnel, part of an exploded bomb dropped by the RAF near Schölz Altenhof in 1941. It weighed seven pounds, was twenty-one inches in length and had been fashioned into a crest. The face of it was inscribed in gold script:

Englische Sprengbombe abnurf 14.4.41
im Schölz Altenhof

The Tels office in Hanover was situated in Heiligergeist Strasse (Holy Ghost Street) and not many Germans knew of its existence. The first of the German staff to welcome me was 'Fat Elli', who fifteen years earlier had been a slim Fräulein well over six feet tall but was now enormous. She was the only one left from the former office in Sterling House.

The Telecommunications Group was a relic from the days of the Control Commission Germany and had been formed initially to supervise the restoration of the devastated telephone and teleprinter network. Its members were seconded GPO technicians, few of whom had any engineering qualifications. They were attracted by the generous pay and allowances given to civilians as an incentive to work in drab post-war Germany. Not the least of these inducements was the granting of officer status to the more senior of them, and this was resented amongst service people – particularly when they were granted superior housing accommodation which they retained for the duration of their tenure, unlike serving soldiers, who waited months for a quarter.

With the demise of the CCG these civilians were absorbed into the Army with responsibility for running the static communications within the British Zone under the overall command of the CSO.

The group, under its controller, was based at Rheindahlen, with detachments at Bielefeld, Berlin, Düsseldorf, Hanover and Sennelager, each of them supervised by a civilian senior tels officer. The military backbone of the organisation consisted of at least one retired military officer at each detachment, every one of whom had served in Royal Signals for an average period of thirty-three years.

The nominal head of the Hanover detachment was a civilian named Frere Wallond who had been trained by the GPO at Maidstone and was a bit of an oddity. One of his peculiarities was that he never smoked during office hours, but on reaching home he chain-smoked. He also objected to staff slipping out to the hairdresser in working time, when the barber was slack. His belief was that one-third of one's hair grew while at work and the remaining two-thirds in leisure or sleeping-time, so it was quite in order to visit the hairdresser during office hours for every third hair trim!

One trouble with taking over from someone *in absentia* is that questions cannot be asked and consequently no answers given, so I spent the first week compiling a completely new set of references. We were about to leave the office on the Friday of my first week when Frere Wallond asked me to remain behind for an urgent incoming telephone message.

It was bad news and concerned Edith's mother, who that morning had collapsed on an outing and died from a stroke. He asked if I wished to accompany her home for the funeral but I declined and returned to our quarter at Brunswick to console her. Later in the evening I received a telephone call from a friend of mine working with Movement Control at Gütersloh, saying that an empty RAF Hastings bomber was leaving there at 6 a.m. and if I could get my wife there by then she was assured of a space.

The evening was spent packing, and after an early start we covered the seventy-five miles to the airport with time to spare. Edith was the only passenger and the load master offered to drop her off at Brize Norton or Lyneham. She chose Lyneham because of its fast train service from nearby Swindon to London.

Geographically ours was the largest area in BAOR and extended from the River Weser to the Danish border and from Holland to East Germany. It also contained the largest concentration of British forces in Germany, with the 7th Armoured Division located at Verden, 2nd Division at Bünde and the 4th at Herford, all of them deployed to discourage an attack from the East.

The *raison d'être* for my post as Signals Works Services Officer was to minimise the drain on Treasury funds caused by the indiscriminate use of the telephone service. This involved strict control over the duration of calls, recovering the cost of calls fraudulently declared as official when in fact they were of a private nature, and restricting the numbers of telephones in use by units to the scale laid down by HQ BAOR.

This was essential because additional telephones imposed an extra workload on the operators, leading, like Parkinson's Law, to the provision of extra positions on the switchboards, all of which were rented from the Germans.

The switchboards – operated by efficient female German operators, all of whom were bilingual – varied in size according to the formation they served. The largest were at Verden and Hanover, but they all had something in common in that they were antiquated and needed constant maintenance by the Deutsche Bundespost technicians.

Private calls were permitted, provided the caller declared them as such, and their cost was recovered from his unit paymaster each month. Suspect calls were those made to civilian establishments or individuals and declared as official, either unwittingly or fraudulently. My staff had a list of suspect extension numbers and invariably these calls were challenged and their cost recovered.

A regiment with an enviable record of telephone discipline was The Royal Scots Greys, stationed at Fallingbostel, whose adjutant, HRH The Duke of Kent, was punctilious in declaring every call he made to Buckingham Palace as private.

One of the drawbacks in allowing soldiers to make private telephone calls on repayment was that some did not appreciate their cost. On one occasion the supervisor of the Osnabrück exchange reported that a young private had incurred a charge of £109 on a call he had made to a pen-pal living on the western seaboard of the USA.

I noticed one month that the Royal Scots had made a large number of official calls to musical publishing agencies, and when questioned the regiment's explanation was that their bandmaster had composed and recorded 'Amazing Grace' and they were trying to promote it. When I pointed out that the band fund would benefit from the royalties accruing from the sale of the disc and therefore any telephone calls resulting from the promotion should be charged to it, they accepted the argument and paid up.

Eventually we were given a quarter in Dickens Strasse. I took it over from a CIA agent who ranked as a major in the US Army. After checking the inventory I made a cursory inspection of the rooms, and on opening a wardrobe door discovered it to be full of his civilian suits, which his German wife had forgotten to pack. He was annoyed and she was upset, so to placate her he rushed to the shopping centre and bought her a box of very expensive chocolates called Sprengels.

The house was in a quiet cul-de-sac bordering on magnificent rose gardens, which in turn fringed the Stadthalle built to replace the one destroyed in the war. This superbly designed municipal building contained a huge banqueting-room and a ballroom, and could seat hundreds of people in its conference centre. The ballroom was a popular venue at carnival times, such as Rosé Montag which followed Lent, and dancing continued there until dawn. But Hanover lacked the spectacular street processions seen further south in the Rhineland areas of Cologne and Düsseldorf. The Hanoverians were mainly of peasant stock, staid and less excitable than their southern neighbours. They preferred to drink beer rather than wine, and paid no heed to the ditty:

> *If the Rhine was made of wine,*
> *Then a fish I'd sooner be.*

Their preference for lager was amply catered for by the number of beer cellars in the city, the most popular being the Löwenbrau on Georg Strasse, not five minutes' walk from the main railway station. Like the Hofbrauhaus in Munich, beer was carried in litre tankards by strong-armed German women and set down on the scrubbed wooden tables. Entertainment was provided by a band dressed in Bavarian costume playing the accompaniment to German *lieds* in which the Germans joined in with gusto.

The Löwenbrau was a very popular venue at *Messe* time, when industrialists from all over the world visited Hanover to attend the great trade fair. On one occasion a lady friend of ours on a visit from England asked if she could take over the conductor's baton, went through the motions of leading the band, and ended up with thunderous applause from the merrymakers.

Some of the revellers had their luggage with them and said that they were leaving for Ostend on the Warsaw express, but rather than pay for hotel accommodation on their last night they preferred to enjoy themselves at the beer-cellar and sleep off their hangover on the train. The express always arrived at Hanover Station punctually at 5.30 a.m., and no one found any difficulty in finding a seat. Normally, the only passengers on board were pensioners from East Germany, past their useful working life; they were permitted to return to their relatives in the West so that Willi Brandt's Government footed the bill for their pensions.

I travelled on the train once or twice and remember conversing with a German doctor who, as we crossed the Rhine bridge on the outskirts of Cologne, pointed to the murky waters of the river below us and remarked drily as we passed the eau-de-Cologne factory, 'That is German enterprise for you! They pump up water from the Rhine, filter it, add a few drops of scent and sell it in decorative miniature bottles as 4711.'

We made full use of the caravan during the holidays and weekends, revisiting Austria and camping at Jesolo, where a launch carried us across the water to Venice, and despite my previous knowledge of the island I succeeded in getting us lost.

On one of our visits to the Harz Mountains we found an idyllic camping-site near the small town of Bad Sachsa, and were so impressed that we rented a permanent plot and left the caravan standing on it. I could see no point in towing it back when all we needed to do was travel up on Friday evening stocked up with provisions for the weekend.

A mink farm had been established on the outskirts of the town. The mammals were displayed in cages nailed to trees so that wealthy Germans could decide which matching skins they preferred to make up their fur wraps or coats. The minks were caged in the open and were left all day in the heat of the sun without a drop of drinking-water, and I felt anger at the callous way they were treated by the farmer. It was nauseating to see them lick up each other's urine to assuage their thirst.

The winter with its long nights was boring, but to alleviate this there was a good deal of social life, with house parties and mess functions supplementing the entertainment provided in the local cinemas and theatres. The Germans had made rapid strides in developing coloured television, and their PAL system was eventually adopted by the BBC under licence.

An annual event televised from Osnabrück was 'the Clown of Osnabrück', although 'Jester' would have been a more appropriate title. It involved aspiring poets conjuring up and reciting, in the vernacular, witty stories of past events, and the rhymester raising the most laughter was adjudged the clown. I watched one of these performances live in a large studio containing many distinguished guests, including Franz Joseph Strauss, the State Premier – and uncrowned King – of Bavaria. Seated next to him was Denis Healey, then the British Secretary of State for Defence, who was visiting the NATO Forces in Germany; I heard him address Herr Strauss familiarly as 'Franz Joseph'. The Germans do not take kindly to being addressed by their Christian names except by close friends, preferring the more formal 'Herr Chancellor', 'Herr Minister' or 'Herr General', and this undue familiarity took the Premier aback. When he spoke to the Defence Secretary he addressed him as 'Mr Healey', with emphasis on the Mr.

It was over twenty years since the formation of the Telecommunications Liaison Group, and the staff recruited from the GPO to organise the restoration of the communications network were now out of touch with modern engineering techniques. The Germans had made rapid strides in technological development. At a time when the GPO was still striving to introduce subscriber trunk dialling, it was technically possible to dial overseas numbers from a call-box in any hamlet in Germany – but not in practice, because they had not yet designed a meter to cost calls. Meanwhile, back in Kent it was not possible to call numbers outside the county without the help of the trunk operators at Canterbury or Maidstone!

The seconded GPO staff were also ageing but, being civilians, they were permitted to serve until their sixty-fifth birthday – unlike civil servants, who were retired at sixty unless they opted to continue working in a lower grade.

Clearly, some fresh blood was needed. When the controller retired, the vacancy was advertised in the GPO technical journals and resulted in a York-based engineer named Brabham joining the group. This caused resentment among some members of the old guard who had aspirations to the top job.

One of the more interesting duties associated with my job was meeting the Commander-in-Chief's train. It had belonged to Adolf Hitler until its capture by the British in the later stages of the war, and was fitted with sleeping-berths, an office, a kitchen and a conference room.

Because of his dual roles as C-in-C BAOR and Northern Army Group, he often met the commanders of NATO forces halfway between his and their HQs to discuss military strategy, and rather than waste time travelling by car he used the train, which was linked by radio to his base.

Whenever the rendezvous was to be in our area of North Germany we were advised of it and took steps to have the train connected by a direct line to the nearest civilian telephone exchange, as a back-up to the radio link. It was my responsibility to see it installed.

The train invariably travelled at night when the railway network was relatively free of traffic, enabling the commander to rest, and arrived at its destination at an early hour. I always travelled up by car on the previous day and, after booking into a local hotel, made a reconnaissance of the siding at which the train was to be berthed. One of my first acts as soon as the telephone was connected was to telephone Edith on my home extension – and the second to eat a hearty breakfast prepared by the general's kitchen staff.

During my later years at Hanover the train was used by General Sir John Hackett, who as a brigadier commanded the 4th Parachute Brigade in its valiant stand against overwhelming enemy forces at Arnhem. The general was a brilliant linguist who had no need for an interpreter when chairing NATO conferences, and on retirement he was appointed a university lecturer and became an author and broadcaster. I saw him on one BBC current affairs programme when an intellectual spoke disparagingly of the military approach to problems. Sir John deflated him by remarking, 'But I am a professor, you know.'

There was no lack of social life at Hanover, most of it based on the garrison officers' mess in the form of curry lunches, dances and entertaining local dignitaries. HM Consul General held a garden party annually at his home and attendance at this function was obligatory, but as honorary membership of our mess had been conferred upon him we were no strangers to each other.

I applied for an extension of service in April 1969, which was approved with the proviso that no further continuation would be considered. Hitherto there had been a tacit understanding that after six years anyone proficient at his job and medically fit could continue on a yearly basis until reaching the age of sixty-five, thus qualifying for an additional Civil Service pension.

At about this time Pat, now serving as a WPC with the

Kent police force, announced her intention of marrying a fellow police officer, and the wedding was arranged for June. Her fiancé's parents lived at Blean, a small village near to Canterbury, and Edith decided to travel home to meet them before the big event. She was so impressed with that area of Kent that we decided to buy a property there, and I agreed to the purchase of a bungalow in the village of Chestfield, which lies within a triangle bordered by Canterbury, Whitstable and Herne Bay.

The formalities were completed before the banns were called for the third time of asking, enabling us to invite relatives to stay there prior to the wedding. Our guests included Dick Hoyle and his new wife Ann, John Lawrence-Brown and Bid, and my sister Cerrie, who brought her Dutch husband along. Dick had settled in Herne Bay after serving with the Kenya police until the colony was granted independence when he lost no time in collecting his severance pay. After that he moved to Tanzania and Uganda as assistant commissioner until they in turn became independent and he was given a golden handshake from each of them.

John, as a peace-time member of the Kenya Regiment, was called up at the outset of the Mau Mau emergency, and fearing for the safety of his family at Langata, sent Bid and the children to England to complete their education. He too had spent long enough in East Africa and saw no future working for the Lands Office, so he accepted the generous offer made by the Crown Agents as compensation for his loss of employment.

One of the guests greeted us with the news that her son had gained a place on an educational cruise on the *Nevasa*, the troop-ship on which we had sailed home from Singapore. It appeared that she had been reprieved from the ship-breaker's yard and the British India Line chartered her to take groups of a thousand children for a fortnight's holiday at sea under the command of Captain Francis-Downer – a wartime hero – and I was pleased that such a fine vessel had been put to such good use.

Before we returned to Germany arrangements were made for the bungalow to be let to a local doctor, who expected to occupy it for at least a year whilst his own house was being built. Collection of rent and upkeep of the property was left to an agent.

On returning to Germany my wife was offered the position of secretary to the psychiatrist at the military hospital in Hanover, which was a challenge and involved learning medical terms – but one which she thoroughly enjoyed.

At last, and not before time, someone at Rheindahlen realised that the Telecommunication Group had become a law unto itself, and it was absorbed into No. 4 Signal Group, headed by Colonel Eric Bardell, an officer with considerable experience of staff duties and communications. This, of course, was resented by the hard liners, who muttered about coming under military control, but at least those of us serving as SWS officers had access to him should any local difficulties arise.

In the autumn of 1970 our agent advised us that the doctor's new house was ready for occupation and asked if we wanted to re-let it. After some discussion Edith decided that as our three children were now in England she preferred to be near to them, and we decided that she would reoccupy our house. I remained at Dickens Strasse for a few months then moved into the garrison mess on finding that shopping, cooking and bed-making were becoming tiresome.

My annual leave amounted to only fifteen days, some of which could be added to bank holidays, and I found this insufficient to make regular visits home. Things came to a head with the postal strike of 1971 when I was out of touch with my family for weeks, and I wrote to Eric Bardell announcing my intention to resign.

Colonel Bardell was concerned about finding a suitable replacement. I assured him that he would receive at least the obligatory three months' notice to allow him time to advertise the post. His letter concluded with the words: 'For my part I would be delighted if you would complete the full tour as I am more than happy with the way you get things done.'

It was three months before my relief arrived in the person of Major Eric Buirski, whom I had first met in Kenya in 1948 when he commanded Northern Area

Signal Troop. Eric had joined the British Army in India in 1935 and had served continuously until 1971. Soon after submitting his application for the post of RO III at Hanover, he was shocked and incredulous when told that he was not registered as a British citizen and to be considered for the job he would have to pay a substantial sum to take out British nationality.

Slips like this do occur. My granddaughter recently applied for a passport, giving her mother's place of birth as Nairobi, and it took a lot of correspondence to persuade the bureaucrats that Linda was of British parentage. Because of this I always advised my son Bryan, also born in Nairobi, to submit a photograph when applying for a job.

My last ten days at Hanover were hectic and I was dined out at the garrison mess, the civilian mess and by the group, presented by the former with a crystal decanter filled with vintage port and by the latter with a neatly designed barometer.

I also received a warm tribute from Eric Bardell, which read:

Dear Tommy,
I am writing on the occasion of your departure from BAOR to thank you for your loyal and devoted service as a retired officer. You have done a first class job as SWS Officer at Hanover and I am most grateful to you for all you have contributed.

All members of 4 Signal Group join me in wishing you a safe journey home, a smooth transition to life in the United Kingdom and a long and happy retirement.

There was some financial reward, too, for a few days after arriving home a letter reached me from the Director General of Defence Accounts enclosing a cheque for £183.45 in respect of a gratuity awarded to me for 5½ years service with the Department!

After a total of 39 years spent in the service of the Crown, 30½ of them abroad and at least a year on troopships, I was now a civilian.

27

RETIREMENT

Alderley Cottage, the chalet house that we bought in Chestfield, was well built and had gained the Ideal Homes Exhibition accolade for design in the early 1950s when wartime building restrictions were lifted. It was surrounded by a large landscaped garden mainly laid to lawn, fringed with borders in which shrubs and a variety of fruit-trees were planted, but it was badly in need of attention.

My Irish neighbour told me that the drainage was poor because of the clay subsoil and advised me to dig a deep trench between our properties to drain away the surface water which settled after heavy rain. It dawned upon me later that it also served to make his lawn less soggy!

Edith worked in the mornings at the Canterbury Cricket Club, where she acted as an aide to Leslie Ames, the famous all-rounder who by that time had retired from professional cricket and become the club manager. The Kent team was then riding high in the County Championship and the sponsored one-day matches now coming into popularity. The club employed eminent cricketers such as Colin Cowdrey, Alan Knott, Brian Luckhurst, Derek Underwood and Mike Denness but they were often unavailable to play for their county as they were representing their country in test matches.

It was not long before callers arrived to test my reaction to joining the local ward of the Tory party, to invite me to join the Chestfield Golf Club and to sound me out about putting my name forward as a prospective city councillor. Some even hinted that I was suitable material for appointment as a Justice of the Peace, but these approaches clashed with my main objective of restoring the garden.

When I left Germany I tipped the scales at over fourteen stones, the result of leading a sedentary life and drinking too much German lager, but within a few months I was down to twelve by dint of digging and other manual work, and felt fitter for it.

After a year at home we both needed a holiday and I learnt that the Cricketers, a small but reputable travel agency, was organising a visit to Corfu in Greece, which is the birthplace of HRH Prince Philip. Because we were late in applying, we were told that accommodation in the seaside taverna was fully taken up but we were offered a bedroom in a flat on higher ground. Supper was taken in the taverna, where we met our fellow guests. They included a Captain of Invalids from the Royal Hospital Chelsea, a retired police superintendent who had served in the Gambia until it gained its independence and a taciturn solicitor from Kings Lynn.

At night it was too risky to negotiate the narrow track to the taverna so we found a modest café near our apartment where we could drink wine and sample local dishes. On hearing that we would soon be leaving the island, the owner invited us to a special farewell dinner and served us with freshly caught fish and copious quantities of retsina.

By the time we left the fiery liquor was having its effect. We reached our apartment but as I groped in the darkness for the key-hole, I slipped on the wet terrace and felt a nauseating pain in my hip. I lapsed into unconsciousness before crawling into bed. A Greek doctor was called in and diagnosed a fractured femur. He advised against admitting me to the local hospital as conditions were primitive and patients depended on food brought in by relatives. On being told that I was returning home on Monday he arranged for an ambulance to take me to the airport and I was lowered on to three aircraft seats.

I was met by an ambulance crew at Gatwick and then whisked away to Crawley Hospital. An x-ray revealed that there was no fracture but my hip was badly bruised. I was lent a pair of crutches and they were in constant use for the next few weeks.

My son, Bryan, had emigrated to Sydney, Australia. He invited us there for a holiday, and we accepted his invitation. The flight from Heathrow started off badly. The ground catering staff called a lightning strike so the jumbo-jet left the airport without rations. We therefore had to make an unscheduled stop at Frankfürt to collect emergency meals, but by the time they were served most of us were famished.

As a result of the diversion and a stop at Perth for immigration formalities, the flight took thirty hours. Bryan met us at Sydney and in his enthusiasm took us on a tour of the city, though all we wanted was to sleep off the jetlag. After a day or two I was in need of exercise and traversed the Sydney Harbour Bridge in both directions. The bridge had once been a favourite spot for would-be suicides but Dannert wire had been erected to deter them.

Bryan then proposed that we should visit Queensland, driving along the old coastal road which skirted New-castle, the centre of the coalmining region, and passing through places with quaint names such as Sugarloaf Point, Smoky Cape, Coffs Harbour and Point Danger. We reached Broad Beach where the Australians had made the mistake of chopping down the palm trees and were cultivating coarse grass to prevent soil erosion.

On our return to New South Wales we rented an apartment at Manly, a suburb of Sydney, and it was there that I nearly lost my life. I had ventured out for a swim in the safe-bathing area, but found myself drawn into deeper water. My fear was of being dashed against the massive shelf-fish encrusted drainage pipes which emptied flood water into the ocean, but at last I found a footing and was able to inch myself ashore, despite the undertow, only to collapse from exhaustion at the water's edge. My plight was noticed by the beach guards who gave me a whiff of oxygen before taking me to Manly Hospital for a check-up-. I was fortunate that the sharks were elsewhere that day!

It was some years later that we realised our ambition to visit the Gambia, that small strip of land bordered by Senegal, which the retired police superintendent had told us about. Edith and I had joined a party that was spending ten days there before enjoying a spell in Sierra Leone. When we landed at Yundum Airport we realised how underdeveloped and impoverished it was. It had once been one of the centres of the slave trade. Following the publicity engendered by Alex Haley's book, *Roots,* a Swedish tourist company had set up a holiday centre on the banks of the River Gambia, and it was here that we spent the next ten days.

We sailed up-river to the village where Haley's ancestors were born and found intricate wood-carvings being sold at exorbitant prices at wayside stalls. However, I had learnt to bargain in India and the vendors were happy to part with their wares for half the asking price.

The humidity at Freetown was insufferable but our air-conditioned, colonial-type hotel was comfortable. We visited a village near to a mangrove swamp and paddled out to a crocodile-infested lagoon – after being assured by the canoe-men that the reptiles fed only at night.

A year later we visited South Africa, flying via Nairobi were we suffered the indignity of being sprayed with insecticide. Once air-borne, the view beneath us was magnificent. The peaks of Mount Kenya and Mount Kilimanjaro glistened in the early morning sunshine which reflected from the snow that capped them. Our route took us to Johannesburg, prior to taking a flight to Durban.

Part of our itinerary included a coach trip to Cape Town, travelling along the Garden Route through Pieter-maritzburg, the region where the tribal Zulus had their home, and then on to Umtata, in the homeland of Transkei. Our route then took us through East London, Port Elizabeth and the Kouga Mountains to George and Mossel Bay. As we approached Cape Town, we were nearing the end of our thousand-mile coach trip. With pride the courier pointed out the hospital where Dr Barnard had carried out the world's first heart-transplant operation, before dropping us off at our respective hotels.

We hired a car and toured the wine-growing area of Stellenbosch and admired the Dutch-style bungalows built on the estates. We ascended Table Mountain in a cable-car and looked down on Robben Island where Nelson

Mandela and other political prisoners had spent years in internment.

At the end of our stay we flew from Cape Town to Johannesburg in a European airbus, and then transferred to a British Airways jumbo-jet to London, Heathrow. The captain of our plane announced that the weather forecast was good and predicted a smooth landing. However, this announcement proved to be the first of many. As we approached London the captain was refused permission to land as Heathrow was shrouded in freezing fog and so we diverted to Prestwick. On arrival we were faced with a baggage-handlers' strike. Half of the suitcases had been removed by clerical staff when word was passed around that the fog had cleared in London. The baggage was then reloaded and we took off for Heathrow, but after circling London for thirty minutes, the captain announced that the weather had closed in again, and that he was approaching the end of his permitted flying time. So, we returned to Prestwick, the only airport in the United Kingdom still open.

By now the passengers were disgruntled. It was with relief that we heard that British Rail was providing a special train to take us to Euston Station. However, we arrived too late to catch the last train home, but the airline made amends by accommodating us in the Cunarder Hotel.

Our next venture was a voyage to Australia on the *Mikhail Lermontov*, a 20,000 ton vessel on charter to CTC Lines. The English cruise-director, Peter Warren, was responsible for our entertainment and arranged deck and indoor games with his Russian counterpart and also provided a talented team of dancers with music from two orchestras.

A storm in the Atlantic delayed our arrival at Kingston, Jamaica. When we did finally arrive the duty-free shop was closed, but a friendly Jamaican policeman ordered the manager to open up, at the same time advising us to buy some bottles of Jamaican rum. As we were behind schedule the captain lost no time in setting off across the Caribbean Sea for the Canal Zone and after two days we reached Colon, on the Atlantic side of the Panama Canal.

The *Mikhail Lermontov* took nine hours to traverse the canal, after which the captain headed for the port of Bilbao. On docking we were allowed a few hours shore leave to visit Panama City but not before being given dire warnings about the activities of pickpockets and muggers. We drove to the city centre in taxis, to find a seething mass of humanity, where, sure enough, the pickpockets were busy. One of the Australians even had his reading-glasses snatched.

We then headed for Tahiti and crossed the equator on the last day of November 1984. Each of us was handed an elaborate diploma signed by Captain Oganov, representing King Neptune. The diploma certified that we had covered 7,240 nautical miles, had proved to be very able sailors and were now admitted to the Kingdom of Neptune. The ship then followed a south-westerly course towards the French-owned Society Islands. Tahiti, the largest of them, had once been offered to Queen Victoria by its inhabitants, on the condition that she sailed out to accept their gift.

We left Tahiti and commenced the penultimate leg of the voyage to Auckland, New Zealand. We were due to arrive in Sydney two days before Christmas and some of the Australians were becoming noticeably festive. We were granted shore leave at Auckland and, as a mark of respect, we visited the military museum where we were impressed with the diversity of theatres of war in which the New Zealand servicemen had been engaged. Two days before leaving Auckland we entered the Tasman Sea. As we prepared for bed, a mighty wave struck the ship, sweeping the water carafe and glasses from the table. When we awoke the ship was berthed and Bryan was at the dockside to greet us.

He took us to Blackheath, a small township in the Blue Mountains, where we settled into a bungalow belonging to one of his friends. The Blackheath Memorial Park, built to commemorate the Australians who fell in both world wars, was only a short walk away. It contained a huge swimming pool, so we spent most of our time there. The local people were very hospitable and had no objection to guests arriving with cases of Foster's.

During our stay we visited the Jenolan Caves, thought to have originated as coral reefs on the sea-bed before geological changes raised them to their present level of nearly 4,000 feet above sea level. On our way back along the Megalong Valley, we stopped at one of the barbecue sites within the reserve. No sooner had Bryan cooked his steaks than swarms of tiny flies appeared from nowhere. To make matters worse, we were the only picnickers at this site so they concentrated solely on us.

Our package also included a return flight on Philippine Airways, and we asked for a stopover in Manila. We were booked into the Mid Town Hotel on a bed and breakfast basis but, so lavish was the breakfast, there was no need for lunch.

Our first free day was spent on a mini-coach tour of Manila, commencing with a visit to the war memorial and the godowns at the docks, where thousands of Americans had died from disease or malnutrition. Our guide then showed us the elegance of the shopping and residential areas, and we were allowed a glimpse of President Marcos' palace before moving on to some of the worst slum areas I have ever seen. The guide was scathing about 'abuse of power', claiming this was responsible for the stark poverty of the lower classes. Finally we ended up at a memorial park where thousands of US servicemen had been interred; headstones erected by the US War Graves Commission marked their burial place.

The Mid Town Hotel was well situated and had a rooftop swimming pool where the air was reasonably fresh. However, at ground level the hundreds of taxis passing to and fro, all of them emitting noxious diesel-engine fumes, made life insufferable. We were therefore not sorry to leave Manila behind us, nor to disembark from the plane which had flown a tedious route with stops at Bangkok, Karachi and Rome.

We were beginning to tire of travelling long distances and decided to take winter holidays in the Canary Islands, roughly on the same latitude as Florida and warmed by sea-tempered breezes wafted in from Morocco. We spent subsequent winters in Tenerife, the Grand Canaria and Lanzerote but as time went on these places became less and less attractive.

In the spring of 1988 I heard that the Geest Line was offering berths to a limited number of passengers wishing to visit the Windward Islands. We were lucky in our bid and were offered a passage on the *MV Geestport,* one of four vessels which carried bananas from the plantations to its distribution centres throughout Britain. It was an ultra-modern ship which had taken part in the recovery of South Georgia from the Argentine intruders.

In late August we left from Barry in South Glamorganshire. As usual the first night on board was spent settling in and meeting the ship's officers and fellow passengers. *The Geestport* was under the command of Captain Mike Davis and the administrative arrangements were under the purser, a Welshman with the unusual name of St Claire. He disclosed to us that in his early youth he had acted as bell-boy to Tommy Farr, the ex-miner and boxing-booth fighter who became heavyweight boxing champion of the UK.

Of the twelve passengers, four were unattached ladies and the remaining couples had diverse backgrounds. The most imposing of them was a retired supertanker captain who had run away to sea at the age of fourteen and jumped ship at Boston, USA. He earned a living washing dishes in a restaurant until US Immigration officials caught up with him and he was deported. His wife never drank tap water, claiming that she had caught typhoid fever (in England of all places) through drinking mains water. Then there was the diminutive ex-squadron leader, who was said to have been a flyweight boxing champion of the RAF. He didn't appear to have gained an ounce in weight since his last bout, despite having a voracious appetite. One of the ladies was reputed to be a Dame, and had spent her life at Eton, providing a shoulder for the younger boys to cry on when life at the public school became difficult. The ship's officers kept a watchful eye on an elderly spinster who was said to be accident prone. It was rumoured that she was courting a self-inflicted injury in order to claim substantial compensation from the ship's insurers.

We neared the Azores and passed Flores, glistening in

the sunlight, and continued an uneventful crossing of the Atlantic until making our landfall at St John's Antigua. A short mini-bus ride took us to Shirley Heights, overlooking Nelson's Dockyard which we left at noon, departing for St Lucia. According to the former tanker captain, the main attraction here was Bagshaw's Emporium. This was famed for its sea-island cotton fabrics, but having shopped at Tang's in Singapore and seen it all we opted out.

We awoke early on the 4th September to find ourselves at Bridgetown, Barbados. We waited for the torrential rain to stop before going to the Hilton International Hotel on the seafront, where we had a quick swim followed by a few rum punches, taking advantage of 'happy hour'. Meanwhile, the serious business of unloading freight and loading bananas was taking place at the quayside. Once this had been completed we set off for St George's in Grenada. The ship tied up near the Carenge and we made our way towards the shopping centre. Along the way we passed picturesque quays, saw local craftsmen making hats and baskets out of palm leaves as well as seeing stalls selling nothing but fruit and nutmegs. After calling at Randolf's Pub we returned to the ship in readiness for a trip on a catamaran to a nearby secluded island. Food hampers were opened and wine bottles uncorked but the excursion was curtailed by the appearance of threatening rain-clouds.

The quota of bananas from Grenada was loaded by midnight and the ship nosed out of St George's on its way to St Vincent. We were advised not to miss the splendid botanical gardens, which were set in an idyllic part of the island and contained every species of tree and shrub known to exist in the Caribbean. The gardens, occupying twenty acres, are the oldest in the western hemisphere and include a breadfruit tree descended from the original one brought there by Captain Bligh (of the Bounty).

Our taxi driver took us to the ruins of Fort Charlotte, built on a ridge six hundred feet high, whose ancient guns commanded the sea area southwards to the Grenadines. The grounds also contained a women's prison, housing many murderesses. Although the death penalty was still in force, women were usually committed to life imprisonment.

Young Island is known locally as 'Millionaires' Island' and when I saw the price list in the pavilion I understood the reason. The resort is built on a hill, with twenty-nine rustic cottages set on the beaches and hillsides, each surrounded by shrubs and trees thereby ensuring strict privacy. It is not a place where the *hoi polloi* are welcome and access to it is strictly controlled. A ferry, a smaller version of the African Queen, carries passengers the fifty yards from St Vincent, and no one is allowed entry to the island until a corresponding number leave it, thus ensuring that it is never overcrowded.

Our ship soon left for Dominica and we arrived at Roseau on a grey and cheerless morning. The rain fell incessantly and the sea was choppy. Unlike the other ports we had visited, the only protection from the open sea was a concrete mole, but there were signs that smaller vessels had been buffeted against the piers and subsequently sunk. The ship's officers were casting anxious looks at the sky and shore leave was vetoed. We did not know it at the time, but Hurricane Gilbert was approaching rapidly and Dominica was in the eye of the storm. Fortunately for us the hurricane passed over our heads and it was not until we reached home that we learnt of the devastation caused. Gilbert wrought havoc throughout the Caribbean; banana plantations were flattened and homes wrecked as far away as Jamaica. A token cargo was loaded, but as the islanders would not venture out with supplies, Captain Davis was ordered to return to St Lucia for more bananas.

After the storm came the calm, and on leaving our last port of call, a course was set for Barry. When we re-entered the Atlantic the sea was placid and its unruffled surface enabled us to see schools of whales spouting in the warm water, along with shoals of porpoise which played at racing the ship as it sped along.

The highlight of the trip home was the Captain's Farewell Dinner, preceded by cocktails in his spacious day-cabin. As a souvenir, he presented the men with a company tie and the ladies a scarf.

On arrival at Barry our car, freshly polished by the shore staff, was ready to drive away with a case of bananas resting on the rear seat. So ended a memorable voyage shared with congenial companions, served by a dedicated and friendly ship's company.

After Edith successfully underwent open-heart surgery, we thought it was time to relax and I took up mundane things such as participating in the village garden competition, with some success; acting as 'teller' in Parliamentary and local elections, where I was always relieved after my stints by Councillor Arthur Porter, the first Lord Mayor of Canterbury; and helping the local Chestfield Society in its efforts to improve our environment.

Edith had become involved with the Women's Institute and told me that they were trying to arrange a visit to the House of Commons, whereupon I told her that they should set their sights higher and said, 'What about the House of Lords?' She scoffed, but it gave me an idea. Lord Cledwyn of Penrhos was the Leader of the Opposition in the Upper Chamber, and we had attended the same school. I telephoned the Whips' Office, giving my background as 'a boy from Holyhead', and that evening his Lordship phoned and asked me when we wished to visit. A date was arranged and we were ushered into his office, to be received courteously – although he went on to explain that he was opening an important debate on the situation in Israel and could not give us his undivided attention. Despite that he escorted us to the well of the House and left us to see the Lord Chancellor, preceded by the Mace Bearer and followed by dignatories, walk into the Chamber for Prayers. We were then rejoined by Lord Cledwyn, who had arranged for us to be seated 'beneath the Bar', the place where at one time Members of the House, before the law was changed, were arraigned and tried by their fellow peers. His business was now over and we chatted for a while about our upbringing before we thanked him for his kindness.

The Master of Signals, Major-General Peter Bradley, was appointed in 1970 and due to hand over in 1982 after he had nominated his successor to carry out the exacting duties for several years ahead. His choice was Major-General John Badcock, who had already retired and taken up consultancy posts with charitable bodies and in industry.

Perhaps what prompted the Master to ask John Badcock to relieve him was the versatile nature of his Army career. Apart from the senior staff appointments of Deputy Military Secretary and Director of Manning, he is listed in *Who's Who* as a C.B., M.B.E. and a Deputy to the Lord Lieutenant of Kent, Robin Leigh-Pemberton, who until his recent ennoblement was the Governor of the Bank of England. His other appointments included a term of office as Deputy Constable of Dover Castle and Head of the British Defence Liaison Staff in Canberra from 1974-77. Above all, he had been selected as commander of the 2nd Infantry Brigade, consisting of thirteen major units, and nearly equivalent in strength to a division. The Corps has produced many brigadiers, but only three of them have been chosen to command a fighting brigade, and John Badcock's achievements deserve wider recognition than a brief entry in the columns of *Who's Who*.

With the industrial boom of the 1980s in full spate, the Corps was experiencing difficulty in recruiting young officers, and the Master wrote to every retired Signals officer asking for his help. Having thought about it, I felt that one solution was to enlist the aid of school careers masters, and as the Chaucer School in Canterbury had technical leanings I gathered together copies of *The Wire*, our regimental journal, and the more sophisticated *Royal Signals Institution Journal*, in the hope that the sporting and technological prowess of the Corps would arouse their interest. The 1980s were a far cry from the 1930s when the senior Royal Signals officer in what was then the whole of British India was Brigadier Le Cornu, and a brigade was dependent for its communication to division on a pack wireless set carried on a mule, plus a few despatch riders. Prospects for young officers with skills in technology and man-management who passed through staff college were unlimited, and access to the highest general staff appointments was open to them – and many achieved high rank. A Royal Signal Corps luncheon held at Blandford in 1991 was attended by fifteen major-generals, serving or retired, and many more were unable to attend!

During the autumn of 1990 some charitably minded people living in Kent were asked to support a function held at King's School, Canterbury, England's oldest school, to raise funds for the Army Benevolent Fund. The star attraction was the Royal Signals Band, who commenced proceedings by playing on the lawns while the guests were received and refreshments served.

Standing near to me was a tall man wearing a Jimmy badge on his blazer pocket, so we chatted and I learnt that he was Roy Andrews, a long-serving ex-member of the Corps, and he too belonged to the Royal British Legion. We bemoaned the fact that the City of Canterbury, the pre-war home of 4th Divisional Signals, was not represented by a branch of the Royal Signals Association – and at that moment the Master strolled by. I suggested that, with his help, we should set about forming one. General Badcock explained that he was still heavily committed with Corps affairs but the idea had already occurred to him, and when he relinquished his duties in a few months' time he would pursue the matter.

Following a fanfare of trumpets, the guests were ushered into the Shirley Hall to be entertained by the band, who gave a stage performance to suit every taste. Charlie Chester, of 'Cheerful Charlie' fame, gave his services as compère and his wit added to a very enjoyable show. During the interval – spent in the vast dining-hall, where the tables were laden with a surfeit of finger buffet delicacies and there was no shortage of wine, all donated by philanthropical tradespeople – we met people who were loud in their praise of the musicians, and the performance ended to the strains of the Corps March 'Begone Dull Care'.

War-clouds were now gathering in the Middle East following Saddam Hussein's invasion of Kuwait and his defiance of the UN Security Council's ultimatum to withdraw. In response to Kuwait's plea for help and to enforce the UN order, the Allies assembled a military force in Saudi Arabia and warships patrolled the Shatt al Arab. The amateur strategists of the BBC presenting the *Newsnight* programme, aided by pasteboard models depicting the terrain in Iraq, were advising the Chiefs of Staff on the way they should conduct their campaign!

Saddam Hussein was threatening that any incursion

into Iraq would result in the sand being stained with Imperialist blood and that the bodies of the Allied soldiers would be sent home in body bags. Our television screens showed pictures of troops building up for the inevitable showdown, and I felt pleased for the US servicemen whose logistical supplies enabled them to douse themselves with bottled water – unlike the half-gallon per man per day of the brackish stuff we had to be content with almost fifty years earlier.

Some months after Hussein's humiliating defeat, General Badcock invited all ex-members of our Corps to a talk given by a Royal Signals officer who had been involved in the planning of the campaign. It emerged that the Iraqis had been outwitted by Allied Intelligence into believing that the attack when it came would be sea-borne, and his army was outflanked by our armour. Once the breakthrough had been achieved, the British 1st Armoured Division, whose tie I wear with pride, had little difficulty in slicing through the Iraqi forces; and such was its impetus that it could have destroyed the whole of the enemy force had not its advance been called off by the politicians.

After thanking Colonel Adams for his exposition of the role played by our Corps in the Gulf War, the General made a brief announcement that it was proposed to form a branch of the Royal Signals Association in Kent and invited those prepared to help to notify him. An ad hoc committee was formed, much work had to be done, but by early June sufficient progress had been made to call an inaugural meeting – and that is how the East Kent Branch of the RSA came into being.

In January 1993, following correspondence in the *Daily Telegraph* after the death of Sir Evelyn Delves Broughton, I contacted Juanita Carberry and, lest my memory was at fault, asked her to verify the account I had written of the events in Kenya which had occurred so long ago. She responded by inviting me to discuss the saga at her home in Chelsea, tastefully furnished and adorned with many mementos of her days in Kenya, including an ornate chest which came from Zanzibar. In her later life she had heeded the call of the sea and was the first woman to have been granted a union card as a 'seaman'.

On retirement Juanita had devoted her time to voluntary work for the Mission for Seamen in Mombasa, but after starting a new life in England she has been active in promoting the welfare of wildlife and in particular exposing the cruelty caused to bears who are trained to dance by being forced to walk on hot embers. Juanita confirmed that my record of life in Kenya was correct, apart from a few minor details, and these have now been put right.

In appreciation for her help I invited her to one of our branch functions, where she met and chatted to some old Kenya hands, including Major Donald Robathan, now eighty-three years old, who had been commissioned in 1928 and served in the East Africa Signal Corps on its formation in September 1939.

Our branch is flourishing under the able guidance and sponsorship of its Honorary Secretary, John Badcock, aided by a willing committee. Fifty members promised to attend the Remembrance Service at Canterbury Cathedral, and to march past the saluting-base behind the branch standard. I was proud to have been chosen to lay the wreath at the memorial and lead our contingent past the Lord Mayor and other civic dignitaries on our march from the cathedral.

The weather forecast for Sunday 14th November, Remembrance Day, was gloomy. As the veterans and other organisations gathered in Canterbury's Longport there was a threat of rain carried by the south-westerly winds blowing in over the Straits of Dover. The parade, led by the band and drums of the Princess of Wales' Royal Regiment, marched to the cathedral, and the wreath-bearers peeled off to the Royal British Legion memorial in the Buttermarket.

The ship's bell of HMS *Canterbury* pealed out to denote the start of the two minutes' silence. Standards were lowered, and after the Last Post and Reveille the wreath-layers rejoined their comrades in the nave. The address was given by the receiver general of the cathedral, Rear Admiral David Macey, its theme being cheerfulness, courage and consideration for others. In a lighter moment he recalled the Falklands War story of a Royal Marines sergeant who had fought with his platoon from Goose Green to Port Stanley, and on entering its boundary noticed a discarded broken bottle. He picked it up and remarked to his men: 'Someone was bloody careless to drop that there. It could hurt somebody.'